GW00750417

de Havilland
DH.60 MOTH
'The World's Most Successful Light Aeroplane'

To the memory of
Captain Hubert Stanford Broad MBE AFC

Without his courage, willingness, devotion,
enthusiasm, initiative, cheerfulness and inherent
professional skills, much of this story might
not have evolved for the telling.

de Havilland DH.60 Moth
© Stuart W McKay MBE, 2005

ISBN 1 85780 212 8

First published in 2005 by Midland Publishing
4 Watling Drive, Hinckley, LE10 3EY, England
Tel: 01455 254 490 Fax: 01455 254 495

Midland Publishing is an imprint of
Ian Allan Publishing Ltd

Design and concept © Midland Publishing
and Stephen Thompson Associates
Layout by Sue Bushell

Printed in England by Ian Allan Printing Ltd
Riverdene Business Park, Molesey Road
Hersham, Surrey, KT12 4RG

Worldwide distribution (except North America):
Midland Counties Publications
4 Watling Drive, Hinckley, LE10 3EY, England
Tel: 01455 254 450 Fax: 01455 233737
E-mail: midlandbooks@compuserve.com
www.midlandcountiessuperstore.com

North America trade distribution:
Specialty Press Publishers & Wholesalers Inc
39966 Grand Avenue
North Branch, MN 55056, USA
Tel: 651 277 1400 Fax: 651 277 1203
Toll free telephone: 800 895 4585
www.specialtypress.com

Photograph on previous page:
By the end of the 1929 King's Cup, the Sealed
Gipsy Engine test aircraft, G-EBTD, had
accumulated 485 hours and 42,000 miles of
travel. *DH Moth Club Archive*

Title page, opposite:
Once owned by Sir Pyers Mostyn in Nairobi,
DH.60G G-AABJ later became part of the
training fleet of the Brooklands School of
Flying. Note the navigation lights on the upper
mainplanes and the trailing edge of the rudder,
and the small drogue being streamed to
indicate that the pilot, under the blind flying
hood, is receiving instruction. *Richard Riding*

CONTENTS

Photographic Contributions
My thanks to the following who have provided specific
illustrations or have allowed me to sift through their pho-
tographic collections and to select images with which to
reinforce and illustrate this history of the world's most
practical and successful light aeroplane, the de Havilland
DH.60 Moth: Clive Abbott; The Aeroplane; John Allan;
Gilles Auliard; Vasco d'Avillez; BAE Systems (Barry Guess
and Mike Fielding); Gordon Bain; Steve Barratt; Michael
Banaki; Vincent Berinati; Bombardier Aerospace; Bruce
Bosher; Eric Brorup; Alan Butler; Arne Butteberg; Peter
Capon; Ian Castle; Jerry Chisum; Ed Clark; Christopher
Clarkson; Tom Cole; John Collier; Dr John Collings-
Wells; Mrs Jan Cooper; Darryl Cott;

Mrs Hannah Crane; George Cull; Terry Dann; Eric Dar-
rah; Jan den Das; Leslie Dickson; Colin Dodds; Victor
Dorée; Barry Dowsett; John Ellis; Ken Ellis; Ivor
Faulconer; Flight; Ben French; William Frogley; Erich
Gandet; Peter Gould; Jennifer Gradidge; John Green-
land; Richard Grundy; Harlan Gurney; Mrs Joan Hamp-
ton; Ted Hawes; Charles Holland; Mike Hooks; Mrs
Carol Horton; Fred Hotson; Nevill Jackson; Roger Jack-
son (The A J Jackson Collection); Tony Jenkins; Mike
Jerram; Craig Justo; W K Kilsby; Colonel Knut Kinne;
John King; Henry Labouchere; Stephen Lally; LAN Chile;
Wolf Letsch; David Macready; Marshall Aerospace (Terry
Holloway); Watt Martin; John Mayer; David McIntosh;
Jack Meaden; Mark Miller; Ken Molson; Hamish Monro;

Hylton Murray-Philipson; Jim Musty; National Archives
(Paul Johnson); Dennis Neville; Jaap Niestadt; Bjornar
Noras; Michael Oakey; Bill Oliver; Ian Oliver; David A
Page; Harold Pearce; Desmond Penrose; Ray Polando
(Malta Aviation Museum); Dr Ace Powers; David Reader;
Nigel Reid; Rab Richards; Richard Riding; Eino Ritaranta;
Stan Roberts; David Salter; Gerry Schwam; Phil Shaw;
Shell Aviation (Iain Jack); Edwin Shipley; Short Bros;
Michael Souch; Philip Stevens; Alex Stocker; Gordon
Store; Mike Stroud; Pat Swoffer; Rusty Tack; Chris
Tucker; Ulster Folk and Transport Museum; Mike Vaisey;
Arvo Vercamer; Monica Walsh (RAAF Museum); David
Walters; David Watson; Reg Webster; David Welch; Jan
White; Bruce Winley; David Yates.

de Havilland
DH.60 MOTH
'The World's Most Successful Light Aeroplane'

Stuart McKay MBE

MIDLAND
An imprint of
Ian Allan Publishing

INTRODUCTION

Captain Geoffrey de Havilland put pencil to paper to draw up his revolutionary vision of the ideal light aeroplane suitable for purchase and operation by the 'ordinary citizen' in 1924. He did so against a background of experience, ability, confidence, practical involvement and some financial assurance. But only two years previously, the state of the business had presented a very different picture.

By the age of 42, 'The Captain' as he was known respectfully amongst his colleagues, or 'DH' throughout the aviation industry, had been for four years, chief designer, test pilot and director of the Company that bore his name on the gates of the muddy little aerodrome at Stag Lane, on the outskirts of North London. Fifty-nine design projects had carried the DH numeric before this current fancy and more besides when his earliest inspirations at Farnborough were added to those created for the Aircraft Manufacturing Company at Hendon. It was here that the 'DH' matriculation began at the suggestion of the Airco chairman, George Holt Thomas, and first appeared when aircraft were designated as 'DE H' followed by a type number.

It was a programme of refurbishment and conversion of cheap, war-surplus DH.9s that provided much of the early work for the fledgling de Havilland Aircraft Company Ltd after its incorporation on 25th September 1920. Following the failure of the high-wing DH.29 transport in 1921, work was accelerated on the DH.34, a single-engined biplane airliner, designed against a specification laid down by Daimler Hire Ltd, who ordered eight machines off the drawing board. Modest factory extensions were necessary to accommodate the vital production and money was desperately short. The task of achieving financial security was a top priority and an effort was made to increase share capital, but results fell well short of the £35,000 required.

At this, possibly the lowest point in the fortunes of the still young company, the future of de Havilland was assured by the arrival of the definitive fairytale white knight. He came in the form of Alan S Butler, a young man who actively participated in sport, sailing and flying, who had inherited a family fortune and was anxious to develop business interests in aviation. Following a meeting at Stag Lane in 1922, Alan Butler contracted with the de Havilland Aircraft Company for the design and construction of an aeroplane to his own specification, the DH.37. In 1924 he invested heavily in the business, taking on the role of Chairman.

Freed of immediate business concerns, 'The Captain' was able to pay greater attention to the more practical matters concerning the design which would mature into what was hailed as 'the most practical and successful light aeroplane which the world has so far seen.' Her number was DH.60, and her type name was Moth.

ACKNOWLEDGEMENTS

To write the story of an aeroplane whose ideal was born during the early years of the Twentieth Century and whose children continue to exploit the full potential of flight, requires the careful study and interpretation not only of contemporaneously recorded and published facts, but also the occasionally bewildering contents of long-archived files and documents, discovered sometimes by chance, else liberated as the result of casual third-party contact or diligent research. Any author is privileged when private papers are graciously offered for rare scrutiny in the interests of recording an accurate history, and I admit to being extremely fortunate and am very grateful in this respect.

This manuscript has been constructed from a myriad fragments drawn together from all corners of the world, supplied willingly and enthusiastically over a number of years. I record my appreciation of the contribution offered by each of the following, and tender my apologies to those whose names I may, inadvertently, have omitted.

Clive Abbott; Ron Hedges, Barry Guess and Mike Fielding for access to the Heritage archive of BAE Systems; Garry Bisshopp; Bruce Bosher; Philip Bremridge; Richard M Clarkson; Vernon Clarkson; Darryl Cott; Colin Cruddas; Bill Taylor, Mark Miller, John Reid and Chris Lee-McCloud of de Havilland Support Ltd; Leslie Dickson; Colin Dodds; Gordon Evans; Malcolm Fillmore; Mrs Eva Fitzpatrick; David Freeman; William Frogley; Philip Gordon Marshall; Peter Gould; John Greenland; Wendy Gubbels; Mrs Pam Guess; Phil Hagger; Mrs Patricia Hammond; Mrs Joan Hampton; Sir Robert Hardingham; Ted Hawes; Bertil Henrikson; Mike Hooks; Ron Hope; Mrs Carol Horton; Fred Hotson; Roger Jackson; Phil Jarrett; John King; Colonel Knut Kinne; Henry Labouchere; Ken Lavanchy; Stan Lupton; Jack Meaden; Michael Oakey; Alex Ogston; Bill Oliver; Bo Vincent Petersen; Peter Elliott of the Royal Air Force Museum; Mike Ramsden; Richard Riding; Eino Ritaranta; Helena Ruokolainen; Hugh Scanlan; Gerry Schwam; Philippa Smith of the Scott Polar Research Institute; Rodney Silk; Colin Smith; Michael Souch; Ron Souch; Gordon Store; Michael Stroud; Nick Stroud; Rusty Tack; Chris Tucker; David Watson; David Welch; Bruce Winley; Jack Woods.

To my friends Desmond Penrose and Michael Vaisey, my special thanks for spending much time and effort in scrutinising the manuscript as it evolved and for keeping me on track.

Stuart McKay
Berkhamsted, June 2005

BEFORE 1925

THE AERO CLUB, founded in England in 1901 at the suggestion of a lady passenger during a balloon flight over Sidcup, Kent, initially and appropriately shared accommodation with the Automobile Club, but later moved to its own premises in Piccadilly.

A retired Royal Navy officer, Lieutenant Commander Harold Perrin was engaged as full-time Secretary in April 1906, and in 1910 the Aero Club was granted Royal status. From typical gentlemen's 'club' facilities in London, the Royal Aero Club (RAeC), under Perrin's capable direction, gradually evolved to a position from which it administered and controlled all civil 'sporting' flying activity in Great Britain, even to the extent of examining for and issuing pilot certificates.

Flying Schools had been formed around the earliest aeroplanes capable of sustained flight and often the establishments were operated by the machine manufacturer or their agents, ever optimistic in their attempts to persuade a pupil into the role of owner. These organisations rarely had a social aspect that might classify them as 'clubs' in the accepted sense, apart perhaps from the London Aero Club at Hendon which, under the management of Claude Grahame-White, became a gathering place for London Society.

Some of the 55,000 wartime machines built in Great Britain alone were sold 'as standing' and formed the basis of the popular travelling circuses, offering spectacle and the opportunity to joyride to a war-weary but acutely air-minded general public. War-surplus training aeroplanes continued their trade with civilian flying schools and converted bombers became lumbering transports for carriage of passengers, freight and mail. Enormous stocks of spare parts were scrapped or sold as cheap lots, including the remnants of the 41,000 aero engines built in

Great Britain between 1914 and 1918 – which could be acquired for very little money.

The Department of Civil Aviation, constituted within the Air Ministry in February 1919, was formed to police the technical integrity of all civil aircraft in Great Britain, in addition to introducing and enforcing flying legislation and providing aerodromes and en-route facilities. By establishing 'standards' in the aftermath of the First World War, the new Department was quick to eliminate any scheme for design and manufacture of which it disapproved: a policy which quickly and inevitably led to its being charged with bureaucratic interference.

Several attempts to satisfy the private sporting-owner market were judged to be too soon after the Armistice, and failed when they coincided with the post-war depression. The Royal Aero Club's first post-war association with competitive flying was in October 1922 when the RAeC Gliding Committee organised a meeting at Itford Hill near Lewes in Sussex, in support of which the *Daily Mail* was encouraged to donate a £1,000 prize.

Only six weeks separated the formal confirmation of the meeting and the opening day

during which time 35 entries were received, although only 13 machines eventually flew at Itford. Of these, two were identical gliders entered by the de Havilland Aircraft Company, the DH.52s *Sibylla* flown by Company test pilot Captain Hubert Broad, and *Margon* entered and flown by Daimler Hire pilot Captain E D C 'Buller' Herne.

On the first day of the competition, 16th October 1922, *Sibylla* was launched by bungee rope but a little over two minutes later landed back and was damaged to the extent that she took no further part in the programme. Herne's flight in *Margon,* which bettered Broad's by 20secs, ended when he ran into a hedge on landing. Three days later during *Margon's* first launch following repairs and a major effort in conversion to wing warping, the machine fell gently back to earth from 30ft when both wings collapsed simultaneously outboard of the centre section, the parachute-style descent of the wreckage saving Herne from any injury. Both gliders were the product of precious resources ill-afforded by the still young and optimistic de Havilland Aircraft Company based at Stag Lane Aerodrome, Edgware, North London, and after Itford both were scrapped.

Stag Lane Aerodrome on Derby Day in May 1923 with DH.9s of the de Havilland Aeroplane Hire Service awaiting arrival of news film for onward distribution. The new Erecting Shop at the top of the picture was the first of the permanent buildings to be commissioned by the de Havilland Aircraft Company, supplemented by a number of reconditioned Bessoneaux hangars which were imported. de Havilland

Following what was regarded as the success of the Itford meeting, the Royal Aero Club devised a formula for another event it organised exactly a year later at Lympne Aerodrome in Kent: a competition for gliders fitted with a small power unit. These machines, 'motor gliders' or 'avionettes,' were seen as a logical development enabling sustainable cross-country flights. The formula appeared to point towards a new class of light sporting aeroplane of high efficiency, operating on minimal power.

The rules for the 1923 Lympne Motor Glider Competition dictated that engines should be limited to 750cc, although the pilots were permitted and encouraged to contribute motive power themselves. The winner would be the machine flying furthest around a triangular course, having been fuelled with but a single gallon of petrol. Flying was to be preceded by a series of trials conducted on the ground to assess the ease of de-rigging and transporting the machines.

The *Daily Mail* again provided a prize of £1,000 and the Duke of Sutherland, Under Secretary of State for Air, offered a further £500, restricted to a British pilot flying a British-built aeroplane. To ensure that the whole competition was not entirely directed towards fuel economy, additional cash prizes were added for elements of performance, reliability and speed.

When the entry list closed on 1st October 1923, one week before the start, the organisers were faced with the prospect of 27 machines, including two from France and a further pair from Belgium. De Havilland's entry was the DH.53, announced only a month before the competition was due to start. The single-seat monoplane was hardly a glider, more a conventional, powered, light aeroplane, fitted with a Douglas twin-cylinder motor and had an inherently poor glide ratio should the engine choose to stop! Two machines were built for the competition, one for Major Harold Hemming, entered on behalf of de Havilland benefactor Alan Butler, and the other shared between Captain de Havilland and Hubert Broad.

Due to some administrative muddle, it was discovered that the span of the DH.53's tailplane exceeded the width of the gateway offered up in the ground handling tests. The company's instant solution was to crop and make good both tips, seemingly without any apparent detriment to the flying characteristics of the type.

Unsettled weather undoubtedly distorted some of the 'economy' results and it was not possible to complete all the competitions. In the prevailing gusty conditions the English Electric Wren and Shackleton ANEC (Air Navigation and Engineering Company) equally achieved 87.5 track miles on their gallon of petrol, an economy exceeded on some multiple laps flown during less windy conditions, and consequently shared first prize.

Neither of the DH.53s won a prize in any category although the type was by far the closest to the still largely undefined specification for a sporting light aeroplane. Hubert Broad had entertained all present with an outstanding display of aerobatics and Hemming had been doing well in the distance (reliability) competition until a broken crankshaft cost him his lead. Nevertheless, the DH.53 was the only one of the 1923 Lympne competitors to go into production. A total of 15 machines, mostly for the Royal Air Force, were built.

In December, re-engined with the more reliable Blackburne engine of only 698cc, Alan Cobham flew DH.53 G-EBHX from Stag Lane to Brussels via Croydon and Lympne in appalling winter weather, to show the aeroplane at the Brussels Automobile Exhibition. Although the return journey was abandoned at Ghent due to unacceptably strong headwinds and the aeroplane returned to England by ship, Geoffrey de Havilland and the design and sales offices of his Company were, as a result of tough practical experience, hardening the specification for their ideal private-owner machine.

Aeroplane 'clubs' formed by groups of like-minded enthusiasts in the early post-war years centred largely on the construction and operation of flying models, apart from fostering a healthy general interest in all other branches of aviation. By the end of 1923, a group closely connected with the Avro Company in Newton Heath, Manchester, had built a full-size glider they designed themselves and were considering construction of another, possibly to be fitted with a Blackburne engine. In December 1923 they announced that under the name of the Lancashire Aero Club they were seeking new members and considering affiliation to the Royal Aero Club.

Coincidental with the Lancashire Club's consolidation, *Flight* published a letter signed simply 'R Preston,' calling for enthusiasts to consider the formation of a 'Light Plane and Glider Club' near London, to which 'flying and non-flying persons would be welcome'. The author was Captain Rupert Preston, later to become Secretary of the Household Brigade Flying Club and, as the retired Colonel 'Mossy' Preston, a future stalwart in the long-term affairs of the Royal Aero Club.

Basic details of the Light Aeroplane Trials proposed for 1924 were announced early in January, but were not followed by detailed Conditions until March. The competition was limited to two-seater light aeroplanes with dual controls, powered by one or more engines of not more than 1,100cc total capacity, and was again scheduled for Lympne Aerodrome, beginning on 10th September. The first two days before the Trials proper were to be devoted to 'Eliminating Tests' in order to prove that not only were the machines capable of controlled flight exercised from either cockpit, but that their ground handling was relatively straightforward too.

'For this test,' read the Conditions, 'the aeroplane must be presented to the officials fully erected. It must then be dismantled or folded in such a manner as to permit of its being transported in one journey, without the use of any extraneous tackle, over a distance of not more than 25 yards, and placed in a shed 10ft in width. It must then be taken outside the shed and re-erected. Two persons only will be allowed to handle the aeroplane throughout this test, and the time occupied must not exceed two hours.'

The Air Ministry established a prize fund of £3,000 which at first sight some considered generous, but as the year unfolded, and Regulations and Supplementaries were published, others began to question this view. The managing director of one manufacturer who wished to remain anonymous, believed some ten companies might enter perhaps fifteen machines, whereas an opinion in *Flight* believed fifty. The director estimated the cost of preparing an aeroplane to be about £1,000 with the prospect of winning a top prize of £2,000, or possibly nothing at all. Built to the exacting requirements of the Air Ministry's Aeronautical Inspection Directorate (AID), he believed the sale price of a machine to be about £800, 'and much too expensive for anybody to buy at, now'.

Whoever the anonymous commentator was, no entries were received, as might have been expected, from Handley Page, Fairey or Gloucestershire Aircraft, whilst English Electric claimed they were too busy repairing a damaged prototype. The de Havilland Company was not to be represented either.

One aviation paper, after a scrupulous analysis of the Regulations, commented: 'They have evidently been drawn up with very considerable care in order to ensure that only a machine having a good all-round performance shall win the chief prizes, so that it seems fairly safe to prophesy on general principles, that the eventual prize-winners will prove to be out-and-out freaks. If this is the case it will be all to the good, however disappointed the Air Ministry may be'.

Captain Geoffrey de Havilland had outlined his private views in a casual conversation with Stanley Spooner, Editor of *Flight*, during the summer of 1924. Spooner had subsequently published an editorial in which he expressed his belief that, if they had wanted to, the de Havilland Company could have produced a machine for the 1924 Trials which would have put up a splendid performance. The Company could have justified the not unreasonable financial speculation, he continued, due to the level of prize money available. That they had declined to do so was, therefore, due to other factors, and when these had been explained, he wrote, he experienced not a small degree of surprise.

According to Spooner's editorial, Captain de Havilland's opinion was that 'the type of machine that will result from the competitions will have no practical utility afterwards'. The Editor doubted whether such a view would be shared by the majority of designers, but he was willing neither to accept it nor reject it. On the question of engines, he gathered that The Captain had come to the conclusion that 'if a really reliable, strong, useful and safe machine is to be produced, the actual engine power for a two-seater should not be less than 50bhp. The reserve of power then available would allow a machine to fly quite strongly even when its engine was not running at its best.

With only 1,100cc, the margin is so small as to put a very heavy strain on the engine, and the reliability is likely to suffer'.

In the middle of July, the RAeC announced a postponement of the Lympne Competition, which was rescheduled to run from 27th September to 4th October. *Flight* attributed the delay to the 'demands of the Air Ministry in the way of engine alterations to conform to their ideas, and the considerable delay in getting engines ready for the aircraft manufacturers who have been hung-up'. Geoffrey de Havilland also was allowed to exercise his right of reply with a letter published in *Flight*:

'You refer to a conversation in which I expressed certain views of the light aeroplane. I had no idea at the time that these remarks would be published, and in view of the fact that they may appear disparaging to the light aeroplane, I should like to make the position clear.

'The design and construction of new machines is a very costly business, and it was not considered policy to embark on the design of a new-type machine, rather highly experimental, when there was little production work going through the shops, and when the type in question was of doubtful value with the specified engine power, as a future production type.

'One has great confidence in the light aeroplane becoming a popular and important type with certain definite modifications as regards engine power.

'The forthcoming trials will be invaluable in providing useful information on many interesting points in design.'

Spooner's own opinions seem to have changed, for only a week before the Lympne Trials he wrote: 'Whether the Air Ministry were wise in limiting the cylinder capacity to 1,100cc when it is generally admitted that this will not be sufficient for practical work afterwards, is, perhaps, a point open to discussion, and may appear to be rather a waste of time and money, as engines of larger capacity will have to be developed next year.'

The Air Ministry signalled their interest in the structured development of a nationally supported light aeroplane movement when the Director General of Civil Aviation, Sir Sefton Brancker, briefed representatives of the press on 3rd June 1924, and a letter was received at the Royal Aero Club in July suggesting a meeting to discuss the foundation of 'Light Aeroplane Clubs'. Subsequent to discussions with RAeC Committee member Lieutenant Colonel Maurice Darby, Managing Director of the Aircraft Disposal Company (ADC) and Club Secretary Harold Perrin, it was suggested the RAeC might be responsible for the organisation of clubs in the London District, and was to negotiate with its affiliated clubs in Manchester, Glasgow and Birmingham. The Air Ministry issued a statement in August:

'The Air Council have been greatly impressed with the aeronautical possibilities opened up by the development of the light aeroplane, in which this country leads the way, and in addition to offering prizes for a competition open to two-seater light aeroplanes, which will be held at Lympne Aerodrome next month, they are anxious that full advantage should be secured to the country from the progress which is being made with this type of aircraft.

'The Air Council have reached the conclusion that these advantages can best be secured by encouraging with the help of county and municipal authorities, the formation of light aeroplane clubs throughout the country, and they are now prepared to assist financially, for a period of two years, the establishment of ten light aeroplane flying clubs whose constitution is approved.

'In the first instance it is proposed to endeavour to secure the formation of such clubs in the leading commercial centres of the country, and an Air Ministry representative will shortly visit likely centres with a view to discussing the details of the scheme which has been prepared with the local authorities and hearing their views on the subject.

'Under the scheme, the Air Ministry proposes to make to each club an initial grant, suitably secured, for the provision of approved types of light aeroplanes selected by the club, and an annual grant for two years towards the expenses of maintenance and the purchase of material and spares.

'The club will be required to put up financial or other contributions to, at least, an equivalent amount, and to insure against loss or damage to equipment provided out of funds supplied by the Air Ministry.

'The club will be required to make its own financial arrangements for suitable aerodrome facilities and the necessary shed accommodation, and to employ one or more qualified air pilot instructors and ground engineers.

'The club will be responsible for the management of the undertaking and for the maintenance of the aircraft, but periodic inspection will be undertaken by the Air Ministry.

'The Air Ministry will also make a grant to each club in respect of each member who qualifies for the issue of a private pilot's licence on club aircraft.

'The possibility of putting this scheme into operation at some date next year depends on the measure of success attained by the aircraft entered for the government competition for two-seater light aeroplanes, referred to above.

'So far as the London area is concerned the Royal Aero Club has undertaken to submit proposals.'

Designed and built around a cheap, surplus, 90hp RAF 1A engine in 1922, the DH.51 was a two-bay three seater, but proved to be too large and cumbersome for the average pilot to manoeuvre on the ground without an army of helpers. Alan Butler

The DH.51 G-EBIM was converted into a DH.51A in 1924 when she was fitted with single-bay, reduced-span mainplanes, incorporating automatic, camber-changing flaps. In this shot, without any other reference to size, the configuration of the DH.60 can be clearly seen. de Havilland

Driven by the Director General of Civil Aviation, Sir Sefton Brancker, the statement was a clear indication of substantial interest and intent: a government department was not only offering start-up funds and a grant in respect of all new pilot licence holders, but was prepared to liaise with local authorities in an effort to ensure support and the provision of adequate facilities from which to operate. The Air Ministry hoped that the winner of the 1924 Lympne Trials would become the natural choice with which to equip their embryonic light aeroplane club movement, but events proved otherwise.

Government funds had not been voted without a very specific purpose in mind. The Air Ministry was anxious to acquire a light aeroplane that would be suitable for basic training of civilian pilots at minimum cost, and to attract and keep current a substantial number of practising pilots who, in effect, would become an emergency reserve for the Royal Air Force and supporting services. The scheme of subsidy, it was hoped, would bridge the gap between actual operating costs and what club members might reason-

ably be expected to pay. C G Grey had something to say about the proposals soon after the announcement, when he wrote in *The Aeroplane:*

'It is fairly evident that flying is much too expensive a game ever to become a sport on the 'one man, one aeroplane' basis. People talk glibly about the light aeroplane becoming the motor-cycle of the air but they always forget that the cheapest possible aeroplane costs roughly five times as much as a good motor-cycle and probably ten times as much to run.'

Eighteen aeroplanes were entered for the 1924 Lympne Trials, nineteen if one counted a Parnell Pixie which could be flown either as a monoplane or as a biplane, but which was only accepted, after a ruling by officials on the day, in the biplane configuration. At 10.00am on Saturday, 27th September, fourteen light aeroplanes were available for scrutiny by the judges, the others having been withdrawn or simply not been made ready in time.

Following the weekend's Eliminating Tests only eight competitors remained, most

others having failed to complete the flying element due to engine failures in the air or on the ground. As Geoffrey de Havilland had predicted, the limitations of motors of low power mated to heavy airframes, attempting to perform at a constant peak in taxing conditions of strong winds and turbulence, became increasingly obvious.

Blame for this decimation was apportioned almost equally between the Royal Aero Club for agreeing to such complicated Regulations and then rigidly enforcing them, and the Air Ministry. The bureaucrats were particularly heavily criticised for interfering in the approval processes for engine development at a time when a power unit of 1,100cc, the maximum specified, did not yet exist. In the limited time available, engine suppliers were forced to design and construct new or much modified units and then deliver them, without adequate testing, to airframe manufacturers who were desperate to install them. Two further failures on the first competition day reduced the finalists to six by Tuesday, four of which were fitted with what proved to be the most successful and reliable of the small engines, the 1,095cc Bristol Cherub.

At the end of the Trials, the winner of the £2,000 first prize was declared to be the Beardmore Wee Bee monoplane with the low-wing Bristol Brownie in second place. Although the Air Ministry congratulated the Royal Aero Club on the efficiency with which the competition had been conducted, and everybody agreed that it was an enjoyable and productive week, the most important result of all was confirmation that engines of 1,100cc were simply not sufficient for any two-seat light aeroplane to be considered a practical proposition.

Was it anything but coincidence that amongst the pages of reports and analysis published in early October, there appeared substantial advertising for the 'Avro Training Landplane, Type 504K Mk II' and, from de Havilland 'A two seater aeroplane of moderate power and adequate performance – the DH.51'? The Company was reminding all concerned that it had despatched DH.51 G-EBIM to Lympne where, during the week of the competition, she had carried aloft 'a number of distinguished passengers'.

The contract to build an aeroplane to a specification laid down by Alan Butler, resulted not only in the DH.37 of 1922, powered by a 275hp Rolls-Royce Falcon engine (later a 300hp ADC Nimbus), but also desperately-needed finance and a business partnership that lasted for almost 30 years. de Havilland

Alan Butler learned to fly on a Mono Avro at Hounslow Heath in 1918 and progressed to a civilianised Bristol Fighter at Filton a year later. He became one of the first postwar private owners when he acquired a Bristol Tourer in 1920. The DH.37 G-EBDO, designed and built for him to special commission by the de Havilland Aircraft Company in 1922, at a cost of £2,600, confirmed he was far removed from the profile of the 'average' owner. He had become Chairman of the firm by the time the DH.51 was introduced in 1924, a big three-seater, two-bay biplane, intended as a touring machine, and constructed around a 90hp RAF 1A engine. But as much as the DH.53 was too small, the DH.51 proved to be too big and too heavy to be a serious contender for the private owner market and only three were constructed.

Visitors to Lympne were also treated to a display of aerobatics by an RAF pilot flying his own Austin Whippet, that precocious invention of 1919. An observer of the scene recorded his view which opened another avenue for debate:

'It may be argued that the Austin Whippet is not a light 'plane, but then, as its owner very pertinently asked at the Buchanan Lecture at the Royal Aeronautical Society recently, when is a light 'plane not a light 'plane? It is true that the machine's 45hp Anzani engine has considerably more than the 1,100cc capacity permitted at Lympne, but at any rate the Whippet is a low-power machine, and until the light 'plane class has been officially defined, may be regarded as such.'

A few days after the 1924 competition had been won and lost, the Air Ministry issued a formidable statement:

'The two-seater Dual Control Light Aeroplane Competition which concluded at Lympne on 4th October, has resulted in the production of new aeroplanes and engines of extreme interest and value from a practical and technical point of view. The aeroplanes, which were all widely divergent in design, proved themselves to be thoroughly efficient and satisfactory, and the power plant showed itself capable of carrying out all the tests prescribed, including the 10-hours' reliability test. On the other hand, it was found necessary to run the engines at such a high speed in order to secure the maximum competition performance, that a loss of reliability was the inevitable result.

'The Air Ministry is, therefore, reviewing the whole of the engine position with a view to obtaining the necessary technical data, free from the adverse conditions inherent in a competition of this nature.

'The Air Ministry considers that the results so far achieved warrant the formation of a small number of light aeroplane clubs, but does not feel justified in recommending the adoption of any existing types of dual control aeroplane for the use of such clubs until the engine question has been further explored. It will, therefore, be necessary for prospective members, or, in the case of clubs which are formed, the active members, to realise that some delay must unavoidably occur before clubs can be fully equipped. Those interested will be kept fully informed of developments in order that they can arrange their definite programmes as early as possible.'

Although the choice of a light aeroplane suitable for the Air Ministry's subsidised clubs had been deferred following analysis of the 1924 Lympne Trial results, and further tests still to be completed by RAF test pilots at Martlesham Heath, the selection process to choose ten clubs continued. The Royal Aero Club had already agreed to represent the 'formation of light 'plane clubs in the London District' assuming prematurely and incorrectly that these would be in the plural.

The RAeC Committee decided to form a 'Light Aeroplane Section' with the prospect of headquarters at either Hendon or Brooklands, and announced their hope that 'two-seater, dual-control flying would be available at a charge not exceeding £1.10s per hour, including the cost of instruction, oil and petrol, damage to machine and third party insurance. It is hoped to have the aeroplanes available for use by 31st March next year'.

By November, following re-appraisal, the Air Ministry had reduced its offer from ten subsidised clubs to six, and officials from each of those provisionally chosen were invited to a meeting in London where terms and conditions were discussed. The six were the Royal Aero Club, representing the London District, Midland Aero Club, Birmingham, and the Light Aeroplane Clubs of Glasgow, Lancashire, Newcastle-upon-Tyne, and Yorkshire.

Delegates were advised that amongst other provisions, the Air Ministry was prepared to make an initial grant of £2,000 to each club for the purchase of a machine and an annual subscription of £500 for two years towards running expenses. A grant of £10 would be paid in respect of each pilot's certificate issued to a member who had trained on the club's aeroplanes. On their part, the club would be required to provide aerodrome accommodation, at least one pilot instructor and ground engineer, and arrange financial contributions at least equivalent to that provided by the Air Ministry.

No specification for a suitable aeroplane could be agreed at the meeting and the ideal size of engine caused a diversity of opinion, some believing that an affordable motor of not more than 40hp would be more than adequate, particularly if allied to an efficient airframe.

To maintain the impetus of the club movement, the RAeC supported a suggestion that part of the grant should be allowed for the purchase of an existing two-seater, dual-control type, and that the Air Ministry might even consider the loan of RAF standard instructional machines, the clubs undertaking the necessary insurance, but the idea was rejected.

While the Air Ministry continued to consider its options, one correspondent summed up the engine situation: 'It is a problem requiring the most careful consideration, as the whole future of the light 'plane movement may very well be marred by a wrong decision'.

JANUARY TO JUNE 1925

EARLY IN 1925, the de Havilland Aircraft Company released details of their new 14-passenger airliner, the DH.54 Highclere. The press was advised that in the event of a forced landing on water, the entire undercarriage could be jettisoned and, with a lower fuselage designed to be watertight, the machine was expected to be able to float on an even keel.

The Company was much more reluctant to talk about their other current project except to say it was the Type 60, a two-seater school machine equipped with a new 60hp engine, which they hoped would be suitable for use by the light aeroplane clubs. Measured against the loose contemporary definition, the aeroplane was bound to fall outside the light aeroplane class, an apparent inconvenience which seemed to cause the designers not the slightest misgivings.

In anticipation of an expansion of their business, the de Havilland Company had initiated a major redevelopment programme at Stag Lane Aerodrome late in 1924, and a visit by an aeronautical correspondent in January 1925 discovered new and improved facilities for the drawing office, wood mill, wing assembly area, erecting shop and flight shed.

Captain de Havilland wrote to the Air Ministry on 15th January, his letter outlining brief details of his Company's new project, its engine and estimated performance:

'The machine is a two-seater dual-control biplane with folding wings. (Folding is really easy and can be done in three minutes). Simple in construction with standard factors of safety, but built of more commercial materials than is the case with military machines. Finish will be good but not elaborate, and by these methods we hope to reduce the cost considerably. We are building the first two machines in this way and will submit them for your Inspection when finished.

'Besides being a very suitable Flying Club machine, it will have sufficient performance for touring, mail carrying etc, and it should make a good training machine.

'I thought you might like to hear about this machine in view of the interest you have taken in Light Aeroplanes generally. It is, of course, realised that any future for this particular machine will depend on the actual performance of the first ones made. We anticipate having the first one flying by the end of February.'

Meanwhile, still anticipating early decisions from the Air Ministry, the six clubs selected to receive an official subsidy were much involved in their own domestic organisation. The Lancashire Aero Club formed a number of sub-committees, each headed by an expert, to cover matters from flying to finance, and from furbishing of a headquarters to aeroplane construction.

The Midland Aero Club, with roots dating back to 1909, had been responsible for the organisation of aviation meetings before the First World War and amongst their influential officers could be counted the Lord Mayor of Birmingham. Apart from continuing negotiations on their own behalf for club machines to operate from Dunstall Park, the committee was seeking approval for the use of the Air Ministry's facilities at the conveniently placed Castle Bromwich Aerodrome.

The Light Aeroplane Section of the Royal Aero Club was advised on 7th January that they would be permitted use of the Hendon Aerodrome, but for only one year. The Glasgow Club remained strangely quiet and although the Newcastle-upon-Tyne Light 'Plane Club reported that 'nothing of a definitive nature has taken place,' their committee had arranged a programme of lectures and organised a temporary headquarters at the County Hotel.

The aviation papers published during the first week of February 1925 carried de Havilland's official announcement of their new aeroplane. Two sentences only, set one above the other in the middle of an otherwise blank page, had dramatic effect:

'The DH two-seater light aeroplane is now in an advanced stage of construction and will be flying early in March.

'Those interested in the de Havilland Moth (the DH Type 60), 60hp Cirrus engine, are invited to apply for particulars.'

While the aviation press waited expectantly for the release of technical details, they could report that progress in the matter of the light 'plane clubs had reached 'a deadlock'. The Air Ministry was still undecided about the choice of engine but confirmed that the types trialled at Lympne in 1924 could not be considered suitable.

To break the *impasse*, a meeting was called for 7th February at which representatives from all the six clubs gathered together in Leeds, hosted by the Yorkshire Club, to discuss the way forward. It was agreed that 'light plane' was in urgent need of definition. How opportune it was for the delegates collectively to debate the merits of the recently announced DH.60, more details of which were just beginning to trickle through.

Might this new aeroplane provide the solution to their problems? At first sight it was not hopeful. The DH.60 was the de Havilland company's commercial interpretation of what they considered a training aeroplane which could also be owned privately, should be: cheap to build, simple to maintain, easy and safe to fly, robust and practical. At 60hp, the engine was believed by the designers adequate for the task and endowed with the necessary reserves. However, de Havilland knowingly had built the first prototypes of their DH.60 without seeking Aeronautical Inspection Directorate (AID) 'supervision,' not that it was necessary except for aircraft scheduled for military ownership'. Could 'approval' be sought retrospectively? The issue of a Certificate of Airworthiness, it was suggested by some, must surely be delayed. Then there was the question of the engine! A new power unit tested only on the bench, rated at 60hp, and with a cylinder capacity more than four times the limit set for the 1924 Trials. Could such a machine seriously be accepted by authority as a 'light plane?' Many thought not.

Abreast of the situation, the de Havilland publicity machine, driven from Stag Lane by Business Manager Francis St Barbe, geared itself for a major press campaign. Only a few days before the DH.60 first prototype flew, a further simple message radiated from the pages of the aviation papers, taking care not to provide a hint of a price:

'The DH.60 two-seater light aeroplane is being produced for the school, the flying club and the private owner. Simplicity, robustness and ease of handling and maintenance are features which have been most carefully considered in its design.

The de Havilland Moth will not be a delicate and frail craft requiring highly skilled

A rare air-to-air view of the prototype DH.60 Moth, G-EBKT, being flown by Hubert Broad with a lady passenger in the front seat, both occupants almost hidden by the high fuselage side and little cut-away around the cockpits. de Havilland

Prototype DH.60 Moth G-EBKT at Stag Lane in March 1925. The shot well illustrates the prevailing state of the surface and why the airfield had such a poor reputation for winter operations. *Flight*

attention. It will be as sturdy and lasting as the modern light car.

'The first cost of the DH.60 will be low and its upkeep correspondingly cheap and simple.'

Progress in constructing the first DH.60 Moth had been more rapid than anticipated and she was ready for engine runs about a week earlier than expected. Allocated work's number 168, she was registered G-EBKT on 10th February. At the same time, the second airframe built in parallel (169) was registered G-EBKU.

To maintain pressure on the government, C C Walker, Technical Director, suggested to the Air Ministry on 19th February that they might purchase G-EBKU (no model name was yet mentioned) and if confirmed within seven days, '...we can definitely guarantee to complete this machine and have it ready for flight, complete with engine, by 1st March'.

It took until 11th March for the Air Ministry's Director of Contracts to reject the offer, partly on account of the fact that no funds were available within the current financial year, but the Department of Technical Development (DTD) showed interest and suggested that, if the engine passed its Type Test and the aeroplane qualified for a Certificate of Airworthiness (C of A), they were prepared to offer test facilities at Martlesham Heath. 'In this suggestion, if so, when replying will you please state what value you will place on the machine for the purpose of compensation in the event of loss during the test'.

On Friday, 20th February, ADC Cirrus I engine No 1 was finally installed in the bearers of G-EBKT. On delivery, the engine had been fitted with an induction pipe which carried the carburettor behind the rearmost cylinder, level with the top of the crankcase. This was the arrangement suggested by Captain de Havilland, but engine designer Frank Halford was not convinced and, after reviewing the installation, a new induction system was fitted with the carburettor mounted on the side, where it remained thereafter. The following day, after a change of main jets to encourage richness, a ground-run of ten minutes was concluded with some satisfaction.

The weight schedule, written up the morning after the first flight, indicated that, less petrol and oil and unpainted, the tare weight of G-EBKT was 764 lb, derived from a weighing system graduated in the imperial units of hundredweights, quarters, pounds and ounces.

The weather over the north London suburb of Edgware on the afternoon of Sunday, 22nd February 1925, was cold and dull with overcast skies. The wind, drifting from the south-east, scarcely disturbed the wind-stocking, but had increased to about 10mph after the doors of the erecting shop were finally closed against the gathering evening gloom. By that time, Geoffrey de Havilland had successfully flown the aeroplane he had designed to, as nearly as possible, his ideal private owner specification.

The DH.60, her wooden fuselage painted in primer only, had been trundled out onto the muddy aerodrome in the early afternoon and the engine test-run again before the historic first flight which lasted for twenty minutes. Captain de Havilland reported on landing that, apart from an indication of fluctuating engine revolutions, all appeared to be as well as expected. The carburettor main jet was changed again in a further effort to increase the richness and following a satisfactory ground check, The Captain took off with Hubert Broad in the front seat. They landed fifteen minutes later and the aeroplane was put away.

She remained unflown for the next four days, a situation dictated by wet weather as much as a planned programme, during which period her fuselage was painted a very dark blue and sign-written with her name *Moth*. All her flying surfaces were left clear-doped, permitting a translucent view of the simple structure beneath.

Further tests were made on 26th February (Broad) and 28th (de Havilland), and by the time G-EBKT was flown by Hubert Broad for the benefit of the Air Ministry on 2nd March, she had accumulated a grand total flight time of ten minutes less than two hours.

This nose-on view of prototype DH.60 Moth G-EBKT illustrates the narrow track undercarriage and very thin wheels, creating a fragile and spindly appearance. On first appearance, the mainplanes and empennage were all clear-doped which permitted the simplicity of the structure to be observed. *Flight*

will be thinking of Paris. And he will not want to take all day getting there; he will want a cruising speed of at least 80mph. And they will need to take weekend luggage: allow 50 lb for that. Also, they will need to use small fields from time to time and to climb above bad weather. The performance will have to be good.'

Geoffrey de Havilland admitted he had so specified his new light aeroplane for three basic reasons. When he flew the DH.53 from Stag Lane to Lympne in 1923 he immediately realised that the specification was directed too far towards the miniature and not truly practical aeroplane. Secondly, the DH.51, built around a cheap engine, went too far the other way. The third and most enduring reason was quite simple. 'I wanted one for my own use,' he said.

The specification for the 1924 Light Aeroplane Trials was, he believed, badly flawed and rather than enter a design with what he considered no future practical application, effort had been directed, in the little wooden hut which served as Stag Lane office for him, Works Manager Frank Hearle, and Company Secretary Wilfred Nixon, towards the 'ideal' machine.

First, the engine had to be closely defined and got right. Frank Halford at the Aircraft Disposal Company was consulted, and together he and Geoffrey de Havilland decided that a surplus Vee-eight, 120hp Renault, cut in half to form a four-cylinder, in-line, air-cooled engine utilising the same crankshaft and cylinders, but with a new crankcase and cylinder head, should result in a comfortable 65hp.

Having defined the power unit, Geoffrey de Havilland was enabled to make his own commercial decisions on the type of airframe to which it should be attached. In his autobiography *Sky Fever*, he confessed that such matters had dominated his thoughts for a long time. Above all, he enthused, with few hampering official regulations to bother about he had a wonderful feeling of freedom that encouraged early belief in the success of the venture.

'I had visualised the finished aeroplane long before the design was started, and the working drawings quickly began to appear. It was an all-wood biplane with four inter-wing struts in all, instead of the more usual eight. The wings were arranged

to fold back along the sides of the fuselage, safely and easily, the time for the whole operation being two minutes. The aeroplane could then be housed in a shed of normal garage size, or the tail could be attached to the rear of a car for towing. It had a plywood fuselage with very adequate cockpits for two people, the passenger being in front; dual control; and very important, a locker behind the pilot for light baggage and tool kit. The landing gear was simple and could take a pretty bad landing. The petrol tank above the centre section held 15 gallons and an extra tank could be fitted in the front cockpit.

'Although I did the main layouts and General Arrangement drawings, the members of the drawing office soon shared my enthusiasm so that the project became a co-operative one, with many useful ideas contributed by all of us.

'The new light aeroplane was intended, above all, for the amateur, for the week-end flyer, and for instruction. Simplicity and safety were of paramount importance. For the same reason, I did not feel it was suitable or good sales policy to give it only a numeral. A name had to be found, and many ideas were put forward before my enthusiasm for natural history, which remained as strong as ever, led me to seek the solution in entomology. It suddenly struck me that the name Moth *was just right. It had the right sound, was appropriate, easy to remember and might well lead to a series of Moths, all named after British insects.'*

Credit for the specification was later claimed by Alan Cobham who said he was asked his views after the expedition to Brussels in the DH.53, and forthrightly expressed his opinion on the matter:

'First of all it must be a two-seater. That young man will not want to fly by himself; he will want to take his girl-friend. Then it must have a range of about 350 miles. He will not want to take his girl to Brighton; he

What, then, had the de Havilland Company created from distillation of all the opinion and debate, analysis of the needs of the amateur pilot and private owner, and the overwhelming enthusiasm of the club movement to provide flying training at an affordable level? The answer was a light aeroplane built against a background of common sense and total reality.

The 'chief characteristics' of the DH.60 were assembled by the Design Office on 22nd January 1925 and, in part, revealed the following:

- Max chord, top and bottom planes, 4ft 3in
- Angle of incidence 3.5°
- Dihedral angle 3.5°
- Span, top and bottom planes 29ft 0in
- Area of top planes incl centre section 118.9ft²
- Area of bottom planes 110.4ft²
- Stagger 3in
- Gap 4ft 10in
- Ground angle 11.25°
- Width of fuselage 2ft 1.25in
- Wing section (special) 8.25% (Mod. DH.9)
- Load all-up 1,350 lb
- Wing loading 5.89 lb/ft²

Perhaps erroneously, the list suggests that the area of the top planes also includes ailerons for there is no mention of ailerons against data for the lower planes. Throughout its design life the production standard DH.60 only ever carried ailerons on the lower planes although some experiments were conducted with ailerons fitted to both upper and lower mainplanes simultaneously.

During construction every component part of the airframe had been check-weighed and the results noted in units of pounds and ounces. Grouped appropriately with unit weights rounded up, the basic weight of G-EBKT was gradually determined:

- Wing structure 193 lb
- Empennage 41 lb
- Fuselage 193 lb
- Engine unit 346 lb
  (The weight of the Cirrus I engine had been estimated at 300 lb)
- Undercarriage 52 lb

The cockpit area of G-EBKT with the small door flapped down, facilitating entry to the front seat which is directly underneath the fuel tank. The fuel cock control is attached to the starboard centre section strut; the windscreens are tiny and there is no built-in baggage locker. *Flight*

- Petrol tank 18 lb
- Crew (standard weights) 330 lb
- Fuel and oil (standard weights) 121 lb
- Machine fully loaded 1,298 lb

From the same detailed weighing schedule it was established whether items were already painted or not; whether units were weighed with all fittings attached or plain; if metal fittings were drilled or wooden components 'taped, trimmed or varnished'. The seat in the rear cockpit was described as '3 ply with aluminium bound edges' at 3 lb 4oz but the passenger seat was aluminium sheet weighing only 2 lb. Windscreens, 'celluloid and aluminium' were recorded at only 4oz each and a single Palmer wheel, 480 x 75, with bush, tyre and canvas cover was recorded at 8 lb 4oz but was later replaced by the larger 600 x 75 at 13 lb 12oz. A de Havilland propeller, DH5120/1 manufactured in mahogany weighed 8 lb 12oz but was replaced later by the DH5124, some 2 lb lighter.

The all-important engine and key for the whole enterprise had been developed from an unlikely ancestry. The British Government's Aircraft Disposal Board had been established to oversee the sale of over 10,000 surplus airframes, 30,000 engines and thousands of tons of spare parts, all of which had been delivered to the Ministry of Munitions too late for use in the recent war. They were subsequently stored in four major centres, one of which was at Waddon, near Croydon.

The Board had begun to auction off these properties but in an indiscriminate manner which the surviving elements of the aircraft industry thought potentially hazardous to their businesses. After lobbying, the government agreed to a privately funded company acquiring the entire stock against an agreed financial settlement and, on 4th March 1920, the Aircraft Disposal Company (ADC), was registered, the brainchild of Frederick Handley Page.

Between then and 30th July 1925 when, as the result of increased trading, the company was re-constituted as ADC Aircraft Limited, 2,000 aircraft and 3,000 war surplus engines were sold raising £1.25 million for the British Treasury, three times as much as anticipated.

In 1913 Frank Halford, who learned to fly at Brooklands and at the age of 19 became an accomplished instructor, was recruited as an engine examiner by the newly created Inspection Department at the Royal Aircraft Factory, Farnborough. Geoffrey de Havilland, a Farnborough-based designer and test pilot, was under pressure to join the same Department as Inspector of Aircraft but, early in 1914, left the Factory altogether to pursue his designing interests with Airco at Hendon. Before he departed de Havilland and Halford had been introduced by Geoffrey's brother Hereward.

On the outbreak of the First World War Halford joined the Army and was posted to service in France. However, he was seconded to the Aeronautical Inspection Directorate (AID) and, in 1915, was appointed to assist the Arrol Johnston Company at Dumfries with an aero-engine development contract awarded by Farnborough. The Beardmore engine programme aided by Halford and under the direction of Arrol Johnston's chief engineer T C Pullinger, became the famous 230hp 'BHP,' the 'H' recognising Halford's contribution. Later, this was developed as their first production aero engine by the Armstrong Siddeley company under the name 'Puma,' and 3,200 units were eventually constructed and married to the ubiquitous and successful DH.4 and DH.9, a union which brought Halford and de Havilland into a close and harmonious working relationship.

In the latter years of the war Halford worked on engine supercharging with Harry Ricardo and, leaving the Army with the rank of Major, became a partner in H Ricardo Ltd, for whom he raced a Ricardo-Triumph motorcycle in the 1921 Isle of Man TT. In 1923 he set up in private practice as a design consultant in London as a direct result of which the 'Halford Special' built in 1924 was raced at Brooklands. That same year he shifted his office to Croydon where he was employed by ADC as a consultant in support of their endeavours to liquidate stock.

Halford was immediately tasked by ADC with making some of the engines, many of French lineage, more easily disposable, even at the risk of limited re-design. He chose as an early candidate an 80hp, eight-cylinder air-cooled Renault which he instinctively knew should be capable of producing more power in view of its size. By designing new cylinder heads in aluminium alloy and introducing twin overhead valves, he encouraged the developed power up to 140hp at 2,000rpm. The modified engine was renamed the ADC-Renault, later 'Airdisco' and in 1924 was fitted to the DH.51.

Designed against the formula devised by Halford and de Havilland their new prototype 'running' engine was assembled at the Waddon works of ADC and initially known as a 'half-Airdisco' or 'upright-four' eventually acquired a new name, 'Cirrus'. Design work, led largely by John Brodie, had been started only nine weeks before the first engine was bench-tested, when it developed 27hp on the RAC Rating, 60hp at 1,800rpm and 65hp at 2,000rpm, hence the contemporary designation of the engine as a '27/60' Cirrus.

In view of its private owner operating potential the engine was fitted with a mechanical self-starter. A geared clutch and ratchet lever attached to the port side of the engine was connected to a spring device on the back of the crankshaft, activated by a cable routed from a floor-mounted hand lever on the starboard side of the rear cockpit. When the lever was pulled, the cable caused the spring to wind up, and when released the stored energy was sufficient to turn the crankshaft through several revolutions. Although it was a commendable idea included in all marketing and promotion material and fitted to some early production Moths, in reality the starter proved to be more of a nuisance. The device eventually was removed from G-EBKT and subsequently offered only as an option.

Early press reports insisted on likening the new aero engine to that in the modern motor car and suggested that as the construction of the Cirrus engine 'is of the simplest and most straightforward' then 'maintenance should be well within the capabilities of the average motorist'. The ADC Company was keen to impress that reliability had been their chief objective combined with the introduction of progressive features, accessibility and low cost of maintenance. 'The engine lifts the light aeroplane from the experimental stage into the sphere of practical utility,' they rightly proclaimed.

The first running engine was fitted with a single impulse magneto, but it was already recognised that a dual system was likely to be an AID requirement, and all production cylinder heads were manufactured with provision for two sparking plugs. The technical specification was released to the press early in 1925:

The 27/60hp ADC Cirrus I Engine

Specification

- *Type: 4 cylinder, vertical, air cooled*
- *Bore: 105mm. Stroke: 130mm*
- *Capacity: 4.5 litres*
- *Normal hp: 60hp at 1,800rpm*
- *Maximum hp: 65hp at 2,000rpm*
- *Petrol consumption: 0.627 pints per hp per hour. (20 miles per gallon)*
- *Oil consumption: 0.013 pints per hp per hour. (1 to 1.5 pints per hour*
- *Weight dry: 286 lb (approx)*
- *Oil base (wet) capacity: 12 pints (Total capacity 20 pints)*
- *Airscrew: driven at direct speed*
- *Ignition: magneto with impulse starter*
- *Rotation: right hand tractor*
- *Overhaul life: 300 hours*

General Description

Cylinders: *cylinders and cylinder heads are separate, the cylinders being of cast iron and the cylinder heads of aluminium, with air cooling fins cast on each. The cylinders are spigoted into the crankcase and into the heads, the joint in heads being made by copper and asbestos washers. The complete cylinder with head is secured to the crankcase by means of four studs projecting from the crankcase and passing through holes in the cylinder head.*

Valves: *both inlet and exhaust valves are of the overhead type and are operated by rocking levers and push rods.*

Pistons: *the pistons are of aluminium and fitted with two cast iron piston rings and hardened steel gudgeon pin. The gudgeon pin is fixed to the small end of the connecting rod by a tapered bolt.*

Connecting rods: *the connecting rods are made of steel; the big ends are lined with white metal.*

Crankshaft: *the crankshaft proper has four throws and is carried in five bearings, the centre and two intermediate being gun metal, lined with white metal, and the outer ones ball bearings. An extension, or the propeller shaft, is bolted on to the forward end of the crankshaft. Another ball bearing, together with a thrust race, is provided for this extension.*

Crankcase: *the crankcase is an aluminium casting and is divided into two portions horizontally along the centre line of the crankshaft, the upper portion containing the bearings, camshaft and gears, the lower half forming an oil base and containing the oil pump, strainer and oil pressure relief valve. A small extension is bolted to the front of the top half of the crankcase, which acts as an oil filler and to which the breather pipes are attached.*

Camshaft: *the camshaft is driven off the end of the crankshaft through the medium of hardened steel gears. The gears are supported between ball bearings. Provision is made to*

couple the tachometer drive to the end of the camshaft. A spiral gear on the centre of the camshaft is arranged to drive the oil pump.

Inlet pipes: *the inlet or induction manifold is of copper with branches to each inlet valve port. A heater muff is provided, a pipe being taken from the exhaust manifold to this muff. The joints are made with copper and asbestos washers.*

Oil pump: *the oil pump which is arranged at the lowest part of the base so that it is always flooded or self primed with oil. The oil pump which is a gear type, forces the oil through a gauze filter which is arranged horizontally just above the pump, thence through the main delivery pipe to the oil gallery arranged on the port side of the engine. The oil gallery is connected to passages cast in the top half of the crankcase which runs to the centre and intermediate bearings, the oil is thus forced under pressure direct to each bearing. Castrol 'C' oil is recommended. The oil filter should be cleaned after every 20 hours' running.*

Oil pressure: *Provision is made for connecting the oil pressure gauge through the 'T' piece fitted in the oil pipe line to the timing gears. Pressure should be maintained at about 10 lb when the engine is hot. A relief valve is fitted but should only come into operation when starting up cold, as the oil pressure will then mount up to 25/30 lb due to the oil being very much thicker, and requiring much more effort to force it through the various passages. Pressure is registered on the gauge behind the engine, fitted to the top cowl of the fuselage.*

Ignition system: *the magneto fitted is the type G4 with impulse starter made by the BTH Company.*

Carburettor: *the standard carburettor is the Zenith 42 FS1, main jet 250; compensating jet 240. (Original specification).*

Technical descriptions of the new Moth appeared in all the aviation papers, but perhaps the best appeared a little after the initial euphoria when the correspondent had had time carefully to distil a considered review. His work was published towards the end of 1925 in *The Automobile Engineer*:

'*The fuselage construction follows very closely normal de Havilland practice, being three-ply covering on spruce longerons and web-member bracing. This type of body design, which may be termed semi-monocoque, has much to commend it. Its chief advantages are as follows:*

a. *It is cheap to produce both in small and large quantities. On account of the ease with which the two sides may be built up complete on a single jig, it lends itself admirably to quantity production.*
b. *Experience with machines having this type of fuselage, which have flown up to 200,000 miles shows that they retain their trim without maintenance.*

The Cirrus I engine from the starboard side showing the position of a single magneto, centrally mounted carburettor, induction pipe and exposed valve rocker gear. ADC

c. A clean exterior is obtained without any extra fairing.

d. Machines of this type have proved themselves to be remarkably safe in a crash.

e. Maximum strength is obtained at a very reasonable weight; also all members are amply duplicated.

f. The type lends itself to easy and cheap repair.

Past experience has brought to light two points which require watching. It is important that all edges of three-ply should be covered with glued tape and well painted or varnished, as a protection against damp. Also, all pockets which can possibly retain oil discharged from the engine breathers must either be filled in or should be provided with drain holes. These points have received attention.

'The wing structure follows normal practice and is of the single bay type. All structural members are of spruce, streamline wires being used externally and flexible cables internally for tension bracing. Although no wires are actually duplicated, in the event of a broken wire a very effective duplication actually comes into operation. If, for instance, a flying wire severs, its load is transmitted through the drift cables and incidence bracing to the other flying wire. In a full-scale test carried out on the ground to determine the effectiveness of this theory, the wing structure of the Moth retained its angle of incidence at the overhang within 1.25°. With an overload of 50%, all wires have a reasonably high factor of safety, calculated on the assumption that with a wire cut they sustain maximum load. This disposes of a very common criticism: why do not designers duplicate flying wires? Many pilots have landed fully loaded machines in safety with a broken flying wire.

'The extension wings have been designed to fold back, thereby enabling the machine to be wheeled through a doorway ten feet wide. The folding gear is of the simplest order, it being only necessary to clip the two jury struts into position, with-draw the four spring-loaded locking bolts, and fold the wings back, locking them in position by special catches provided. In this condition the machine can be towed behind a car with the greatest ease.

'The undercarriage is of the rubber-in-compression type, with radius rods and cross-bracing cables in front of a compression leg. In practice this arrangement would appear to have most of the advantages and qualities, from shock-absorbing point of view, of the oleo damped gear. The natural hysteresis of the rubber, combined with the friction of the sliding pistons and discs, provides sufficient rebound damping, the undercarriage retaining at the same time simplicity and needing the minimum of attention.

'The empennage is of the very simplest type. While the tailplane is fixed in flight, it can, of course, be adjusted on the ground to give correct trim. Longitudinal trim during flight is controlled by spring loaded gear installed in the pilot's cockpit (not fitted until April), and connected to the control stick. The machine can therefore easily be flown hands off at any speed. The fin is of cantilever construction, and following tests with the prototype, now carries a balanced rudder of the well-known DH shape. It has been found in practice that the rudder gives ample control when taxying on the ground.

'Attached to the lower part of the fin-post the tailskid is of the non-steering type sprung with ⅜in rubber cord like many of its forebears. Engineers practised in the art are able to replace a broken cord with a new one in about three minutes. The tailskid shoe is easily detachable for renewal when worn. A stirrup fitting is provided on the tailskid to engage with the lifting handle which is used when the machine has to be moved with the wings folded.

'Up-to-date practice is conformed to in the arrangement of the controls. Ball-races are employed throughout on the aileron and elevator controls, while pulleys have been entirely eliminated, levers being substituted in all cases. No cable touches any part of the structure throughout its length; the chance of cables fraying is therefore reduced to a minimum. The elevators are interconnected by a counter-shaft inside the rear fuselage, to reduce the chance of individual flutter and the mechanism can be inspected through a hole in the port side. The elevators are controlled by cables led from the aft cockpit inside the fuselage to a bell-crank lever at the after end, from which rods connect up to kingposts on the underside of the elevators. Two doors allow access to the tailskid bungee. Complete dual control is fitted. The forward control stick can, however, be removed, and the control gear completely enclosed when the pilot only is flying the machine. The forward rudder-bar is also easily disconnected. Due to distribution of load and the centre of gravity, when the Moth is flown solo the pilot must occupy the rear seat. (Early Moths were controlled with "sticks" fitted with spade grips, but these were later discontinued on civil machines).

'The two ailerons which act on the lower planes only are operated by the de Havilland patent differential gear, which is housed inside the lower planes and connected by two cables to the controls within the fuselage. Explained quite briefly, the differential aileron gear functions so that when the control stick is moved, say, to the starboard, the port aileron will travel down through a considerably smaller angle than the starboard aileron will move upwards. In this way a balancing effect is obtained which should result in a lighter control. Further, in addition to the rolling moment imposed on the machine by the movement of differentially controlled ailerons, a yawing moment in the right direction is also set up, which enables a smaller rudder to be employed. (The aileron differential gear was patented by the de Havilland Aircraft Company in 1922 [No 184317] with designer Arthur Hagg named jointly).

'Located inside the top centre section plane, the petrol tank is well streamlined, and supplies fuel by simple gravity to the carburettor through Petroflex piping. A three-way two-level cock is fitted to the petrol tank, giving a reserve supply of 1.25 gallons, sufficient for about 20 minutes, the total capacity of the tank being 15 gallons. A float operated gauge is fitted, and this has been found in practice to be very reliable. The makers recommend that the petrol filter should be cleaned out every day; the drain cock on the petrol tank sump should be turned on every day and if necessary cleared with a wire in order to release any water or foreign matter in the sump.

'The engine is mounted direct on the top longerons by cast aluminium brackets bolted direct to the crank case. The engine cowling is simple, quickly detachable, and forms an efficient streamlining to the forward part of the fuselage. A baffle, fixed to the port top cowling, deflects part of the slipstream between the rear cylinders, and provides ample cooling. In practice it has been found that the Moth can be climbed full throttle on the hottest day, for a considerable length of time, without any suggestion of over-heating.

'For special long-distance flights up to 750 miles non-stop, an extra petrol tank may be fitted in the passenger's seat. This is provided with a hand pump by which the pilot can replenish the gravity tank while in flight.'

Additional Technical Specification was listed for the DH.60:

Performance (at 1,255 lb): speed, full throttle near ground, 90mph. Speed, cruising at 1,800rpm, 75mph. Speed, stalling, 40mph. Rate of climb, ground level, 440ft. per. min. Time to climb to 5,000ft, 14.75min. Ceiling (absolute), 13,000ft.

Minimum factors of safety: normal flight C.P. forward, 5.5; normal flight C.P. aft, 4.0; worst wire cut C.P. forward 2.75; worst wire cut C.P. aft, 2.0; limiting nose dive, 1.25. These factors cover the normal type of stunting that this type of machine could reasonably be expected to perform.

Within a week of the maiden flight, one perceptive correspondent summed up the situation with a remarkably accurate and insightful prediction: 'We may look forward to the day when there are low-power aeroplanes, light 'planes, lighter 'planes and slightly lighter 'planes. The one great thing achieved at the moment is that we have got away from the capacity rating, and that some other figure, probably the total weight, will form the basis of the future light aeroplane as a class.'

On 26th February 1925, during his Parliamentary presentation of the Air Estimates, the Secretary of State for Air, Sir Samuel Hoare, touched on the problems encountered in establishing the promised light aeroplane clubs without an engine suitable for a two-seat training machine. However, he said that he had reason for hoping that in the course of the summer, a beginning would be made with an experiment that may prove very valuable in the matter of training pilots and of diffusing an air sense throughout the nation.

For the first time in history, the Air Estimates included a sum voted for 'assistance to light aeroplane clubs'. The £22,000 declared was still considered insufficient by many, even when compared to the proposals as originally announced, but with only six clubs now to be subsidised instead of ten, it was generally agreed that something could be started in real earnest.

St Barbe invited the press to Stag Lane on 3rd and 4th March in a move to guarantee maximum coverage from journals publishing at the end of that week. Neither engine nor airframe having yet passed their Air Ministry acceptance tests, the few short flights available were limited to within a three-mile radius of the aerodrome. There was no 'hands-on' experience to report because the front control stick had been removed, but one astute airman noted how very little rudder was necessary after time spent with his head in the cockpit studying movement of the controls. 'Every detail showed the impress of a pilot designer'. He also thought the tiny front windscreen was not wholly adequate. The writer was in no position to discuss these observations with Hubert Broad for G-EBKT was still lacking any form of inter-cockpit communication, although a Gosport system was fitted, as intended, a few days afterwards.

The sculpted cockpits of the Moth were not fitted with doors, apart from a modest flap hinged to the top longeron on the port side which let down to permit entry from the wing-walkway to the front seat situated underneath the petrol tank. As the Cirrus engine's exhaust ports were on this same side, the exhaust pipe was routed across the front decking ahead of the windscreen and secured to the starboard side of the fuselage. The pilot occupying the rear seat needed to be athletic to climb over the fixed surround, a feature which was not to be revised for some considerable time.

Following a prolonged period of heavy rain, the aerodrome surface which through-out Stag Lane's entire history suffered regular saturation due to its saucer-like disposition on London clay, was described as 'deplorable' and 'nothing but a quagmire'. To some extent the atrocious conditions proved a benefit, for few observers believed any of the Lympne two-seater trialists could possibly have got off. The Moth demonstrated it had ample reserves of power to cope with the situation, an attribute it surely needed if ever it were to be considered a practical all-weather proposition.

A journalist who had reported on the construction of the Moth flew two trips in poor weather with Hubert Broad early the following month. 'Though the weather was reputed to be very bumpy the bumps were scarcely felt at all, owing to the ease with which they could be corrected'. He continued, 'Admittedly as a training machine the Moth will be no encourager of the ham-fisted type of pupil. But pilots trained on this machine will have the enormous advantage of acquiring from the start that lightness of handling which, it must be confessed, was very difficult to impart to pupils on the heavy handed instructional machines which were formerly so much in use'.

The aircraft was also put through a spinning routine. 'As expected, stalling the Moth leads to no alarming drop but merely to that slight sinking feeling which is not surprising as she is controllable at 40mph. When coaxed into a spin she spins fairly fast, owing to the short span, but a straightened rudder brings her out instantly. An adjustable spring on the joy-stick, fore-and-aft, takes the place of the adjustable tail actually found on larger machines, so that for touring purposes the machine is as suitable as for instructional.'

The Aeronautical Correspondent of the *London Times* noted that Hubert Broad had shown the aeroplane's powers by 'looping, spinning and carrying out turns with perfect ease' although due to a misunderstanding at the time an aerobatic C of A had not been applied for. The Moth took longer to get off due to the aerodrome being waterlogged, he noted, and Captain Broad was forced to climb out in order to lift the tail round into the strong wind, but the larger school machines, DH.9s, had been stopped from operating altogether. Assisted by a briefing from de Havilland's Business Manager, no doubt, the same correspondent was able to advise the nation that 'the Moth is the most promising contribution yet made to the difficult problem of getting the youth of the nation into the air, for while it is something more than a light aeroplane, it is considerably less than the normal full size machine'. Part of the report was quoted prominently in full page advertisements for the Moth which appeared in aviation papers shortly afterwards. Earlier issues had carried photographs selected from a series taken imme-diately after G-EBKT had been painted, but before her introduction to the press. In what appeared to have been an interlude of bright sunshine, the aeroplane's tailskid was attached to the back shelf of an open Bull-nose Morris and, driven by Hubert Broad in trilby hat, overcoat, collar and tie, accompanied by a pretty young lady in flying suit and fur-trimmed leather helmet, believed to be film actress Estelle Brody, commenced a tour of Colindale, Burnt Oak and Stone Grove, negotiating with care what little traffic was encountered on the Edgware Road. On the aerodrome, the happy couple were photographed effortlessly and dispassionately locking the folding wings into the rigged position and putting on board a set of golf clubs, but to be accommodated who knows where? As a publicity stunt it was outstandingly successful and nobody with an interest could have failed to notice just how practical and adaptable this new aeroplane appeared to be.

Broad resumed testing on 4th March with a low-speed solo flight of sixty minutes and with the ignition slightly retarded. The following morning he flew for almost an hour with 200 lb of ballast in the front cockpit and later that day climbed to 10,000ft carrying C C Walker, Chief Engineer, acting as observer. The purpose of the 'trial' was recorded as 'short climbs at 60mph with various throttle openings. Short glides at same speed with engine ticking over'. It was logged that, on average, petrol consumption was about four gallons per hour. Broad noted that there was 'too much surging in atmosphere for good test' and that his touchdown speed was 41mph. So far it was the longest flight lasting 1hr 20min. Six additional flights were logged by Broad on 6th, 7th and 10th March on which occasion he flew with W T W Ballantyne as observer in three separate tests, climbing to and descending from 10,000ft at prescribed speeds, in weather conditions that were described as clear and cold but bumpy below 5,000ft.

Broad's logbook does not record his test flight with Ballantyne on 18th March after a new Zenith triple diffuser carburettor had been fitted, or several later tests. The climb on this date was discontinued at 6,400ft after the engine began to mis-fire due to over-richness, and black smoke was seen coming from the exhaust pipe. Nor was their flight of 24th March logged. For this, G-EBKT had been fitted with larger windscreens but at 9,000ft the engine became very rough with reducing rpm, causing the crew to make an early return to Stag Lane. Eric Mitchell rectified the problem by decarbonising the heads and changing a plug.

For the next several weeks, Broad continued with his freelance career working for much of April in support of both Handley Page and Gloster. On 20th April, flying a

DH.9, he crashed the aeroplane on landing at Cricklewood in an effort to avoid a goal-post, but was unhurt. In his absence the test flying programme at Stag Lane was continued by Captain de Havilland with Hessell Tiltman as observer.

As a result of lobbying by representatives of the aero clubs who, together with officials from the Air Ministry, had been invited by the de Havilland Company to view the Moth at Stag Lane, and under the subhead of the £22,000 voted in the 1925 Air Estimates, the Air Ministry announced its latest financial package early in March. Inevitably, this was not universally welcomed, but was regarded as a significant improvement over previous offers. Essentially, each club was to receive a maximum of £2,000 in the first year to cover the purchase of two 'light planes', one spare engine and sundry operational equipment. In addition, the Air Ministry agreed to pay £1,000 per annum for two years for maintenance, half the cost of a replacement machine should a club suffer an accidental total loss, and a payment of £10 for each pilot trained *ab initio* to licence standard within the club.

The major dissatisfaction stemmed from the apparent allocation of the first year's cash grant to the purchase of just two aeroplanes. A club with 200 members, for example, might consider this ratio inadequate and prospectively damaging to enthusiasm if heavy bookings were to result in long waiting lists for flights. But realising this was likely to be the best offer made prior to the definition of a 'light plane' and the provision of an approved engine, the clubs accepted the new terms during a conference held at the Royal Aero Club on 18th March. St Barbe's reaction was immediate promotion of the DH.53 and DH.60 together as 'Complementary Flying Club Equipment'.

'The DH.53 Humming Bird can be looped, spun and rolled, and it behaves and is handled in exactly the same way as full sized machines'. And in support of the DH.60, an earlier message was repeated lest anybody might have forgotten that the de Havilland Moth 'is as sturdy and lasting as the modern light car'.

Having established a financial framework within which to operate, J F Barnes, Secretary of the Yorkshire Aeroplane Club, enquired of the de Havilland Aircraft Company on 26th March, details of the current position regarding certification of the DH.60 Moth and her Cirrus engine. St Barbe answered by return:

'We beg to advise you that the Certificate of Airworthiness for the Moth has not yet come to hand, as the Air Ministry Airworthiness Department has not yet completed its investigations into the design. There is no doubt, however, that the machine will qualify for the document in question, and it is expected that this matter will be cleared up in the course of a few days.

'The Cirrus engine is now undergoing its type trials at the works of its makers, The Aircraft Disposal Company. It is undergoing this test in an extraordinarily successful manner and very shortly should be certified as airworthy. (It will probably qualify not only for a civil licence, but will also be suitable for military use).

'As soon as the engine is approved, the first Moth will leave for Martlesham Heath, where its flying trials will be carried out'.

The Yorkshire Club secretary was additionally advised by Tender No 185 that the standard selling specification for an early production Moth was as follows:

To supply one de Havilland Moth two-seater light aeroplane (DH Type 60) fitted with 27-60hp Cirrus engine, complete with the following instrument equipment:

2 Air-speed Indicators – pitot head.
1 Revolution Indicator and drive.
1 Aneroid.
1 Oil Pressure Gauge.
1 Inclinometer.

Fitted with hand starter in pilot's cockpit and painted in any colours. Registered and accompanied by a British Air Ministry Certificate of Airworthiness.
Per each. Nett price £885.

Specification of materials:
To Designer's Specification.

System of Inspection and Examination: *Our own Inspection Department under the supervision of the British Air Ministry Aeronautical Inspection Directorate.*

Terms of payment: *20% cash with order – remainder upon production of Certificate of Airworthiness proving completion of aircraft and its readiness for delivery.*

Delivery programme: *Deliveries will be effected in rotation – normal delivery 8 weeks.*

The quoted price of a DH.60 Moth, ex-Stag Lane works, erected and ready for flight, at £885 might have shocked the Editor of *Flight* who in his paper published only three weeks previously had accepted that the demonstrated performance of the new aeroplane was 'most satisfactory'. But, he continued: 'we do not know what the de Havilland Aircraft Company intends to charge for the Moth, and it seems doubtful whether any definite figure can be quoted at the moment, as much will obviously depend upon the number of orders received. It does, however, appear probable that if built in batches of 50 or so, the machine could be produced to sell at about £500'.

From 1st April a slight change of emphasis resulted in the company's advertisements promoting figures for weight and performance, and the following week, the wording was again carefully considered. 'A school aeroplane of simple and robust construction, of good performance, and exceptionally economical to run', was the message carried simultaneously in English, French, Spanish and German.

ADC completed a 100-hour run in pursuit of an Air Ministry Type Approval on a test-bed Cirrus engine during the first week of April 1925. No problems were encountered and the fears that the rear cylinders might be susceptible to overheating were

Press day at Stag Lane on 4th March 1925. While members of the Press inspect the prototype DH.60, others interview Chief Engineer Charles Walker. General Manager Frank Hearle is at centre left wearing a bowler hat and light coloured raincoat.
BAE Systems

allayed following a prolonged run with a conventional propeller.

The prototype Moth meanwhile was still accumulating flight time in support of her application for an airworthiness certificate and, while manufacturer's engine tests continued, the three-mile flight limit necessitated her travelling by lorry from Stag Lane to the ADC works on Croydon Airport. During unloading, a plank broke when she was being rolled off the back of the transport, and the airframe was damaged in the subsequent heavy landing which also broke her propeller. During repairs undertaken at Stag Lane the opportunity was taken to fit the larger Dunlop 600 x 75 wheels, spring catches on the wing-folding pins and a spring-loaded trimmer for the elevator controls. Other minor details and the final 'lead paint' finish applied to the fuselage all contributed to a new tare weight of 798 lb.

Captain de Havilland and Hessell Tiltman recommenced performance flight testing on 15th April with a new DH5120 propeller of 6ft diameter and 4.6ft pitch and the following day G-EBKT was airborne with a special muff attached to the intake manifold and a lagged exhaust pipe. It was noted that when operating in cold air, the engine produced about 80rpm more than in hot.

A meeting hosted by the Air Ministry on 31st March and attended by officials from the Royal Aero Club, Society of British Aircraft Constructors and the principal engine manufacturers, was convened to discuss the Two-Seater Light Aeroplane Competition for 1925. Their decision was to limit entrants to aeroplanes with engines weighing no more than 170 lb. Later detail confirmed that both aeroplane and engine must be of British manufacture, the competing pilots must be British subjects, and the declared task would be to complete about 1,000 miles of flying split into multiple stages. Most importantly, in view of the major shift in emphasis regards engine specification, and following review of the mistakes of the recent past when it was accepted that insufficient development time had been allowed, it was announced that there would in fact be no Competition in 1925 at all, and all effort was to be directed towards August of the following year.

Criticism was immediately heaped onto the heads of those responsible for these decisions and doubts were expressed whether, at 170 lb, the formula would produce the type of engine or class of machine generally required. But another decision of considerable significance was made at the same time. The Air Ministry advised the Royal Aero Club that it would be pleased for them to act as agents for the purchase of aircraft on behalf of the light aeroplane clubs, and it agreed, however reluctantly, that the de Havilland DH.60 Moth with its 60hp ADC Cirrus I engine was its approved choice.

The Royal Aero Club placed orders on the de Havilland Aircraft Company immediately after a delegate's meeting on 16th April, which called for two DH.60 Moths and one spare Cirrus I engine each for the Lancashire Aero Club, Newcastle-upon-Tyne Light Aeroplane Club, and their own Light Aeroplane Section. The Glasgow Club was suffering from lack of support and excused itself from the scheme for the time being. The requirements of the remaining two clubs, Midland and Yorkshire, were not confirmed, but it was expected that they would agree to take DH.60 Moths also. All orders were expected to be satisfied by deliveries from Stag Lane in early June. In the event, the Yorkshire Aeroplane Club ordered only one Moth, and no spare engine, whereas the Midland Club followed the precedent of the other four.

St Barbe's advertising agency ensured the news received maximum exposure in whole page advertisements booked against the earliest available press opportunities. There was no great extravagance, just a picture of the prototype and a simple statement that the Moth two-seater light aeroplane was to be used by the Air Ministry's selected clubs. How very inspired then, having secured the British club order, immediately to promote the virtues of the DH.60 as seen by an American correspondent writing for *Aero Digest* magazine in New York. Set against a photograph of the Trilby-hatted Hubert Broad, his lady companion, G-EBKT and a set of golf clubs, readers were advised that:

'Our English cousins are demonstrating to a sceptical world that a really fine aeroplane can fulfil the optimistic promises made for it. The de Havilland Moth, for example, proves to be capable of a reasonable speed range, is ruggedly built and the fortunate selection of a trustworthy low-powered engine places it in the practical class of light aeroplanes. The machine's ability to rise from and alight upon rather unfavourable terrain with relatively little difficulty makes it an ideal one-man ship for cross-country travel.'

On 21st April, the day after his DH.9 crash at Cricklewood, Hubert Broad demonstrated G-EBKT to members of the Canadian Air Board at Stag Lane, squeezing four flights into a 35min schedule. Captain de Havilland flew 'KT on each of the next five days and Alan Butler made a solo flight in her 'around Stag Lane' on 24th. On 29th April, Broad was cleared to take her to Cranwell to inspect the aerodrome in preparation for flying his prospective mount, the Gloster III, in the Schneider Trophy Contest scheduled for Baltimore in the late autumn.

Following return to Stag Lane, a new carburettor and induction system were fitted in addition to modification of the washers on some cylinder head holding-down studs.

The work was completed in time for a series of demonstration flights to be recorded on 1st May flown by Broad, followed by another week of routine testing with a DH5124 propeller ('constructed in mahogany, diameter 5.58ft and pitch 4.8ft with Air Ministry metal tip No 12 modified as indicated on the drawing to 26g thickness and a width of 0.75in instead of 1.0in') by both Broad and Captain de Havilland. On 10th May Broad landed G-EBKT on Byfleet Golf Course, although there is no indication that this was anything but a premeditated exercise.

After measuring the attitude of the machine in the glide at various speeds between 45-65mph, using the 'top rail' as reference, Tiltman's report concluded: 'The angles indicate that this machine has a normal gliding angle, ie. the same as the machines DH.9 (standard), DH.51, and does not have the characteristics of the DH.37 and DH.34'.

The aeroplane clubs continued to make plans anticipating delivery of their Moths in the early summer. The Lancashire Aero Club received word from the Avro Company who assured them of a hangar and use of their Woodford Aerodrome, 'entirely without charges of any kind'.

The Royal Aero Club agreed to form a separate company to operate the machines allocated to the London District of their Light Aeroplane Section, initially known as the London Light Aeroplane Club. Incorporated as the London Aero Club Ltd, but operating as the London Aeroplane Club, headquarters were established with some surprise at Stag Lane, and not at Hendon as had been confidently predicted. It is believed the suggestion that they should settle at Stag Lane was made by Frank Hearle, the Works' Manager, and was fully endorsed by the Club and the Company, both of whom could see enormous practical advantages and mutual benefit.

St Barbe booked the order for nine DH.60 Moths which was received from the Royal Aero Club. The first of them was registered G-EBLI (183), on behalf of the London Club on 29th May, but the remaining eight were not registered to their operating companies until 22nd June and in the following order:

184	G-EBLR	Light Planes (Lancashire) Ltd, Woodford
185	G-EBLS	Yorkshire Aeroplane Club Ltd, Roundhay
186	G-EBLT	Midland Aero Club Ltd, Castle Bromwich
187	G-EBLU	London Aero Club Ltd, Stag Lane
188	G-EBLV	Light Planes (Lancashire) Ltd, Woodford
189	G-EBLW	Midland Aero Club Ltd, Castle Bromwich
190	G-EBLX	Newcastle-upon-Tyne Light Aeroplane Club Ltd, Cramlington

191 G-EBLY Newcastle-upon-Tyne Light
              Aeroplane Club Ltd,
              Cramlington

At the beginning of May, the Aircraft Disposal Company confirmed that the Cirrus engine had successfully passed the British Air Ministry Type Test of 100 hours, 'to date, the first and only British low powered aero engine to do so'. The order of test was quantified by the makers:

- 10 hours on Heenan and Froude Brake.
  54hp at 1,800rpm.

- 50 hours on calibrated propeller.
  54.5hp at 1,820rpm.

- 39 hours on Heenan and Froude Brake.
  54hp at 1,800rpm.

- 1 hour on Heenan and Froude Brake.
  Full throttle at normal revs.
  61hp at 1,800rpm.

- 1 hour on Heenan and Froude Brake.
  At high revs, 2.080rpm.

- 1 hour on Heenan and Froude Brake.
  High power and high revs.
  68.25hp at 1,980rpm.

The engine had run faultlessly and not a single spark plug was changed, a point not lost on those who championed the cause of single ignition.

With the DH.60 and her Cirrus engine launched into what the de Havilland Aircraft Company hoped would be an expanding and profitable market and with the blessing of the Air Ministry, it was time for the Company to raise as much public awareness as it could. Support and encouragement were needed for a new candidate to fill the sixth subsidised position made vacant by the temporary withdrawal of the Glasgow Club, and to ensure that they too ordered Moths. In the event, this sixth position was not allocated until the following year when on 8th June 1926, two DH.60 Moths, G-EBOH (269) and G-EBOI (270), were registered to the Hampshire Aeroplane Club Ltd, operating from the Avro aerodrome at Hamble.

Alan Cobham, a publicity-conscious pilot employed as Manager of the de Havilland Aeroplane Hire Service, took little persuasion to make, in May, a live wireless transmission on the still new airwaves of the British Broadcasting Company, in which he was heard offering flying instruction, supposedly in a Moth, to London actress Heather Thatcher. One listener believed that although Cobham's voice on occasions rivalled that of well known comedian Harry Tate, the whole business was in reality an excellent piece of propaganda for flying, even though the entire 'lesson' had taken place in the shadow of a DH.51 in the erecting shop at Stag Lane.

By the end of April the prototype motor had logged a total running time of forty hours in sixty flights. The longest single non-stop trip of 2hr 35min was flown on 29th April, the day before the change of carburettor. Some maximum weight circuits of Stag Lane on 2nd May with larger diameter mainwheels and flown by Broad and Tiltman confirmed that the DH5124 propeller was satisfactory after which a further 14hr running time was added. This included two 20min flight checks by Alan Cobham on 28th May during which G-EBKT was credited with passing the 5,000 mile mark, a contemporary measure of the degree of use, and valued as more relevant than flying hours. That evening, Cobham landed G-EBKT at Croydon Airport; the following morning he had a very early breakfast and at a few minutes before 5.00am he took off again bound non-stop for Zurich.

Part of the preparation for the flight, to which St Barbe had made some allusion during the press demonstration at Stag Lane on 2nd March, included the installation of a 25-gallon capacity long-range petrol tank in the front cockpit which, with the windscreen removed, was then faired over. Fuel was hand-pumped against a regular schedule to the main tank in the centre section, which for this exercise had been changed to increase capacity to 19 gallons.

The Moth followed the familiar railway line to Lympne Aerodrome, circled overhead to be observed, and crossed the English Channel to strike the French coast at St Inglevert, where an identical performance concluded the cross-Channel protocols. From that point it was a matter of flying in a direct line straight to Zurich; where in spite of a cloud-impeded crossing of the Vosges mountains, Cobham arrived without further incident after a flight of six hours. Following a forty-five minute turn-round during which both man and machine were refreshed, the Moth was headed back to Croydon where, due to the influence of headwinds, touchdown was not achieved until seven and three quarter hours later. Due to the strength of the wind, much of the latter part of the return flight had been conducted at low level, often at about 100ft, where turbulence caused extreme discomfort.

Zurich was chosen as a target partly because it was situated almost exactly 500 miles from Croydon, and a round-trip figure of 1,000 miles was considered of significance when judged by the public. The flight in each direction had been made solo but clearly demonstrated the ease with which such a journey could be undertaken by two people in a Moth, refuelling as necessary en-route. It was not the first return flight from London to Zurich accomplished in a day, neither was it the longest non-stop solo flight in an aeroplane of its class, but it achieved all that was expected in terms of publicity. In a total running time of 14hr 35min, the Cirrus engine had consumed 56 gallons of petrol and 14 pints of oil, at a direct operating cost compared with contemporary prices of less than half that charged by public transport, and with a considerable saving in time.

The day following G-EBKT's return to Croydon, Frederick Handley Page wrote a congratulatory letter to C C Walker, not wasting the opportunity to promote his Company's new and patented invention, the leading edge slot:

'Hearty congratulations on the firm's success with the Moth flown by Cobham. I wish more people would do it. I cannot, of course, forbear to add that with the slotted control on it, it will be improved, but that is, perhaps, my fanaticism. However, when you have got it on you had better send St Barbe down here to book an order for one of the machines. Let me be quite clear, please. Send St Barbe after it has flown with it on, not to promise to fit it and fly it after I have placed an order.

Apart from all these remarks, many congratulations. You have done more good for civil aviation by this flight than by most things that have happened hitherto.'

The DH.60 Moth was described in the inevitable follow-up advertising as 'the most practical and successful light aeroplane which the world has so far seen' and the flight itself was 'a convincing demonstration of the practicability of the Moth for serious travel'. Subsequent maintenance work on Cirrus engine No 1 revealed the need to replace three valve rocker brackets, a job which was completed on 3rd June. The following day, Alan Cobham, accompanied by Lieutenant Colonel Ivo Edwardes of the Air Ministry as passenger, took G-EBKT off from Stag Lane bound for Tempelhof Airport, Berlin. Flying near Middelharnis in The Netherlands, the engine stopped due to fuel starvation, and G-EBKT was damaged when the undercarriage collapsed as she ran into a shallow ditch after an otherwise successful forced landing on rough ground.

The cause of the engine failure was blamed on an air lock in a small-diameter supply pipe which prevented fuel from being pumped out of the small auxiliary tank into the main. The engine had logged a running time of 3hr 45min on the day of the accident, which equated to maximum endurance when using the standard supply of 15 gallons. While Colonel Edwardes went on to Berlin by train, Cobham arranged for G-EBKT to be transferred to Antwerp by barge, from where she was subsequently carried back to England by ship.

On 8th June 1925 the engine was removed from 'KT after 73 hours and relocated in the vacant bearers of the DH.60 Moth second prototype G-EBKU.

JULY TO DECEMBER 1925

THE SECOND prototype DH.60 Moth G-EBKU (169), was commissioned at Stag Lane on 13th June. The engine was situated four inches further back in the bearers and at her check-weighing, completed on 16th June, G-EBKU recorded a tare weight of 787 lb, eleven pounds lighter than the first prototype. The fuselage was painted mid-blue, complemented initially with clear doped wings and tail. The exhaust system was more conveniently routed along the port side of the fuselage, and the front cockpit door was repositioned to the starboard side, a significant change that became the production standard and was applied to 'KT in retrospect. But neither G-EBKT nor G-EBKU were built with external access to storage space in the decking behind the rear cockpit and were not subsequently modified to accept a door in this position when the convenience was recognised.

After prototype G-EBKT had been painted, she carried the legend 'DH MOTH' on the front fuselage sides. Later this titling was removed and both she and her sister were adorned with the blocked-in planform of a moth in the same location, well forward of the front cockpit, the letters 'D' and 'H' superimposed on the left and right wings respectively. Early production aeroplanes had the legend 'MOTH' in block capital letters added underneath the stylised insect. At a later date the moth became more subtle

with elegantly crafted letters 'DH' placed just above the artwork and this layout was maintained until the advent of the famous six-point star. Although modified slightly in colour and size over the years, the star became the standard fuselage insignia for all DH.60 Moths, with transfers of the Company's angular badge in black and gold applied to both sides of all four wooden interplane struts, a distinguishing feature which was quickly copied by competing manufacturers.

The rudder fitted to G-EBKU was redesigned to accommodate an aerodynamic balance, a feature which was applied retrospectively to 'KT prior to July's King's Cup Air Race. The rounded shape remained a classical identification for the entire range of de Havilland's light aeroplanes, including the later biplane twins.

In view of Cobham's accident with G-EBKT in June, and as a precaution against fuel locks, the internal diameter of the gravity-feed pipe from the main tank to the carburettor was increased. At a later date, a foot-tread frame was let into the front fuselage side forward of the 'Moth' insignia, to assist when climbing up to the fuel tank and although the majority of these remained as 'open' orifices, some were fitted with a spring-loaded cover-plate.

G-EBKU's maiden flight, conducted by Captain de Havilland, lasted for three quar-

ters of an hour and she logged two hours the next day, 14th June, which was a Sunday. There followed an intensive programme of trials during which she flew on each of the next twelve consecutive days excepting 21st June, but accumulated only 15 hours in a total of 48 mostly local flights. Hubert Broad flew 'KU for ten minutes on 15th June, taking time off from a heavy programme with the DH.54 Highclere commercial airliner. The previous day he had flown a DH.9 to and from Paris on behalf of the *Daily Mail*, during which he had logged his 3,000th flying hour. On 23rd June, G-EBKU flew nine times and on that date qualified for a Certificate of Airworthiness (C of A). Two days later, exactly three weeks after her altercation with a ditch in The Netherlands, G-EBKT also was issued with her Certificate.

Due to a misunderstanding, de Havilland had applied for and had been granted, a Normal Category C of A at a maximum weight of 1,350 lb, but aerobatics were not authorised. Both prototype Moths had been built using Grade A spruce, but the Company declared that all subsequent aircraft would use the lower specification Grade B. Following investigation by the Structural Strength Branch at RAE Farnborough, a series of modifications was detailed in order for production aircraft built from Grade B materials to qualify for an aerobatic C of A at 1,250 lb. For a structural weight increase estimated at 50 lb, all mainspars were to be strengthened, also the elevator spars, elevator connecting rods and ends, and the connecting rods between control sticks. Until such times that the C of A was reclassified, all pilots were to be made aware of the non-aerobatic limitations which it was realised would restrict the type's training capabilities.

In an attempt to placate the Director of Technical Development, St Barbe issued an assurance that the DH.60 had been designed and built to aerobatic requirements but the Ministry remained sceptical, believing that, for aerobatics, the aircraft was under-strength. The matter was not to

Second prototype DH.60 Moth, G-EBKU, also appeared with clear-doped flying surfaces but was fitted with a balanced rudder and an exhaust system on the port side before her first flight. DH Moth Club Archive

G-EBKT with her retro-fitted balanced rudder, running-up against chocks under the care of RAF personnel at Croydon in July 1925, prior to taking off in the King's Cup Air Race. DH Moth Club Archive

be resolved until the end of the year when, following further modifications to the bottom front spar, the DH.60 Moth was officially cleared for aerobatics at a weight of 1,280 lb.

Hubert Broad delivered G-EBKT to Martlesham Heath for tests, as invited, but not until after the value of the aeroplane had been agreed in case of a total loss. Francis St Barbe had advised the Air Ministry: 'For your information we value this machine at £2,000, which figure is half the total amount which we have spent in designing and constructing the first aircraft of this new type'. After a week's consideration St Barbe revised the figure downwards to £1,200, agreeing that the Company would take the risk on the difference between the two valuations.

Two weeks prior to the maiden flight of G-EBKU, the Royal Aero Club (RAeC) was still considering the Draft Regulations for the 1926 Two-seater Light Aeroplane Competition.

The argument over what was a light aeroplane as opposed to a 'heavy' light aeroplane continued to exercise the thoughts of some who wanted to renew old arguments and believed that in 1925, it was 'surely possible for machines of modern design, in conjunction with the more efficient engines of today to fly with ample margins as a single or two-seater on 12hp or less'. But the debate concerning minimal horsepower was already lost to practical reasoning.

In June the RAeC was able to announce terms and conditions of membership for the London Aeroplane Club, 'formed with the object of bringing together as members of the Club, persons interested in flying, and for the purpose of providing and maintaining aeroplanes for the use and instruction of Members of the Club'. Membership was open to British subjects only, was to consist of Ordinary and Associate Members and, in an emancipated age, was open to 'both sexes'. Details of flying charges were circulated by the Secretary:

Two-seater dual control. £1.10s per flying hour, which charge includes the cost of instruction, oil and petrol, damage to aeroplane and third party insurance.

Single seater. £1 per flying hour, which includes the cost of oil and petrol, damage to aeroplane and third party insurance. The minimum time for which aeroplanes may be hired will be half an hour. Subject to the prior claims of instructional and solo flying, Associate Members will be permitted to hire aeroplanes for passenger flying at the rate of £1.10s per flying hour.

It is hoped to be able to commence flying instruction early in July. Two DH Moth machines have been acquired out of the grant made by the Air Council, and fully qualified pilot instructors will be available to give flying instruction to the members daily, including Sundays.

It is hoped that members who are able to do so, will attend at the aerodrome during the week so as to reduce as far as possible any overcrowding at the weekends. The acquisition of additional machines depends on the extent to which the scheme is supported.'

The Midland Aero Club announced its proposed terms on 13th July. Whilst hoping to take delivery of its first two Moths by the end of the month, the committee was already considering limiting membership to about 1,000 'including ladies'. It proved to be a hugely over-optimistic view.

The Lancashire Aero Club produced the first issue of its monthly bulletin *The Elevator* in July and, in a section intended to be less than serious, posed the question: 'How long (or short), will it take to crash a Moth, and who will be the culprit (or victim)?'. The bulletin also made some of the earliest references to flying members being known as 'Mothers'.

Both prototype DH.60 Moths were entered in the 1925 King's Cup Air Race and positioned to Croydon on 2nd July to start early the following morning. In preparation, the engine fitted to G-EBKU was top-overhauled at a little over 90 hours accumulated running time. Additional work included routing the exhaust pipe of each aircraft vertically down behind the engine, inside the cowlings; fitting KLG F15 sparking plugs into the exhaust side of the cylinder heads; the removal of externally mounted oil pressure

indicators and the installation of a 4:1 rev-counter drive onto the back of the crankshaft.

Flown as normal two-seaters with passengers on board, Alan Cobham flying G-EBKT entered by Lord Wakefield, and Captain de Havilland in 'KU, took off at 6.00am bound for Harrogate and quickly disappeared from the view of the few early riser spectators, flying into a thick ground mist, sustained by a stiff wind blowing off the North Sea. Both Moths subsequently made precautionary landings due to the visibility but, abandoning the Race, found their way back to Stag Lane later that day. It was an unfortunate beginning but all was not completely lost.

In view of the disappointment of the King's Cup, in which only three of the fourteen starters completed the course, the 'Croydon Stakes Consolation Handicap' was organised for Saturday 4th July in which five of the 'retired' King's Cup entrants were invited to take part. Alan Cobham in 'KT was joined by Wally Hope flying 'KU, racing against an Airdisco Avro 548A, a Lynx Avro 504N and a DH.51. The course took in 523 miles of the original King's Cup route, flying from Croydon to Bristol, Shotwick, Blackpool and Harrogate, before the final leg back to Croydon.

The 'Consolation Handicap' which became the 'Race Round England' in de Havilland's post-event publicity, was won by the DH.51 G-EBIQ flown by Colonel The Master of Sempill, with Alan Cobham second and Wally Hope in fourth place at a much reduced average speed. It was later discovered that during his aggregated airborne time of slightly less than seven hours, Hope had been flying with a wildly inaccurate compass from which all the magnets were later found to be missing.

Both prototype Moths continued their racing careers at the Bank Holiday meeting

organised by the Royal Aero Club during the first three days of August at Lympne, 'an aerodrome with many attractions from the competitors' point of view'. There were to be no laurels for the advertising agents to exploit this time. In Heat 2 of the International Handicap, a 100 mile race on 3rd August, 'KT and 'KU flown by Alan Cobham and Hubert Broad respectively, finished in second and third positions, separated in time by fifteen seconds. In the Final, Broad could manage only fourth place, and appeared over the finishing line without a sign of Cobham who had been flying at very low level. Broad took off again in 'KU, only to find that 'KT had forced-landed in a wheat field on the last lap and had overturned on touchdown, fortunately without injury to her crew.

Under the professional name *Dickie,* Croydon-based aviation artist Charles Couper Dickson explained the mishap in a strip cartoon published in *The Aeroplane,* showing the crop growing higher on each lap, Cobham the perfectionist not varying his height by an inch. Charles Dickson was later engaged by the de Havilland Company to design their press advertisements and Wally Hope flew him from Croydon to Stag Lane to discuss the campaign in person with Captain de Havilland and his senior colleagues.

While G-EBKT was being dismantled, Colonel Sempill flew 'KU in the 100-mile Grosvenor Challenge Cup Handicap but retired on the last lap due to engine problems, although he was already well down in the field and unlikely to have gained a place. On return to Stag Lane, 'KU's engine was dismantled for inspection and a new ball-race was fitted to the crankshaft in addition to a new oil pump and three cylinder heads. Repairs were also effected to the induction

pipe, a component which was to be the source of many problems.

Prior to the Lympne meeting, the aviation press had been enthusiastic about a new prospect: an inter-club race open only to Moths. 'As all the machines will be of one type and all with the same type of engine, competitors will of course, tune up their engines to maximum pitch, while cornering and course-keeping by the pilot will also play an important part. For pure sport there is little doubt that such a race is vastly more entertaining than any handicap in which a variety of types and powers take part'. Entirely the opposite view was taken later when the press blamed the coming of the Moth for a decline in the popularity of the King's Cup. 'The light aeroplane led many thousands to take a practical interest in flying but it also led to a swarm of entries for the great handicap race, all more or less indistinguishable to the non-technical public. It was all a very natural and a very desirable development but it inevitably robbed the Race of much of its interest!'

A spate of engine problems caused anticipated deliveries to run behind schedule, but Stag Lane at the end of July was gripped with activity as the first batch of club aeroplanes was prepared for qualification for Certificates of Airworthiness. On 20th July Hubert Broad test flew G-EBLR, the first of the two Moths scheduled for the Lancashire Aero Club at Woodford. The aeroplane was tested again the following day together with G-EBLI, the first for the London Aeroplane Club whose premises were being prepared near the aerodrome's main entrance.

G-EBLI was credited as the first production machine, painted grey with silver-doped wings. She had been weighed as early

The first two prototype DH.60 Moths, G-EBKT and G-EBKU, both in standard two-seat configuration, ready to start the 1925 King's Cup Air Race from Croydon early on the morning of 3rd July 1925, flown by Alan Cobham and Geoffrey de Havilland. DH Moth Club Archive

as 16th June when her tare weight was recorded as 817 lb, a modest increase over the prototypes but which now included jury struts and control stick centralising jig, seat cushions, safety belts and speaking tubes.

On 25th July, Broad found it necessary to fly both aeroplanes again, and G-EBLS (Yorkshire Aeroplane Club) and G-EBLT (Midland Aero Club), were added to his daily quota. Publicity photographs were prepared which featured G-EBLI, 'LR, 'LS and 'LT all standing in line on the aerodrome's notoriously muddy surface.

There was still speculation that 'even in fairly large batches' the cost of a Moth was likely to remain between £800 and £900 per aircraft. It was not until late August 1926 when ADC Aircraft announced a price reduction from £300 to £260 for a dual magneto Cirrus I engine, that de Havilland's published advertising included a price of £795 ex-works for a new standard Moth.

The London Aeroplane Club was scheduled to open on 19th August and the Royal Aero Club was keen to use the occasion at Stag Lane to launch and promote the new light aeroplane movement. The Lancashire Aero Club was equally anxious to begin subsidised operations and was prepared to receive its first Moth at Woodford Aerodrome by the end of July, according to committee chairman John Leeming, who wrote a graphic account of the times in his book *Airdays.*

'It had been decided that, as Chairman of the Club, I should go to London and fly with de Havilland's pilot in the machine to Woodford. So on the evening of 27th July I departed for town, and the following day presented myself at Stag Lane. The first thing that greeted me when I arrived was the news that the engine of our machine had suddenly developed some trouble. Broad had taken the machine up for a test flight during the morning, and as soon as he landed mechanics had been set to work to discover what was causing a mysterious loss of revs. (There is no record of this flight in Hubert Broad's logbook.)

'De Havilland had no other machine that they could send. There were only three Moths in existence at that time and their own test Moth, G-EBKT had gone that morning to Coventry. At five o'clock, two hours before we were due at Woodford, the mechanics discovered the trouble. It was serious; it would take two days to put right. At 5.25pm, just as I had accepted the inevitable and was about to wire Woodford, G-EBKT roared over Stag Lane. We did some very hurried talking and arranging during the next few minutes. If 'KT was not our proper machine it was at least a Moth. Probably few at Woodford would realise that a change had been made, and once more bluff might save the situation. If 'KT was flown there, formally accepted, and then flown quietly back again the next day, our own Moth could be delivered without fuss as soon as it was ready.

A shot of four of the first DH.60 Moths allocated to the new flying clubs, awaiting delivery from Stag Lane: G-EBLI (London); G-EBLR (Lancashire); G-EBLS (Yorkshire) and G-EBLT (Midland). BAE Systems

'St Barbe explained the situation to the pilot who had just landed and introduced me to him. Alan Cobham was his name. Cobham was tired after a double journey to Coventry and back, but as soon as he understood the position he agreed to fly to Woodford.

'We landed there at 7.30pm after an uneventful flight in perfect weather and there was quite a large crowd to see the first Moth arrive. Only Tom Prince gave any trouble. "Have you signed for this machine?" he demanded. "They've framed us. They've palmed off an old machine on you. I tell you it's one painted up. It's been used. It's not new! We must not take delivery!"

'I managed to hush him in the end, and the next day the local press reported and applauded the safe arrival of the Club's first Moth. That evening my telephone rang and at the other end was a much concerned and very worried member. "I went down", he stuttered, "thought I would just have another look at it, and the Moth's gone! It's gone! Just isn't there! The farmer says two men came about eleven o'clock this morning, and one of them flew it away!"'

Broad test-flew G-EBLR on 21st July (and again on 25th) confirming, perhaps, the questioned serviceability. G-EBLR did not receive her Certificate of Airworthiness until 13th August, in company with G-EBLS and G-EBLT scheduled for the Yorkshire and Midland clubs respectively, and the two Moths for the London Aeroplane Club, G-EBLI and G-EBLU.

Sir Philip Sassoon, Under-Secretary of State for Air, declared the London Aeroplane Club 'open' on Wednesday, 19th August 1925, only six months after the first

flight of the prototype Moth. In an unusually acerbic caption to a photograph of the opening ceremony held outside the Club shed, *The Aeroplane* declared 'this is what Lancashire did yesterday' and continued, 'entirely unsung, the Lancashire Club has been open for months. It has built itself one light aeroplane, and flown it, and took delivery of its first Moth a month ago'. Although this statement perpetuated the myth, there was evident bad feeling over what was suspected to be manipulation of publicity in favour of the capital city's Aeroplane Club.

In view of the apparent controversy it was unfortunate perhaps, that in his inaugural speech Sir Philip Sassoon should congratulate the Committee and members of the Club, as reported in *The Aeroplane* 'as having won for London and rightly for London, the first Light Aeroplane Club in the country'. The *Flight* reporter's shorthand notes recorded Sir Philip as giving the London Club 'the credit and distinction' of being first. However differently the speech was reported, it was evidence for those who suspected subterfuge.

Following the Under Secretary's flight with Chief Pilot Instructor Captain F G M Sparks in G-EBLU, a ballot drew 15 more names of Club members to whom instructional slots of 30 minutes were allocated. David Kittel, who was drawn first, gave up his place to allow Mrs Sophie Eliott-Lynn the honour of being the first Club member to receive flying instruction. Mrs Eliott-Lynn, an accomplished athlete and one-time Olympic javelin thrower, went solo on 18th October and completed her 'certificate qualification flights' only twelve days later. The first member from any of the subsidised clubs to obtain his 'A' Certificate following local training was the London Club's Guy

Warwick, qualifying on the same day as Mrs Eliott-Lynn's solo efforts.

Peter Capon, an office boy and tracer employed in the Drawing Office at Stag Lane in 1925, later wrote:

'At that date I owned a quarter plate camera and was "invited" to take photographs of de Havilland's civil aircraft for their Certificates of Airworthiness. Thus I also doubled as semi-official photographer and, in my spare time, did all the weighing of bits and pieces and complete aircraft.

Every Certificate required that it should contain a "side view quarter plate photograph clearly showing the registration". For this fringe benefit I was paid two shillings and three pence for every print supplied. Bob Loader, from the Business Office, used to sign my petty cash chitty.'

The London Club's two pilot instructors, Frank Sparks and Charles Witcombe, endorsed the suitability of the Moth aeroplane when their views were aired in a de Havilland advertisement published at the beginning of September. Between them, the two instructors had flown 45 hours during the Club's first week of operation, and Sparks noted that 'not the slightest adjustment has been necessary to aircraft or engine, and I am now confident that the Moths will stand up to the particularly exacting service to which we shall submit them'. 'Sparky', a member of the Territorial Cavalry during the First World War, had transferred to the Royal Flying Corps on the grounds that he believed the cavalry was too dangerous!

The Yorkshire Club was still without a base aerodrome, although a site near Leeds was being investigated when their first light blue Moth, G-EBLS, was delivered on 18th August, the day before the ceremony at Stag Lane. Flown by Reginald Kenworthy with Club Secretary I F Barnes as passenger,

G-EBLS left Stag Lane at 10.45am, carrying a letter from the Lord Mayor of London to the Lord Mayor of Harrogate, but permission to land at Harrogate had been refused, so the fraternal greeting was carried on to the Blackburn works aerodrome at Roundhay, Leeds, where the reception committee welcomed their guests at 1.00pm.

The second of the Lancashire Moths, dark blue and silver G-EBLV, joined G-EBLR at Woodford on 29th August. She was delivered from Stag Lane by Alan Cobham who had routed via Coventry to check progress on the Armstrong Siddeley Jaguar engine, scheduled for his DH.50 flight to the Cape in November. In an effort to maintain momentum the Lancashire Club had organised an Open Day to coincide with the delivery during which their 'L-P-W Monoplane', soon to be used for teaching Club members to run 'straights' across the aerodrome, was on display alongside their Avro 504K. Bert Hinkler was credited with a fine exhibition of 'trick' flying in the Avro while Alan Cobham executed 'several consecutive loops' in the Moth.

Reporting that the London Aeroplane Club had completed its first 100 hours of flying instruction on 8th September, one paper noted that the only 'mishap' suffered by either Moth had been a punctured tyre. The report went on to attribute this good record to the instructors, the ground engineer, the boy helper and the 'class of pupil who are receiving instruction'.

Meanwhile there was a hint that the second of the green and silver Moths for the Midland Aero Club, G-EBLW (189), and both the red aeroplanes scheduled for the Newcastle Aero Club, G-EBLX (190) and G-EBLY (191), were delayed through a shortage of engines. Certificates of Airworthiness for the trio were not in fact issued until 9th, 13th and 28th September respectively. G-EBLW eventually was delivered to

Castle Bromwich on 25th September whilst G-EBLX arrived at Cramlington Aerodrome, Newcastle on the 15th. The Newcastle Club had only recently moved to the 82-acre site from their previous base at Gosforth when 'LX landed there in the late afternoon flown by club chairman Baxter Ellis with Captain Herbert Leete as passenger. The trio had refuelled on their way from Stag Lane at Brough, temporary home to the Yorkshire Club, and arrived after a total flight time of a little over three hours. At the time, Ellis was the only member of the club to hold an 'A' licence. The second Moth, G-EBLY, was delivered by the club's pilot instructor G F E Harrison on 7th October in a flight seriously hampered by autumnal fog.

The aerodrome and Club facilities at Cramlington were not officially opened until 21st November when, on a raw winter's day, the city's Lord Mayor ably performed the ceremony. His daughter christened the two aeroplanes *Bernicia* and *Novocastria* before most members of the official party were taken aloft, and then entertained to tea. Within a fortnight, both aeroplanes were marooned in their hangar by a 7ft snowdrift and had to be dug out before they could be used for sporadic sorties between successions of storms.

By mid-December it was found necessary to remove Cirrus engine No 13 from G-EBLX and to fit the spare, although the measure was described as precautionary. Both Moths had been delivered with self-starters fitted, but Club pilots were unimpressed when engines which had stopped in mid-air as the result of throttling down, failed to start again when the cockpit levers were tugged with growing urgency and frustration.

And there, for the moment, deliveries to satisfy the first round of the Air Ministry's scheme of subsidised light aeroplane clubs were halted. The Hampshire Aeroplane Club, filling the position of the reluctant Scottish Club, did not receive G-EBOH (269) and G-EBOI (270) until 7th August 1926, during which interval the Sales Office at Stag Lane had been busy booking the first of the independent orders.

During the next 14 years, encouraged by the subsidy scheme, private ownership grew from just 16 aeroplanes in 1925 to 590 by 1939, and the number of clubs increased from five to 71, for a total government expenditure of £682,000, which in the light of subsequent events, was regarded as a very worthwhile investment.

Scenes at the Lancashire Aero Club at Woodford on 29th August 1925, following delivery of the Club's second Moth, G-EBLV, by Alan Cobham. Note the potentially dangerous attitude adopted by a right-handed propeller swinger when attempting to start a right hand rotation Cirrus engine.
DH Moth Club Archive

Coincident with the 1925 Stag Lane factory expansion and re-organisation which, due to very wet weather transformed the open ground around the works into a quagmire, the Company initiated regular meetings under the chairmanship of General Manager Frank Hearle. These were an early attempt to monitor the records for design, production, inspection, sales and service of the Moth aeroplane. Suggestions for improvements from clients and employees, channelled through departmental representatives, were conveyed to the Management Committee where they received the fullest consideration. This opportunity became more essential when Moths were exported to operate under abnormal conditions of 'climate, geography or circumstance'.

Although the subsidised club system was now in full flight, a spate of correspondence published in the late summer of 1925 continued to question the definition of a 'light aeroplane' and the total number of Moths likely to be made available under the Air Ministry scheme. 'I am convinced that a club cannot be carried on for long if the costs are high and the number of members thereby limited. This does not appear to be the method which will achieve the objects of the Light Aeroplane Club Scheme,' wrote *Aeroen* in a letter published by *Flight*.

Was it anything more than professional interest or personal concern that took the Director of Civil Aviation, Sir Sefton Brancker, to the London Aeroplane Club on 24th October? His Saturday visit allowed him to meet officials, pilot instructors and members under training, when the matters of upkeep and running expenses were openly discussed.

The reason for delayed delivery of Moths in September, attributed speculatively to shortages in engine supply, was more likely to have been due to de Havilland's investigation of an unexpected spate of misfiring. Chief Engineer Charles Walker analysed the problem making a specific note of the influence of climate.

'The early work with the Moth induction system produced some interesting vagaries. When G-EBKT appeared in February 1925, it was decided to fit a straight induction pipe with the carburettor at the end and branches to the engine. The system recommended by the makers of the Cirrus engine, and used on the type test, was similar to that now in use, that is, the carburettor in the middle. The straight pipe was tried because it was simpler and cheaper and gave rather more revolutions all-out. It also lent itself rather well to air heating, as the intake pipe could be led quite easily to the back of the rear cylinder.

'This straight induction pipe was used on Moths for the first six months under all sorts of conditions and with entirely satisfactory results.

'Quite suddenly in September, one of the London Club Moths started missing badly at certain throttle positions. Investigations at once took place, during which another Moth started the same complaint. Several new machines were coming out at this time, and all were at first correct, but the missing and irregular running spread like an epidemic. One Moth which started for Newcastle developed the trouble en-route. This could always be cured temporarily by making some small alteration in the position of the intake pipe, but it was liable to recur, and it was, therefore, decided to fit the present standard induction system, and avoid all possibility of future trouble.

'Later investigations showed that at low revolutions the mixture was rich in the rear cylinder, and as the engine was opened out this condition travelled forward until when all-out, the front cylinder was getting more than its share at the expense of the others.

'When one thinks of 10,000ft altitude in February, damp and dry days at ground level, and numerous other variations of the European climate, one begins to wonder what condition of temperature, pressure and humidity had been escaped in the first seven months, or whether all brands of petrol suddenly altered in September, 1925.'

Following delivery of the initial orders on behalf of the Light Aeroplane Clubs, the next machine off the line, No 192, was allocated to the Controller of Civil Aviation, Australia. Issued with her Certificate of Airworthiness (C of A) at Stag Lane on 15th September, she was delivered by sea to the Larkin Aircraft Supply Company at Essendon Aerodrome, Melbourne. Registered G-AUAE at the beginning of November in the name of the Civil Aviation Branch of the Department of Defence, G-AUAE was put on static display at the Melbourne Motor Show where she became the centre of attention due to numerous wing-folding exercises and was publicly demonstrated at Essendon on 28th November, flown by Captain E J Jones. The Moth was used by the Civil Aviation Branch during the next two years for conducting pilot and instructor flight tests at various locations around the country.

The grey-painted Moths of the London Aeroplane Club (LAC) were well camouflaged when flying in the murky skies north of the capital and the fuselages were later painted brown and eventually yellow when the LAC immediately attracted the label of 'The Mustard Club' after a sales promotion scheme for Colman's famous preparation, and the aeroplanes became known to all at Stag Lane as 'Yellow Perils'.

During their formative years, the clubs appeared to be offering a pleasant social environment together with the opportunities to participate in an exciting and new 'dare-devil'

activity, very much a part of Twenties' culture. When, fifty years after, he was questioned on his motives for joining an aeroplane club, Victor Dorée pondered for a while before suggesting that club flying was a new experience suddenly available to the general public, and he and his contemporaries had already finished with roller skating!

As the result of experience gained with maintenance of the club aircraft, which were worked hard within a harsh environment, the ground engineers were able quickly to report back to the manufacturer details of the most obvious problems. Although the Moth was a design much publicised as devoid of pulleys, the substituted ball races suffered from an ingestion of dust and mud until measures were taken to protect them.

There was no method of lubricating the inner sliding portion of the main undercarriage compression legs except by dismantling the whole system, which for an aircraft engaged mostly on daily circuits and landings was not infrequent. This challenge was accepted by the Design Department which also re-designed the axle and later provided a new, strengthened tail skid system not based on elastic cord.

For instruments connected to the pitot-static system, more durable rubber tubing was requested, plus some consideration to be given to improving access to the back of the installed instruments other than by slithering upside-down onto the cockpit floor. The tubing issue was resolved easily enough, but the other never was. It was suggested too that the engine oil pressure gauge and revolution counter be moved from their position on the fuselage front decking, just behind the engine, where they were difficult enough to read even when not subject to extreme vibration, to a new position inside the cockpit.

The Midland Aero Club was declared open by the Lord Mayor of Birmingham on 6th October in a ceremony held in the Club hangar at Castle Bromwich. Lieutenant Colonel Francis Shelmerdine, representing the Air Ministry, formally presented the Club with its two DH.60 Moths, G-EBLT and G-EBLW, after which the chief pilot instructor Captain William McDonough, recruited from the recently defunct Northern Airlines, 'entertained the spectators with some splendid exhibition flying' in company with two Armstrong Whitworth Siskins which were visiting from Coventry. During the next two months, the Club reported that both Moths were available simultaneously for only five weeks due to the incorporation of 'various modifications'. Flying was also hampered due to the fact that Birmingham Parks Committee still utilised the 'aerodrome' for sports activities every Saturday.

The basic test for a pilot's 'A' (private) licence, as opposed to a 'B' commercial licence, was a climb to 6,000ft overhead the

DH.60 G-EBMF, the second Moth to be delivered to a British private owner, and customised to accommodate a suitcase in a hold behind the rear seat, not accessible from outside the aircraft. Note the appearance of a 'moth' emblem above the name on the front fuselage. Richard Riding

airfield, when power would be shut off, and the aeroplane glided down to land within 100ft of a marker, often within a circle described in the middle of the landing area. Occasional blips of engine warming throttle were permitted but 'rumbling,' using motor assistance, was considered unsporting. In addition, five consecutive figures-of-eight were required to be flown overhead the aerodrome at 1,000ft without variation of height. The requirements were set by the Royal Aero Club, and each candidate was observed by a RAeC nominee standing watching on the airfield, usually a resident instructor.

During the qualifying solo flight tests for her 'A' licence on 30th October, Sophie Eliott-Lynn lost sight of Stag Lane Aerodrome from 1,000ft due to rapidly deteriorating visibility. Retreating westward at heights up to 6,000ft, she put down her Moth three times in search of her bearings before landing finally near Slough from where Charles Witcombe retrieved the aeroplane the following day. Although not admissible for the purposes of qualifying for her certificate, the pilot was complimented on having proved herself thoroughly capable of handling the Moth by selecting suitable places for putting down and getting off.

Moth No 193, registered G-EBME to Rex Mundy, qualified for her C of A at Stag Lane on 31st October, the first of all the private owner machines. Both G-EBME and G-EBMF (194), for Wing Commander A Wynn, both had 'accommodation' for a large suitcase built into the decking behind the rear cockpit, the first design change in support of customisation.

On later production models a hinged door opening upwards on the starboard side provided external access to the rear locker. Apart from a brief period when access was possible only from inside the rear cockpit the external door was to remain an essential feature on all future marques of the DH.60 Moth. The space proved an ideal receptor for an auxiliary fuel tank once the suitability of the aeroplane for long distance record breaking had been recognised.

Mundy's aircraft had been acquired to allow him and his business colleague Laurence Hope, universally known as 'Wally', to travel to the Sudan to take part in a big-game hunt, but the trip was postponed in favour of a European tour. The following year, Mundy and Hope formed Air Taxis Limited, operating Moths from a small shed near the main gate at Stag Lane.

On 5th November, the Lancashire Aero Club arranged a luncheon party at the Midland Hotel, Manchester. Invited were a number of prominent business people, and as principal guests, Sir Samual Hoare, Secretary of State for Air, Sir Sefton Brancker, Director General of Civil Aviation, Sir William Letts of Crossley Motors, and Sir Charles Wakefield. By the end of the party, paid for by two club members due to a worrying shortage of funds, Sir William had promised the gift of an Avro, and Sir Charles, having accepted the position of Club President, offered another Moth.

Within a few days of the party, G-EBLV was badly damaged when she overturned at Woodford. Club Chairman John Leeming, anxious to practise out of sight of critical eyes, landed on a remote area of the aerodrome which was still establishing after re-seeding and was very soft. The thin wheels dug into the surface and the aeroplane turned slowly over onto her back. Leeming had forgotten to fasten his lap strap and fell out of the cockpit, witnessed only by a farmer and two horses ploughing the adjacent field.

It was the Club Chairman again who was responsible for the crash of G-EBLR on 26th December which nearly wrote her off. Following an acknowledged alcoholic lunch, several club members organised an impromptu landing competition. After drawing lots, Leeming was the first to go, but he became mesmerised by the target, a circle of whitewash splashed onto the frozen surface, and without attempting to flare, flew straight into the ground. The Lancashire Club must have been relieved to accept Sir Charles Wakefield's gifted Moth, G-EBMQ (201), which was handed over during a short ceremony at Stag Lane on 2nd February 1926, at which Leeming, harbouring a feeling of guilt perhaps, represented the new owners.

Soon after returning from his Schneider Trophy expedition to Baltimore, Hubert Broad flew a DH.60, probably G-EBKU, to Martlesham Heath on 24th November 1925, where a number of RAF test pilots flew her. Broad returned to Stag Lane the same day in preparation for imminent flight trials of the Jaguar-engined DH.9J.

Victor Dorée proposed that the LAC should purchase another Moth, and offered to put up £20 if other members would pledge similar sums. Major K M Beaumont, Will Hay, K V Wright and Sophie Eliott-Lynn, sharing a pledge with another member, all agreed to support the idea.

Club endorsements were used to publicise the Moth whenever possible and Major S A Packman, pilot instructor of the Newcastle Aero Club received credit for a timely quote in December:

'The completion of the Club's first 100 hours flying on two DH.60 Moth Machines with no replacements other than two tail skid shock absorbers is, I consider, a fitting occasion to comment upon the complete suitability of this type as a training machine. Its stability, ease of control, manoeuvrability, economic and trouble-free running, place it in the front rank of its class.'

The de Havilland copy writers could have asked for little better although the weekly club report published just beyond the first 100 hours referred to the fitting of a new exhaust pipe to G-EBLX. 'The engine now runs like a Rolls-Royce. This is a distinct improvement upon the Ford-like rattle of the old pipe in its latter days. It fell off almost at the moment the delivery sheet was being signed in respect of the new one'.

To the engineers working daily on Cirrus motors, matters were not routine. They discovered that the most regularly checked items, petrol and oil filters, were, to quote one club chief engineer, 'rather inaccessibly placed'. In order to speed the job they were forced to use spanners specially adapted for the task, leading de Havilland eventually to provide a tool-roll with each new aircraft sold, including many Moth-specific items. The engineers at the London Club evolved an engine schedule which they recommended for use at any similarly busy organisation:

Schedule A. After 5 hours' flying.
Valve gear checked and oiled.
Petrol filter cleaned (main).
Contact breaker checked.

Schedule B. After 10 hours' flying.
Sparking plugs to be cleaned.
Distributors to be checked.
Oil filter to be cleaned.

Schedule C. After 30 hours' flying.
Oil system to be drained and flushed out and fitted with fresh oil.
Filter under float chamber, float chamber and jet chambers to be cleaned.
Propeller bolts and tightness of boss on shaft to be checked.
Petrol flow to be taken.

Schedule D. After 120 hours' flying.
Engine to be top overhauled.
(Decarbonising and valve grinding).
Change all joints in the oil system.

The schedule time for complete overhaul had been fixed provisionally at 240 hours but was expected to be increased after further experience was recorded.

Throughout the summer and into winter, G-EBKU had been extensively flown whenever the weather was suitable and regular checks were completed resulting in replacement of many engine top end parts. In early August a complete strip-down permitted a new ball race to be fitted on the rear of the crankshaft. To assist Captain de Havilland and Hubert Broad, Wally Hope was recruited in October for routine flight testing.

On 25th November a redesigned heater pipe was fitted with the connection moved from the centre of the manifold to the rear. By 4th December, the prototype Cirrus I engine had logged 206 hours when a new rear section of the copper induction mani-

fold was fitted by Bob Hardingham and Eric Mitchell. Eight days later, after a further six hours flying time, it was found to be cracked and was replaced. During inspection on 17th December at 222 hours, the manifold was discovered to be broken again. Worse still, a crack was found in the top of the crankcase on the starboard side, opposite No 3 cylinder, and the engine was removed under the supervision of Jim Norman and handed over to the shops.

For the de Havilland Business Manager the year ended on a high note. Orders were beginning to flow into St Barbe's office from British based private owners and, perhaps more importantly, from interests overseas. The important first sale to South America was achieved when Moth No 196 qualified for her Certificate at Stag Lane on 20th December. Unregistered, the Moth was shipped to Morrison and Company, a merchant service operating in Valparaiso, Chile, ostensibly for local flying training but in reality she had been procured on behalf of the military for assessment.

Two days before Christmas, Colonel Sempill left Stag Lane in a Moth for a demonstration tour of the Irish Free State, flying directly to Dublin, a route which involved a water crossing of 70 miles. The weather which had already caused a delay in departure remained cold and foggy but the tour was completed successfully. On the return journey to Stag Lane, following a shorter sea crossing which made landfall at Stranraer, Sempill landed on a sandbank off the Lancashire coast to top up the main tank with fuel carried on board in tins.

On Christmas Eve the de Havilland Company announced that the DH.60 Moth had been selected as the standard equipment for the light aeroplane clubs in the Common-

wealth of Australia. The Australian Government too had recognised the value of building up a reserve of civilian pilots, and would place on loan with Divisions of the Australian Aero Club, government aerodromes and sheds, workshops and facilities. In addition a bounty of £20 was to be paid for every pupil who qualified for a licence. A cabled order had been sent to Stag Lane for the supply of six Moths to be delivered as soon as possible.

Having successfully launched the Moth, the Design Department at Stag Lane was already looking at developments. Concerned about the possible difficulties in sourcing spar-grade wood and the government's decision only to purchase metal aircraft for the military, investigations had begun in November against the designation DH.60A for wings constructed around 16G tubular Dural spars to specification 2T4, of 2.735in diameter, rolled to produce a parallel-sided cross-section with half round ends. The geometry of the biplane rigging called for the interplane struts to be moved outboard by 3in from the original position but otherwise there appeared to be no major changes.

In January 1926 nine spar test specimens were delivered to Stag Lane but inspection revealed inconsistencies in dimensions and weight and there were additional problems in that four pieces appeared to be not entirely straight. Work continued into 1926 and by March, overhang tests were being applied to a top front spar. The Company maintained an interest which eventually developed into limited flight testing of specimen structures for both wings and tailplanes, but in the meantime, other important developments were to take a greater priority.

JANUARY TO DECEMBER 1926

THE DE HAVILLAND School of Flying adopted house colours of deep maroon for the fuselages of the aircraft on the fleet, with silver wings and empennage as standard. Two DH.60 delivery positions were reserved for the School late in 1925: G-EBMP (198) was registered to the de Havilland Company on 27th November and G-EBMV (235) on 11th December. In addition to their primary duties as training machines, in the early days of Moth production, most School aircraft were to be widely flown in support of Company promotions. G-EBKU eventually joined the fleet too, on 22nd April 1926, with the prototype Cirrus engine overhauled and back in her mountings. Hubert Broad test flew G-EBMO (197), a new aircraft allocated to the Sales Department, on 18th January 1926 and the following day demonstrated her to visitors from Japan.

Equipped with its Cirrus Moths and five civil-registered DH.9s, the de Havilland School of Flying and Reserve Flying School issued an authoritative joint prospectus at the beginning of 1926. In support of three basic courses tailored to the needs of the Military Instructor, Commercial Pilot and Beginner or Private Pilot, the school offered 'Refresher Courses' for which machines could be hired by the hour, with or without the services of an instructor. Although the DH.9s were an important part of the business, employed only to service the Reserve contract, it was the newer type which was featured more prominently in the document. Under the heading of 'Equipment' the authors were keen to reveal that having opened with one preliminary training machine in 1920, the school had gradually expanded and widened its sphere of activities, building up a reputation for sound and reliable flying instruction 'until at the present time it is the largest and most completely equipped Civilian Flying Training Organisation in the British Empire'. They continued:

'Elementary flying is taught on de Havilland Moth two-seater light aeroplanes fitted with 27/60hp Cirrus engines. The Moth was evolved after continued close scrutiny of training requirements and it represents the most modern school aeroplane. It is easy to fly and is of a type which instils instant confidence into pupils. Unlike many aeroplanes used for training, the Moth has no inherent peculiarities of behaviour which are confusing and mystifying to learners. On the other hand, the characteristics and flying qualities of the Moth are such that pilots taught on them in the early stages of their training can pass with equal ease to small, fast, highly manoeuvrable machines or to high-powered transport types. All the aircraft are fitted with dual control, so that during the early flights the pupils may follow the movements of the control column and rudder bar as the Instructor causes the machine to perform simple evolutions.'

Compared to the London Aeroplane Club's fees, the de Havilland School rates might have appeared disproportionate, but this was an unsubsidised business aimed primarily at satisfying the requirements of the Air Ministry. For civilians, the DH.60 Moths were charged at £5 per flying hour with an instructor but £8 per hour solo, the difference being explained so: 'The charges for solo flying include an insurance premium which relieves the pupil of all liability in respect of damage to the aircraft and Third Party claims up to £1,000. Personal accident

Four maroon and silver DH.60 Moths of the de Havilland School of Flying pose with staff instructors at Stag Lane. Chief Instructor Captain A S White is on the extreme left. Standing by the propeller at right is the School's Chief Engineer, ex-Farnborough Apprentice Bob Hardingham who, as Sir Robert Hardingham, was later head of the ARB. de Havilland

is not, however, covered by the premium, but pupils may arrange their own cover at low rates'. The School advertised trial lessons on a Moth aeroplane at two guineas and offered special terms to purchasers of private Moths when instruction at the School was charged at 25% less than the published schedule.

Knowing there to be a list of 100 prospective members still waiting to join the London Aeroplane Club, the Company seized the opportunity of attracting business at the best commercial rate. It was also an ideal situation in which to utilise early production DH.60 Moths and to monitor their in-service careers whilst accumulating funds.

The Air Ministry took a stand at the annual Schoolboys' Exhibition held in London in January, before the end of the Christmas holidays, from where they invited essays on the subject of methods for advancing aviation. De Havilland decided to join forces and, in addition to exhibiting a Moth, to offer prizes to essayists: first prize was a flight of 100 miles in a Moth or an hour's flying instruction, plus several minor awards of 'flips'. Some aviation papers mischievously linked the Air Ministry's attendance at the Exhibition with recent news that they had placed an order with de Havilland for 'one entire machine'.

The first casualty of the year 1926 amongst light aeroplane club Moths was Newcastle's G-EBLY which was damaged on landing at Cramlington during the wintry weather experienced on Wednesday 6th January. Based near a major sea port there was nothing more natural than to despatch her to London on board her namesake, the Tyne-Tees steamer *Bernicia* who sailed with her precious deck cargo a week after the mishap.

The London Club did not move to Hendon as Harold Perrin was predicting before Christmas and the threatened acquisition of an Avro Baby was abandoned. On 8th January the LAC recorded the year's second club casualty when Colonel Turner, flying G-EBLU, hit a hedge whilst practising short field landings at Stag Lane, and the Moth was damaged beyond economical repair.

De Havilland launched a major advertising campaign effective from the New Year, largely entrusted to Bob Loader. Each week until early March, whole page displays featured a different element in the design and construction of the Moth. Diagrams and sectional drawings were accompanied by short, concise sentences promoting the convenience, simplicity and safety of the aeroplane. After running for four weeks, readers anxious to learn more were instead confronted with a stylistic view of an inverted Moth flying straight out of the page. The only text read: 'The de Havilland Moth has the Aerobatic Certificate of Airworthiness'. It was clever, tasteful and full of drama that could not be ignored by anyone who previously had questioned the integrity of the design and construction.

For those who contacted the company asking for further information, the Business Office was happy to supply a specification sheet which included details of instruments, loose equipment and optional extras such as a Hughes compass, telephones complete with all tubes, mouthpieces, Y pieces and one helmet set, engine tool kit, watch with holder, and engine, propeller and cockpit covers. There was also news that the aircraft was now priced at £795 (ex-works, unpacked and ready for flight) with an additional six guineas payable to the Air Ministry for the issue of Certificates of Registration and Airworthiness. All covered surfaces were painted aluminium; fuselage, cowling, struts, tank and undercarriage would be supplied in either Royal Blue or Ensign Red. Alternatives could be supplied at extra cost and as most customers took this option the stricture of 'standard colours' was soon abandoned.

The Yorkshire Light Aeroplane Club left their temporary home since August with the Blackburn Aircraft Company at Roundhay Aerodrome, Leeds, and moved into their new quarters at Sherburn-in-Elmet on 20th January 1926. That the success of the light aeroplane movement was positively in the national interest was amply demonstrated by the wholehearted support of local dignitaries, the Lord Mayor and Lady Mayoress, officials from Leeds University, local Members of Parliament, and the Director General of Civil Aviation, Sir Sefton Brancker. A luncheon was hosted in the city by the Lord Mayor and, due to the shortage of daylight, all the speeches were made during the meal to enable guests to hurry out to the aerodrome where Sir Sefton declared the new site open and, in spite of a substantial covering of snow, flights were arranged in the Club's only Moth, G-EBLS. Brancker's lunchtime speech must have heartened those who heard him say that the light aeroplane movement was one of the most important moves in British aviation during the last few years. 'It was the government's endeavour to encourage light aeroplane clubs with as little red tape and as little control as possible by giving financial support', he said.

De Havilland was very aware that, in order to grow, their after-sales service had to be ultra-efficient and tailored to customer needs at all times. They received good press from an incident which occurred at Cramlington just before noon on Saturday 30th January. The Newcastle Club's G-EBLY was already out of action and under repair at Stag Lane, when 'LX suffered a broken propeller. A new one was delivered overnight and the machine was airworthy again by 10.30am on Sunday, much to the relief of the flying members and the Club's treasurer in particular.

Following a period of purely civil activity, January 1926 was a month much devoted to military interest in the Moth. The Royal Australian Air Force had ordered two DH.60s in June 1925 for evaluation by No 1 Flying Training School at Point Cook. The first of these, No 199, flew on 13th January, and was handed over at Stag Lane the following day. The aeroplane was issued with civilian documentation but taken on RAAF charge at Point Cook as A7-1 in March. The second machine, No 200, was test flown on 28th January, and accompanied her sister to Victoria where she became A7-2. In June, both aircraft were discovered by Major Hereward de Havilland, still in their packing cases at Point Cook, where he was advised that they would not be erected immediately as a training course was then in progress, and it was wished the pupils should keep their minds on their work and not on Moths! Although A7-1 crashed at Point Cook in November 1926 and A7-2 was written off by No 3 Squadron at Richmond, they had achieved their primary task: that of successful evaluation as initial trainers for military pilots. However, it was considered that with the Cirrus I engine the aircraft was underpowered, but that could be rectified. More importantly for the Exchequer, in comparison with the other most suitable candidate, the Lynx-powered Avro 504N, the Cirrus Moth was about half the price.

'Billy' Sempill's dramatic flight to Dublin just before Christmas resulted in a Moth demonstration to representatives of the Government of the Irish Free State at Stag Lane on 16th January, after which an order was placed for delivery of four machines in July (Nos 264-267). Broad's demonstration of G-EBMO to the Company's Japanese visitors three days later helped to secure an order for a single aeroplane, No 274, delivered to de Havilland's Japanese agent, Mitsubishi Shoji Kaisha Ltd, at Stag Lane in November. The all-silver machine was shipped to Japan and absorbed into the Imperial Army for evaluation, although no further orders were forthcoming. Shortly before the handover, HIH Prince Chibu, brother of the Emperor of Japan, was treated to a conducted tour of the Stag Lane factory and a flight with Colonel Sempill in a Moth.

The first of the six Australian Light Aeroplane Club Moths was flown in February. G-AUAJ (241) was followed into the air by G-AUAK (242) on leap year day. Together with G-AUAF (243) and G-AUAG (244), the machines were issued with Certificates of Airworthiness at Stag Lane in April prior to shipment to Australia. G-AUAH (245) and G-AUAL (246) were certificated in London in May. All six machines ordered by the Controller of Civil Aviation, were registered to the Civil Aviation Branch, Department of Defence. G-AUAF, 'AG and 'AL were allocated to the Australian Aero Club (Victorian

Section) at Essendon whilst G-AUAH, 'AJ and 'AL went to the New South Wales Section operating from Mascot.

Supported by RAAF fighters and bombers, 'AE, 'AG and 'AL all took part in an Aero Club Display at Essendon on 21st August 1926, when 'AL was flown by Alan Cobham who had arrived in his DH.50J G-EBFO six days previously. The August date is regarded as that upon which co-ordinated club activity began in Australia.

G-AUAF crashed during an air display at Essendon in August 1927, 'UG went down at Ballarat in July 1934, and the other four led complicated, accident-prone lives. G-AUAJ was broken up for spares when in service with 2 EFTS as A7-114 in 1940; G-AUAK (VH-UAK) never recovered from the abandonment of yet another major rebuilding programme. She had suffered a bizarre accident in 1931 when, during the search for a missing swimmer in Botany Bay, she was caught in her own slipstream while circling at low level and the main wheels touched the surface of the water, causing her to stall. Salvaged and dried out, 'UK finally crashed at Mascot in 1941 and her mortal remains were due to have been amalgamated with those of G-AUAH (VH-UAH), another Moth which had suffered a dunking in the sea off Ettalong Beach in November 1941. G-AUAL (VH-UAL) was lucky to have survived until 1936 when she hit a tree on the Northern Golf Links near Essendon two days before Christmas.

DH.60 Moth G-EBMV (235) was subjected to a heavy test schedule initiated by Broad on 2nd February 1926. The Cirrus I engine was fitted with what was described as a 'Duplex carburettor and induction system' and also high compression cylinder heads 'for comparison'. Captain de Havilland acted in the unaccustomed position of flight

test observer to Broad on 5th March. All the tests were scheduled at the constant trial weight of 1,240 lb adjusted to 1,225 lb 'obtained by omitting two gallons of petrol'. Three days later, Broad and Ballantyne repeated the tests with a different propeller, DH5120/3, of 6ft diameter and finer pitch than previously.

The Captain and Richard Clarkson flew the aeroplane on 24th March in a climbing speed trial with yet another propeller, a DH5128/1 (D. 6ft 6in P. 3.95ft), manufactured from mahogany and with a brass sheathing, and the engine built up with standard compression cylinder heads and a Duplex carburettor. Three days later, carrying C C Walker as observer, Captain de Havilland flew G-EBMV fitted with a Fairey-Reed metal propeller and on 1st April, Broad and Ballantyne resumed climb tests to 10,000ft after the same propeller had been subjected to a reduction in diameter and alteration to the blade section.

What might have been a spectacle was unfortunately disrupted by the weather on 13th March when Alan Cobham arrived back in England from Cape Town in the DH.50J G-EBFO. The plan was for a group of aeroplanes including six Moths to fly out from Croydon, rendezvous over Sevenoaks, and escort Cobham back to a growing spontaneous reception. However, in very murky conditions, the Moth formation missed him altogether and, led by Captain de Havilland with Mrs Gladys Cobham on board, the welcoming committee groped its way back to Croydon only to discover that G-EBFO was already there and her pilot was being urged to get back to Stag Lane as quickly as possible in advance of an audience with the King.

The British summer season of 1926 was the first in which organisers of aviation meetings could be reasonably assured of

any substantial numerical support by Moths drawn from both flying clubs and the growing number of private owners. It was a brave decision by the Lancashire Aero Club to arrange the country's first public flying meeting to be organised by a light aeroplane club, at Woodford, so early in the year.

A crowd of 15,000 spectators attended the meeting whose programme was dominated by local Moths flown by the Club's instructors and including G-EBMQ (201), the Lancashire Club's newest Moth, presented by Sir Charles Wakefield. They were joined by Hubert Broad who had travelled up from Stag Lane in the almost new G-EBMV and was credited with a 'fine exhibition flight' to complement Neville Stack's 'display of stunting'. It was an important start for the light aeroplane movement and vital that the public would go home well satisfied after their Sunday afternoon out.

Air Vice-Marshal Sir Geoffrey Salmond, a VIP guest at the meeting, was reported to have said that if light aeroplane clubs were growing up all over the country there would be a greater sense of flying, and a greater appreciation of flying men. Sir William Letts, Managing Director of A V Roe and Co, hoped that the club facilities offered by his company at Woodford would lead to the training of many pilots, not for the purposes of war, but for peace and the progress of science, and the human race. However, the irrevocable link between the subsidised clubs and the military was demonstrated a few weeks later when a Moth from the Newcastle Club flew to the Ponteland Rifle Range where it carried out Infantry Contact Patrol exercises with the Northumberland Fusiliers, during which members of the battalion were instructed on how to fire at low flying 'enemy' aircraft.

On 27th April 1926, the de Havilland School's G-EBMP was flown across the fields to Cricklewood for her first recorded visit to the Handley Page works, where discussion centred on the adoption of slots. It was a

The black and silver DH.60 G-EBMU *Silvry II* owned by David Kittel. The mass of the extra paint on the wings caused concern in the de Havilland Weights Department. Note the style of windscreen. The fuel cock lever can be seen on the port cabane strut; rudder cables are duplicated. The wire connecting the leading edge, root end of the port lower wing and the bottom of the rear cabane strut is to support the lower wing when folded. The devices mounted on the fuselage side between the front cockpit and the exhaust pipe, are the early style of fixed length jury strut. The only explanations for the strange shape of the lower of the two struts are that it fits on the port side and takes into account the exhaust pipe, or, that it fits on the starboard side, and allows the front cockpit door to be opened when the wings are folded. DH Moth Club Archive

The first DH.60 Moth ordered by the Air Ministry was J8030, seen here at Stag Lane prior to application of the serial number. The aircraft was despatched to Martlesham Heath and used for trials with Handley Page slots fitted to the lower mainplanes and activated by the ailerons. Peter Capon

short trip which Broad was to make on a regular basis. The Handley Page Aircraft Company had been experimenting with slats hinged to the leading edge of wings for some years, and had patented the invention. When extended, the slat formed a 'slot' through which air was accelerated, providing a sufficient degree of extra lift at low forward speed to delay the stall by a few miles per hour. This was considered to be particularly advantageous when landing and of especial benefit to pilots under training. Factors which ruled against the universal fitting of slats were the costs of installation, the additional weight penalty, and the not inconsiderable royalty payment demanded by Handley Page for each commission.

Following his letter to de Havilland in May 1925 promising to buy a Moth, Frederick Handley Page instead persuaded the Air Ministry to order a machine and to equip her with the company's patented slot apparatus. J8030 (233), was first flown, less slots, from Stag Lane by Hubert Broad on 13th April. The happy marriage with the device in its final form was to prove beneficial to the reputation of the Moth as an established training aeroplane. By the time the master patents on the slot invention expired ten years later, the Handley Page Company had received more than £750,000 in royalties.

DH.60 Moth J8030 was the first of three ordered by the Air Ministry against contract number 103092, a parsimony sniped at by the press. The request to tender had been placed in October 1925, originally for one Cirrus-powered DH.60 Moth landplane and an additional set of lower mainplanes

J8030 in a heated workshop at Martlesham Heath fitted with her new lower mainplanes complete with leading edge slot devices. The mechanism was activated by a link to the aileron control box on the underside of the wing. National Archive. Crown copyright

accommodating Handley Page Autoslots. De Havilland quoted £975 as the delivered price of the aircraft and £600 for the design, manufacture and delivery of the lower wings which included flight testing before hand-over. The Company was also anxious to establish the regime of Inspection required by the Director of Contracts at the Air Ministry:

'We are writing to ask that, should it be decided to favour us with your Contract, you will accept the aircraft manufactured under the Inspection procedure governing civil aircraft. That is to say, with a Certificate of Airworthiness instead of full Service Inspection. This request is being put forward because, in view of the quantity of

Moth machines in use, we are holding considerable stocks of components and we are drawing from these stocks to produce complete aircraft; these stocks have been manufactured under our approved Inspection Department in the usual way for civil aircraft, and have not therefore been submitted to complete AID Inspection.

'Should you insist on full Service Inspection it would be necessary to lay down a special machine, which would mean that we could not offer such rapid delivery or such a prompt service of replacements.'

The agreed contract called for the aircraft to be a 'standard Moth' with a Certificate of Airworthiness. The Company subsequently

revised its quotation for the supply of J8030 to £900, with £500 for the pair of lower wings fitted with slats manufactured from L.16 aluminium over a wooden core. At this stage in development, the 'autoslots' were still believed to be most efficient when operated in association with ailerons which on the Moth were fitted to the lower mainplanes only. Martlesham Heath described how the system worked:

'The connections between the differential sprocket gear and slot, and between differential gear and aileron, is by means of tubular rods fitted with self-aligning ball bearing ends, the movement of the slot and the aileron being simultaneous. As at present fitted, the slot is fully open when the aileron is right down, but the relative movement of the slot and the aileron can, however, be altered by the adjustment holes provided in the sprocket gear on the mainplane. If it is desired to revert to direct instead of differential control, this can be done by fitting a new aileron lever on the present sprocket gear.'

The other two aircraft, J8031 (247) and J8032 (248), were tested at Stag Lane by Broad on 31st March, and on 10th and 12th April respectively were positioned directly to the Central Flying School (CFS) to begin an evaluation process.

J8030 was inspected at Stag Lane on 22nd March when several minor criticisms were recorded amongst which were that the windscreens were celluloid and should be changed for Triplex units, considering that the aircraft was for Service use, and no compasses were fitted in either cockpit. Following flight tests with standard wings and then with slotted lower mainplanes, she was delivered to the Aircraft and Armament Experimental Establishment (A&AEE) at Martlesham Heath on 28th April, arriving with standard wings and a single-ignition Cirrus engine complete with a ratchet self-starter system fitted in the rear cockpit.

On receipt by A&AEE, there was initial consternation at the absence of slotted wings but the experimental set was later located in the Stores, booked in as a separate delivery from the manufacturer. It was also established that the Air Ministry had called for a dual ignition system and de Havilland agreed to change the engine at an additional cost of £25 for which purpose J8030 was returned to Stag Lane in May.

In summary, following flight trials, Establishment test pilots Squadron Leader English, Flight Lieutenant Sorley and Flying Officer King reported that:

'The aircraft is very easy to fly and in respect of handling qualities is very suitable for instructional purposes, particularly when fitted with the ailerons with slots, which almost eliminate risk of a serious accident through inadvertent stalling. It is,

however, under-powered, and the take-off run is too long, and the rate of climb off the ground too slow to make a suitable aircraft for use on small aerodromes, or on larger aerodromes when there are objects to be cleared at the boundary.

There is a fall-off in rate of climb with the ailerons with slots (which is due to the increased total weight of 33 lb due to the installation) and no appreciable difference in level speeds. The slots do not therefore have any appreciable effect on the total drag in straight flying.'

During her trials the aircraft had suffered two punctures, a fact which her assessors believed unlikely to have occurred had bigger tyres been fitted, more suited to cope with hard surfaces. Her sister aircraft J8031 was loaned to 2 FTS Digby from November 1926 but was returned to CFS by September 1927 and immediately offered for public sale. She was acquired by the Hampshire Aeroplane Club at Hamble to whom she was delivered following civilianisation as G-EBVD at Stag Lane. The Moth led an active life with a number of different owners and survived until 1949 when she was scrapped near Croydon. J8032 was detached from CFS to 5 FTS Sealand where she was struck off charge in November 1927.

Victor Dorée's 1925 Christmas party initiative on behalf of the London Aeroplane Club proved worthwhile when the petroleum distributing companies, guided by the Royal Aero Club, established a fund from which they donated £200 towards the cost of a third Club Moth. Identical sums were presented to Newcastle and the Lancashire Club who chose to spend their windfall on the refurbishment of a Renault-powered Avro 504K. In February 1926, with a total of £420 pledged by members, the London Club placed an order for a new Moth against delivery promised for late March. A donation of £50 received from Captain de Havilland helped to boost the total to £675 but by the end of March the club was still £100 short. Small donations continued to trickle in for several more weeks until the £795 was safely gathered together. On Friday 30th April, DH.60 Moth G-EBNP (280) joined the LAC fleet.

The replacement for the crashed G-EBLU, supplied under the terms of the Air Ministry scheme of subsidy, was G-EBMF (194), a second hand machine originally delivered to Wing Commander Wynn, the second private owner of a Moth at Stag Lane to whom she had been handed over in December 1925. She was formally sold to the London Aero Club Ltd on 17th April and delivered seven days later for immediate weekend service.

The arrival of the two new Moths allowed G-EBLI to be withdrawn for overhaul and installation of the club's spare engine which had been converted to dual ignition. Pressure on bookings was eased as more mem-

bers bought Moths of their own. With production-standard aeroplanes now available to them, de Havilland released their first prototype Moth from the shackles of experimental flying. Norman Jones and Sophie Eliott-Lynn jointly purchased G-EBKT from de Havilland and on the morning of Sunday 28th March flew 22 members of the Middlesex Women's Athletic Association on local joyrides. During April alone, Mrs Eliott-Lynn flew just over 52 hours, a figure to be compared with the London Club's total of 70 hours on one machine in the same period. Further good news was the announcement that the Duke of Sutherland had agreed to donate another Moth to the Club and G-EBNY (263), was formally presented on 10th July following the conclusion of the King's Cup Air Race at Hendon. Almost coincidentally, the London Club passed 1,000 flying hours, the first of the subsidised Clubs to do so.

The Newcastle Club appeared to be experiencing more than its share of difficulties and G-EBLY was again in trouble on 2nd April. The following report by the Club Secretary serves to illustrate the determination to succeed and the effort and spirit of co-operation which prevailed:

'One of the club's most careful pilots miscalculated slightly when landing, breaking a wheel and gently turning the machine over on to its back. As is usual in such cases, this took place in the furthest corner of the aerodrome. The only spare required which was not available was a rudder, and Major Packman got on to the telephone right away in an effort to obtain one. The Lancashire Club very kindly offered to supply one from a machine. Owing to holidays it was not safe to trust to having this forwarded by rail, so Mr J Edmundson set off for Manchester, accompanied by Major Packman, to bring the rudder up, leaving Cramlington at about 5.00pm and returning at 6.30am on Saturday.

'Meanwhile, Mr Brown had a team at work assisting him to make the necessary replacements up to a late hour, fitting a new axle, centre section, cylinder head, cowling etc. Work was re-commenced on Saturday morning with the result that the machine was being tested by Major Packman before 5.00pm on Saturday. Considering that the machine had to be almost completely dismantled, this was a very good performance.'

Britain's General Strike began on 3rd May, industrial action that had a particularly debilitating effect on transport. In addition to machines operated by the Royal Air Force and Imperial Airways, light aeroplane club machines were immediately volunteered for the public service. Wally Hope, operating a DH.9 provided by de Havilland, was even sworn in as a flying Special Constable.

Mrs Sophie Eliot-Lynn and Norman Jones took joint ownership of the prototype DH.60 G-EBKT in March 1926 and she was repainted pale blue. In April, Mrs Eliott-Lynn flew the aeroplane for almost 52 hours. The rudder cable can be seen still as a heavy-duty single strand. Sir Robert Hardingham

The government was particularly anxious that factual news should be disseminated as quickly as possible in an effort to eliminate false rumours concerning the current situation and likely developments. To that effect, the rapid distribution of newspapers was considered an absolute priority, and transport by air was the ideal solution.

Harold Perrin recalled that 'the immediate result was that Mr G T Witcombe, one of the London Aeroplane Club instructors, had the task of flying to Woodford, near Manchester, carrying one of the directors of the *Daily Mail*. That journey accomplished, the machine on its return to London carried out the first task of newspaper distribution, delivering copies of the *Daily Mail* at Lichfield, Stoke, Stone and Macclesfield.'

Aeroplanes gathered at Lympne, each to receive bundles of newspapers printed in Paris and delivered to the aerodrome by Imperial Airways for onward distribution. Two London Aeroplane Club Moths detached there were joined by the irrepressible Sophie Eliott-Lynn in her own G-EBKT. Small bundles of papers printed secretly in Newcastle were dropped into surrounding villages from the local Aero Club Moths operating from Cramlington, and supplies were later carried in bulk for distribution in London. Alternative titles were delivered to Newcastle by Moths of the Lancashire Aero Club, and a secret printing in Plymouth led to a distribution fleet gathering at Yeovil.

It was necessary to mount an armed guard on the aeroplanes in some areas once local pickets had discovered their strike-breaking potential. Jan Michie, resident engineer to the London Aeroplane Club, travelled with the Club's Moths to Lympne and, during the daytime lull in activities there, took the opportunity to complete the tests for his RAeS Aviator's Certificate.

Divided into regions, Great Britain's 'Southern Section' air service was administered by Harold Perrin. At the end of the strike, Perrin reported that seven Moths in his section had covered 15,275 miles, in addition to those flown by ten Avros, eight DH.9s and two Bristols, about 50,000 miles altogether, flown by a fleet which eventually grew to 30 aeroplanes. The London Club had flown 98 hours, Newcastle 49 and Lancashire 25.

The Secretary of the Newcastle Aero Club summed it up succinctly: 'Apart from financial considerations the work has brought much prestige and a greater realisation of the importance of aircraft among the people of the district.'

During the same Whitsuntide extended weekend, Colonel The Master of Sempill, accompanied by his wife, left Stag Lane in de Havilland School Moth G-EBMV (235), and during the next five days, flew 800 miles around Wales and the West Country, 'landing when and where I wished and never going near an aerodrome or aeroplane hangar'. Each night the Moth was housed in a farm shed or barn else folded and picketed, whilst petrol was obtained from local garages. On two occasions, at Borth in West Wales and Instow in Devonshire, the aeroplane was put down on the sandy beaches. The tour was perfect publicity for the Moth and details were written up and published under the titling of a 'practical demonstration,' ensuring that details of petrol and oil consumption were compared with that of a medium-sized car.

An almost identical situation surrounded Sir John Rhodes' tour in his Moth G-EBNM (249), between 3rd and 6th August when he flew a 792-mile circular tour from Stag Lane to include the English Midlands and South Coast. All aeroplane expenses included, a detailed report averaged the running cost at 2.48 pence per mile, and again laid heavy emphasis on the favourable comparison with motoring. A de Havilland advertisement, which appeared soon after, implored readers to 'Avoid overcrowded roads and recapture the joy of travel by owning a Moth two-seater light aeroplane'.

Sophie Eliott-Lynn who completed all her training on Moths with the London Aeroplane Club was the first member to satisfy the requirements for a 'B' commercial licence. Her night-flying test was completed on Monday 31st May at Stag Lane and, in celebration jointly with Mrs Sherwood Kelly, the two ladies organised an 'At Home' at the aerodrome for 200 guests on 1st June during which time more than half were taken

for flights in just three Moths. The guest-list was studded with society names in addition to the leading aviators of the day, and the two Moths undergoing trials at the Central Flying School were amongst a bevy of visiting aeroplanes.

Stag Lane was soon to host another aristocratic lady when Mary du Caurroy, Duchess of Bedford, became a de Havilland customer. Her first flight at the age of 61 was taken on 11th June when she was flown by Moth from Croydon to Woburn by Sydney St Barbe, who chose to land, without realising it, in the Bison Enclosure. The Duchess recorded in her diary that 'there was a little wind but not enough to make things unpleasant and I enjoyed the experience enormously without the slightest feeling of apprehension, nausea or cold. In fact all was pleasant except the noise!'

On 15th July, the Duchess again flew from Croydon to Woburn with Hubert Broad in G-EBKT, and was impressed to learn that only the week before, Broad had won the King's Cup Air Race in a similar machine (G-EBMO), at an average speed of over 90mph. From this time, the Duchess hired Moths to fly between her engagements whenever possible, until and inevitably, she placed an order with de Havilland for the supply of an aeroplane of her own. G-EBRI (405) was registered to Her Grace, The Duchess of Bedford at Woburn Abbey, in May 1927, a few days following her return from a 4,500 mile European tour, flown with her new personal pilot Captain Charles Barnard, in Geoffrey Cunliffe's hired Moth G-EBPM (353).

Recording the aeroplane's performance was a task still exercising the Design Department at Stag Lane and on 18th June, G-EBMP (198) was engaged for a series of climbing trials using a single ignition Cirrus I engine fed on 'Power Spirit'. Each of the three

In August 1926, Sir John Rhodes and his wife flew almost 800 miles, touring England, at an aeroplane operating cost of less than three pence per mile. The open locker door reveals the spaciousness of the now standard, externally accessible luggage compartment. *Flight*

'Fuel, oil, aircraft and engine replacements and general supplies can be provided at the current retail prices.

'Major adjustments, overhauls, repairs etc, can be executed and charged for on a cost plus profit basis. If required an estimate can be submitted before the work is undertaken.

'It will be appreciated that the charges for ground engineer's examination and cleaning are calculated as occurring during normal working hours and therefore, if these services are required at other times, an additional charge covering the overtime of any employee may be necessary. Prior notice during week-ends or other times when the de Havilland establishment is closed should be given when skilled attention is required. Furthermore, it should be remembered that no landing fees whatever are charged at Stag Lane Aerodrome.

'This Service is the first of its kind ever put on a basis within reach of the pockets of the ordinary person who can afford to run a motor car.'

planned ascents were to be made with a different propeller: a standard cruising propeller, DH5120/3; a 'climbing propeller' DH5130/1 and a Fairey-Reed Dural blade, 32730A/3. The atmosphere was described by Richard Clarkson as 'too surgy' for meaningful results and he considered that engine rpm was down, but the observations were noted and compared with those obtained on 29th June when Broad piloted G-EBNY (263), 'a standard production Moth' in conditions then recorded as 'warm, close and calm'.

As part of a general expansion of facilities at Stag Lane, on Mid-Summer Day 1926, the de Havilland Company continued its important motoring analogies when it officially unveiled the 'Aero Garage' for which basic details had been announced at the end of the previous year. This was a scheme designed specifically for the convenience of the private owner and garages were in such demand that new blocks continued to be erected at Stag Lane until 1930 after which, during a four-year period, the aerodrome

was slowly run-down due to the establishment of the new site at Hatfield, where Moth garages were an early and popular feature. The lock-up units were designed around the folded dimensions of the DH.60 Moth and the de Havilland Company marketed the buildings too, including erection at any suitable location.

'Suitable housing accommodation and attendance is provided at Stag Lane Aerodrome for a monthly charge of £2.10s.0d per machine. (Accommodation at government aerodromes at this time was charged at £10 per month). The de Havilland charge includes assistance in removal of the machine from the hangar, starting the engine, fuelling etc.

'Qualified ground engineers are available to examine the aircraft, engine and accessories. Minor adjustments are attended to and the daily certificate signed. The fee for this examination is 7s.6d.

'External cleaning of the aircraft, cleaning its cockpits etc, costs 7s.6d a time.

The 1926 King's Cup Air Race was flown from Hendon on 9th and 10th July. The format varied from previous years in that two laps of about 740 miles each were flown each day, the laps alternating between Hendon-Martlesham-Cambridge and Hendon-Coventry-Brockworth. Of 14 starters, five were Moths joined by two other de Havilland types, a DH.51 flown by Colonel Sempill and Company chairman Alan Butler in his Nimbus-engined DH.37A, G-EBDO.

Of the Moths, only Captain William McDonough in the Midland Club's green and silver G-EBLW was not from Stag Lane, where all club flying was suspended on 10th July on account of the Race and in anticipation of the Duke of Sutherland's presentation of a new Moth at Hendon. McDonough's competition was from Captain de Havilland himself in the heavily prepared G-EBNO (261), Hubert Broad in G-EBMO (197), Frank Sparks with the London Club's G-EBLI (183), and Wally Hope flying G-EBME (193).

But there was to be no clean sweep for de Havilland's advertising agents to promote,

The Stag Lane Aero Garage was opened in a blaze of publicity on 24th June 1926, offering private lock-up facilities for six folded Moths. They were to be the first of many built at Stag Lane, but there never were enough to satisfy demand before the airfield closed to club and private owner operations in 1933. LNA

although Broad did win the Race in the red and white G-EBMO, covering Sunday's 1,480 mile course in a flying time of 16hr 22min 40sec, a margin of just 22sec separating him from a Vickers Vixen in second place. Initially, the agents opted for a small panel announcing the win, let into pre-planned advertisements covering the delivery of four Moths to the Air Corps of the Irish Free State. Wally Hope, who was unwell and landed at Oxford on the first day, retired from the Race, as did the DH.51 and the DH.37A, leaving the two standard club Moths to carry the Company flag and be numbered amongst the total of only five finishers.

Later, the de Havilland Company and ADC Aircraft Ltd took joint advertising space to emphasise that Broad's win had been in an aeroplane which 'except for the removal of unessential features offering resistance, was in every respect a standard machine'. The Mk I Cirrus engine was said to have 'run unfalteringly at full throttle' for the duration.

A month after the race, de Havilland provided details of some of the 'unessential features' which had been modified to preserve the 'standard' specification:

'In order to give the machine sufficient range to deal with emergency conditions on the long course an extra 8 gallon petrol tank was fitted in the front cockpit, its contents being transferred (by means of a Vickers pump) to the standard gravity tank as fuel was consumed. The front cockpit was faired in and the windscreen removed. To the rear cockpit a long sloping windscreen was fitted and the size of the opening reduced. The spring bolts, with handles for wing folding at the front spar roots, were replaced by ordinary bolts, and the planes were faired into the fuselage by means of doped fabric. The exhaust pipes were entirely removed. The petrol tank was covered with fabric doped on to the centre section in order to provide as clean an air-flow as possible, and the same measures were adopted where the tailplane and fin joined the fuselage. The extension handle to the petrol cock was removed and the stepping-board on the bottom plane taken away. The revolution indicator and oil pressure gauge were fitted on the rear dashboard instead of externally behind the engine.'

During the King's Cup Geoffrey de Havilland had been forced down at Chelmsford with a broken oil pipe, a great disappointment as the light blue and silver G-EBNO had been prepared especially with the prototype Cirrus II engine. Other obvious changes included fairing of the front cockpit and a special streamlined exhaust collector box which sat on top of the cylinder heads.

The starboard side of the Cirrus II engine showing the dual magneto installation and the square section induction manifold. ADC

ADC Aircraft Ltd, embarked on a major advertising campaign after the Race, offering dual ignition Cirrus I engines at a new, reduced price of £260 each, unpacked, ex-works, a saving of £40 per unit.

Introduction of the Cirrus Mk II engine was the first major change to the specification of the DH.60 Moth since production and sales had been authorised in 1925, although a number of minor modifications had been incorporated, each with the aim of increasing the machine's 'robustness under hard wear'.

It was generally agreed that the reliability of, and confidence in, the Cirrus I engine had played a major part in the success of the DH.60 Moth. Introduction of the Mk II now offered owners a choice. At about the same weight as the Mk I, 268 lb, the new engine was accepted easily into the existing airframe, and at maximum speed (2,000rpm) developed 84hp, an increase of 29%. At cruising revolutions (1,800rpm), power was rated at 78hp. A new 6ft diameter propeller, DH5132/1, had been designed in May when the speed assumptions had been 83mph and 75mph respectively.

Frank Halford, ADC and de Havilland all agreed that the Mk II would not replace the Mk I but rather would offer a choice to customers. With a view to increasing export orders, the additional power was seen as the key to improved take-off and climb performance from small or congested fields and hot or high-elevation aerodromes. Consideration was also shown towards a seaplane application and, with small changes to the crankcase, even to a pusher configuration. Some relatively minor modifications incorporated by Frank Halford were the first of the several steps that lead directly to production of a completely new unit of de Havilland specification two years later.

The Cirrus II was fitted with standard cast-iron cylinder barrels and aluminium heads. The rocking levers were carried on a separate steel bracket, bolted to the platform provided on top of the cylinder head. Phosphor bronze replaced steel valve seats and the pistons, increased in diameter by 5mm, carried three rings closely spaced at the top. Apart from small changes to the crankshaft and thrust bearing, and the use of forged aluminium connecting rods, probably for the first time in aero engine practice, according to John Brodie, the most radical re-design was to the induction manifold in an effort to eliminate any recurrence of the unexpected difficulties experienced by operators of early Cirrus I models. The new manifold, heated by exhaust gases, was of a different shape and serviced from a dual carburettor, with one induction passage supplying the two inner cylinders, and another the two outers. Unusually, the two outer branches were flexibly connected to the fixed centre portion by short lengths of rubber pipe secured by Jubilee clips. The carburettor was fed with ram air by a pipe leading from the top right hand side of the cowling.

On the Monday morning following the King's Cup, 'Billy' Sempill was back at Stag Lane in company with Hubert Broad, Harold Hemming and Frank Courtney, the quartet of pilots booked to deliver the four DH.60 Moths ordered by the Irish Free State Army Air Corps. The aeroplanes were painted white overall with green, white and orange vertical rudder stripes, and were scheduled for the training of officers and cadets at Baldonnel Aerodrome near Dublin. To cope with what was expected to be soft grass airfields, the Irish Moths were fitted with Palmer tyres of greater width than standard. The significance of the heavily publicised gathering was that this was the

Captain Geoffrey de Havilland flying G-EBNO during the severe winter weather which enveloped Great Britain at the end of 1926. Originally the test bed for the Mk II Cirrus engine, The Captain used G-EBNO as his personal aircraft until August 1927.
BAE Systems

first export delivery of Moths by air, a task successfully accomplished in four and a half hours, operating via Sealand for refuelling before the water crossing.

Hemming flew with Captain Frederick Tymms in the front cockpit who was monitoring a new type of light aeroplane compass. Passing over an interesting geographical feature, Hemming had difficulty in drawing Tymms' attention to the fact, but by stretching forward just managed to tap him on the head, at which point the engine stopped. Flying at low level, Hemming had little time to select an appropriate field, and put down safely only after a violent sideslip. Rolling to a halt, he discovered that when bending forward, his coat sleeve had managed to turn off the ignition switches.

Unfortunately, apart from '25' (266), which was withdrawn from use in 1935, their service life with 'A' Flight of the School of Aeronautics, Baldonnel, was short. '23' (264), and '24' (265), crashed under unrecorded circumstances in July and June 1928 respectively. '26' (267), lasted barely a year, crashing in June 1927. Although 14 civil DH.60 Moths were later registered in Ireland, 'A' Flight did not replace its losses.

Seven thousand members and guests of London's fashionable Roehampton Country Club welcomed four Moths and a DH.51 into their grounds on 17th July when a display of aerobatics was followed by an 'aerial golf tournament' – in essence a low-level flour-bombing competition. Hubert Broad had first flown into the grounds on 25th June to check for any difficulties, but none was obvious and the event was a great success. It was another all-de Havilland publicity coup, and the Company expressed a wish that other similar establishments should follow the good example set by Roehampton.

The Duchess of Bedford now started to travel by Moth as often as she could in preference to taking a journey by train. It was no surprise that the press dubbed her, respectfully,

The Flying Duchess and closely followed her newsworthy activities. An expedition in August was described by Lettice Curtis in her biography of the Duchess, *Winged Odyssey*:

'Broad collected her from Woburn to lunch with friends at Lyndhurst. After diverting to view the Mauritania *in Southampton Water, the largest passenger ship then afloat, they landed on Lyndhurst golf course. They left again at 3.45pm and flew home via Netley, Hayling Island and Bosham where they circled Mr Ogilvie (the resident surgeon in the Duchess' hospital at Woburn) who in his boat was taking part in the local regatta. They then made their way via Chichester, Hindhead and Windsor, arriving at Woburn at 5.20pm.'*

Throughout the summer and into the late autumn Captain de Havilland, flying with Richard Clarkson as observer, tested a number of different propeller designs during climb trials in the prototype Cirrus II Moth G-EBNO. The aim was to produce substantive figures which could be compared with a 'standard Mk I Moth' before the new '1927 Model' was unveiled in January.

The Hampshire Aeroplane Club, sixth of the subsidised clubs and well established at Hamble, replacing Glasgow who were still organising themselves, took delivery of their two allocated Moths, G-EBOH (269) and G-EBOI (270), just after 6.00pm on Saturday 7th August. Flown by Frank Sparks, and Captain G I Thomson, newly appointed instructor of the Hampshire Club, the pair had left Stag Lane at 4.00pm and routed via Brooklands to pick-up a passenger, thence overhead and around Winchester and Southampton to announce themselves. On arrival at Hamble, waiting club members quickly christened G-EBOH *Gee-Bo* and G-EBOI *Gee-Boy*, before Thomson brought the day's proceedings to an end with the most important trip of the day, a flight with the reporter from the local newspaper.

During the First World War a printed bulletin called the *DH Gazette* had been produced 'in the field' followed by the monthly *Air-co Rag* which continued until 1920. With the Stag Lane business now consolidated, the *DH Gazette* was reborn in August 1926 with the declared intention of advising recipients of 'doings' at Stag Lane, improvements in existing designs, and of forging a link between users of de Havilland aeroplanes in all parts of the world. Priced at 4d per copy, issues appeared spasmodically due to the part-time attentions of the Editor but, from June 1928, the price was increased to 6d and in November, Oscar Cooke took up the Editorial position in a full-time capacity. Now under the control of St Barbe, the *DH Gazette* was a magazine with a more clearly defined mission: business! The contents were to focus more on the universal use of the Moth and other de Havilland products rather than the partisan approach to events in Great Britain and to social life at Stag Lane in particular.

Perhaps to combine the importance of the engineers' view and to publicise the recognised strengths as well as the correctable deficiencies of the DH.60 Moth, the August 1926 issue of the *DH Gazette* was allowed to carry a feature by the London Club engineer Jan Michie, concerning the maintenance of the type which he said was in his opinion, after a year's personal experience, probably the easiest machine yet produced to keep in flying order.

Michie reported that carelessness when 'sucking in' had caused one or two 'narrow shaves'. These incidents were largely due to the fact that the aeroplane could be handled and started by one person, aided by the efficiency of the impulse mechanism built into the BTH magnetos. He advised caution when dealing with propellers, suggesting that ignition switches should be treated always as live. The Editor added a note to advise readers that the problems had been caused by a batch of faulty switches, all of which had since been replaced.

But there always was and would continue to be, dangers in mishandling propellers. The following April, Lady Mary Bailey was almost scalped when at Stag Lane the engine of her Moth fired and the propeller blade struck her a glancing blow on the head. Not discouraged, after a short convalescence she returned to flying, if anything with an even greater intensity of purpose, and well beyond the boundaries of Stag Lane Aerodrome.

Michie's suggestion that a self-starter should be added as a matter of safety was also noted by the Editor who advised that the Design Department was already devoting its attention to the matter. There was nothing to remind readers that a self-starter had been installed in the prototype Moth and several other production aircraft since, later mostly removed by popular request.

Administered under the Competition Rules of the Royal Aero Club, a two-day Air Race meeting was held at Ensbury Park Racecourse, near Bournemouth, on 21st and 22nd August. Eight race categories were announced in advance, three of which were limited exclusively to Moths. The London, Midland and Hampshire Clubs were all strongly represented with the London Aeroplane Club suspending operations at Stag Lane in favour of sending all four of its Moths to Bournemouth. One wit suggested that the name of the south coast resort should be changed to 'Bournemoth'! Although private Moth owners were lacking, their cause was led by Captain de Havilland, Sophie Eliott-Lynn and Wally Hope, with two de Havilland directors sponsoring entries to be flown by Hubert Broad.

Including flour bombing, Moths were credited with wins in nine of ten events. Although considered a success, the crowds of spectators were thinner than anticipated and the size of the temporary aerodrome was clearly marginal for some of the bigger machines. Apart from some difficult landings caused by the strength and direction of the wind on Sunday, there were no incidents apart from the one occasion on Saturday when Rex Stocken hit a tree with the wingtip of the Hampshire Club's new Moth G-EBOH during an overtaking manoeuvre. Stocken managed to maintain control and to finish his heat; the badly damaged wing was replaced overnight for the Moth to continue with her racing career the following day.

In the midst of all this practical aviation stood the spectre of the Lympne Trials scheduled for the second week of September! Following the Air Ministry meeting on 31st March 1925, with the Moth already launched and well into flight testing, it had been announced that a further series of two-seater light aeroplane Trials was to take place at Lympne. The planned delay until 1926 was to permit new engines to be designed and tested such that their amalgamation with appropriate airframes would be accomplished most expeditiously and result only in proven aircraft reporting at Lympne.

Engines, the target for severe criticism in 1924, were to be limited not by capacity but to a total weight of 170 lb, to include ignition equipment, airscrew hub, and, in the case of water-cooled engines, pipes and liquids. It was believed this formula would result in the emergence of 'honest engines' of between 80hp and 100hp, but probably concentrated at the lower end of the range.

The announcement was anathema to those who still firmly believed that very small engines mounted in increasingly efficient glider-type airframes was the way forward for the 'light aeroplane' so defined. At a dry weight of 260 lb, the Cirrus I, already acknowledged as the most practical power unit of its type, was ruled completely out of contention.

In June 1925 the *Daily Mail* had announced it was providing £5,000 in prize money for the Trials 'to encourage the production for popular use, of moderate priced, low-powered light aeroplanes of improved types' but when the list of competitors for 1926 was published at the beginning of September, only 16 machines were entered, three of which, the Blackburn Bluebird, Avro Avian and de Havilland Moth, all nominated the new Armstrong Siddeley Genet engine as powerplant. The Editor of *Flight* was less than impressed:

'It will be observed that there is a somewhat disappointingly small number of new machines entered, quite a large proportion being the two-seaters of the 1925 Lympne competition. Generally speaking, the new types appear to have been entered by private clubs or individuals, and the aircraft industry as a whole has not come forward as might have been expected ... As far as we are aware the Genet engine has not yet passed its type tests ... doubtless it will in good time before the competition, as it is one of the stipulations that all engines used in the competition must have passed their Air Ministry tests.'

Scant attention was paid to a French Light Aeroplane Competition which was conducted at Orly in mid-August. Although international, only eight competitors took part, British interests being represented by Mrs Eliott-Lynn in G-EBKT. A marking system that rewarded the Moth with no points in the 'all wood construction' category, no points for not carrying a parachute, maximum equal marks for engine starting, yet an advantage of only two marks in the 'folding and dismantling' time trial in which she achieved the necessary targets in a quarter of the time of her nearest competitor, conspired to leave her in seventh place, just ahead of a 25hp Anzani powered Pander which was unable to complete some of the categories at all.

The de Havilland Company accepted the challenge presented by the 1926 Trial's engine weight limitation and in concert with their rivals Avro and Blackburn, opted for the left-hand tractor Genet, a compact radial weighing in at just two pounds inside the 170 lb limit set by the Rules, a qualifying factor which was to prove disastrous in the final outcome. A Fairey-Reed duralumin propeller replaced the more familiar wooden blades of de Havilland design. The 'Genet Moth' so presented by de Havilland, factory number 271, was registered G-EBOU to the company in July 1926 and painted silver with a red top decking was test flown by Broad on 3rd September. The C of A was issued five days later and on 9th September Broad flew her to Lympne for the 'eliminating trials' where she became 'No 2'.

The engine complete with propeller, cowlings, filled oil tank, mounting plates, fireproof bulkhead and exhaust pipes totalled 230 lb. Weighed on 6th September, the tare weight of G-EBOU was 720 lb, 143 lb lighter than a standard model Cirrus Moth and assisted by a main fuel tank reduced in capacity to 12 gallons. It was not quite the

Members of the de Havilland team with DH.60 Genet Moth G-EBOU at the Lympne Light Aeroplane Trials in September 1926. The aircraft was disqualified from the Trials after a ballast weight was not replaced after a forced landing. DH Moth Club Archive

patronising attempt to comply with the Regulations as it might have seemed, for de Havilland already had sights on another high profile development which would of necessity feature the Genet engine and its capabilities for operating whilst inverted.

According to Armstrong Siddeley, the Genet I engine was rated at 65hp and the Genet II and IIA of 1930 at 80hp. Throughout her public life, press reports of Genet Moth activity quote her engine to be 75hp. All references to the mating of the Genet engine with the Moth airframe in surviving de Havilland documentation and reflected throughout available Air Ministry papers, consistently quote 60hp, the figure adopted from this point.

Technical details of the 'Genet Moth' released necessarily to officials caused a flurry of interest. The press analysis of her declared empty weight at 735 lb and load carrying capacity of 700 lb indicated a heavy points score, giving her 'a very good chance' in the competition. The new Avro Avian was credited with a useful load of 828 lb and, therefore, a ratio to structural weight that was thought difficult to equal.

On the first day of the eliminating trials, Broad failed to clear the 25ft imaginary barriers used to assess take-off distance and initial climb, and he and team manager Bob Loader protested that taking off uphill, a direction dictated by the strong southerly wind, imposed an additional and unfair burden. To compensate for the runway slope, the marker flags representing the barrier were lowered by five feet, and on Friday evening the Genet Moth soared over, following the earlier success of the Bluebird. After immense anticipation, the Avro crew was unable to start the engine of the Avian which remained grounded.

The following day, during the landing trials, the Bluebird suffered minor damage to an undercarriage strut but whilst under repair another fitting inadvertently was bent and Royal Aero Club officials assessed the additional job as a 'major repair,' not permitted under the Rules, thus eliminating Blackburn's competition. Broad meanwhile completed the landing test by coming to rest in the Genet Moth within the stipulated 125 yards from the theoretical hedge. During one of several earlier attempts he had asked his front seat passenger, one of the Company's engineering support party, Eric Mitchell, to stand up on his seat during short finals to act as an air-brake. At the end of the day only nine competitors remained to begin the Trials proper on 12th September.

In the event, Bert Hinkler's Avian was plagued with constant leaks from an aluminium petrol tank, but was eliminated after a forced landing with a broken magneto drive shaft which could not be repaired within the time allowed. The Genet Moth

suffered an exactly similar problem, but repairs were effected in the field to allow the aeroplane to complete the course before the deadline. It was later discovered that a lead ballast weight was missing from the cockpit, either left inadvertently at the site of the forced landing, or taken by a souvenir hunter, as a result of which G-EBOU was technically disqualified. Ironically, the identical fault which had led to the loss of the two most practical aeroplanes in the Trials was failure of the drive to the single magneto. Armstrong Siddeley had been restrained from fitting a second magneto in order to comply with the upper weight limit imposed by the Regulations.

Stanley Spooner, who appeared to have an obsession for designing light aeroplanes against minimum cost rather than any other level of practicability, but who equally was an admirer of all offerings from the Avro camp, wrote scathingly in his post Trial editorial: 'A competition, the regulations for which rule out what is admitted to be the finest two-seater low-powered aeroplane in the world (the Avro Avian) is obviously wrong!'

Not surprisingly, de Havilland retaliated immediately with an advertising campaign quoting a statement published in *The Times* at the conclusion of the 1926 Trials: 'The fact remains that since 1924, the only two-seater aircraft which has made any headway, and which is at present the approved aircraft for training novices in the State-aided flying clubs, is the DH Moth'. Under the heading 'The Real Owner Pilot's Aeroplane', the de Havilland copywriters continued their analogy with motoring:

The needs of the man, or woman, who requires an aeroplane as a practical vehicle were carefully considered in the design of the Moth: comfort, space for plenty of luggage, easy and effective controls, an engine which the man in the street can keep in perfect order, and above all, the robustness and reliability that are expected in a good automobile were taken to be of more importance than freakish performance, such as is generally encouraged by technical competitions...'

Charles Walker summed up what was seen by many as the near-futility of the whole exercise:

'Whatever may be the conditions of a competition, and those in question have raised a good deal of criticism, there is always a certain amount of valuable technical information to be gleaned when aircraft are gathered together in competition. This information may already be in existence, but a competition focuses attention on certain points (and, incidentally, obscures others) in a way that nothing else will do.

'As regards our own entry, this being a practically standard Moth with an engine

rendering it eligible for the competition, could not hope to do very well in a competition calling for highly specialised qualities. It may be said, however, that we were very satisfied with the speed at which it was lapping in the Grosvenor Cup of nearly 99mph and also with its other qualities. Another unusual feature in the Genet Moth was that the mileage per gallon seemed steadily to improve as the speed was increased. Broad continued this improvement up to 81mph before his disqualification, and was then doing well over 20 miles to the gallon.

'It is perhaps being wise after the event, but one may say that in a competition having no spectacular value, much more interesting technical information would be gained had the general conditions been such that machines could have been penalised more and eliminated and disqualified less.'

Having flown without great success in any of the air races held at Lympne on Saturday 18th September, so concluding the generally uninspiring events of the week, Hubert Broad flew the Genet Moth back to Stag Lane on the following Thursday where she was immediately exercised in climb speed trials to 7,000ft.

The de Havilland Company continued to progress their studies of tubular metal main spars and on 9th September the Design Office compiled a basic schedule of weights for 'metal planes' again under the designation DH.60A, a term later used erroneously by Hereward de Havilland and some commentators to describe the Cirrus II powered model. Spars were to be manufactured in 16 gauge alloy with ash plugs in the ends. Compared with wooden mainplanes the 'metal planes' were estimated to be about 23 lb heavier.

The plan had advanced sufficiently by the end of 1926 that a complete set of mainplanes and an experimental tailplane had been manufactured and fitted to G-EBOS (268), designated a DH.60A but in all other respects a standard DH School Cirrus I Moth which had qualified for a C of A in July. The aircraft was weighed in her new configuration on 9th February 1927 when the tare weight was recorded as 903 lb.

The degree of flight testing undertaken is unclear but, in August 1927, G-EBOS was sold to a private owner at Stag Lane, Miss Sicele O'Brien. Almost certainly standard mainplanes had been refitted, as the recorded tare weight at the aircraft's sale was 880 lb. In October 1928 G-EBOS spun into the ground at Mole Mount Golf Course near Mill Hill, badly injuring Miss O'Brien and her passenger, Mildred Leith. The enquiry into the accident revealed that the front and rear rudder bars had not been connected together prior to what was intended to be an instructional flight.

Hereward de Havilland joined those engaged in flight testing on 22nd September when he and Richard Clarkson took up the de Havilland School's Cirrus I powered G-EBOT (272), in an effort to collect further climb and speed performance data with a propeller, DH5132/1, scheduled for the Mk II Cirrus and quoted to be 'fast revving'. The exercise was later repeated in separate flights on the same day by Geoffrey de Havilland and by Broad in G-EBNO with a Z64 metal propeller. Collected data was later analysed and used as the basis for design in December 1926 of a four-bladed wooden propeller of 6ft diameter and 4ft 1.5in pitch (DH5144/1) scheduled for the Cirrus II although there is no evidence that an example was ever manufactured or flight tested.

Supported by a crowd of 20,000, the Lancashire Aero Club's second Air Pageant of the year at Woodford on 26th September was organised to celebrate their first 12 months of operation. The Avro Company seized the opportunity to field the latest version of its already outdated Gosport, now fitted with a 100hp Alpha radial engine of recent Avro design and manufacture, and both Avro and Blackburn displayed their Genet-powered Avian and Bluebird respectively.

Together with G-EBOU, these two other veterans of Lympne competed in Woodford's Open Handicap Air Race. Broad flying the Genet Moth lost badly to the Avian and Bluebird owing, it was believed, to the fact that the Moth's cowlings permitted the radial engine to run too cold with the result that it started missing, a symptom also experienced by Bert Hinkler when flying the Avian at Lympne.

While Broad was coping with the Genet Moth at Woodford, his successful King's Cup Moth, the crimson and white G-EBMO, had been loaned to Colonel Sempill who was waiting patiently for a change in the weather before beginning a fantasy journey. Leaving a small field near the village of Sennen in Cornwall early on the morning of 29th September, and with a 12-hour endurance thanks to the long-range tank situated in the front cockpit, 'Billy' Sempill flew round the nearby Land's End Hotel before setting the first of many courses that would take him to John O'Groats, 600 straight-line miles away. Although the famous route had been covered many times previously in almost every imaginable manner, nobody before had flown directly between the two landmarks.

Carrying 50 gallons of fuel and sufficient oil, a non-stop flight was planned, but the Cirrus engine began to run rich as G-EBMO approached Wrexham, and a considered diversion into the RAF aerodrome at Sealand soon established that the carburettor float was full of petrol. With the problem quickly rectified, the journey was resumed and without further incident the Moth was

landed at Duncansby Head, a common grazing ground alongside the John O'Groats Hotel, 8hr and 14min flying time from Land's End.

Moths first appeared in the showrooms of two London stores in October. At the premises of S T Lea, 141 New Bond Street, amongst the more usual stock of Austin, Sunbeam and Rolls-Royce motor cars, Sam Lea, having secured 'the London concession for de Havilland aircraft of all types', carefully positioned DH.60 Moth G-EBPG (359), one set of wings folded back against the fuselage and the other removed altogether. A young salesman was engaged, fresh from school at Merchant Taylors, with a brief to promote the de Havilland School of Flying in addition to aeroplanes. He later was coached by DH instructors on the ground, and at weekends in the air. Against a background of orchestrated publicity, Mr George Groves arrived in an 18-50 Crossley Six to be welcomed by the Sales Manager of Crossley Motors Ltd, ostensibly to buy the aeroplane on behalf of his old friend the Rajah of Bhong.

The whole episode may have been a charade. Were not Crossley Motors major shareholders in the Avro Company? Neither G-EBPG nor any other Moth was ever registered in the name of the Rajah, and after standing in the showroom for some months, G-EBPG was returned to Stag Lane.

London's Selfridges Department Store arranged a Moth as a window display in Oxford Street as part of a promotional Flying Week in the autumn of 1926. The second prototype Moth G-EBKU (169), offered for sale by de Havilland, was positioned with her tail near the left side of the window, while the fuselage flanked by folded wings, nosed into the far right hand corner, presenting the best possible viewing angle, and cleverly enhanced by a huge mirror positioned on the right hand wall. A notice along the top of the window explained that the Moth was displayed 'with wings folded ready for the garage'. In addition to two dummy aviators modelling flying clothing, some photographs and brochures and an advertisement for the de Havilland School of Flying, the most prominently displayed caption announced that 'Full particulars of garaging, oil consumption, mileage, landing facilities, etc, are obtainable from the Motor Cycle Department on the First Floor'.

Allegedly, at some later date, Mr Gordon Selfridge, travelling in the USA, was asked what was new in his London store, and on the spur of the moment confessed he had started an Aviation Department. There being no such plan, he was forced to call his son in England immediately, and insist that a new Department was created as quickly as possible.

Genet Moth G-EBOU was aired briefly on 20th October prior to delivery to Croydon, where, in a highly polished condition, she

was paraded for inspection at the Dominion Premiers' Demonstration on 23rd October. Two British ministers who were photographed taking a close interest were Secretary of State for Air, Sir Samuel Hoare, and the Chancellor of the Exchequer, Mr Winston Churchill.

At the Company's request, G-EBOU was positioned to Martlesham Heath for performance testing, arriving on 30th November following payment of the standard £20 test fee. Due to delays with paperwork, test flying did not commence until early January 1927 and then at an agreed all-up weight of 1,267 lb.

The acceptance and success of the Moth airframe tied to the ADC Cirrus engine created mild concern amongst the directors of the de Havilland Company. They realised that their future strategies could entirely be dictated by an influence outside of their immediate control, and it was unwise to tie themselves to a sole supplier of power units. Disregarding the Genet which was a specialised case, there was every reason for the company to seek an alternative to the current supply of Cirrus engines from ADC Aircraft Ltd, and negotiations with Frank Halford resulted in the first ideas for an entirely new powerplant going onto the drawing board on Thursday, 29th October, 1926.

Close co-operation with Short Bros, and a wide experience of operating many of their earlier designs as seaplanes, coupled with the additional power now available through the Mk II Cirrus engine, inevitably led de Havilland into fitting a DH.60 Moth with a 'float chassis' in November. The airframe selected was No 273, and she was carried by lorry to Short's Rochester works on the River Medway where two duralumin floats originally designed for the Short Mussel were attached. The airframe had been modified for her nautical role by the introduction of several stainless steel fittings, including the wires and rods bracing the float chassis, and the leading edges of the lower mainplanes were sheeted with 3-ply for added durability.

The aeroplane carried no registration letters as the plan was to send her to the United States almost immediately, accompanied by the newly knighted Sir Alan Cobham, where she would become the property of Mr Kenneth B Walton of Haverfold, Pennsylvania, and be evaluated for possible licence production. The legend 'DH MOTH' was painted full span on top and bottom wings, on both fuselage sides and across the rudder.

The 'Moth Seaplane' listed by the manufacturer as an 'Exhibition Machine' and fitted with production Cirrus II engine No 6, was first flown from the Medway at Rochester by Hubert Broad on 15th November. The Company publicists welcomed the opportunities presented by the now familiar DH.60 shape in a new configuration and

Hinaidi Aerodrome, Baghdad, just before Christmas 1926, where Stack and Leete's former RAF Squadrons, Nos 55 and 70, were still in residence equipped with DH.9As and the troop-carrying Vickers Victoria. Stephen Lally

Chancellor of the Exchequer, Winston Churchill, and Mr W L MacKenzie King, Canadian Prime Minister, inspecting Genet Moth G-EBOU at the Dominion Premiers' Demonstration at Croydon Aerodrome on 23rd October 1926. The Air Ministry subsequently bought six Genet Moths and the Canadian Air Force, two. The display board quotes the engine rating at 70hp. BAE Systems

soon ensured the world was fully informed:

'Already acknowledged to be the most practical small aeroplane, the Moth in its new form, equipped with Short-built duralumin floats and the Mk II Cirrus engine, enters a new sphere, that of a light seaplane. For training, club flying, patrol work or private touring it is in a class by itself. With pilot and passenger it leaves the water after a short run, it is delightful to handle in the air and easy to manoeuvre on the water. An ordinary boathouse is sufficiently large to house it and it costs no more to run than a small launch.'

Following Broad's initial trials, Alan Cobham accompanied by his wife, Gladys, flew the new Moth while still wearing the general attire appropriate for an official guest at the civil ceremonies which earlier had surrounded the naming of the DH.50J G-EBOP *Pelican*. Two days later the Cobhams sailed for New York on board RMS *Homeric*, taking Moth 273 with them, fully rigged and loaded into the hold. The plan was for the seaplane to be lowered onto the water at Quarantine near Ellis Island, to fly up the Hudson River for a conventional wheeled undercarriage to be attached at Newark, and then on to Washington DC.

On arrival in the USA on 25th November, to Cobham's immense frustration and embarrassment, in choppy surface conditions the seaplane Moth refused to leave the water. To lighten the load, Lady Cobham and her luggage vacated the machine but the reduced weight made no difference. DH MOTH was towed by motor launch with the Cobhams on board along the river to Battery Point, where the seaplane was lifted safely onto dry land in the presence of the owner and reception committee from the Aero-

nautical Chamber of Commerce. Cobham was furious and wrote afterwards: 'The episode did nothing to improve my relations with the (de Havilland) Company, which were already strained'.

On 2nd December 1926 in bitterly cold conditions and running into a persistent headwind, DH MOTH was flown by Cobham and his pregnant wife from Miller Field, New Dorp, Staten Island, to Mustin Field, serving the US Navy Yard in Philadelphia, where they stayed the night, resuming the journey to Boling Field, Anacostia, Washington DC the next day. 'It was pleasant to arrive and be in a warm house', Cobham wrote, adding with a touch of cynicism, perhaps, 'and to see the purchaser testing his Moth and pronouncing it marvellous'.

DH MOTH was demonstrated around Washington on 4th December, carrying United States mail, the envelopes initialled or, more rarely, signed by Alan J Cobham, and hand cancelled with a cachet reading 'Cobham First United States Overland Flight, New York-Philadelphia-Washington. DH Moth Airplane'. The flights were described as 'Peri-Columbia Demonstrations' and for the benefit of members of the Senate and House of Representatives, Cobham is believed to have executed a 'touch and go' on Lexington Avenue.

It was Cobham's last association with the aeroplane. While he embarked on a lecture tour, following a reception by President Coolidge, the Moth was flown by Kenneth Walton to the Huff Daland plant at Bristol, Pennsylvania, where she was allocated civilian licence number '1026'. The Huff Daland Airplane Company Inc was considering the production of a popularly-priced two-seater aircraft based on a modern air-cooled engine of up to 80hp and had distributed a

questionnaire to prospective customers. By 10th December, 145 replies had been received and the company needed to decide whether to design its own machine or to negotiate with de Havilland for the rights to manufacture the Moth under licence.

However, no American investment was forthcoming and plans to manufacture or even market the Moth in the United States were abandoned. In October 1927, Walton sold the aeroplane to Canada where she was registered G-CAIL to Western Canada Airways of Winnipeg. Re-registered to Commercial Airways, Regina, on 5th March 1929, G-CAIL was destroyed by fire near Lac La Rouge the following day.

Cobham was particularly angry with de Havilland, believing the Company knew the Moth seaplane might have take-off problems on rough water, but had failed to advise him. Testing at Rochester had been brief and under relatively calm conditions, and the company had already publicly admitted that the Mussel floats were something of a 'makeshift'. The episode was quietly forgotten, probably all having realised that matters had been badly rushed to ensure that the aeroplane's delivery to her American owner would coincide with the publicity generated by Alan Cobham's lecture tour. The *DH Gazette* could only comment optimistically: 'When the float undercarriage which has been specially designed and is now being built for the Moth at Messrs Short Brother's Works, is completed, there is every indication that the results will be even more satisfactory'.

At about the time late in 1925 that the Lancashire Aero Club were being promised another Moth by Sir Charles Wakefield, the club decided to engage a full-time salaried instructor. Club Chairman John Leeming

The first Moth Seaplane, No 273, was fitted with Short Mussel floats as an interim measure, and demonstrated by Alan Cobham from the River Medway at Rochester in November 1926. Short Bros

offered the post to a former RAF pilot, T Neville Stack, an accomplished musician then playing as a drummer in a band at one of London's exclusive night spots, the Kit Kat Club.

The following year Stack and one of his unpaid instructors, Bernard Leete, a former RFC and RAF colleague whose squadron had been based alongside Stack's at Hinaidi in Iraq for three years, decided, during a train journey from Manchester to London, that each would acquire a Moth and, in company, fly a substantial distance rather in the manner of a touring holiday. Apart from Cobham's flight to Zurich and Bert Hinkler's epic trip to Italy in the Avro Baby, until that time no other extended flights in civilian light aeroplanes had ever been attempted. They hoped their adventure would result in recognition of the type as a practical long-distance vehicle, and possibly even create a new record. Secretly they were thinking of Australia.

With self-confessed naivety, the tourists approached Francis St Barbe and asked for the de Havilland Company to present them with two free Moths. Not surprisingly, the request was refused, but the Business Manager offered them a pair of used machines which had recently been retired from service. Leete acquired the second prototype G-EBKU and she was converted to a single-seater with a 20 gallon fuel tank installed in the front cockpit. Stack purchased G-EBMO, Broad's King's Cup victor, and she was similarly prepared and fitted up with Cirrus II engine No 1. St Barbe's package also included a spare propeller for each Moth to be carried slung under the fuselage, a number of engine spares and a tool kit. The inclusive price was £1,200, and both aeroplanes were registered to their new owners on 6th November 1926 in preparation for departure nine days later.

Prior to her sale, G-EBKU had been operating with the de Havilland School of Flying with the prototype Mk I Cirrus engine installed. This unit was removed in June 1926 and replaced by Cirrus II No 41. With a total recorded time of almost exactly 300 hours, the displaced Cirrus I was installed in DH.60 Moth G-EBMP (198), and test flown on 15th June. G-EBMP remained in service with the de Havilland School until late summer 1927, when the engine was transferred to another School Moth, G-EBOT (272), probably at the time she was sold to Winifred Spooner in August that year. G-EBOT passed to new owners at Woodley from 1928 and Broxbourne in August 1931, where she was destroyed in a crash in December. Unless the unit had been

changed again, she may have taken the historic old engine with her.

Although planning extended to about a year, not until shortly before their departure did Stack and Leete reveal their intended destination to be Cairo, possibly extending to India, whereupon the British press latched onto the assumption that either the flight was to be made non-stop in a daring record attempt, or landings were to be made at every intermediate city, a suggestion quickly disabused by Stack's statement that the flight was 'a holiday jaunt and not a Cook's tour'.

Although the weather was far from suitable, Stack and Leete left a muddy Stag Lane during the early afternoon of Tuesday 16th November. Leete struggled into Lympne in 'KU with a badly missing engine, where both Moths became weather-bound. Bob Hardingham and a colleague, who were summoned from Stag Lane, diagnosed 'KU's trouble as air locking and realigned all the petrol piping in both Moths to prevent a repetition. During this time, by good fortune, 'foreign matter' was discovered in one petrol tank on G-EBMO, necessitating taking down and flushing out the whole of the fuel system.

Continuous bad weather and a heavy social programme were features of the subsequent expedition as far as Malta, which was reached on 30th November. The arrival of the two Moths at Hal Far Aerodrome was the first by any civilian crew during a flight to the East and was already a deal further than Zurich or Rome. Leete later remembered that during a meeting at Stag Lane, St Barbe had quipped that if the pair were to reach Malta, 'de Havilland would give you the Earth'. Later, when reminded, St Barbe could not remember making any such promise!

Storm conditions prevailed for a week and the sea crossing to Khoma in Tripoli was not achieved until 8th December. The appalling weather persisted until 12th December when the two Moths arrived at Heliopolis, Cairo, where the pilots were welcomed and given 'a grand time'.

The plan now was to fly on to Karachi, utilising RAF facilities en-route as far as possible. Leaving Cairo on 14th December, they landed at Amman due to a strong headwind, where they discovered a magneto on G-EBKU had seized, but they continued next day across the desert, relying on the remaining good one. Operating via Rutbah Wells, they reached Hinaidi, Baghdad, two days later, the first civilians to cross the Syrian Desert via the Air Mail Route. On 19th December, Stack was prevailed upon to perform an exhibition of 'trick flying' during the Baghdad Races which is reported to have left 'an outstanding impression'. Three years previously, Stack had been an officer with No 55 Squadron and Leete with No 70 Squadron, both of which units were still resident at Hinaidi. The Depot workshops cut a new drive-sprocket for 'KU's magneto before the tourists left to spend Christmas with No 84 Squadron at Shaibah.

On Boxing Day, crossing the top of the Persian Gulf near Bandar Dilam, G-EBKU suffered oiled plugs and Leete put her down. Watching from above, Stack observed the execution of the forced landing. 'The manner in which he picked out the only piece of ground and the judgement shown in gliding to and landing on it was a remarkably good piece of piloting.'

At Bushire, both engines were top-over-hauled during which a crack was found in one of 'MO's cylinder heads. Having no spares, the crack was filled with Hermetite and the flight continued through dust-laden air to Drigh Road Aerodrome, Karachi, where the travellers arrived on 8th January 1927. The journey from Stag Lane had occupied 54 days, covered 5,541 miles, and achieved everything that had been anticipated. Neville Stack and Bernard Leete, both officers in the RAF Reserve, were each awarded the Air Force Cross. Their safe arrival in India created enormous local interest, and the public welcome was believed to have been the largest ever seen in Karachi,

Stag Lane Aerodrome at the end of 1926. The expansion and consolidation of the site has been immense since the first permanent buildings were erected only three years previously. The building with the domed roof just above the compass base is Alan Butler's private hangar. de Havilland

with special train and bus services laid on to convey the crowds to the RAF aerodrome.

In India the decision was made not to proceed to Australia after all. Two new engines were considered an essential part of the scheme, but the two pilots were already 'stumped' financially, and neither de Havilland nor ADC Aircraft seemed inclined jointly or separately to offer anything except publicity. The two Moths left Karachi on 15th February, heading for Lahore and Delhi, each pilot carrying 10 lb of mail, the stamps franked with a special cachet to commemorate the first mails to be flown across India by light aeroplane.

G-EBKU was flown leisurely to the Punjab in March 1927, where she was engaged in a number of air experience flights. With Lady Hailey, wife of the Governor of the Punjab in the front seat, and flown by Bernard Leete, she collided with overhead wires when landing at Lahore on 2nd April. Although pilot and passenger were only slightly hurt, the world's first certificated Moth was damaged beyond economical repair.

Having abandoned the Australia flight, Stack returned to England leaving G-EBMO to be flown in and around North West India and the Punjab by Leete. The aeroplane was later transferred to a new owner and flown extensively throughout the country but was never registered locally. In July 1927 she suffered a fate similar to her old travelling companion when being flown by Flight Lieutenant W H Vetch. She collided with overhead wires whilst demonstrating at Shillong polo ground in Assam, and injured four spectators when she fell to the ground, writing herself off.

Tragedy struck at the London Aeroplane Club on 22nd November 1926 when G-EBNP,

the aeroplane purchased by member subscription, spun into the aerodrome from 3,000ft, killing newly-qualified pilot Jan Michie, the Club's ground engineer, and putting pilot instructor Sydney St Barbe out of action for four months. On 4th November the unfortunate aeroplane had been taxied into a ditch prior to a solo flight by Colonel 'Mossy' Preston. Only eleven days before the fatal accident, de Havilland had published statistics which revealed that worldwide, Moths had flown 580,000 miles in about 8,280 hours. They put heavy emphasis on their statement that 'no serious accident on a Moth has ever been recorded'. It was an unhappy coincidence that when the record was broken, the accident occurred on home ground.

In the second week of December, a meeting in the Selbourne Town Hall, Johannesburg, inaugurated the first light aeroplane club in South Africa. Under the Chairmanship of Mr A L Palmer, Mayor of Johannesburg, who was the first to sign his name, those attending voted for what was becoming a familiar resolution:

'That this meeting of citizens convened by the Mayor of Johannesburg is definitely of the opinion that for national reasons the time has arrived for the active promotion and encouragement of aviation in this country, and to that end, and in order to provide members of both sexes of this community with the necessary facilities at a reasonable cost, agrees to establish forthwith a flying club to be known as the Johannesburg Light Aeroplane Club.'

There can be little doubt that, apart from her construction and almost unrivalled ability to satisfy the market specification, much of the success of the DH.60 Moth was due to the

acknowledged business acumen of Francis St Barbe. His relentless promotion of the aeroplane ensured that the type was soon recognised all over the world, and few publicity opportunities were missed. The name *'Moth'* was the registered trademark of John Moreton and Company Ltd, a machinery manufacturer of Wolverhampton. By what persuasion St Barbe managed to transfer the long-established mark to the permanent custody of the de Havilland Aircraft Company is lost to history and the walls of his Stag Lane office. The news was circulated in *The Trade Marks Journal* as a matter of basic fact:

'475591. Aircraft included in Class 6, and Seaplanes. The de Havilland Aircraft Company Limited, Stag Lane Aerodrome, Stag Lane, Edgware, Middlesex. Manufacturers. 15th December, 1926.'

Registration of the Trade Mark was believed to be the first in the world applied in respect to 'aircraft and seaplanes' and was another piece of typical St Barbe logic, but he qualified his achievement:

'Although the registration of this trademark will not prevent competitors from copying features of Moth aeroplanes which have not been patented, it does enable us to offer to our clients the protection which the law allows to goods sold under the Trade Mark Acts, and we are happy that we can now say, equally with those in more ancient and established industries: refuse worthless imitations.'

In general, the situation was healthy. At the end of the year in which Moths had been first allocated to its fleet, the de Havilland School of Flying reported that 46 *ab initio* pilots had been trained with an average of seven hours dual instruction to first solo. In Great Britain, 135 *ab initio* pupils had qualified on Moths at the flying clubs. Maintenance costs for the Moth were estimated at 0.7d per mile, while for a six month period, August 1925 to February 1926, the London Club's engine and airframe replacement costs represented only 0.19d for every mile flown.

At the sixth Annual General Meeting of the Company conducted at Stag Lane on 30th December under the chairmanship of Captain de Havilland in the temporary absence of Alan Butler, his report was full of optimism:

'The reliability and economical running of the Moth has been conclusively established by its record with the various Clubs, on our own School, and in the hands of the private owners, and we are confident that this type of aeroplane has a most promising future.'

JANUARY TO MARCH 1927

THE YEAR 1927 began with a fanfare of praise for the Moth and her achievements during the previous 12 months. *'When the so-called light aeroplane comes into its own and popularises flying and enables us to get off those awful crowded roads of ours most of the credit for the revolution will be due to the de Havilland Moth. One can only hope that when that happy time comes the de Havilland Company will have been able to get their manufacturing costs down so that they may be able to hold their present leading position on price as well as on quality and, as may be seen, their price has already been dropped for 1927.'*

It was true! De Havilland announced 'the 1927 Model Moth' in the manner of a new motor car, bombarded the aviation press with substantial advertising, and even distributed loose inserts with selected papers. If anything, greater emphasis was put on the better performance as the result of the installation of the newly-available 85hp Cirrus Mk II engine than on the reduction in price from £795 to £730 ex-works. An increase in the provision of loose equipment now included a complete set of engine, cockpit and propeller covers at no additional charge. In addition to the supply of a tail lifting lever and control stick jig, the composition of the tool kit was improved to include an adjustable spanner, screwdriver, pliers and special spanners for sparking plugs, filters and propeller. A new telescopic jury-strut was included, and a set of tools for more serious engine work and an owner's name plate were available as optional extras. Palmer wheels, 650 x 125, could be supplied in preference to Dunlop stock which was the new 600 x 100 or original 'small wheel' and special seats were specified for owners wishing to wear 'Irvin' type parachutes.

A H Bell, Secretary of the Newcastle Aero Club, suggested that 'the improvements in finish, details of design, comfort of pilot and passenger, the absence of instruments out-

side of the cockpits and above all, the climb and the speed, still with the same low landing speed, are a revelation!'

The Air Ministry's Accidents Investigation Sub Committee sat for one of its regular meetings on 18th January 1927 under the Chairmanship of Lieutenant Colonel Mervyn O'Gorman. It was O'Gorman, in his capacity of Superintendent of the Royal Aircraft Factory at Farnborough in 1910, who had agreed to buy Geoffrey de Havilland's first successful aeroplane for £400 and to employ him as a designer and test pilot. Now he was to go on record by asking Squadron Leader A T Williams of No 2 Flying Training School, Digby, whether it was a disadvantage that a (Reserve) pupil should learn to fly on a type (DH.60 Moth) that was not in use in the Service. Williams replied that he thought it was.

Between April and December 1926, the two schools authorised to provide *ab initio* training for Reserve Officers had completed 31 courses, 14 of these on Moths with the de Havilland School at Stag Lane and the remainder at Bristol. During the same period, de Havilland had provided 88 courses for Reserve Officer training from a national total of 362 shared between five civil schools.

The Sales Office at Stag Lane hoped that most of the difficulties experienced with the

Cirrus I had been eliminated in the Cirrus II, which had increased in capacity from 4.5 litres to 4.94 litres. Dual ignition was now standard, provided as before by BTH AG4 magnetos. Although the weight had been reduced marginally by 6 lb and the power increased, the unit was still very 'tall' at 904mm, sitting high in its mountings.

De Havilland was pleased to promote 'customer' improvements in the airframe too. The 'hatch' to the baggage locker previously integrated with the rear decking as believed to be most practical, surprisingly was replaced to permit access only from inside the rear cockpit. It was recognised that on several occasions pilots had taken off with the rear door unlatched, causing it to fly open and cause local damage. Although this situation was attributed to sheer carelessness or bad communication with aerodrome staff that assisted on departure, the manufacturer bowed to feedback. But the customer was not always right and the greater view was that this configuration was grossly inconvenient and in due course the external locker door was re-introduced. In the rear cockpit a pocket was provided above a new design of instrument board for the stowage of gloves, maps, powderpuffs or pipes! An opinion expressed in the aviation press was that 'the Moth has now reached a stage when it is not a question of

G-EBPM was unveiled as the '1927 Model Moth' and in addition to an increase in loose equipment and installation of the Cirrus II engine as standard, was offered with a reduced price tag. Richard Riding

a machine that will do its job with an engine of such and such power, but what sort of little comforts, what minor refinements, what colour schemes etc, would the purchaser like. That in itself marks, we think, the evolution of the private owner's aeroplane'.

The price reduction was attributed to the efficiency and mass throughput of component production using an elaborate system of jigging situated within an area of the factory set aside solely for the purpose, and the easy access to all parts and materials in the erecting shop. Fuselage sides were built in jigs to facilitate both manufacture and interchangeability in case of major repair. All wooden longerons and cross members were located in slots, ready to receive the ply skin which was glued, tacked and screwed into place: a traditional method of construction applied to all wooden structures designed by de Havilland. Wings were assembled from 'kits' of loose parts collected together from the stores on trolleys designed, for example, to hold just the exact number of ribs for the job without the need to count, plus all the associated metal parts, clips, screws and gimps.

With the re-organisation came staff promotions: Albert Brant became Assistant Works Manager under Frank Hearle and Bert Groombridge became Production Engineer. Edwin Hancock's appointment as Superintendent of the new 'Development Department' was seen as a popular move. At the beginning of the year, output was measured at three aircraft per fortnight.

There were some detail aerodynamic changes too. The 1927 Moth wingspan was increased by 12in to 30ft and the length from 23ft 6in to 23ft 8.5in. Changes were

necessary in the structure of the rear fuselage to eliminate the counter shaft associated with the elevators, the two halves of which were now joined by plates bolted through their spars to become what was termed 'continuous'. The fuel sight gauge remained on top of the tank, visible only to the occupant of the rear cockpit who also had sole control of the fuel on-off cock, now moved from the rear cross spar of the centre section to the port side cabane strut. Although the tare weight only increased from 855 lb to 890 lb, the maximum all-up weight rose from 1,350 lb to 1,550 lb. Stagger was increased by half an inch and chord by almost 2.5in. Apart from revised main ribs the most significant structural changes to the wings were the replacement of wooden compression struts by steel tubes and the change from tapered spar roots with steel 'U-plates' to a parallel-sided section with a slot cut to take the root-end fittings. An experiment with oval section steel tube interplane struts which had been tried in October 1926 was not pursued. In Australia, the authorities insisted that the front flying wires be increased from quarter to five-sixteenths diameter.

Although the first of the Mk II Moths were supplied with the same small, rounded mica windscreens, the height was increased on later deliveries, the shape and size of Moth windscreens and their applicability to front and rear cockpits becoming a subject of continuing evolution during the next few years.

Captain de Havilland put pen to paper and emphasised that his words were written from the view of a private owner although he included some comforting technical and safety details:

'There are people who get much pleasure in adjusting, oiling, cleaning and fitting odd accessories for comfort or efficiency to their cars. I can spend hours in this way, and owning a light aeroplane at once gave a new interest in this direction. You cannot of course, make big alterations and it is best not to try modifying any structural part, and in any case it should not be necessary. As regards strength, the Moth has a very high factor of safety. Its breaking load in the air is the equivalent of 50 people (fortunately you cannot get them all in) and if a front or rear flying wire were to fracture (this has not occurred in 800,000 miles of Moth flying) the load is taken via the incidence wires between the outer struts in the remaining flying wire.*

'Duplication is carried out in this way wherever necessary, including the controls, and, therefore, it is carrying matters too far to suggest a duplicated control failing, but, if this extraordinary event happened, say, to the rudder, it would be easily possible to keep directional control by throttling down the engine, in order to eliminate propeller torque and slip, and controlling on the ailerons. This can be tried at any time by detaching the spring on the left side of the rudder bar, which should, normally, be adjusted to take all loads off the feet when cruising. It will be found that by throttling and taking the feet off the rudder bar the machine can be landed with precision by the use of ailerons alone. And vice versa, the rudder can be used to control the machine laterally.'*

Introducing the new Moth, the *DH Gazette* laid heavy emphasis on the headline fact that 'the ranks of the private owners are swelling', and identified the most recent developments:

'The first private owner in Great Britain to take delivery in 1927 was the Hon. Geoffrey Cunliffe (G-EBPM/353), who has recently learned to fly at the de Havilland School. Lord Charles Ossulston, who has lately been acting as instructor for the Newcastle Aero Club, has also taken delivery of his Royal Blue Moth (G-EBPT/361). He is keeping it at Chillingham Castle in Northumberland, and intends to use it in connection with his business of managing his father's estates. Lady Bailey has chosen an all-silver scheme for her Moth (G-EBPU/373) which will be ready soon. Mr Maurice Burton has ordered a Moth Seaplane (G-EBRH/404), for delivery in the spring. He intends to use it for coastal touring, a

The Moth's wooden fuselage frame was built in a substantial jig which led to efficiency in manufacture and guaranteed interchangeability of component parts during major servicing or repair.
de Havilland

delightfully pleasant form of air travel. Among the Moths despatched overseas recently is one which Major Allister Miller has taken to South Africa (G-UAAA/362), and another (356), shipped to Major Shirley Kingsley in the Argentine where it will be used for practical demonstration purposes.'

Maurice Burton's seaplane was described in one paper as the equivalent of the first privately-owned air yacht, and was supplied with a hand starter and 'other necessary equipment required by the private owner of a seaplane'. Only lacking was the experience of the owner who had recently qualified for his licence on landplanes at Stag Lane.

The customer list could hardly be described as representative of the 'man in the street' around which the whole philosophy of the Moth light aeroplane had been engineered, but these were early days. The purchase price of a new Moth, yet to be reduced further, was still about three times the average annual salary of a working man, and then there was upkeep and running costs to add on too. However, the second-hand value of machines, once early owners started to trade up or had decided to leave the movement, was relatively poor which fact opened up the prospect of ownership for many more individuals and small clubs.

The London Aeroplane Club replaced G-EBNP by purchasing the old prototype G-EBKT from Sophie Eliott-Lynn and the aeroplane was delivered on 10th January. The following day Captain Reggie Spooner forced landed her into a ploughed field where she turned gently over onto her back, sustaining minimal damage, and thanks to the efforts of the engineering staff was back in commission four days later.

In Australia the Sydney Aero Club was dismantling one of its Moths and, together with a spare engine and an uncovered wing, preparing them for exhibition at the Motor Show held over a nine day period in the middle of their busy flying season. The aircraft was displayed on a corner plot under cover with the starboard wings folded back and surrounded by models and notice boards carrying information and messages of encouragement aimed at prospective members.

Meanwhile, the press discovered that Major Hereward de Havilland was already on his way to Australia with a brief to investigate the prospect of establishing a factory there for the erection and later production of Moths.

The Newcastle Club received G-EBLY from Stag Lane on 22 January 1927, repaired after she had collided with a fence when attempting to take off from Cramlington on 21st November. It was the aircraft's second enforced visit to the place of her birth and was to be her last. The aircraft had been back in service for only a month when during a

series of practice solo circuits at Cramlington on 22nd February, the engine stopped at a height of about 300ft after take-off. The pilot, J D Irving, in attempting to turn back towards the aerodrome, almost inevitably stalled the aircraft which hit the ground in a flat attitude astride a fence, breaking his arm and wrecking the aeroplane.

Although there was no loss of life, the Accident Investigations Branch of the Air Ministry was quickly on the scene where the inspector was advised that before his last take-off, the pilot had turned the fuel cock to the 'reserve' position which allowed fuel to be drawn from a sump forming the lowest part of the standard petrol tank. When the wreckage was examined in detail the inspector reported that he was able to retrieve about half a pint of water from the front portion of the tank although almost all the fuel remaining at the time of the crash landing had escaped. It was also found that the main filter chamber and the feed pipes were practically full of water and there was a quantity of water but no petrol in the carburettor.

Having joined the subsidised circle later than most, the Hampshire Club was already making great strides and by February had appointed a full-time salaried secretary. At the time the Newcastle Moth G-EBLY was crashing and breaking her pilot's arm, Hampshire's pupil pilot the Hon H R Grosvenor was going solo. He broke both a Club record and a Club rule (by consent) by reaching this position after only five and a half hours' instruction, most of which had been flown with his left arm in a sling, the result of damage inflicted when riding in a steeplechase.

Major Hereward de Havilland arrived in Perth, Western Australia, on board RMS *Otranto* on 7th February 1927. He had been accompanied by a dismantled DH.60 Cirrus II Moth (G-EBPP/355), painted white with scarlet lettering whose construction he had closely supervised at Stag Lane. The aeroplane was erected and test flown at Maylands Aerodrome before a crowd estimated at about 4,000 before he set off on 24th February for Melbourne with Eric Harrison, taking up an appointment with the Australian AID, as passenger. Following the Trans Continental Railway for much of the way and flying into a constant headwind, the aircraft landed at Melbourne four days later, having covered the 2,000 miles in a flying time of 33hr 31min.

The arrival of the Stag Lane team received substantial coverage in the newspapers and with his two colleagues, P L Taylor who was nominated Works' Superintendent and F R Bedford, Company Secretary, Major de Havilland soon opened talks with de Havilland's local representatives, Gilbert Lodge and Company, concerning the prospect of erecting Moths received in dismantled condition from the parent company in England. If matters progressed satisfactorily,

local production from scratch was considered logical, especially as the type was now in regular use with the Royal Australian Air Force and light aeroplane clubs which continued to spring up all over the country and by February 1927 included those of South Australia, Queensland, New South Wales, Victoria and Geelong.

One of the newest Clubs, the Qantas-operated Longreach Light Aeroplane Club based at Eagle Farm near Brisbane, received the first Moth to be imported into Queensland and already had a waiting list for flying instruction. In an effort to avoid the worst heat of the day, lessons began at 5.30am. On the last day of 1926 a pupil on his first solo from Eagle Farm was reported to have 'completely lost his head' after hitting an air pocket and crashed G-AUFJ (278), 'with the engine on'. Although the pilot was uninjured, the Moth was badly damaged and the Club management suggested that in future all pupils should be subjected to a test to discover if their nervous systems reacted quickly or not! The aircraft was rebuilt in September 1927, fitted with a Cirrus II engine, and sold two years later to a new owner in Miles, Queensland who wrote her off within weeks of taking delivery. Another Brisbane pupil made a 'pancake landing' in June when flying G-AUFL (352), but worse was to follow on 18th July in Perth when, during the pilot's fourth solo flight, G-AUFI (277), spun down from 2,000ft and hit electrical cables supplying power to the tramway system. The Moth's fall was arrested but the aircraft caught fire and was destroyed.

DH.60 Moths G-AUFI, 'FJ and 'FK (277-279), had been supplied in kit form from Stag Lane early in 1926. Two had been delivered for assembly by West Australian Airways at Maylands Aerodrome, Perth, (G-AUFI and 'FK) and the third, G-AUFJ, was completed by Qantas at Longreach, both companies having taken up distribution agencies.

Hereward de Havilland and his team registered the de Havilland Aircraft Pty Ltd in Victoria on 7th March 1927. An office was established in Little Collins Street and after a long search a far from ideal galvanised iron warehouse of 6,000ft^2 was secured as the Company base in Whiteman Street, South Melbourne. When the first Moth (363) arrived, somewhat unexpectedly, in its packing case from England, the main doors to the establishment could not be opened due to a sagging roof and the big box on its trailer had to be left in the street overnight. Following assembly the Moth, with wings folded, was towed behind a Morris Cowley car early in the morning to Essendon Aerodrome, seven miles away, where she was flight tested as G-AUFT on 9th April on behalf of her new owner, Sun Newspapers of Sydney, who were to use her to distribute pictures of the opening of the new Federal Capital site at

Canberra. Who would have known at the time that as one of many subsequent adventures, she would be flown by Jim Mollison back to England in record time in 1931?

The first advertising on behalf of the Australian company appeared in mid April:

'The de Havilland Moth. The new vehicle for the pastoralist, the agriculturist, the prospector, the commercial traveller, the doctor and the tourist.'

In addition to what had already appeared in European promotions, the copywriters suggested the Moth could be flown from 'a paddock of normal size' which might have raised some confusion in Australian interpretation. The price of £825 (Australian) was 'ready to fly away from the Melbourne depot' although it was clearly indicated that ex-Stag Lane Aerodrome, the aeroplane was priced at £730 Sterling.

The Australian demonstrator Moth G-EBPP was re-registered locally as G-AUPP

in May and following a flying visit to Sydney was 'quickly snatched' by Messrs P Berry and H T Hammond and registered to Golden Aircraft Company of Mascot, a company operating a passenger joyride and air taxi service at 1s.9d per mile. Named *The Golden Moth* after application of her new colour scheme she was the victim of several forced landings due to engine failure and was sold to a new owner at Geelong in January 1929. Re-registered VH-UPP in January 1931, the aircraft stalled in a turn at low level and was completely wrecked.

The general importance of the growth of the flying club movement in Great Britain, now expanded well beyond the six clubs in receipt of the Air Ministry subsidy, was reflected at the launch of the proposal for a 'Norwich and East Anglia Flying Club' at Mousehold Aerodrome, Norwich, on a dismally wet and cloudy day on 25th February. Not only were all the civic dignitaries in attendance and fully supportive, but

Colonel Ivo Edwardes, Technical Advisor to Sir Sefton Brancker, flew up from Stag Lane with Hubert Broad in the Genet Moth to represent the Air Ministry. Lady Mary Bailey also flew from Stag Lane in her Moth, G-EBPU (373), her first long cross-country; Leslie Irvin arrived in his maroon Moth G-EBNX (262), from his private aerodrome near Letchworth, and RAF Moths flew in from Wittering and Martlesham Heath to join other Service types which kept the circuit busy all day.

RAF Moth J8030 (233), indulged in 'a fine display of aerobatic flying' by Flying Officer J Summers, was still fitted with her experimental Handley Page slots on the lower wings. As a gesture of support, both the London and Hampshire Clubs sent Moths, the former flown by CFI Frank Sparks who took 30 joyriders up during the course of the afternoon. Bad weather had defeated the arrival of a Moth from Newcastle but the Yorkshire Club had sent G-EBNN from Sherburn. Due to a shortage of petrol the crew had put down at Elmham near King's Lynn where they landed alongside a garage to refuel. The field was wet and the surface sticky and after a take-off run of 300 yards G-EBNN lifted off but her undercarriage just clipped a hedge and the Moth stalled, landing on her nose in the adjacent field. Hearing of their plight, the Lord Mayor of Norwich sent his car to collect the two pilots, Messrs Barnes and Wayman, to convey them to the public meeting.

The assembly agreed that a committee be appointed to arrange the details of forming a club. Before the formalities came to an end, the Lord Mayor, acting as Chairman of the meeting, revealed that two leading citizens, James Hardy and Henry Holmes, had agreed to purchase a new Moth and present it to the new Club while Colonel Edwardes announced that, in addition to the six subsidised Aero Clubs, the Air Ministry was already considering the approval of a further eight.

The Structural Strength Branch of the Airworthiness Department of the Royal Aircraft Establishment at Farnborough was tasked with checking de Havilland's application of 21st March 1927 for a Certificate of Airworthiness for Cirrus II Moth G-EBQJ (371),

An official at Waddon Aerodrome (Croydon), starting the Cirrus engine of Dennis Rooke's DH.60 Moth G-EBQJ, before his departure for Australia on 24th May 1927. Photopress

configured as a seaplane, fitted with Short floats at Rochester and test flown from the River Medway by Hubert Broad. On 28th March climb and speed tests were recorded at 10,000ft with Hessell Tiltman acting as observer. Tiltman noted that, operating at a weight of 1,480 lb, the take-off run to unstuck in a 10mph wind, was only 15 seconds.

As a new model, the Moth Seaplane appeared to have been shelved when in April, G-EBQJ was sold to Dennis Rooke, converted to landplane configuration and issued with a Certificate of Airworthiness on 21st May. Rooke was originally scheduled to take G-EBQX (385), but that aeroplane was not expected to be ready for the May departure date chosen by Rooke for his flight home to Australia. Instead, 'QX was gifted to the new Norwich Club by the two benevolent citizens.

Four days after certification Rooke quietly and unostentatiously left Croydon but his aircraft was forced down in the Libyan Desert with an engine problem. According to contemporary reports, Rooke had no emergency supplies with him and worked on the engine without food or water for three days, 'packing the pistons' with strips of material torn from his shorts. On 20th June the aircraft was damaged in unfortunate circumstances when landing at Karachi. On that day, Rooke had flown 1,250 miles from Basra and, arriving in near-darkness having been delayed by Customs' formalities in the Persian Gulf, at first mistook a military parade ground for the aerodrome. Unluckily the tailskid collided with an earth bank after successfully landing on a cricket ground only 180ft long.

Examination showed that four longerons were broken but plans were made to graft on the undamaged rear fuselage of Neville Stack's G-EBMO (197), which had conveniently and only recently crashed at Shillong. Following repair the journey was continued. Between Karachi and Cawnpore, Rooke was forced down several times but on 24th July the aircraft reached Allahabad having landed on a sandbank in the Middle Ganges. She got off again after a four hour struggle with the engine and only after Rooke had offloaded all his personal kit in an effort to reduce weight. The accumulated

delays had resulted in the arrival of the Monsoon which grounded Rooke for a fortnight near Gaya, Bahir. G-EBQJ crashed into a palm tree when taking off from the aerodrome at Aurangabad bound for Calcutta on 4th August. The aircraft was wrecked and Rooke, who was taken to hospital in an unconscious condition, afterwards returned to England.

The Hampshire Club had already announced that by May 1927 it was hoping to have a Moth Seaplane in operation when it would become the first aero club in the world (probably) to offer such equipment to its members. However, the proposed Seaplane Handicap Race scheduled for the Club's spring pageant was postponed until the autumn 'at the request of several intending competitors'. If they were relying on the loan of Maurice Burton's G-EBRH they

would have been disappointed. Following flight trials with her Short floats on the River Medway in July the seaplane was delivered to her owner at Southampton and moored in The Solent. On 4th September, Burton and the Short test pilot John Lankaster Parker were on their way to the International Aero Show in Copenhagen when G-EBRH overturned on touchdown at the Danish Naval Flying Base near Kastrup. Neither pilot was injured but the seaplane was a total loss. Nothing further was heard from the Hampshire Club about their marine ambitions.

Much seaplane acceptance and performance testing was carried out by Hubert Broad with Richard Clarkson flying as observer in the front seat, reliant solely on the aircraft's basic instruments: a sealed aneroid in a clipboard and a thermometer attached to the port, front, interplane strut.

Maurice Burton became the first private owner of a Moth Seaplane when he took delivery of G-EBRH during the summer of 1927, but the aircraft was wrecked when she overturned on touchdown at the Danish Naval Flying Base near Kastrup on 4th September. Mike Hooks

Both Broad and Clarkson liked the people at Shorts where the production sheds ran two lines in parallel: one for flying boats and the other for double-decker London buses.

During his time at Farnborough in 1911, Geoffrey de Havilland had flown an FE.2 fitted with a single plywood float, from Fleet Pond, three miles from the Factory. Perhaps the background knowledge so gained was the reason why almost all de Havilland aeroplane types built at Stag Lane were at some stage in their development tested on a float chassis, either from Rochester or very occasionally from a large lake on the west side of the Edgware Road between Hendon and Cricklewood known as the Welsh Harp. Experience with Moth Seaplanes G-EBQJ and G-EBRH was not to be dismissed for, as light aeroplane clubs continued to be formed at an apparently accelerating pace around the world, in April 1927 the Ex-Services' Flying Association based in Singapore broadcast a proposal to set up a club based on the island. It seemed almost certain that, if anything could be sourced, the most ideal equipment would be a light seaplane, and a Moth was a prime candidate. The Club was soon re-named the Singapore Flying Club and an approach to the Harbour Board requesting land for the erection of a shed was viewed favourably. Meanwhile, Club officials tackled the prospect of raising the necessary funds. Noting the views of the Hampshire Club, perhaps, Singapore also declared an intention to be the first Flying Club in the world to train exclusively on seaplanes.

The Forestry Branch of the Ontario Provincial Government in Canada thought it could well deploy light seaplanes also, to replace the less agile and more expensive machines already employed by the Air Service for forest survey and fire detection patrols. Four Moth Seaplanes were ordered

in April followed by another order for one aircraft from Pacific Airways of Vancouver for similar work in British Columbia, and another required by the Department of Marine and Fisheries to be used in connection with the Hudson Straits ice patrol. Rumours immediately spread that the de Havilland Company were considering establishing an assembly and service depot in Canada, similar to the one already organised in Australia.

This sudden spate of interest led to another feast of advertising, this time highlighting both the landplane and the Moth Seaplane which was ideal for 'Forest fire patrol; exploration; prospecting; mail carrying; fishery protection; touring and all forms of rapid transport'. The Seaplane was advertised at £1,150 ex-works, ready to fly, with packing and delivery to the London Docks charged at £40 extra.

A story fed back to the Stag Lane publicity machine came from South Africa. The company had already reported that Major Allister Miller had shipped a Moth to Cape Town in February 'having searched Europe and America for an aeroplane which would fill his requirements as a private owner in South Africa'. His Moth had been issued with her C of A at Stag Lane late in January and registered G-UAAA in South Africa on 14th April, the first light aeroplane in the country. On arrival in Cape Town, Miller had the Moth offloaded from her ship onto the Esplanade where she was erected and, without concern, flown off the narrow promenade directly to Wynberg Aerodrome. For a few days G-UAAA, *The Point*, was displayed in the showrooms of the city's Chrysler motor car dealership, having been towed there behind Miller's own badged model. On 15th April, accompanied by the Motoring Correspondent of the *Natal*

The Hampshire Aeroplane Club was probably the first to introduce 'Utility Races' when they organised the Hampshire Air Pageant at Hamble in June 1927, which involved a pilot manoeuvring his aircraft through a confined space or simulated garage marked out on the ground, prior to rigging the aeroplane and flying a circuit or engaging in other novelty activities.
DH Moth Club Archive

Advertiser, J E Dunn, Miller took off from Wynberg Aerodrome on a 2,400 mile tour of the Union, returning to Cape Town nine days later. Dunn filed a comprehensive description of the tour ending with a tribute to his host:

'Major Miller, as is well known, has for years past worked hard to get proper recognition for civil aviation in South Africa and by this tour he has done wonders in a week. He has roused the public at last so that they are beginning to realise the possibilities of air transport in this country of big distances.'

In a letter to Francis St Barbe at Stag Lane, Miller wrote: 'On the performance of the machine and the engine I have nothing but praise; she is a most perfect outfit. I was particularly impressed with the performance at Johannesburg which is 6,000ft high. I took off with the greatest ease fully loaded to 1,350lb'.

Attended by 20,000 spectators and supported by the South African Air Force, the Johannesburg Light Plane Club raised considerable funds from its June 1927 air show at Baragwanath which, added to £400 already on deposit, was sufficient to purchase their first DH.60X Moth G-UAAD (432), supplied through the local de Havilland agent, John Veasey, in August. The aircraft was present at Baragwanath on 29th October when the Club was inaugurated, in

Following arrival at Wynberg Aerodrome in April 1927, G-UAAA was towed into Cape Town for display in the showrooms of the city's Chrysler dealership. de Havilland

company with a second Club DH.60X, G-EBSR (422), re-registered G-UAAO in August the following year and ZS-AAO in January 1929, when G-UAAD became ZS-AAD.

The late summer of 1927 saw the formation of further light aeroplane clubs at Capetown, East London, Port Elizabeth and Durban. East London almost immediately ordered a Moth which was registered to them in November as G-UAAB (435), shipped on board the *City of Alexandria* in December and named *Allister M* in honour of their champion.

After all the fuss and bother generated by those who wished to define a 'light aeroplane' the Federation Aéronautique Internationale (FAI) adopted a classification for light aeroplanes for record purposes which would be effective from 1st May 1927. Three Classes were to be established based on weight empty:

- First Category. Two seater aeroplanes. Weight empty not more than 400kg. (For every record attempt a person had to be in each seat).
- Second Category. Single seat aeroplanes. Weight empty not more than 200kg.
- Third Category. Single seat aeroplanes. Weight empty above 200kg but not more than 350kg.

Under earlier draft proposals it had appeared that the Genet-engined Moth, for example, might have been in a different category from other Moths, but the Categories to be effective from May were welcomed as being entirely practical.

While Frank Halford was still immersed in the design phase of a new light aero engine commissioned by the de Havilland Aircraft Company, who were themselves designing a small aeroplane in which to flight test it, a new company was formed, 'Cirrus Aero-Engines Ltd'. Acquiring 'goodwill of that part only of the business of ADC Aircraft Ltd, which is concerned with the manufacture of Cirrus aero engines; and in conjunction therewith, the registered trade-mark, Cirrus, No 453271, in Class 6'.

Informed sources believed production of the Cirrus engine would be re-organised to occupy a defined area of the ADC Aircraft works, much in the manner that de Havilland had established a dedicated and efficient Moth shop at Stag Lane, and by laying down batches of 100 engines at a time, so reduce the unit cost. A major cost reduction would be achieved, it was suggested, if the Air Ministry permitted random selection of say, one in ten engines for complete strip-down inspection after running, rather than the current practice of stripping every single unit.

The de Havilland Aircraft Company was quick to seize the initiative when the Norfolk Club formed. While waiting for delivery of the machine donated by their benefactors, Stag Lane made arrangements for the loan of a Moth which in March was put 'on view' in the Norwich Market Place. The Club's own Moth, G-EBQX (385), was delivered on 8th June and badly damaged in an accident on the aerodrome on 30th August. During the five weeks she was under repair at Stag Lane, de Havilland again loaned a Moth, the venerable G-EBMP (198), which had worked with the de Havilland School of Flying since January 1926, and after Norwich was to join the London Aeroplane Club as a permanent replacement aircraft.

Was Norwich aware that in February 1927, East Anglia already had an aero club? In the neighbouring county the Suffolk Aeroplane Club, founded at Ipswich in 1926, had purchased a Blackburn Bluebird helped by a generous cash donation from none other than Sir Charles Wakefield and were already looking for a second machine. Meanwhile, Sir Charles' famous lubricants company, C C Wakefield, was distributing a booklet entitled *Flying for All*, a compendium of articles first published in the national daily newspaper, *The Morning Post*. Anybody interested in club flying, in particular, was advised to contact the company for a free copy.

The de Havilland publicity machine picked up a gear in the spring of 1927, taking double page advertisements to confirm, in case anybody was in doubt, that the Moth was the aeroplane making Britain airminded. The copywriters could easily have substituted 'the world' as requests for the Company's brochures and price lists poured daily onto Francis St Barbe's desk, having arrived from all corners of the Empire and elsewhere.

Relentlessly, St Barbe exploited every opportunity for publicity. One popular story, probably true, suggested that St Barbe, who often flew with Hubert Broad to demonstrate the Moth at pageants and club open days, was on one occasion flying above the Great North Road and descended to very low level to identify expensive sports cars. They found a driver who appeared to want to race. When the car was held up in a congested area the Moth got ahead and landed in a suitable field by the side of the road, waiting for the car to catch up, which it did and the driver stopped. He was advised that the petrol consumption of his car and the Moth were about the same as were the running expenses, but the Moth was faster. The three adjourned to a local hostelry where the driver of the car, it is said, was persuaded to make a commitment to buy a Moth.

Appended to the company advertising published at Easter – 'As cheap as a car to run and maintain and cheaper than many to buy!' – St Barbe gave notice that de Havilland had joined the retail trade. 'For the convenience of those interested who are unable to visit Stag Lane Aerodrome, a Moth is now exhibited at the showrooms of William Whiteley Ltd, Queen's Road, London W2. Deferred payments arranged.'

The aircraft is claimed to have been sold within ten days of going on display in the Motor Department following which a second machine was ordered from de Havilland and advertised for sale against the following rates:

Cash price £730

or

£230 cash deposit

and

12 monthly payments of £47.5s (total £797)

or

18 monthly payments of £32.5s (total £810.10s)

or

24 monthly payments of £24.15s (total £824).

This second aircraft at William Whiteley's
Moth Emporium was the dark red and silver
Cirrus II Moth G-EBPQ (357). Following her
return unsold to de Havilland, she had been
engaged on 4th April in climb performance
trials flown from Stag Lane by Captain de
Havilland with Hessell Tiltman acting as
observer, but they were unable to climb
through a cloud layer with a base at 800ft so
further trials that day were abandoned. Two
days later the aircraft qualified for her C of A
and in May was registered to Gosport-based
Lieutenant Llewellyn Richardson RN who,
with his brother as passenger, flew from
Stag Lane to Malta and back in August. The
following April, Richardson, a pilot with a
Blackburn Dart squadron, landed the Moth
on the deck of the aircraft carrier HMS *Furious* off Portsmouth.

The exhibition of Moths in departmental
stores, a trend started by Selfridges and
endorsed by Sam Lea in his Crossley Motors'
showroom in the autumn of 1926, led a
number of other prestigious houses with the
necessary asset of large windows, to offer
Moths as part of their standard retail inventory. G-EBPR (358) appeared in the
Bournemouth showrooms of de Havilland's
southern agent, Motor Macs Ltd, in April at
the same time that G-EBPS (360) went on
display with the Voss Motor Car Co Ltd at
their premises in the Adelphi Hotel, Liverpool. Both aeroplanes later went into service
with the de Havilland School at Stag Lane.

With no prospect of immediate subsidy,
new flying clubs continued to spring up in
almost every major city, supported by civic
leaders and members of the business community. While aeroplanes could be funded
and purchased, aerodrome facilities were
often the bigger problem. The Nottingham
Aero Club could do no better than quote its
headquarters' address as care of the United
Services Club in the city but were hopeful of
Air Ministry approval to lodge at Hucknall
Aerodrome. Hubert Broad, shy and retiring
at the best of times, was persuaded to give a
lecture at the city's University College on
3rd February entitled 'Flying for all. The
story of the Moth', a presentation illustrated
with lantern slides.

Having failed to establish a subsidised
Scottish Flying Club in 1925, a further
attempt was made in April 1927. As part of a
publicity campaign organised in Glasgow,
Broad flew a Moth to the city with the famous
amateur boxer the Marquis of Douglas and
Clydesdale as passenger. Broad lectured to
the Glasgow Rotary Club on 5th April and

the following day flew back to Stag Lane via
Woodford carrying a senior reporter from
The Glasgow Evening Times, W J Cumming.
The next day, with John Yoxall, chief photographer of *Flight*, as passenger, Broad flew
DH.60 Moth G-EBNO to Filton for the inaugural meeting of the Bristol and Wessex
Aeroplane Club in the Victoria Rooms,
Clifton. By way of publicity, in the pouring
rain, the aircraft was towed through the
streets of Bristol behind an open-topped
Hampton light car using a tail trolley borrowed from the Bristol Aeroplane Company.

The meeting was addressed by the
Deputy Director of Civil Aviation, Colonel F
G L Bertram who, like his colleague at Norwich, held out no hope of an immediate
government subsidy.

Sir Charles Wakefield offered one sixth of
the cost of a new Moth, generosity matched
by George Parnall who further volunteered
use of his company aerodrome at Yate where
there was a suitable shed and 'at least one
aeroplane that might possibly be of service...'

Many of the newly forming clubs, free to
choose any 'flying equipment' they liked,
looked to the acquisition of Moths, mostly
new ones manufactured at Stag Lane. Those
who had been supplied with Moths as part
of the plan in 1925 had few complaints. The
Newcastle Aero Club admitted that they had
been fortunate 'in not suffering many
crashes' but they had seen both their aircraft
under major repair at Stag Lane, each out of
action for many weeks. Perhaps it was not so
surprising, therefore, that 'at the end of our
first twelve months' running, when each
machine was dismantled and thoroughly
examined for the purpose of obtaining
renewal of certificates of airworthiness, we
were very agreeably surprised to find that

practically nothing needed attention. The
opportunity was taken to replace certain fittings by modified types but apart from this
the heaviest item of expense was for cleaning materials, painting, etc'.

Although the servicing and repair of Moths
was to become a major part of the de Havilland business, some aircraft were placed
beyond redemption as a result of lack of
piloting experience more often than
mechanical failure.

The Hampshire Club temporarily lost
G-EBOI on 8th March with only 168 hours in
the logbook. The Club chairman, an 'A'
licence holder with fewer than eight hours on
Moths, elected to sit in the front seat while a
pilot with only two previous solo flights
indulged in authorised landing practice. On
the third take-off the 'passenger' in the front
cockpit became concerned about trees looming directly ahead, took control and started a
tight, over-ruddered turn to the left. G-EBOI
entered a spiral dive and crashed into a field
adjoining the aerodrome.

When considering the crash at the meeting of the Accidents Investigation Sub-Committee convened on 11th April, the
Chairman, Major Cooper, reminded all
members that the petrol tank on a Moth was
secured by wires so that in the event of an
accident the tank would be thrown clear. In
one recent investigation the tank had been
found some 12ft from the wrecked fuselage,
intact and full of petrol. The Chairman asked
whether such a system might even be appropriate to some of the fast military 'scouts'
then in service? But de Havilland were
already planning to eliminate the system, for
which design 'improvement' the Company
was to attract an equal degree of criticism.

APRIL TO AUGUST 1927

A NEW WORLD of opportunities was opened for the light aeroplane on 30th March 1927 when the de Havilland Company delivered DH.60 Cirrus II Moth G-EBQE (370) to Shell-Mex Ltd. The aeroplane was handed over in a simple ceremony on a cold and windy day at Stag Lane. Painted gold overall with red trim, struts, undercarriage and letters, G-EBQE was named *Arom* by the wife of Shell-Mex's Assistant General Manager. Standing on some clumsy wooden staging erected for the occasion, instead of the usual champagne baptism, Mrs George Wilson poured two gallons of Premium Spirit from a trademark gold can into the aircraft's gold-painted petrol tank.

Arom is acknowledged to be the first business aircraft in Great Britain and she was to be extensively flown between Shell-serviced facilities at home and in Europe by Captain 'Jerry' Shaw, late Chief Pilot of Aircraft Transport and Travel Ltd (AT&T) and now manager of the Shell-Mex Aviation Department. *Arom* was purchased very much as a business tool, a fact emphasised in a short speech of acceptance by the debonair George Wilson who reported that his company was now satisfied that the light aeroplane had reached a high degree of development, and that its use offered many advantages in respect of time saved, reasonable first cost and running expenses. To the mutual advantage of both de Havilland and Shell the naming ceremony was filmed by the Gaumont organisation and shown as part of their famous newsreels in cinemas all over the country for the next several days.

Her first business trip on 27th April took *Arom* from her Croydon base to the Blackburn Aircraft Company at Brough from where the Genet-engined Bluebird was being marketed as a serious competitor to the Moth but at an extra cost of £45. A lady pilot with the Yorkshire Club whose fleet included a side-by-seat Bluebird described the type as being like a bus when compared with the Moth's sports car performance. De Havilland always nurtured reservations over the side-by-side configuration, a view probably vindicated by the poor commercial performance of a cabin biplane designed in 1934, the DH.87 Hornet Moth, which Captain de Havilland always claimed was the result of over-enthusiasm on the part of the Sales Department, and was built against his better judgement.

Arom led an active life in her first season attending country-wide pageants, displays and race meetings as the light aeroplane movement continued healthily to expand. Jerry Shaw, a keen golfer, was a participant in the first aerial golfers' meeting at the

Mrs George Wilson, wife of Shell-Mex's Assistant General Manager, pouring two gallons of Premium Spirit into the tank of the company's first business aircraft, the gold-painted Cirrus II Moth G-EBQE, during a naming ceremony at Stag Lane on 30th March 1927. *Flight*

As part of a publicity campaign in support of a flying club for Bristol, G-EBNO was displayed in a city square and later towed through the streets behind a Hampton car using a tail trolley borrowed from the Bristol Aeroplane Company at Filton. BAE Systems

Royal West Norfolk Club at Brancaster. All players had to fly 100 miles, land on the golf course and play 18 holes. First prize, a cup, went to G-EBQE and its pilot, a 'plus two' player. In June, Charles Barnard and Gordon Aston, of motoring fame, set off from Stag Lane at 9.00am to play 72 holes. They flew to Sunningdale where they played their first round and at 3.00pm they started their second on the Royal Liverpool links at Hoylake, Cheshire. Just after 8.00pm they were enjoying dinner at St Andrews where the next morning they completed their third round on the Royal and Ancient Course before taking off for Brancaster where after the final round, Aston was declared the winner. Back at Stag Lane having flown about 800 miles, the pair suggested that a safe landing was possible on any course throughout the British Isles, which would now be open to golfers trying to escape from weekend congestion.

The Genet Moth G-EBOU had been refurbished at Stag Lane and on Maundy Thursday, 14th April 1927, was re-weighed to reveal a 58 lb weight increase, largely attributed to the installation of dual ignition, 600 x 75 Palmer wheels, jury struts, parachute seats and a doping pump with associated piping. It is possible she was fitted with new wings at this time, as in her Lympne Trial configuration her span was only 29ft and not representative of the current specification. Elsewhere in the Stag Lane works six Genet-powered aircraft ordered for the RAF's Central Flying School Aerobatic Team were nearing completion.

David Kittel, an early private owner of a Moth, the black and silver G-EBMU (234) *Silvry II* (Kittel's car was *Silvry I*), also used his aeroplane for business and at Easter flew via Ostend and Brussels to Cologne, returning home after a leisurely flight along the Rhine to Hangelar for a short stay then on to Rotterdam. The journey was assisted by an internationally recognised carnet issued by the Royal Aero Club (RAeC), 'eliminating the necessity of making substantial Customs' deposits and opening the way to much easier Continental access to travellers in light aeroplanes'.

On his return to England Kittel said that for the outward trip he had navigated on an Ordnance Survey map of four miles to the inch, but from Cologne he had access only to a basic road map which was so confusing that approaching Rotterdam he became completely lost. Clearly, some thought would need to be given to assist an 'average person' like himself with no particular knowledge of map reading or navigation he suggested. With the ability of so many private owners now to make similar trips, it was a very valid observation.

For the 1927 Easter holiday break, the Royal Aero Club announced that the first of the season's aviation meetings was to be their second programme of Races organised at the Ensbury Park Racecourse on the outskirts of Bournemouth. Entries were invited from private owners and the light aeroplane clubs for up to 12 places in each of 12 events.

De Havilland disclosed that, for the benefit of Moth owners, the Company's Bournemouth agent, Motor Macs Ltd, of Holdenhurst Road, would be parking a van bearing the inscription 'Moth Service' at a prominent location at the race course. 'It will carry a full range of Moth and Cirrus engine spares, and will be the headquarters for a Service Staff which will be specially augmented by engineers from Stag Lane Aerodrome. We hope that any Moth owner requiring assistance will hail one of the men with Moth badges on their white coats.'

A mobile Moth Service facility was to be made available at almost all significant meetings thereafter, with the capability of satisfying quite major needs, including the provisioning of mainplanes, control surfaces and undercarriages, propellers and complete engines.

The Company became sufficiently involved with the regularity of Moths taking part in races for the Sales Department to publish a number of *do's and do nots* applicable to man and machine:

- Read and understand the Aerodrome Rules before taxying to the starting line.
- Having passed the post do not zoom or turn sharply.
- Keep straight on your course at an even altitude.
- Keep your eyes wide open all the time.

For the good of the aeroplane the basic hints were:

- Drain the mineral oil from the engine sump and replace it by Castrol 'R' or Shell Superheavy 'A'. When engines are run at high revolutions for long periods it is always well to use a vegetable oil of high viscosity.
- Watch your petrol gauge. The rate of consumption at full throttle is much higher than at cruising revolutions. Many pilots turn their petrol taps to the 'reserve' position before starting in a race, thus avoiding an interruption of fuel supply to the carburettor in rapid turns owing to the inlet of the main supply pipe being uncovered while the petrol 'slops about' in the tank.

A week before the first Bournemouth race, 'The Boscombe Stakes,' scheduled for 2.30pm on Good Friday, 15th April, the RAeC was able to publish detailed lists of entrants, nominated pilots, and aircraft by type and individual registration. It was immediately evident that, once again, Moths would dominate the event, completely outnumbering all other types.

The publicity generated was not all as predicted. The owners of the racecourse and the organisers were again severely criticised for running the meeting through a solemn religious festival – although no racing actually took place on Easter Sunday there were flying demonstrations. Squadron Leader Walter Longton landed after one gallop round the pylons to discover that his Bluebird was peppered with 70 small holes. These were the result of being fired at by a shotgun wielded by a red-bearded farmer who was subsequently arrested, charged with attempted murder, tried and acquitted.

In the second heat of the second race on the first day, Geoffrey de Havilland flew Moth G-EBQH (276), which was identified as a DH.60X and described in the programme as a 'Special Machine'. At the end of the third lap, The Captain made obvious preparations to land but a commotion on the ground caused him to realise there was still a lap to go. He managed to overtake Bernard Leete who was flying Lady Bailey's Moth G-EBPU, to finish first, and he also won the final, this time completing an extra fifth lap to make absolutely certain.

Excellent handicapping produced some exciting finishes as aircraft flew low and fast along the home straight but in front of a poor crowd. Almost no advertising was taken in the local area to promote the meeting and a follow-my-leader procession of 15 racing aeroplanes along the sea front from Poole to Boscombe on Easter Monday did little to improve matters.

Amongst the flying community the racing meeting was regarded as a complete success, the most competitive and entertaining event of its kind for many years and surely the sign of even better times to come. Of the 19 heats and finals for which the type was eligible, a Moth took first place in nine. The 'sameness' of the racing attracted some criticism in the same paragraphs that praised the idea of mostly equally matched types flying in competition.

The Hampshire Aeroplane Club secured headlines on the final day when their only serviceable Moth, G-EBOH, took off with the petrol tap not fully open. The engine, nine hours off her last overhaul, coughed and finally died as the aircraft strove for height just outside the boundary. During the curving glide back towards the landing ground, G-EBOH fractionally failed to clear a corrugated iron fence and was demolished in the impact, fortunately without injury to either occupant, one of whom was the Club's Chief Instructor. G-EBOH had flown just over 200 hours since delivery to Hamble in August 1926.

De Havilland's 'Special' Moth, the designated DH.60X G-EBQH, had flown for the first time shortly before the Easter race meeting at which Captain de Havilland, probably, had outsmarted the handicappers. The designation 'X' meant little except G-EBQH was regarded as 'experimental'. However, the company saw some marketing value in retaining the title. On 4th April with Hessell Tiltman and 50 lb ballast in the front cockpit, taking the weight to within 18 lb of her fully loaded approval of 1,370 lb, Geoffrey de Havilland took off into a strong south westerly wind at Stag Lane on the aircraft's second performance-measuring flight but a cloud base at 700 ft precluded them from achieving anything useful. Broad flew 'QH six days later and on 15th April the aeroplane was romping home at Bournemouth, a clear winner.

The DH.60X incorporated a number of minor structural changes and aerodynamic refinements, few of which were immediately obvious. Marketed initially as the 'Moth Type X' she improved the marque even beyond the '1927 Model' introduced only in January.

The Cirrus II engine sat several inches lower in the bearers in an effort to improve the pilots' view forward through taller, frameless windscreens, and associated with the new induction system, the carburettor received its air supply through an aperture in the starboard side of the cowling nose bowl. At the opposite end of the fuselage, modifications to the structure were made to accommodate a new non-steerable tailskid bolted to the sternpost. To an elegantly curved cantilever tailplane were attached a pair of interchangeable elevators of increased area. The leading edge of the fin, previously bolted to the rearmost cowling former, was now attached to the tailplane. Improvements were made to the anchorage of the pilot's safety belt, a basic lap strap, patented by de Havilland (GB 297541) in association with Hubert Broad. In recognition of a continuing training role, all the flying control members had been re-stressed for the 'pilot's opposing' case. Strengthened mainplane ribs, tested at Farnborough on 12th April in support of an aerobatic Certificate of Airworthiness, failed well in excess of the required factor of 7.5 with similar results recorded for the modified tailplane and elevators. G-EBQH had tipped the scales at a tare weight of 859 lb, including an allowance of 3 lb for her 'final coat of lead paint' on the fuselage.

The 'gap' between top and bottom wings was increased by 2in to achieve a better gap:chord ratio and greater aerodynamic efficiency. There were other reasons too. The fuel tank had been redesigned into a 19 gallon capacity, low-lift aerofoil section being more streamlined and completely filling the centre section. Its tinned-steel skin was now corrugated longitudinally for additional strength, the required lengths of sheet cleverly formed by passing them through rollers on a mangle-type machine

Designated a DH.60X Moth, the appearance of G-EBQH at Ensbury Park on her first public outing, caused great interest amongst those who recognised her improved features. de Havilland

Hampshire Aeroplane Club Moth G-EBOH lost engine power just after take-off from Ensbury Park Racecourse, Bournemouth, on the final day of the Easter meeting, and just failed to clear a corrugated iron fence when attempting to land back. Seriously damaged, the aeroplane was repaired at Stag Lane and returned to service six weeks later. *Christopher Clarkson*

before they were assembled and solder jointed. Unlike the early tank, which had been concealed within a streamlined fairing and secured to wooden cross spars by adjustable cables, the new all-visible tank rested on steel tube cross spars in the cabane to which it was now firmly bolted. Jack Meaden explained what difference the new aerodynamic shape made:

'The bottom of the tank, previously flat-bottomed and aligned with the underside of the RAF 15 section wing, was now curved downwards 2.5in below it and the curve of the upper surface was flatter by a similar amount. The interplane gap had been decided partly by the requirement for a minimum door-open space of about 2ft under the tank to allow the occupant of the front seat enough room to get in and out, so curving down the bottom of the tank 2.5in required the interplane gap to be increased by a similar amount to maintain the access space. Due to the dihedral, the highest point on the aircraft was not the top of the tank but the upper surface of the top wings near the tips, so the extra gap increased the height from 8ft 7in on the DH.60 to 8ft 9.5in on the DH.60X. This remained the same for the later models still to come.'

The appearance of the DH.60X at Bournemouth had created a great deal of interest and, after a Westland Widgeon II, Widgeon III and Cirrus II-powered Avro Avian, was the fastest aeroplane at the event, but for the 'Racing Correspondent' of the *de Havilland Gazette* it was aircraft from competing manufacturers that drew his attention:

*'The Bournemouth Meeting provided convincing proof that other designers have now recognised these facts, for the products of at least three other manufacturers, all of which might be said to be in the Moth class, took part in the races. In these machines, in some, of course, more than others, it is possible to detect the influence of the Moth, not only in class but also in features of design and methods of construction. Take, for instance, the plywood fuselage construction. This method of fuselage building was introduced many years ago by Captain de Havilland and has always been employed in the Moth. It now seems to be general practice with builders of small aeroplanes, many of whom in earlier models used the now almost obsolete 'stick and wire' type of construction. The centre tank with gravity feed to the engine; the layout of the Moth undercarriage which has proved so success-*ful; the folding wings; control trimming devices; these and many other features of the Moth have been embodied in the new machines, and I venture to forecast that the lowering of the Cirrus engine in the fuselage of the Moth G-EBQH, which Captain de Havilland himself flew at Bournemouth, will set a fashion which will find several devotees.'*

The fashionable aerodrome at Tempelhof, Berlin, was the scene of a handing-over ceremony on St George's Day after Hubert Broad arrived in a DH.60 Moth bearing ferry markings G-W101 (374), with Francis St Barbe as passenger. The aircraft had been purchased by Karl Bercowitz, a prominent German banker, and presented to the Deutscher Sportflieger Klub with headquarters at Staaken. For publicity purposes, during test flying in England, Broad had been photographed standing on the seat in the rear cockpit with both hands held free of the controls in an effort to demonstrate the stability of the aeroplane, but only six weeks after delivery the Moth crashed in Germany killing Alfred Heft, a First World War fighter pilot and former test pilot with Junkers. No reason for the accident was ever made public although Heft was thought not to be comfortable with the lightness of control of the Moth compared with his more usual mounts.

The Raab Katzenstein Company took a licence to build DH.60 Moths at Kassel in August 1927 and bought an engineless airframe kit (445), presumably to assist in this. The licence covered Germany, Austria and Hungary where the aeroplane would be known as the *Motte*. By December 1927 it was reported that a programme had been laid down to build 20 aircraft with firm orders already received for seven. After inspection of drawings and possibly the imported airframe, the Certifying Authority (DVL) concluded that the Moth did not meet German construction requirements and withheld certification of the type until early in 1929 when de Havilland's Berlin-based agent, Alfred Friedrich, began to import Moths from Stag Lane. There is no evidence to suppose that any Moths were afterwards ever built in Germany.

A notable absentee from Bournemouth at Easter was, perhaps, Her Grace, the Duchess of Bedford, who was busy making plans.

A publicity stunt requiring some faith, undertaken by Hubert Broad, was to demonstrate the stability of the DH.60. Having trimmed the aeroplane high over Stag Lane, Broad stood up on his seat with hands and feet off the controls. BAE Systems

On St George's Day 1927, two well-dressed Englishmen, Hubert Broad and Francis St Barbe, delivered Cirrus II Moth No 374 (ferry marked G-W101) to the Deutscher Sportflieger Club at Berlin's Tempelhof Aerodrome. The aeroplane was written off six weeks later. de Havilland

With her personal pilot, Captain Charles Barnard, the Duchess left Woburn Abbey on 24th April in the green and silver first production Cirrus II Moth G-EBPM (353), loaned by the Hon. Geoffrey Cunliffe. During the next three weeks the Moth was to fly south through France and central Spain to Seville where Barnard demonstrated her to King Alfonso of Spain and the Prince of Wales who were attending a local fete.

On they flew, the aerial tourists, across the Straits of Gibraltar to Tangier where they arrived on 1st May, before turning for home via Spain's Mediterranean coast. In addition to a hat box, handbag and leather attaché case carried on the Duchess' knees, Barnard noted that the aircraft was very heavily loaded with three suitcases, four extra tins of petrol, oil and spares, mostly distributed around the Duchess' legs and feet in the front cockpit. In spite of this the Moth crossed mountains at 9,000ft without difficulty when required to do so. It might be worthy of note that when the Bishop of Willochia, South Australia, reported at Stag Lane to be flown to Manchester to preach a sermon that same evening, he was compelled to tie his baggage under the fuselage, between the undercarriage legs!

In Seville the travellers met a former de Havilland employee, F W 'Bill' Hatchett, a First World War pilot and skilled woodworker whom the company had encouraged to leave his Stag Lane workbench to take on occasional test flying duties in refurbished DH9s. In Spain, Hatchett was now a regular pilot on the Seville-Laroche route and he arranged for the manufacture and installation of an additional petrol tank of 6.5 gallons capacity to extend the safe range of G-EBPM, thought to be highly desirable for some of the proposed homeward sectors.

Following unimagined adventures, the 'Flying Duchess' was delivered safely back to Woburn Abbey on 12th May having covered 4,500 miles in a flying time of 54hr 45min. Her arrival at Stag Lane earlier in the day had been greeted by a swarm of newspaper reporters and photographers. It could hardly have been better publicity. The secretary of the Yorkshire Aeroplane Club provided another perfect example:

'On Thursday 26th May Mr Wilson, in the course of his business, had occasion to visit Oxford to collect a Morris Cowley chassis. Saving eight hours over a train journey, he flew down with Mr Mann, under threat of excommunication if the machine were not

returned in time for Saturday's flying, and landed at Port Meadow at 8.30pm. Friday dawned, with mist, rain, and low cloud at Oxford. On ringing up Sherburn they were informed that the weather there was fair and balmy. Whereupon they took thought, folded the wings of the Moth, put the tail up on the hood of the Cowley, and set sail for a sunnier clime.

At Banbury they paused awhile and, refreshed, were inclined to take a more optimistic view of the flying conditions. Moreover the sun came out. The omens being favourable they drove the combination into a suitable field, unfolded the Moth, and Mr Mann flew it back to Sherburn in the very creditable time of two hours.'

In an uncharacteristic display of humour, *Flight* suggested that 'not only is this believed to be the first time that a motor agent has utilised a private aeroplane for the collection of a car from the works, but that Mr Wilson who sells cars for a living and flies a Moth for a hobby, if he lived to be 100, will probably sell Moths for a living in addition to flying one for a hobby'.

Following her refurbishment in April, Genet Moth G-EBOU was delivered to the Central Flying School at Wittering where she was used by pilots posted to the Display Team to invent and perfect manoeuvres and routines prior to delivery of their own aircraft, which were behind schedule.

The necessary mating of the 60hp Genet engine to the Moth airframe in order to conform to the regulations covering the 1926 Lympne Trials had been a success. Unlike the Cirrus engine with its wet sump, the radial Genet engine provided with an appropriate fuel supply could be continuously operated when inverted. The engine also had built a reputation for reliability and smooth running. Combining these features with the strength of a proven airframe enabled the creation of an almost ideal display vehicle at an economical price.

In the hands of Flying Officer Dick Atcherley, some of the aircraft's aerobatic potential was displayed at the Midland Aero Club's 'At Home' at Castle Bromwich on 1st May, where before 5,000 spectators he flew a series of manoeuvres described as 'amazing!'. The reporter for the *de Havilland Gazette* described what he saw:

'Beginning with a series of beautifully executed slow rolls, Mr Atcherley then performed an evolution of which he is reputed to be the inventor, and which had not been seen before by anybody present. Reducing his speed to near stalling he pushes the stick forward and the machine dives on to its back. After flying for a short distance in an inverted position the pilot rolls over right side up. The display was more spectacular than anything of its kind seen at a flying club meeting before. We must warn owners of standard Moths against attempting this stunt for two reasons. Firstly, the pilot has to be firmly held into his seat by strong harness, and secondly, it will be realised that the standard Cirrus engine with its wet sump cannot run in an inverted position. Although structurally identical to the standard machine, G-EBOU is fitted with non-return valves in the air vents of the petrol and oil tanks so that their contents do not escape when the machine is flying wheels-up.'

On 6th May Broad and Tiltman flew a series of timed climbs at near maximum authorised weight in DH.60X G-EBQH to 10,000ft overhead Stag Lane. Two weeks later, Tiltman observed for 'Jimmy' White, the popular chief instructor with the de Havilland School, when two flights were made in the same aeroplane with thermocouples attached to the front and rear cylinders. On 23rd May Broad and Tiltman repeated the exercise in respect of numbers two and three cylinders. The climb programme was then interrupted to allow G-EBQH to go racing during the Whitsun holiday.

Described as the 'first Australian built aircraft', DH.60 Moth VH-UFV was assembled by de Havilland Aircraft (Pty) Ltd from a kit of parts supplied by Stag Lane, augmented by upper mainplanes and empennage constructed in the Company's galvanised-iron warehouse at Whiteman Street, Melbourne. de Havilland

Following the successful flight in April 1927 of the first Moth assembled by the new Australian company at its rat-infested warehouse in Melbourne, a second aircraft was completed in June for delivery to the New South Wales Section of the Australian Aero Club. Registered G-AUFV, the aircraft was based on a kit imported from Stag Lane but incorporating upper mainplanes and a tail assembly constructed in Melbourne. As a result the Moth was allocated Work's number 1A and hailed by the press as the first ever 'Australian built' aircraft.

'Major de Havilland made the first flight at 7.30am from Essendon Aerodrome. Just after 10.00am he left on the delivery flight to Mascot. Near Albury he came down in a vacant paddock to inspect the oil system. This caused some delay and it was 1.30pm when he reached Cootamundra. After refuelling it was too late to reach Mascot before nightfall so he stayed overnight and left Cootamundra at 9.00am arriving at Mascot at 11.30am. Near Picton he had taken the Moth up to 8,000ft because of low lying thick cloud and commented that it was jolly cold up there! In the afternoon of the following day, Saturday 4th June, the Aero Club took formal possession of G-AUFV. Aeroplanes of the Club and some of the members paraded at Mascot Aerodrome for the occasion, which included a christening ceremony when Mrs Hughes, wife of the Club President, named the aircraft Oswald Watt.'

The same apparently successful formula used at Easter was applied to a second air race meeting held at Ensbury Park on the Saturday and Monday of the Whitsun holiday, 4th and 6th June 1927, but tragedy struck on the morning of the first day. Major Harold Hemming was taking off for a test flight in Alan Butler's DH.37A G-EBDO when the aircraft collided with a metal frame used to carry runner and rider details

on horse race days. The aircraft lost a wing, hit a fence and eventually crashed upside-down. Although Hemming survived but with a serious head injury, Claude St John Plevins, passenger in the front seat, died later in hospital. It was the design and construction of this aeroplane to Alan Butler's special order in 1922, which led ultimately under his Chairmanship to financial security for the de Havilland Company and the development of facilities and resource from which, and with confidence, to launch the DH.60 Moth only three years later.

The Bournemouth Whitsun meeting was described by *Flight* as 'a thoroughly ill-fated and disappointing event, the effects of which will take a good deal of living down'. It was quite a different summary from the euphoria which had followed the Easter meeting only a few weeks before.

As raced at Bournemouth by Hubert Broad, G-EBQH was not 'placed' and returned to Stag Lane on Whit Monday evening. Two days later on 8th June, 'The Captain' and Hessell Tiltman climbed to 16,264ft amsl in 68 minutes and 30 seconds: 1,000ft above the declared service ceiling but less than the 18,100ft figure published for the type's absolute height. For the occasion the aircraft was fitted with what was described as a 'standard production cooling cowl'. Lady Mary Bailey familiarised herself with G-EBQH during the next month and on 5th July, with Mrs Louie de Havilland as passenger, climbed the DH.60X to a new world altitude class record of 17,289ft. To comply with the FAI rules, the ladies' weight was augmented with 74 lb of ballast and both were committed to wearing a seat pack parachute. The actual climb was flown at a steady airspeed of 55mph and lasted 90 minutes.

The de Havilland School lost a Moth on Saturday 4th June. Flown by Jimmy White, with Reservist Ronnie Malcolm from the Sales Department in the passenger seat, G-EBPG

(359), was heading for the races at Bournemouth when the crew decided to land at the military airfield at Worthy Down to take a quick rest break. Immediately after taking off again at a height of about 50ft, G-EBPG turned to fly towards the station buildings but when abreast of the hangars the engine lost power and stopped. White put the aeroplane into a steep gliding turn but hit the ground at high speed, breaking the undercarriage, bounced to about 15ft and crashed into the hangar's corner buttress, afterwards bursting into flames. The pilot was slightly injured but Malcolm was unhurt.

The Air Ministry's accident inspectors enjoyed their Whitsun weekend holiday before visiting the site on the following Tuesday. White's version of the accident they found difficult to believe in that, after engine failure and an almost certain collision with the hangar, he said he had steered the Moth so that the engine would pass between the buttresses. Suspicion fell on whether or not the fuel was turned on. Malcolm could remember nothing and White could not confirm whether he had turned the fuel off on arrival.

So ended the short eight week career of G-EBPG, just 45 flying hours from the time she was the star attraction in Sam Lea's motor car emporium in the West End of London.

The Air Ministry contract to equip the Display Team of the Central Flying School, 761499/27, called for the supply of six aircraft (Nos 379-384) to Specification 7/27, powered by 60hp Genet engines, to be fully operational in advance of the 1927 Royal Air Force Display at Hendon in July. It was a close run thing!

The Air Ministry was concerned about the strength of the tube connecting front and rear cockpit control sticks, and of its tendency to vibrate in concert with the parallel rockshaft. The gauge of tube was increased to improve rigidity and a modification introduced which damped vibration by tying the two units together with a leather strap and buckle. Approved for civil aircraft, the Air Ministry accepted the situation only by a late concession granted on 30th June in preference to more dramatic and time-consuming changes proposed by the manufacturer.

By 21st May all six airframes were complete but still awaiting delivery of their engines. When finally they arrived, it was discovered they differed in some detail from the drawings originally supplied to de Havilland with the result that the engine mountings needed modification and re-submission to the Airworthiness Department. Clearance for flight was received on 14th June.

Flying DH.60X G-EBQH, Lady Mary Bailey (right) and Mrs Louie de Havilland, set a world altitude class record of 17,289ft on 5th July 1927, operating from Stag Lane. de Havilland

The Central Flying School Display Team of 1927 flying five of the establishment of six Genet Moth aircraft in close formation. They had little time to perfect their routine between aircraft delivery and the RAF Display at Hendon on 1st July. The upper surface of the top wings and the top of the fuselages were painted bright red for the benefit of the spectators to help identify when the aircraft were inverted.
Sport and General

Having been able to practice solo aerobatics on the Genet Moth G-EBOU for almost eight weeks, the team had barely 14 days in which to perfect their formation routines. Hubert Broad test flew J8816 (380), on 16th June followed by J8818 and J8819 (379 and 383) the next day. Such was the urgency for the aircraft to be handed over that J8820 and J8821 (383 and 382), were weighed, flight tested and delivered to Wittering on the same day, Saturday 18th June.

The aircraft were painted silver with red fuel tank and top surfaces to all horizontal planes and control surfaces in order to provide an indication of when the aircraft were inverted in flight. J8816 was the heaviest at a tare weight of 820 lb, equipped like all the others as a two-seater but delivered with the front cockpit faired over. The lightest was J8817 at 788 lb. Two of the Genet Moths were equipped with full harness in both cockpits, and all had toe straps on the rudder bars in the rear cockpits, a petrol dope cock and a starting magneto. They were cleared for aerobatic and inverted flight on 17th June at the civilian weight of 1,280 lb, later raised under military authority to 1,350 lb.

Reserve pilot in the team was Flying Officer Dermot Boyle who remembers a potentially catastrophic incident during one of the few formation rehearsals:

'We were approaching to land in formation, D'Arcy Greig was leading; I was flying on the left behind Dick Atcherley. At about 500ft the leader's aircraft suddenly assumed a vertical position, pointing straight at the ground, and the whole underside of the fuselage came into full view. It was a most startling sight. The formation immediately broke up in disorder. The cause of this spectacle was that Dick Atcherley's starboard wingtip had touched the top of D'Arcy Greig's elevator, forcing it down, thereby forcing the tail to rise up against Dick's wing tip and thus compounding the danger.'

The wet and miserable summer did not abate even for the RAF Display at Hendon on 1st July. One of the Genet Moths was the mount of the CFS Chief Instructor, Squadron Leader H Smart, who put on a thrilling display of crazy flying:

'...flat turns, switchbacks, flying sideways, skidding and very nearly stalling, that little machine slithered round the aerodrome doing everything that every young pilot is taught not to do, and causing laughs and gasps in all the enclosures...'

But the 'palm of the afternoon' was awarded to the pilots of the CFS Team led by Flight Lieutenant D'Arcy Greig: Flying Officers Beilby, Atcherley, Waghorn and Stainforth. The Editor of the de Havilland Gazette waxed lyrical:

'Taking off with wingtips almost interlocked the flight climbed to about 1,000ft and flew across the aerodrome in close formation then, without separating or splaying outwards, it dived slightly and went over in a perfect loop, finishing in as good formation as it had started. But that was only to whet the appetites of the spectators. Next followed a half roll and the formation flew right across the aerodrome on its back. Another half roll and it was as you were!

'Next came the double bunt, about which many of us had heard but very few had seen. Having regained the height they lost on the inverted glide, the formation came across the aerodrome well throttled down, and just as they were about to stall, the pilots pushed forward their sticks and the Moths dived downwards and under, describing an arc of a circle, the diameter of which I judged to be about 300ft. At no time did the speed seem to be excessive and throughout, the movement of the machines was easy and gentle. On completion of the bunt the formation was again on its back and a slow roll put it again right side up. The final manoeuvre was a spin, in formation, which, as a spectacle, was exceedingly thrilling. For this item the machines were spread out slightly, and at a signal from the leader, they dropped their left wings and commenced to spin down. At about 500ft they came out and rapidly re-collected in a close vee. After one circuit of the aerodrome they landed as they had taken off, wing tip to wing tip, amid the applause of thousands of motor horns.'

For the 1927 Display, the team's aircraft were not fitted with a fuel system which permitted sustained inverted flight; such a system would not be available until the following season when two aircraft formed the nucleus of the CFS 'Inverted Flying Flight'. According to Air Ministry records, by the autumn, J8816 (380) had been delivered to Stag Lane after a brief spell of trials at Martlesham Heath in September alongside J8820. She was converted by de Havilland into a civilian standard aircraft registered G-EDCA, based at Croydon for the exclusive use of the Director General of Civil Aviation until a new Cirrus Moth was allocated. Other records indicate it was J8818 (379) which became G-EDCA until February 1928. Apart from the CFS order, and in spite of their advertising, only two further Genet-powered Moths were built. The Canadian Ministry of Defence took Nos 460 and 461 for use by the advanced flying unit of No 2 Squadron based at Camp Borden, Ontario, where applicants for the posts of flying instructors within the expanding club movement were trained and examined. Both Canadian Genet Moths qualified for Certificates of Airworthiness at Stag Lane on 30th December 1927. Not taken on charge by the RCAF until 17th February and 10th November 1928 respectively as '27' and '28', the first crashed at Angus, Ontario in May 1930 and '28' was struck off charge in January 1932. The civilian Genet Moth G-EBOU was sold to Flight Lieutenant Frank Soden in December 1927, an instructor at CFS, and continued to be based at Wittering.

By June 1927 it was clear that the reorganisation of the Stag Lane factory and standardisation on the more powerful

Bob Loader demonstrating the new style of telescopic jury strut, one end of which was fixed and the other clipped onto the undersurface of the top mainplanes, lying parallel with the root end rib. The struts remained in position at all times, conveniently and essentially placed for when the wings were folded. *Flight*

Cirrus II engine, were together working for more rapid delivery to a growing number of discerning customers. In addition to a programme of replacing Cirrus I engines in some early Moths, production doubled to an average of three new aircraft per week.

One of the first of many owners who upgraded their Moths by fitting the Mk II Cirrus engine was Sir John Rhodes. In June he excelled his previous airborne exercises by flying his Moth, G-EBNM, 1,548 miles to the South of France and back. The trip involved flying 23hr over a period of nine operating days, 'carrying a passenger and two suitcases'. Apart from further promotion of the Moth as a practical long-range vehicle, Sir John published very detailed accounts which identified the total aeroplane expenses at £14.6s.5d, representing just over 2d per mile.

Such trips were still newsworthy and the expanding columns devoted to private flying in the aviation press were fed regular reports from club secretaries concerning whom had arrived from where and in what, the fact that they had taken tea and uplifted petrol, given rides to the following named club members and where they intended landing after departure and for what reason. The gossipy, society news gradually disappeared as additional clubs were formed and many more serious journeys by light aeroplane were planned and executed.

Ivor McClure took delivery of G-EBRU (387), on 11th June and with Oliver Tapper immediately left for France where McClure was to assist the Bentley Team racing that weekend at Le Mans. They landed on the parade ground and impressed the gathered crowd by folding the wings. They were joined at the circuit by Captain Eric Hayes (G-EBQW/378), who had arrived with Mr W W Bentley as passenger and Neville Stack whose own passenger, H E Symons, was able to write up the story of Bentley's historic win for his magazine, *The Motor,* during the flight back to Stag Lane. Eric Hayes usually kept his Moth at Shrewsbury but was a regular visitor to London. As the result of an accident he was forced to keep his left arm in a sling which made it impossible for him to ride a motorcycle or drive a car, although he found he could, without difficulty, manage a Moth.

It was during their French trip that McClure and Tapper crystallised some of their ideas about the type of assistance that might be welcomed by a growing number of itinerant pilots, proposals with which they approached the Automobile Association.

A field adjoining Stag Lane Aerodrome was loaned to the Gaumont British Film Company in June for production of *The Flight Commander*, an adventure set in an outpost of Empire in the Far East, featuring Sir Alan Cobham and a Moth and several other types of aeroplane loaned by de Havilland and the Royal Air Force. According to Stag Lane's own 'Film Critic' who had been offered free tickets for the trade showing, the climax came when Sir Alan 'dropped a well-aimed bomb (properly permitted by authority) to start the rout of the mob, at the same time introducing a useful bit of air-mindedness propaganda'.

Leslie Irvin who had flown Moth G-EBNX (262) from his private airfield near to the Irving Air Chute Company works at Letchworth in Hertfordshire since taking delivery in June 1926, upgraded her to Mk II status and returned to the United States in July 1927, taking the Moth with him to his home town of Kenmore, near Buffalo. A visitor to the Irving factory there was Charles Lindbergh, a four-time user of Irving parachutes, who saw the Moth and was offered the opportunity to fly her at a later date. Whether the appointment was ever kept is unknown, but writing about his life later, Lindbergh mentions that he drove his future wife, Anne, to a town called Falaise where they flew in a Moth, their first flight together in the USA. Leslie Irvin sold his aeroplane in September. Registered NC1686, her eventual fate is unknown.

At the beginning of June the dangers of taxying downwind too fast in a machine not fitted with brakes or a steerable tailskid became evident at Woodford. The pilot leaped out of the cockpit and, by pulling on a wingtip, slewed the aircraft to prevent her from falling into a ditch although one wheel went over the lip and the propeller was broken. Only days later the Lancashire Club lost the first Moth it had received in 1925 when, on 11th June 1927, G-EBLR (184), suffered a broken rocker arm during a cross country flight and having made a satisfactory forced landing in a field at Hale, Cheshire, unluckily collided with a set of iron railings and was wrecked.

The Hampshire Club grounded G-EBOI in June for what it described as 'extensive alterations to the petrol system in an endeavour to cure its unfortunate habit of cutting out when taking off with the tank less than half full'. The exact nature of the 'extensive alterations' was not specified but probably involved a smoothing out of the gravity feed pipe to eliminate tight bends. The 'cutting out' problem was one which had caused considerable alarm. Following the cure of earlier induction trouble, de Havilland identified the new problem as an air lock caused by the breather pipe on the petrol tank. The cure was simply to lengthen the pipe and change its shape relative to the airflow.

Another patent was applied for on 14th June when Geoffrey de Havilland, British Subject, and the de Havilland Aircraft Company, jointly sought patent rights for an air speed indicator.

'This invention consists of improvements in or relating to air speed indicators for aircraft, and has for its object to provide an instrument which will be simple in construction and operation and will be cheap to manufacture and install.'

The 'instrument' was to become known as the 'windy' ASI, a spring-loaded vane which was forced across the face of a graduated scale by the pressure of the airflow, thus crudely measuring airspeed. The device was fixed to the starboard, front interplane strut as an optional extra on all production Moths and the patent, No 277914, was granted on 29th September 1927.

As hours were accumulated on the Cirrus I engine, mechanical problems began to accumulate. The Lancashire Club suffered several failures and the Flying Sub-Committee ruled that no more flying was to be considered on the Club's Cirrus I engines until all known modifications had been incorporated. Their decision was influenced to some extent by a forced landing in mid-June caused by a loose valve seat in an engine only recently overhauled by the makers, and in which two further seats were found to be on the point of coming adrift.

It was recognised that, extensively modified or not, the old engines were getting tired and replacement with the Cirrus II was an enticing prospect. However, an announcement was still awaited from the Air Ministry regarding funding in respect of subsidised operations beyond August and heavy expenditure at this time was to be avoided.

Stung into action by the prospect of tainted publicity, ADC Aircraft published 'unsolicited testimonial ... as further proof of the remarkable robustness of ADC Cirrus

engines'. The testimonial was a letter from Thomas McCracken, Ground Engineer at the Hampshire Club at Hamble:

'One of the Moth machines at this aerodrome crashed in a ploughed field adjoining the aerodrome due to an error of judgement on the part of the pilot.

'The machine hit the earth with the engine running fast and although the machine was wrecked and the engine partly buried in earth, it is gratifying to know that when the engine was removed from the wreckage, the earth washed off, and then mounted in the engine bed of another machine, it was found that the engine had withstood the abuse without causing any damage at all, not even knocking the propeller hub out of truth.

'The engine started up on the first pull and upon being opened up when fitted with a new propeller, it developed its full revolutions and behaved in quite a normal manner, which goes to show how good these Cirrus engines really are.'

The total eclipse of the sun on 29th June was observed by only a few as cloud cover over much of Great Britain obscured the view. Apart from Dr Gerald Merton's Moth G-EBQZ (369), specially equipped with instruments and a camera, and other aircraft chartered by the press, Her Grace the Duchess of Bedford was airborne with Charles Barnard at 3.30am, climbing through 10,000ft of cloud for a perfect view of the spectacle before letting down with great care and 'Bradshawing' back to Woburn at low level.

In June, the first customer for an 'X' type Moth purchased through William Whiteley was A C Morris Jackaman who persuaded the store to take his three-litre Sunbeam in part exchange. The aeroplane, G-EBRT (410) *Peridot I* (there were to be others), was first flown on 2nd July and kept on a private aerodrome at the owner's home near Slough, from where it was regular practice for him to fly to the South Coast for an early morning bathe. On 13th August G-EBRT was flown to Rustington, West Sussex, with Jackaman's brother Nigel in the front seat and where arrival and departure in a large field were to be filmed by prior arrangement. After take-off for return to Slough, the pilot made a sharp, steeply banked turn to the left, downwind, at less than 100ft, presumably playing to the camera, but the aircraft entered a spiral dive and hit the ground at a steep angle, sustaining severe damage.

Following the early success of the Moth, Geoffrey de Havilland recognised instantly that for his Company to depend entirely on

an outside source for the supply of engines was potentially dangerous. It was not unreasonable therefore, to capitalise on the original specification laid down for the Cirrus engine plus the experience gained with its operation, and starting with a blank sheet of paper, to design a new power unit unrestricted in the use of previously designed parts or specified materials, to be manufactured by the de Havilland Company. Frank Halford commented: 'The advantages of doing so were a greater degree of economy, and the increased technical efficiency resulting from the closer co-operation of those respectively responsible for engine and aeroplane production'.

Design work commenced on 29th October 1926, aiming to achieve 100hp at 2,100rpm, a specification agreed after much debate – debate which had also considered whether the engine should be geared or un-geared and of wet or dry oil base. During this period, Frank Halford made proposals for four distinct types of engine, both air and water cooled, before a decision was reached. There is some evidence to suggest that the new engine was to be called *Vampire* but the name eventually chosen was *Gipsy* spelled very specifically with a single 'y'. Two dictionary definitions of *Gipsy* are 'member of a travelling people found throughout Europe' and 'a girl who flouts convention'.

To manufacture the new engine the Company made preparations for additional workshops and dedicated running facilities to be erected at Stag Lane. The first test engine, largely constructed by Sid Weeden and Eric Mitchell, was to be built to a racing standard to achieve 150hp at 3,000rpm and gradually de-rated to 100hp for production models: an unusual path but entirely practical when the ultimate goal was a high level of safety and reliability. A new airframe, the DH.71 Tiger Moth, already under construction for research into streamlining and the

efficient application of low engine power to high-speed flight, was an ideal test vehicle. The revolutionary, all-metal DH.77 Interceptor of 1929 bore a remarkable similarity to the layout and basic shape of the DH.71 and its Napier 'H' engine was another brainchild of Frank Halford.

The first Gipsy engine was running by mid-1927 and, as test-bed trials continued, two DH.71 airframes were completed at Stag Lane in conditions of great secrecy. It was hoped to enter both in the 1927 King's Cup Air Race scheduled for 30th July at Nottingham but delays in certification prevented this. The first DH.71, G-EBQU, was fitted with an 85hp Cirrus II engine and took off from Stag Lane with Hubert Broad at the controls at dawn on 24th June. The aircraft was originally fitted with wings of 19ft span but these were soon exchanged for others of 22ft 6in span in order to wring the best possible advantage from the King's Cup handicap formula. Broad was at first unhappy with the gearing of the controls and described flying the Tiger Moth like standing on a garden roller on one foot with closed eyes! Further flights were made the following day, again very early in the morning to avoid too much attention.

After satisfactory flight trials G-EBQU was re-engined with the racing Gipsy but was withdrawn from the King's Cup. The second DH.71, G-EBRV, was similarly flown with a Cirrus II engine on 28th July, a powerplant which was never replaced.

When compared with the racing engine, the differences in the standard production model involved only cylinder heads, valves, induction pipe and carburettor. The technical specification of the 100hp Gipsy I as first published was:

- *Type*: 4 cylinder, vertical, air cooled.
- *Bore*: 114mm. *Stroke*: 128mm.
- *Capacity*: 5.23 litres.

- *Normal hp*: 90bhp at 1,900rpm.
- *Maximum hp*: 98bhp at 2,100rpm.
- *Petrol consumption*:
  0.59 pints per bhp per hour.
  (5.75 gals per hour, 9/10 throttle, 1,900rpm).
- *Oil consumption*: 0.5 to 0.75 pints per hour.
- *Weight dry*: 285 lb.
- *Oil capacity*: 16 pints.
- *Rotation*: Left hand tractor.
- *Overhaul life*: 450 hours.

The Gipsy I featured cast-iron cylinders with aluminium alloy cylinder heads. The layout was conventional, the crankshaft running in five main bearings in an aluminium alloy crankcase, with the propeller hub keyed to a tapered extension on the nose of the crankshaft.

A major feature distinguishing the Gipsy from the Cirrus engine was the change to left hand rotation. One good theory on why that rotation was chosen argued that it was a convenience as most potential swingers of propellers would do so with their right hand. But it was for a more basic technical reason altogether. With exhaust ports on the left side of the Cirrus, pilots reported that a right hand slipstream had a tendency to spill exhaust gases into the open cockpits. Eric Moult, a member of Frank Halford's design team, explained why on a Cirrus engine, this problem could never be cured:

'The original Renault engine, from which the Cirrus descended, had a spur gear reduction which meant that the crankshaft rotated in the opposite direction from the propeller. The Cirrus had no reduction gear or separate airscrew shaft because the propeller was mounted direct on the crankshaft itself which continued to rotate in the same direction as hitherto. This meant that the Cirrus propeller had to be a Right Hand Tractor (RHT).'

The close cowling of the new Gipsy engine introduced cooling problems which were quickly addressed as Eric Moult remembered:

'With early installations of air cooled engines the cylinders just stuck out in the breeze which was bad for drag and not too good for cooling. With an in-line engine, the front cylinders got the full benefit of the slipstream and the others suffered accordingly. We soon learned that it paid to pick up the air in a duct or scoop and direct it alongside the row of cylinders between which it could escape laterally. In this way a power unit could be cowled to protect it from the elements and the overall drag so reduced.

'There is considerable swirl in the slipstream behind a propeller and this swirl can be used to help cylinder cooling provided the scoop is placed on the windward side of the cylinder bank. A Gipsy engine with its Left Hand Tractor (LHT) propeller has its scoop on the starboard side. In

designing the new aluminium head for the Airdisco, Major Halford decided that the exhaust manifolds should be outside the cowled engine while the cooling scoop and induction manifolds should be in the Vee between the cylinder banks.

'On an individual head this meant that the exhaust ports faced outwards while the inlet ports faced inwards. When the same cylinder head was applied to the 4 cylinder Cirrus, the exhaust manifold was on the port side of the engine and the inlet manifold on the starboard side.

'With the Gipsy both ports came out on one side of the head, the inlet horizontal and the exhaust inclined, thus all the manifolding was on one side of the engine arranged so that the cooling air blew on the backs of the ports for good heat transfer. So one finds the carburettor and manifolds on the port side of a vertical Gipsy whereas they are on opposite sides of the cylinder with a Cirrus.'

After the King's Cup was transferred from Bournemouth, the idea of a 21 lap race was abandoned in favour of three different circuits each based on Hucknall Aerodrome, Nottingham and averaging 540 miles. A combination of poor weather and a handicap formula based on the speed of a DH.60X Moth assessed at 103mph, and which resulted in the handicap speed of another entry with a maximum speed of 180mph to be calculated at 244mph, caused nine of the original 25 entrants to withdraw in protest.

Only six aircraft completed the course and, for the second year in succession, the winner was a Cirrus I-powered Moth, the old G-EBME (193), flown as a private entry by Wally Hope, and averaging a remarkable 92.8mph. The Moth had been modified for the race in great secrecy at Stag Lane where, in friendly rivalry with a de Havilland School Mk II Moth, she had clocked 100mph on test. Hope was delighted with his win which had become a strong ambition and afterwards he revealed some of the details of the modifications:

'The aircraft had been fitted with a new but standard Cirrus I engine, known to deliver full type-test power, less exhaust pipe. As the handicap formula included wingspan, several inches of spar extension were grafted on to the top mainplanes, fitted with new tip bends and re-covered. The centre section fuel tank was removed and the centre plane filled in; a new tank was installed in the front cockpit which was faired over. An acute angled sloping windscreen was fitted to the rear cockpit which had new doors tailored to close up almost around the pilot's neck. Following discussions with the Palmer Company, new wheels were fitted of much smaller diameter than standard and "liberal use was made of fabric, dope and aluminium sheet to cover every drag-creating protuberance".'

The port side view of the Gipsy I engine with the square section induction manifold which proved to be more efficient and considerably cheaper to manufacture than earlier round section castings. de Havilland

Shortly after the race the aircraft was converted back to standard configuration and fitted with a Cirrus II engine. It was sold to the Victorian Section of the Australian Aero Club at Essendon. She was registered G-AUME on 26th January 1928 but exactly eleven months later, on Boxing Day, she crashed following a spin off a steep turn near the ground when the passenger is believed to have jammed the controls, and was destroyed.

De Havilland had prepared five other Moths for the King's Cup Race that year. G-EBPU (373), Mk II Cirrus, and G-EBMV (235), Mk I Cirrus, were modified in a similar fashion. Apart from the carriage of a nine gallon petrol tank in the front cockpit by G-EBPU, both had the strut fairings and wing root foot boards removed; all cracks fabriced over; planes faired into the fuselage; tail faired; no exhaust pipes; standard planes; small windscreens and the front cockpits faired over. The centre section fuel tanks remained in position and unaltered. G-EBRT (410) and G-EBSK (417), Mk II Cirrus, both had small centre section fuel tanks and a nine gallon tank in the front cockpit. Whereas 'SK had short exhaust pipes, 'RT had no exhaust pipes fitted at all. G-EBQH (276), Mk II Cirrus, flew with the front cockpit enclosed, a small centre section fuel tank, engine cowlings identical to those fitted to the DH.71 and 15° of dihedral applied to the top planes, a feature also applied to G-EBRT.

Hubert Broad flew the Cirrus-powered DH.71 G-EBRV to Nottingham on 29th July but retired during the King's Cup the following day due to the instability of the weather which caused him to force land in Lincolnshire and later return to Hucknall Aerodrome. During the morning of Bank Holiday Monday, 2nd August, Broad returned G-EBRV to Stag Lane and, to the intense delight of the Nottingham crowd reappeared at Hucknall in G-EBQU at 6.39pm, having left London at 6.00pm. At half throttle the Tiger Moth had cruised northwards at 163mph and, during his demonstrations at 100ft, reached 185mph. Frank Halford later explained that due to airscrew problems it had been necessary to limit the engine speed to 2,500rpm, giving about 130hp.

The eventual combination of the new powerplant and a tried and trusted Moth airframe was a force against which much of the opposition could only wilt and die, else attempt to survive by inventing imitations, and Francis St Barbe had already warned against those.

In advertising which was published with contemporary King's Cup reports, Blackburn Aircraft announced their new Bluebird II fitted with the Armstrong Siddeley Genet engine. Offered as a landplane at £775 or a seaplane at £935, the Bluebird was described as the only sociable light aeroplane with improved levels of comfort, visibility, performance and of course, side by side seating. The Avro Company left Nottingham empty-handed and had to resort in their advertising to applauding Sophie Eliott-Lynn's performance of 19th July when between dawn (3.30am) and dusk (9.30pm), she had landed an Avian on what was described as 'every usable aerodrome in England as well as 20 fields'.

Between races, the circuit at Nottingham was in constant use by joyriding Moths to which Lord Ossulston alone contributed 30 trips on Sunday afternoon following a taxi flight in the morning, and 70 on Monday. The arrival of Hubert Broad on Bank Holiday Monday evening with the Tiger Moth powered by the new de Havilland engine had been much anticipated. C G Grey, who had introduced Alan Butler to the de Havilland Company in 1922 must have been warmly satisfied to report on the firm's progress in just five years since:

'There must be some significance in the fact that out of six races for the King's Cup four have been won on de Havilland aeroplanes. Either that proves that DH machines are very efficient or very reliable or very fast or very good, somehow or other, which most people know to be true. Or else it means that the de Havilland people are very energetic and enterprising in always putting their machines into races, which is very much in their favour from the point of view of the buyer who wants service.

'Whichever way you look at it the DH people deserve their success, the more so because

probably the firm has the smallest capital of any aircraft firm in the country and is the only British aircraft firm which is selling aeroplanes for civil air transport abroad. Get that into your head and you will see how well the DH Company deserves the distinction and honour of winning the King's Cup.'

Alan Butler was disappointed at his own personal performance in the King's Cup. He had accepted the loan of Captain de Havilland's DH.60X Moth G-EBQH (276) on 14th July and immediately flew to Cranwell where he stayed overnight. During the next two days he flew for eight hours around segments of the King's Cup course familiarising himself, but in conditions of rain and low cloud. It was all in vain; during the race proper on 30th July, G-EBQH was forced landed with a valve problem in her Cirrus II engine.

The reputation of the Moth as a light seaplane resulted in an order from the Canadian Department of Marine and Fisheries for a light aircraft to accompany six Fokker Super Universals as part of the 1927 Hudson Strait Expedition, setting out apparently to study ice patterns in the shipping lanes between the proposed grain port of Churchill on the western edge of Hudson Bay, and Europe. Some years later it was revealed that the main aim of the Expedition had been to explore the potential for establishing military bases in the Strait and to test aeronautical and other equipment.

DH.60X G-CAHK (377) first flew in May and was registered in Ottawa in July. The Expedition set out on 17th July, with the Moth, named *Spirit of the Valley of the Moon*, carried on board the icebreaker CGS *Stanley* By 24th August the aircraft had made five survey flights totalling 14 hours. Against the advice of the Moth pilot, Squadron Leader Thomas Lawrence, the ship's captain decided to offload the aircraft before a secure strip of stony beach at Wakeham Bay had been prepared to receive her. Moored without shelter, the Moth rode out a 12 hour south westerly storm which blew

up overnight, but eventually capsized and was wrecked; only the engine and floats could be salvaged.

Following a visit to Stag Lane by Captain Roy Maxwell, Director of the Ontario Provincial Air Service (OPAS) based at Sault St Marie, an urgent request was made for four aircraft to be supplied equipped with an interchangeable float and wheeled undercarriage as replacements for aging Curtiss HS-2L flying boats, to be engaged on forest fire detection and light freighting duties. Fitted with Short floats the first aircraft, the all-yellow DH.60X G-CAOU (400), was flight tested from Rochester by Hubert Broad on 14th June with Hessell Tiltman carried as observer. With a pilot and full fuel tanks the aircraft was adjudged nose heavy; carrying 80 lb ballast to achieve maximum all-up weight, she proved to be slightly tail heavy.

G-CAOU accompanied by 'OV, 'OW and 'OX (401-403), the first four production DH.60X models, were shipped to Canada on board the *Empress of Australia* which docked on 2nd July. The first OPAS Moth, possibly G-CAOU, was flight tested by Roy Maxwell on 11th July operating from the slipway of the service hangar on the St Mary's River near Sault St Marie. On the same day Major John Leach, Superintendent of Western Flying Operations for the Ontario Government tested the Moth he was scheduled to operate from Sioux Lookout. Three days later G-CAOV was flown by R S Grandy and J H Judd after which all four OPAS Moths were immediately put into service, logging 700 hours in the first four months and leading to an order for six additional machines for delivery from May 1928.

The most important duty of the OPAS Moths was detection and suppression of forest fires over an area of 150 million acres. Prior to the inauguration of the service the average acreage lost to fires was two million but the regular air patrols in 1927 reduced this to a record low of 36,000 acres.

The first four DH.60X Seaplanes displayed a remarkable adaptability to progress which

DH.60X Seaplane G-CAOU was operated by the Ontario Provincial Air Service from July 1927. In March 1929. Along with many contemporaries, the wooden fuselage was replaced by a steel tube frame with a Gipsy I engine, the configuration illustrated in this photograph. Jack Meaden

was responsible for their longevity. Although G-CAOV overturned when touching down on Lac Seul as a result of engine failure in July 1928, G-CAOU, 'OW and 'OX were all rebuilt with steel tube fuselages (DH.60M) and fitted with Gipsy I and later Gipsy II engines. G-CAOU was not sold until 1948 and ended her career as a snowmobile; 'OW was sold in 1949 and 'OX was written off in 1936.

Over a period of several years, de Havilland had experimented (and were to continue the process) with methods of providing heating in open cockpit aircraft. The four Moths supplied to Canada in July 1927 all were fitted with pipes which drew hot air from muffs around the main exhaust and directed it to the area of the rudder bars in both cockpits. A similar system was fitted to G-CAHS (409), a DH.60X Seaplane delivered to Dominion Airways at High River, Alberta, in July. G-CAHS, *Elsie,* was written off when she crashed into English Bay, British Columbia, in March 1928.

Eight Moths from Stag Lane landed in the grounds of the Roehampton Club on 16th July for the second successful aerial garden party. The *de Havilland Gazette* commented that: 'some people still imagine that a pilot has to be disguised to look something between a diver and a Channel swimmer, and they must have been surprised to meet white spats and buttonholes'. The Duchess of Bedford who presented the prizes had arrived in her new emerald green and silver DH.60X G-EBRI (405), which had been delivered to Woburn only three days previously.

The prolonged period of wet weather which disrupted all the British flying meetings during the summer of 1927, dampened the Aerial Fete held in the grounds of Raynham Hall, Norfolk, on 23rd July. Organised by the Marchioness Townshend the event was intended to raise funds for Norwich hospitals in addition to assisting the Norfolk and Norwich Aero Club, and was well supported by many private owners and RAF aircraft and personnel. An exhibition of aerobatics by Bert Hinkler on his Avro Avian was cancelled after it was discovered that the aircraft had a damaged wheel. Hubert Broad offered the loan of a replacement from his Moth but it was a different size and could not be fitted so Broad was asked to take over, stunting his Moth under a lowering cloudbase and in incessant rain.

In spite of the considerable exposure to the major aviation events, the public still wanted to read the 'society' stories and the aviation press was willing to publicise the facts, many of which were still 'firsts' or noteworthy for other reasons. A recurring theme was the ability of the Moth to operate in unusual situations where much general interest and assistance was rendered by local people. In high summer, Norman Hulbert, a London Club member, hired a Moth

from the de Havilland School and flew to Dorset, landing on the lawn of Ferne House near Shaftesbury, home of the Duke of Hamilton. Much local flying over the weekend is reported to have caused 'a sensation'.

Senor Don Juan de la Cierva, designer of the autogiro that bore his name, borrowed a Moth from the Hampshire Club and with Miss Ruwe, a visitor from Los Angeles, flew to the Isle of Wight to visit a friend. The trip was timed to permit a landing on the sandy beach alongside the house from where the folded aeroplane was hauled up an old stone slipway and parked in the road. After an enjoyable day and with the tide now out, the exercise was repeated in reverse and the Moth returned to Hamble.

With the closure of the London Club for staff holidays at the height of the season in August, Francis St Barbe joined Ivor McClure in G-EBRU for a scheduled 14 day tour of 15 European countries. They were detained in Spain as their authorisation had not arrived from the Embassy in London, but escaped when an engine test developed into a full power take-off run after news was received that the necessary permit was 'on its way'.

Due to a misunderstanding by the authorities in Vienna, at the furthest point from Stag Lane, the crew of G-EBRU were unable to locate the Matyasfold Aerodrome at Budapest having arrived in darkness. The airfield had not been advised of their journey and no welcoming lights were shown. McClure landed on a disused parade ground but hit a ditch which took off the undercarriage. The adventure had covered 2,200 miles, half that anticipated, landing in seven countries in eight days.

In mid-August the Duchess of Bedford left for another European tour with Charles Barnard, returning near the end of the month from Naples. In a week the Moth had travelled 3,500 miles, crossed the Alps at 14,000ft and allowing her crew a spectacular view, looking down into the crater of Vesuvius.

The historic Moth prototype, G-EBKT, now fitted with Cirrus I engine No 23, was lost during an outing from Stag Lane on 21st August. The pilot was a young but relatively inexperienced RAF officer, Pilot Officer Stanley Pritchard-Barrett, trained on the Avro 504 and now a Bristol Fighter pilot with a total flying time of just over 100 hours. His total time on Moths was one hour the previous February and a 15 minute check flight with a London Club instructor on the day of the accident. The inspector's report says of *Katie's* last flight:

'*The pilot took off into wind, but when at about 20ft from the ground he turned to the left and made a half circuit of the aerodrome without any appreciable gain in height. He then headed in a Northerly direction, continuing to fly at about the same altitude with the engine very much throttled down until the aeroplane arrived over*

the high ground at Stanmore when he started to circle round a private golf course. On completing a wide turn to the right through 180°, being then very little higher than the tree tops, the pilot opened up the engine and started to climb but the aircraft suddenly fell over, and dived out of control to the ground.'

The Cirrus I engine provided a story of its own. Examination revealed that one of the engine valve guides was a loose fit in the cylinder head and an attempt had been made to effect a cure by coating the guide with soft solder. But this had no influence on the cause of the accident which was due 'to an error of judgement on the part of the pilot causing the aeroplane to stall near the ground'.

G-EBKT had flown about 800hr during the two and a half years since that momentous Sunday in February 1925 when she had performed so well and to the satisfaction of her designer. Perhaps it was ironic that she should have been written off in the same month that the re-negotiated Air Ministry subsidy for the Approved Flying Clubs should come into effect.

The terms of the subsidy were a matter of interest not only to the six clubs already receiving government assistance, but to the many others that had started operations in the recent past. The announcement came on 16th July and was made appropriately enough by Sir Sefton Brancker during celebrations to mark the opening of an extension to the domestic facilities of the Lancashire Aero Club at Woodford.

'The new subsidies are to operate for three years and are then to end. The Air Ministry hopes that three years hence the Clubs will have become self supporting.

'According to the new scheme, £50 is to be paid to each of the Approved Clubs for each pilot qualifying for the 'A' or 'B' Aviator's Certificate.

'In addition to this £50 for new licences, £10 will be paid to each Club for each active member on a Club's list who holds a current certificate. Furthermore a grant of 30 shillings per hour of flying time up to a maximum of 20 hours per annum will be paid to the Club for the flying done by each such individual pilot. Thus each active pilot will be able to earn £40 for his Club.

'The total amount of the subsidy will not exceed £2,000 to any one Club in any one year.'

The new scheme of 'payment by results' was designed to encourage Clubs towards greater efficiency and by the organisation of regular displays, race meetings and 'At Home' weekends, to raise additional funds by taking cash at the gate. Such events always resulted in the recruitment of additional members – after all, was that not the whole idea?

AUGUST TO DECEMBER 1927

AT STAG LANE Aerodrome on 16th August 1927, Lady Mary Bailey cracked a bottle of South African wine against the propeller hub of DH.60 Cirrus II Moth G-EBSO (419). Sponsored by the *Johannesburg Star* newspaper, G-EBSO, named *Dorys* after his fiancée, was to be flown by a young South African Air Force pilot, Lieutenant Richard Bentley, from London to Cape Town.

Bentley had been resident at Stag Lane for three weeks, supervising conversion of his Moth which in its final single-seat configuration had an endurance of eleven hours. He had arranged for supplies of Shell petrol and Castrol R oil to be laid down at strategic points along his planned route and, satisfied that everything was in order, he left Stag Lane at 10.30am on Saturday 1st September.

In spite of his preparations on arrival in Paris he discovered there was no triptyque on board, but an urgent telephone call to the Royal Aero Club in London found Harold Perrin and allowed him sufficient time to get the document onto the 4.30pm Imperial Airways' flight from Croydon. Bentley had his precious paperwork by 7.30pm. From adversity came the best publicity for European air travel.

Richard Bentley arrived at Wynberg Aerodrome, Cape Town, on 28th September where he was met by jubilant crowds. The success of the flight was due largely to the methodical approach of the pilot, who started each new sector early in the morning, rarely flew for more than six hours on any day, spent a relaxing afternoon maintaining his aeroplane, then was early to bed. Almost nothing had been reported on his progress until he reached Johannesburg from where the flight proceeded against very strong headwinds. For the achievement of covering 7,250 miles in 28 days, Flight Lieutenant Bentley was awarded the prestigious 'Britannia Trophy' by the Committee of the Royal Aero Club and the Air Force Cross by the SAAF.

The Australian branch of the de Havilland Company made a special offer to the Aus-

tralian Aero Club in August to supply one complete DH.60 Moth, less engine, in unassembled parts, at a special price of £375, delivered to Melbourne, Perth, Adelaide, Sydney or Brisbane. Details of 'unassembled' were quite specific:

1. Fuselage complete, and already assembled with seats, control unit, safety belts, and all metal fittings excepting instruments and instrument board, the latter being supplied ready for assembly to cockpits.
2. All spars, ribs, diagonals, leading and trailing edges, and other wood parts including packing blocks etc, for wings and empennage ready for assembly after certain holes have been drilled. The spars are ready marked off for ribs and are drilled ready for strut and internal bracing bolts.
3. All metal fittings are supplied ready for fitting with necessary bolts, nuts and pins. All control cables supplied spliced, with turnbuckles and shackles complete.
4. Chassis complete with compression legs and axle already assembled.
5. All engine controls, petrol system, etc, ready for assembly to fuselage.
6. Fabric covers supplied already sewn.

'The only tool required for the completion of the machine are ordinary spanners, pliers etc, available at any aerodrome or amateur workshop. Drawings will be loaned by the company and full details of the various operations of assembly and erection given. Either the new type, DH.60A or the present type can be supplied, and the price quoted covers the complete aeroplane less engine. No extra of any kind need be bought excepting dope and paint.'

It was not quite the £500 fly-way price that C G Grey constantly championed as the maximum for a 'man in the street' aeroplane but it was a significant gesture, and one which the Stag Lane factory appears not to have pursued itself.

The Australian Aero Club annual report until 31st August 1927 revealed the extent to which the Light Aeroplane Clubs had advanced, and in particular the Mascot-based Sydney Club where more pupil pilots had been trained to licence standard in a lower total flying time than that achieved at the most directly comparable organisation, the London Aeroplane Club at Stag Lane. Each of the Sydney Club's Moths loaned by the Australian Government, G-AUAH, 'AJ and 'AK had been completely overhauled and returned to service where they were joined by the Club's self-funded G-AUFV (DHA 1A) *Oswald Watt* in June and G-AUGJ (DHA 3) *Ross Smith* on 24th September. Even this fleet of five aircraft was insufficient to meet the demand for solo flying and at the end of the year a fourth 'loan' aircraft

Dick Bentley taking off from a waterlogged Stag Lane Aerodrome on Saturday, 1st September 1927, bound for Paris, where he discovered he had left vital travel documents in London. Sport and General

was sought from the Civil Aviation Department. At the time, Australia could boast a total of 28 'light aeroplanes' of which 22 were DH.60 Moths.

Francis St Barbe and Hubert Broad flew DH.60 Moth demonstrator G-EBSI (416), from Stag Lane to Copenhagen on 1st September for the first Danish International Meeting and, although his report mentions that the Moths of John Carberry, Viscomte de Sibour and the Moth Seaplane of Maurice Burton had all flown out from England, there was no mention that Burton's Moth G-EBRH (404) had crashed on arrival. It was more noteworthy to St Barbe that Hubert Broad had been placed 2nd on handicap in a local air race and, having removed the exhaust pipe to gain extra speed, failed in the climb competition to achieve more than 11,000ft as the carburettor heater had been disconnected with the exhaust. St Barbe was not slow to circulate the appreciation that, operating under such a handicap, the climb in 15min was still a remarkable achievement. Despite all this, Broad's weekend performance earned him five trophies and St Barbe returned to his office with a smile and a cheque. G-EBSI was left in Denmark, sold to the popular Danish magazine *Ude Og Hjemme* by whom she was pressed immediately into a nationwide propaganda tour.

The City of Norwich was immensely proud of its Aero Club and on 8th September the Lord Mayor and 19 City Councillors flew during what was believed to be the world's first 'Civic Air Meeting'. The fall of darkness prevented even more flights when the lack of a second Moth was plainly evident, a situation impressed on the Lord Mayor and Lady Mayoress when they visited the Club again on the following Sunday to take tea. The Committee had already declared that no member could be allowed to fly for more than 15min; clearly ineffi-

cient use of the aeroplane and frustrating for pilot members and instructors.

Flight Lieutenant David D'Arcy Greig left Wittering at 9.00am on 10th September in the de Havilland School's brand new DH.60X Moth G-EBTD (430) bound for his home town of Elgin in the Scottish Highlands. He was accompanied by an old friend, Flight Lieutenant A E Beilby, an instructor with 5 FTS at Sealand. The trip was newsworthy as no light aeroplane had ever visited the area and G-EBTD was duly aerobatted over the city and Greig's old school, Elgin Academy, before landing alongside the house where the pilots were to be weekend guests. It was important for the light aeroplane movement to continue to emphasise the advantages of air travel and Greig's domestic flight was reviewed as follows:

'The journey to the north, something under 600 miles (when starting from Stag Lane), was covered in eight hours both going and returning; 32 gallons of petrol were used and £2 covered the total cost of the journey. Travellers to Scotland by train will thus be able to compare the costs of travel, greatly in favour of the Moth!'

Already bound not to travel by train if possible, the Duchess of Bedford flew in her Moth from Woburn Abbey to her Scottish home at Cairnsmore House, Kirkcudbrightshire, on 25th September where, in anticipation of many such future journeys, the Duchess had had a permanent landing field and aeroplane shed prepared.

At Woodford the Lancashire Club reported that G-EBLV had been further damaged. During the afternoon of 16th September she had landed on a soft patch in the middle of the aerodrome, standing on her nose, breaking the propeller and bending the cowlings. She was made air-

worthy to fly again one hour later! In avoiding the soft patch that same afternoon she was landed instead near the boundary fence but hit a ridge, losing her undercarriage. The aeroplane was completely rebuilt by the club members using what were described as 'some of the sundry fuselages, empennages, aerofoils and whatnots in the hangar!'. She was then sold to club member John Anderson who had agreed to her continued use by the club. In February 1928, when being flown by her new owner, she was badly damaged again when she encountered severe downdraughts in The Pennines, and was forced to land on a hillside where she overturned.

David Kittel's much travelled Cirrus I Moth G-EBMU was damaged in a landing accident at Stag Lane in August. As a result he traded the aircraft with de Havilland for a new X-type Moth, G-EBTH (439), which was delivered almost immediately, again painted black and silver and called *Silvry 3*. On 18th September Kittel set off on another solo tour of Europe, covering 4,000 miles in 18 days, ranging as far east as Budapest and south to Rome, once more navigating by the use of road maps. His return to Croydon was in company with an Imperial Airways' flight from Paris which allowed direct passage in just under three hours.

Travelling in the opposite direction a few weeks later, Morris Jackaman reached Le Bourget Airport, Paris, one hour and 35 minutes after leaving Croydon in his wife's DH.60X G-EBVK (467). The estimated average ground speed for the trip was 147mph and only just over six gallons of petrol were consumed. Harriet Jackaman had won the new aeroplane in a raffle and it was flown by her husband while his own G-EBRT (410) was being repaired. G-EBVK was sold in April 1928 to Lieutenant Glen Kidston RN, and travelled with him to Malta on board HMS *Courageous*. The aeroplane was subsequently owned by a number of flying schools until December 1934 when she was ditched in the River Thames near Vauxhall Bridge and sank. Recovered, rebuilt and re-engined, G-EBVK later spent time in service with the Herts and Essex Aero Club at Broxbourne.

Such adventures were worthy of considerable publicity and in its assessment of David Kittel's tour, *Flight's* editorial was very positive:

'England is quite a pioneer in this new aspect of aviation, for our tourists do not come across air tourists of other nationali-

An Englishman abroad. Major Shirley Kingsley, the Company's representative in Argentina, with that country's Director of Civil Aviation and other Air Force officers, following a demonstration of the Moth at Buenos Aires in September 1927.
de Havilland

ties. One reason for this perhaps is a lack of foreign development of the light aeroplane of our standard. It must be admitted though that our lead in air touring would not be possible without the capital ground organisation that Europe incidentally provides through its extensive use of commercial aviation.'

After heavy rain fell onto the London clay that was Stag Lane Aerodrome, the surface was frequently turned into a sea of mud and operations with Moths fitted with thin wheels and a straight axle were difficult and, sometimes, impossible. While the Yorkshire Club's G-EBNN was receiving attention with the de Havilland Service Department, her sister G-EBLS flew down from Sherburn to visit. When leaving to return north, her take-off run consumed the whole of the glutinous aerodrome without leaving the ground although she managed to stop within the confines of the adjacent field.

The practicability of the Moth as a method of international transport was to be further proved by a whole troop of aircraft from Stag Lane, who proposed to head off to Italy to support the tenth Schneider Trophy Contest to be flown at Venice Lido on 26th September. Included in the party were Captain de Havilland in G-EBSF (415); Winifred Spooner solo in G-EBOT (272), to which long-range tanks had been fitted; Douglas Mill and Captain Isett in G-EBTI (431); Mrs Maia Carberry with Hubert Broad in G-EBSQ (421), and Alan Butler with Peter Hoare in G-EBQH (276).

Alan Butler left Stag Lane on 21st September, arriving in Padua the following day after a nightstop in Mâcon. The weather was not good from the start and the de Havilland Chairman noted that the cross Channel flight was 'nasty and low' and the sector between Lyons and Turin 'the most unpleasant flight I have ever accomplished, but a wonderful experience'. The return trip was described as 'good but difficult' with much time spent flying above cloud. Winifred Spooner's Italian adventure was even more memorable as she skilfully forced landed G-EBOT in a street in Genoa after the engine failed.

There was more bad news for Sherburn on 23rd September when Captain Anthony Milburn's Moth G-EBRZ (413), with only 43 hours logged, crashed 400 yards off the eastern boundary, killing the lady passenger, Miss Dorothy Ellison. Milburn, one of the country's leading polo players, had received 15 hours' dual instruction at Newcastle before moving to the Yorkshire Club. With a total of about 19 hours solo, on the day in question he was seen to fly the Moth very slowly into the 25mph westerly wind, attempting to 'hover,' a favourite manoeuvre. The aircraft stalled at 500ft, recovered, but spun from 300ft and hit the ground.

Hubert Broad tested another DH.60X Seaplane at Rochester in October, an aircraft fitted with Short duralumin floats. Painted as K-SALF (447), the aircraft was scheduled for demonstration purposes around the Baltic, and at the invitation of the Finnish Minister of Defence, Colonel Solin, accompanied by Broad and Fred Hopkins, a rigger from Stag Lane, she was shipped from Hull to Finland on 2nd November. During erection on the slipway at the ice-covered lake at Helsingfors, the aircraft was enveloped in a heavy fall of snow which froze and had to be scraped off the wings and floats. Just days before the Baltic froze over, demonstration flights were conducted on behalf of the Air Force, Air League, Reserve Corps and the press.

In February 1928 the aircraft was formally registered K-SILA to the Air Defence League of Finland, named *Ilmatar* after the ancient Finnish goddess of the air, and based in Helsinki for which purpose she was converted to a ski-equipped landplane. From June 1928, K-SILA was operated by her resident pilot, Flying Master Heiskala of the Finnish Air Service, on a set of wooden floats designed and manufactured locally at a fraction of the cost of a metal set.

It seems more than probable that the 'unofficial' lettering applied in England was another scheme devised by St Barbe when he concluded who the eventual operators would be. The Moth made a welcome appearance at the Finnish Air Display held on the frozen harbour at Helsingfors on 4th March and, following an agreement signed on 31st March, the country also acquired the rights to manufacture DH.60 Moths under licence in the newly-established State Aircraft Factory (Valtion Lentokonetehdas) at Suomenlinna near Helsinki, from where the first aircraft would emerge the following year.

From 1st October 1927, the de Havilland Aircraft Company Ltd offered a 'Guarantee' in respect of all new Moth aircraft supplied '...by them either direct or through their duly accredited agents, that such machines have been built with all usual and reasonable precautions to secure excellence of material and workmanship'. There was nothing unexpected in what was guaranteed and what was not, but the company ensured that 'it was under no obligation to repair or replace any instruments, tyres, engines, or engine parts or fittings, nor any parts not manufactured directly by them' and also that the Guarantee 'shall apply only to the original purchaser unless notice of a change of ownership is given to the Company and the change duly accepted by them'. It was a sign of maturity and confidence in the product although there may have been growing pressure for such assurance from both private and, particularly, institutional owners.

In South Africa during August, Allister Miller had demonstrated his Moth at a number of airfield locations where new light aeroplane clubs were anticipated, offering dozens of free flights to prospective members. The result was that by October, de Havilland were able to announce the sale of a further eleven Moths to customers in the country. It was suggested that Moths might be used to seed clouds in an effort to break a prolonged drought and to produce rain, whereas in Great Britain a method was required to curtail one of the wettest summers on record.

The year 1927 had been unkind to the earliest Moths. Both prototypes had been crashed, the Newcastle Club lost G-EBLY (191) in February and the Lancashire Club's G-EBLR (184) crashed in June. Now, within days of de Havilland's announcement of its new business initiative in issuing guarantees, although certainly not covered by it, the London Aeroplane Club's G-EBLI (183), spun into the ground from 6,000ft near Stanmore. The pilot, Charles Swan, who was undertaking his solo height test, had already indicated to friends that he was planning to descend in this manner, and observers reported that the aircraft had entered a right hand spin at high altitude which continued vertically until G-EBLI collided with the ground.

On the previous day, 8th October 1927, Mrs Sophie Eliott-Lynn believed she had achieved a world altitude record flying an Avian from Woodford, but a corrected barograph reading indicated she had only equalled Lady Bailey's record which still stood. On 11th October in London, the high-flying Mrs Eliott-Lynn married Sir James Heath and henceforth this qualified engineer and commercial pilot would be better known as Lady Heath.

Unlike many other prospective ventures, the Bristol and Wessex Aeroplane Club had, somewhat against the financial odds, won through. Although it started in the business of flying training on 29th July, it was not officially 'opened' at Filton Aerodrome until 8th October. During his speech, Air Minister Sir Samuel Hoare announced that the level of subsidy enjoyed by six of the country's light aeroplane clubs had been extended to four more: Bristol and Wessex, representing the West of England; Norfolk and Norwich for Eastern England; Nottingham for the Midlands and the Scottish Flying Club at Glasgow, all of whom had chosen Moths as standard equipment.

The Bristol Club's first Moth was DH.60X G-EBSN (418), registered on 23rd July. She lasted less than a year, stalling at 300ft on take-off on 6th May 1928 and killing both instructor and pupil in the crash that followed. Club Chairman Archie Downs-Shaw collected his own DH.60X Moth G-EBST (427) from Stag Lane on 9th September, the

G-AUGM, the DH.60X purchased by public subscription for use by the Rector of Wilconnia, NSW, Australia, to serve a parish the size of the whole of England. Rev F Bate, Secretary of the Colonial and Continental Church Society, accepted the aircraft at Stag Lane on 12th November 1927, after which Mr Bates' son, seen in the front cockpit, was flown in her by Geoffrey Alington. de Havilland

first of several privately-owned Moths to be housed at Filton. Two years later, G-EBST was sold to Sir Malcolm Campbell's dealership at Heston and survived a number of ownerships until she was requisitioned in July 1940, delivered to the RAF at St Athan, and struck off charge there three months later.

The Newcastle Club published a booklet, *Learn to Fly at Cramlington Aerodrome*, in October. Written by the club's pilot instructor J D Parkinson, the booklet covered the club's short history and the costs involved in learning to fly. C G Grey enthused about the publication, praising the compilers, printers, advertisers and Sir Sefton Brancker who wrote the foreword.

John Leeming of the Lancashire Club published a handbook, *The Pilot's A Licence*, the first really practical attempt to put together all the details, not only of how to qualify for a pilot's licence but of how to maintain and renew it. To maximise exposure copies were handled by the Book Department at *The Aeroplane* and, at two shillings a copy post free, 500 copies were sold within a fortnight.

After an embarrassing delay the formation of a Scottish Flying Club was accelerated in September thanks to a publicity campaign assisted by the management of several Glasgow theatres, cinemas and businesses. Having been assured of an Air Ministry subsidy if the business plan was acceptable, the Club Committee approved the purchase of a DH.60X Moth, G-EBUU (471), in October. Only two sites local to Glasgow had been found with potential for development as a club aerodrome, neither of which was liable to be ready for operations in less than a year. An approach to the Air Ministry resulted in the offer to use Moorpark Aerodrome, Renfrew, following which a public meeting was addressed by Sir Sefton Brancker, whose message was, once again, that the community should offer full support.

The club's first aircraft was delivered from Stag Lane on Tuesday 2nd November, flown by DH School Instructor Bob Reeve with Jack Anderson of the *Glasgow Evening News* as passenger. Named *You You*, the Moth was painted red and gold, the colours of the Scottish Standard, and on arrival was displayed in the Glasgow showrooms of Messrs Wylie and Lockhead for the duration of the Scottish Motor Show. Operations began at Renfrew on 3rd December but G-EBUU crashed there on 1st May the following year when an inexperienced pilot realised he was flying the wrong circuit direction and attempted a steep turn whilst reducing power. The aircraft entered a spiral dive and struck the ground. She was replaced almost immediately by DH.60X G-EBYG (337). This aircraft remained in service until March 1930 when she was sold to a private owner at Brooklands who flew her to Kenya in April. After landing in the bush for a lunch break, the aircraft was attacked by hostile natives and set on fire.

Encouraged, perhaps, by the growing public awareness of the practical light aeroplane, a former RAF pilot who had taken Holy Orders, and whose 5,000 parishioners, living on the Darling River in New South Wales, occupied territory several times the size of Great Britain, appealed through British newspapers for funds to buy a Moth. In addition to dispensing pastoral care, Reverend Leonard Daniels was intending to chauffeur the doctor based in Wilconnia around the territory, avoiding bad motor journeys along inadequate tracks.

An early contributor to the appeal was Sam Lea who sent £25 from his erstwhile Moth showroom in New Bond Street. Sufficient money eventually was raised, largely by Rev Daniels himself who had completed a six month lecture tour of England, to permit the Bush Church Aid Society of Sydney to place a firm order with de Havilland. Moth No 453 qualified for her C of A on 11th

November 1927 and was handed over in a ceremony at Stag Lane the following day to the Rev F Bate, Secretary, and other representatives of the Colonial and Continental Church Society. In very bumpy conditions, the aircraft was test flown by Geoffrey Alington who later took Mr Bate's son for a local flight. Painted silver with purple struts, and the legend *Church of England* on the fuselage, the Moth carried the letters G-AUGM at Stag Lane, but was not officially listed as such until April 1928 by which time she had been delivered by sea to Sydney. Re-registered VH-UGM in 1929, the aeroplane was flown by Rev Daniels and his successor, Rev C Kemmis until 7th November 1932 when VH-UGM stalled while landing on a road near Wilconnia Aerodrome. Badly damaged, the Moth was stored until 1934 when she was sold to South Australia Airways. She survived a number of owners until 22nd November 1959 when, due to engine failure, she was fatally damaged in a crash near Melbourne.

There were other notable orders and deliveries late in the year too. The first of two British aircraft to be ordered by an Italian customer since the end of the First World War was delivered to the Italian Government at the beginning of November. Alan Butler positioned DH.60X No 470 to Croydon on 2nd November and, in conditions of 'rain, mist and fog', flew via Lympne to Le Bourget. The following day the aircraft went on to Nice where Alan Butler stayed with friends until 5th when the aircraft was taken on to Milan and handed over to the Regia Aeronautica on Sunday 6th November.

The second aircraft, No 468, was built as a Moth Seaplane and inspected at Rochester on 9th November by the Italian Air Attaché in London, General Guidoni, soon to take up his new appointment as Director General of Aircraft Construction for Regia Aeronautica. Following his flight with Short's test pilot John Lankester-Parker, the aircraft was converted back to a landplane and set off for the sunshine of Rome on Friday 25th November in the capable hands of de Havilland School instructor, Bob Reeve.

Reeve had recently flown DH.60X Moth G-EBUA (438), to wintry Oslo where he had demonstrated the aeroplane to the Norwegian Army at Lillestrom before a technical survey of the type was undertaken at the State Aircraft Factory at Kjeller between 15th

Alan Butler, third from the left, in Milan on Sunday, 6th November, when he handed over to Major de Bernardi, DH.60X No 470, which he had flown from Stag Lane. The Moth was the first British aircraft ordered by an Italian customer since the end of the First World War. *Alan Butler*

and 18th October. Afterwards, he had taken the aircraft on to Copenhagen where she was sold to the Danish newspaper *Ude og Hjemme*. No quick decision was forthcoming from the Norwegian authorities, however, and it was not until after evaluation in service of two civil-registered DH.60M Moths engaged in night postal flights during the summer of 1929 that a decision was made to purchase DH.60Ms for Army, and possibly Navy, training purposes, and to negotiate a licence for the production of further aircraft at Kjeller.

Colonel J L Ralston, Canadian Minister of National Defence, made an announcement in Ottawa on 24th September to confirm that the Canadian Government was to assist in the establishment of light aeroplane clubs in the larger population centres of the Dominion. Two aircraft were to be allocated to each selected club in addition to an airfield or seaplane station plus two spare engines and an instructor. Qualification was the ability to maintain the allocated aircraft and to enrol 30 club members each of whom had expressed a willingness to learn to fly. The government promised to supply an additional aircraft each year for every one funded by the clubs themselves. Although the purchase of the DH.60 Moth type could not be assumed due to intense competition from manufacturers in the USA, an order for ten DH.60X Mk II Moths was placed with de Havilland on 10th November requiring that the aircraft be delivered for operations to begin in the spring of 1928.

Immediately following the Minister's announcement applications for consideration and assistance were received from 15 cities, and clubs were formed in Montreal, Edmonton, Ottawa and Regina. A private citizen pledged a grant of land to create an aerodrome for the Toronto Aeronautical Association; 80 acres were secured by the club forming in Victoria; and the Montreal Club was promised a new aerodrome to be built by the Government at St Hubert on the south side of the St Lawrence River. The Edmonton and Northern Alberta Aero Club devised a series of 30 lectures to be delivered throughout the winter to 90 members already recruited. The club in Vancouver was to be operated by the Air Force Club of British Columbia from a new municipal aerodrome to be built next to the rifle range on Lulu Island.

The ten Moths of the initial order were eventually distributed equally between Toronto, Montreal, Hamilton, Winnipeg and Vancouver Flying Clubs, and a further ten clubs were to be rewarded following settlement of their constitutions and other arrangements.

Western Canada Airways of Winnipeg, recipients of the DH.60 Moth demonstrated in North America by Alan Cobham in 1926, purchased a new DH.60X Seaplane from Stag Lane in 1927. The aircraft, No 434, was despatched from England in October and was registered C-CAIG on 14th December. The new seaplane was to be used for mail delivery and taxi operations but when engaged on a training flight with a new pilot, she stalled and crashed when landing at St Charles only six months later.

When the Midland Club's G-EBLW (189), was returned to Stag Lane in November, it was just for routine overhaul. The Club considered it some kind of record to have flown her for 546 hours of training without an accident, during which time she had carried up and safely down again, eighteen *ab initio* solo pilots.

The Rhodesian Aviation Syndicate of Bulawayo took delivery of their new DH.60X Moth at Stag Lane on 7th November following a demonstration by Bob Reeve. Registered G-EBUO (452), the aircraft was later shipped to Durban, erected there, and flown to Bulawayo where she arrived on 30th December to take up a career in flying training and aerial photography. In August 1930 she was re-registered VP-YAB to the Rhodesian Aviation Company of Bulawayo and crashed there in November 1931.

An aero club was formed in Kenya in July and by November had enrolled 145 members. Their application to the Government of the Colony for assistance in the provision of an aeroplane and a suitable aerodrome was endorsed by the Air Ministry after the Club proposed that it should help in the establishment of a local Air Defence Force,

training pilots, observers, engineers and riggers who would be placed at the disposal of the government in times of national emergency. But it was not until December 1929 that an aeroplane was procured and then due only to the ever philanthropic Sir Charles Wakefield who presented a new DH.60M Moth to what had become the Aero Club of East Africa, based in Nairobi, an aircraft that became part of the Kenya Auxiliary Air Unit in September 1939.

The Aero Club of India, established at the beginning of 1927, encouraged the formation of light aeroplane clubs throughout the sub-continent. A flying club had been formed in Simla on 9th September by 50 members of the Central Legislature; the Delhi Club was constituted on 23rd November followed by others in Calcutta and Allahabad. The choice of equipment was left until after the turn of the New Year when government assistance was expected. Meanwhile, financing their own prospective state flying clubs were the Maharajahs of Patiala and Jodhpur. The exposure of India to the practicalities of the Moth had already been achieved and the potential of the market was not lost on the directors at Stag Lane.

When the order was announced in May 1928, the Indian Aero Club opted for eight Moths with the anticipated new de Havilland engine plus eight spare engines, scheduled for delivery at the end of that year. In preparation, ten Indian pupils were enrolled at the de Havilland School at Stag Lane, some of whom were to be groomed as instructors. Steps were also made to train local engineers, not only for the new clubs, but in advance of a rumour that de Havilland were considering setting up a factory in India similar to the organisation working to capacity in Melbourne. When the aircraft were delivered, mostly in January 1929, one went to Bombay, (VT-AAE, 854), two each to

Leslie Irvin sold his first Moth during a brief interlude of living in his native USA, but on return to England he purchased DH.60X G-EBUW in November 1927. He made history in February 1928 by flying the first light aeroplane in Great Britain to drop a parachutist. In May, Leslie Irvin flew G-EBUW via Berlin to Warsaw to arrange for a new parachute factory to be established there. de Havilland

Karachi (VT-AAA and 'AB, 850 and 851), and Bengal (VT-AAC and 'AD, 852 and 853), and three to Delhi, (VT-AAF, 'AG and 'AH, 855-857). Only one of the batch survived until the war: VT-AAB was impressed as MA941 in 1942, but was struck off charge by November 1944.

In November, de Havilland announced that they were to set up local distribution agencies for Moths within Great Britain. It seemed appropriate that the motor trade should be enrolled and DH.60X G-EBVC (483) was registered to Maude's Motor Mart on 16th November and delivered to the company at its private aerodrome at Stoke Cannon near Exeter in January 1928. The company signified it would be happy to welcome visitors by air. 'We suggest that intending visitors should notify us by telegram or otherwise of the probable time of their arrival and we will then, whenever possible, have our own machine flying over the aerodrome as an indication of its locality.' Already well known in motoring circles, Maude's were to be responsible for sales in Devonshire, Cornwall and Somerset, but the scheme appears not to have met with great success. Flown by Maude's director, E N Hughes on business trips, G-EBVC was sold to Phillips and Powis at Reading in September 1929 and not replaced.

Meanwhile, in Australia, Hereward de Havilland was busily consolidating his firm and in November, accompanied by Captain Scott of the Vacuum Oil Company, flew a Moth on a 4,000 mile tour of New South Wales and Queensland, which saw them operating 'from homestead to homestead'. Following their return to Melbourne, it was

rumoured that seven new owners had been signed up.

Leslie Irvin, who had returned to his native America with Moth G-EBNX in July, was back in England in October and ordered a new DH.60X Moth which was registered G-EBUW (475) in November and delivered in December. On 2nd February 1928, flown by Irvin, G-EBUW became the first light aeroplane in Great Britain, and possibly the world, to drop a parachutist. The jump was made by Mr de Weiss, a company demonstrator, overhead the Irving Air Chute factory at Letchworth, viewed by the workforce, most of whom had never witnessed the practical use of their own product.

The following summer, on 25th May, Leslie Irvin flew G-EBUW to Berlin and from there the following day to Warsaw where, during the course of the next week, he arranged for a new factory to be established to manufacture parachutes for the Polish Air Force. Leaving Warsaw during the morn-

ing of 1st June he flew to stay overnight at Hanover and continued to Letchworth next day, having covered the 880 miles from Warsaw in a total flying time of less than eleven hours.

In order to flight test one of the six prototypes of its new Gipsy I engine, de Havilland took an existing airframe from the School fleet. They selected DH.60X Moth G-EBTD (430) and installed the new powerplant in August. The engine was fitted with a self-starter and enclosed in a modified Cirrus II cowling, a difference not at all obvious to the casual observer. The initial flight trials in September 1927 were conducted in an atmosphere of apparent calm. There were no target dates to be met and nothing to be gained at this stage by creating a lot of publicity. Frank Halford revealed that many different pilots were invited to fly G-EBTD and, within the first 100 hours, to attempt to 'break' the engine, a task which they materially failed to achieve.

At Newcastle on 17th November, G-EBLX was damaged by a fire. Contemporary reports described the aircraft as being in the 'hangar' at the time, probably one of the first occasions when the term was used in preference to 'shed'. The aeroplane trod the well-known path to Stag Lane where the necessary repairs were effected to have her airworthy again by January.

Christian Pitman landed his new Moth G-EBUZ on the playing fields of Eton College on 14th December, to collect his younger brother and return home for the Christmas holidays. This visit by an 'old boy' attracted much attention from other pupils, who believed Christmas had come early. BAE Systems

The promoters of the East Kent Flying Club who had almost abandoned hope in August called a meeting of interested parties in the Town Hall at Hythe on Wednesday 23rd November. They were pleased to announce that an Air Ministry subsidy would be available to the proposed club from 1st January 1928, provided they could finance the purchase and maintenance of their chosen equipment, a DH.60X Moth, and engage and pay staff. The use of accommodation at Lympne Aerodrome suitable for the housing of up to three aircraft had been agreed with the Air Ministry at a nominal rent of £5 per annum.

On 3rd December, Sir Sefton Brancker flew to Lympne in DH.60X Moth G-EBQH with Hubert Broad who took the opportunity to demonstrate the aircraft's recently installed Handley Page slots. The Director General was entertained to lunch by the Club Committee, whose members were considerably more optimistic than previously, but it was not until May 1928 that the Club started operations at Lympne with an ex-de Havilland Company DH.60X demonstrator, G-EBWC (553). As the result of early financial assistance from Earl Beauchamp, Warden of the Cinque Ports and first President of the East Kent Flying Club, the opportunity was taken to relaunch the organisation under what was termed 'the picturesque title' of the Cinque Ports Flying Club.

As an early Christmas present, Christian Pitman took delivery of his DH.60X G-EBUZ (478) on 14th December. Two days later he landed on the playing fields of Eton College, which as an Old Etonian he knew well, to collect his younger brother, before flying home to Bristol for the holidays. The Moth remained in the family only until the following March after which G-EBUZ passed through a number of different hands. Acquired by Lieutenant Iain MacGregor in October 1932, she was flown from Heston to Lucknow, India, the following March. In February 1934 the aeroplane was registered VT-AEE to the promoted Captain MacGregor but was sold locally in May 1935 and cancelled in 1942.

Seasonal goodwill was exhibited late in 1927, when a long overdue contract, many believed, was agreed between the Air Ministry and the de Havilland Company for the purchase of 20 Cirrus II-powered DH.60X Moths. The contract, 806527/27, specified that ten airframes, J9104-J9112, (510-519), were to be supplied less engines, (these to be fitted on receipt by the Royal Air Force at the Home Aircraft Depot, Henlow), with

nine more, J9113-J9121 (520-528), supplied in airworthy condition. The final aircraft (529) was to be a civil example for the Air Council, re-using the personalised registration G-EDCA, for the express use of the Director General of Civil Aviation and replacing his Genet Moth.

At the time the order was placed, the Air Ministry was still debating the merits of providing autoslots for J8818 in her temporary guise as G-EDCA, and as requested by Sir Sefton. They were hesitant due to the understanding that trials with the preferred system of slots on the top mainplanes were still in progress by de Havilland utilising G-EBQH, an aircraft known to have been modified with deeper section spars now standard in all new machines and not applicable to the Director General's mount. The acquisition of the new aircraft solved the problem.

Apart from the flying club aircraft, the three DH.60s purchased for assessment early in 1926 and the six Genet Moths of the CFS Display Team, the 1927 contract was the first substantial military commitment by the Air Ministry. An announcement in *The Times* of 30th December 1927, was headed 'RAF Economy':

'An important step in the direction of economy in equipment and operation has been taken by the Air Ministry in a decision to re-equip No 24 Communication Squadron of the Air Defence of Great Britain with de Havilland Moth light aeroplanes instead of with military machines.

'An order for 20 of the latest Moth types, fitted with 30-80hp Cirrus Mk II air cooled engines, has been given to the de Havilland Company, and delivery will begin in mid-January to Northolt, the aerodrome which serves the Home Defence Headquarters at Uxbridge. At present, Bristol Fighter air-

craft of wartime design are mainly used for the purpose of taking inspecting officers and officials round to the various aerodromes and military centres, and by using Moth two-seater machines, the aeroplane which is the mainstay of the flying clubs and the private owner, the petrol consumption alone will be reduced from about 16 gallons an hour to four gallons without any appreciable loss of speed.

'The economies effected extend beyond mere running costs, for fewer mechanics are needed to handle the machine, its maintenance is much simpler, its folding wings require less hangar space (an important consideration), while its low landing speed and general ease of control mean that if a pilot is forced down anywhere by bad weather, he can get away again from any medium-sized field, without extra assistance.

'The first cost of each machine is only £730, and the spares are correspondingly cheaper, so that from every point of view there is an advantage in using a machine of this class for internal work which does not entail the use of armed aircraft.'

With the exception of the Genet Moths, which were regarded as a special case, DH.60 J8030, languishing at Martlesham Heath, and the 20 DH.60X aircraft now ordered, together proved to be somewhat anomalous as far as the Air Ministry's administrative systems were concerned. J8030 had been built to civil standards and issued with a Certificate of Airworthiness. Spare parts subsequently were ordered as required direct from the manufacturer who was not required to keep a record of modifications applied by the Service and, not unreasonably, refused to update master drawings to incorporate them. The Australians recognised they had a similar problem and wanted the British Air Ministry to provide details of all manufacturers' modifications incorporated since the first deliveries to Australia, a situation quickly resolved by directing the request to the RAAF Liaison Officer based in London. This additional contract for Cirrus Moths hastened the view that formal recognition of the aeroplane as a Service type was essential and a routine was set slowly in motion to regularise the position.

Although contrary to the government's aircraft procurement procedures, led by its earliest discussions with de Havilland over the acquisition of Moths built only to civil standards, the Air Ministry had believed that light aeroplanes like the Moth could be purchased for Service use, categorised similarly to the acquisition of the example quoted in official minutes, Morris cars, providing civil and military specifications remained basically the same. It was not until April 1929 when consideration was given to the purchase of a number of the new Gipsy-engined Moth, and the prospect of fitting the type with Service specification equipment, thus diverging from the specification of the civil model, that the Air Ministry finally decided to adopt their standard policy. Probably the first modification incorporated under the regularised system was the fitting of methyl bromide fire extinguishers. The anomalies of the Genet, DH.60 and DH.60X models would be resolved, officials assured themselves, by attrition or as the aircraft were gradually withdrawn from service.

Reports about the Company which appeared in the aviation press towards the end of the year concentrated on what were seen as four significant facts: Geoffrey de Havilland and Hubert Broad would soon be making a series of high-profile test flights on Moths fitted with Handley Page automatic slots; development of the new Gipsy engine was making good progress; Major Hereward de Havilland was demonstrating a Moth to an Australian church organisation seeking to establish an aerial medical or 'flying doctor' service; and Francis St Barbe was in Canada where it was rumoured a Moth distribution centre was to be set up in either Ottawa or possibly Montreal.

In fact St Barbe was in Toronto and returned from there in December to report to his fellow directors that an ideal business opportunity awaited the company in Canada. Included in the order by the Canadian Department of National Defence for Moths for the Canadian flying clubs, St Barbe had been made aware that two aircraft, DH.60X Moths Nos 456 and 457, flight tested at Stag Lane in November, were for evaluation under Canadian conditions in respect of suitability for RCAF training requirements. The Department was also anxious to confirm de Havilland's arrangements for after-sales service and to discuss future options, especially the choice of engine.

The two evaluation aircraft were allocated civil registrations, G-CYYX (456) and G-CYYW (457), although they only ever displayed the last two letters. G-CYYW was

taken on charge at Ottawa on 13th January 1928 and 'YX at Winnipeg three days later. Both were struck off on 3rd December 1929, although there is no surviving record of what must have been very significant service during their short operational lives.

Ten other aircraft, G-CAKA to G-CAKJ (448-449; 454-455; 458-459; 462-463 and 472-473), qualified for their Cs of A between 1st December 1927 and 9th February 1928. G-CAKA to G-CAKF were taken on charge by the Defence Department in January and February 1928 but, of the last four, G-CAKG, KI and KJ were not taken on charge until 2nd May, and G-CAKH not until 12th June. All were supplied as standard landplanes but, in recognition of their military patronage, each was fitted with parachute seats.

The year 1927, probably, was the most vital in the history of the DH.60 Moth. Both airframe and standard Cirrus powerplant had been honed to a point where reliability was a high expectation; production was efficient, enabling the price to be reduced. Both private ownership and the light aeroplane club movement led mostly with the Moth as standard equipment and supported by governments, was expanding throughout the world; the aeroplane was already in service with national agencies and the military. Plans were in hand for Moths to be assembled and eventually manufactured at more new factories within the Empire and elsewhere. The Gipsy I engine had been successfully flight tested and the Moth had been fitted on an experimental basis with Handley Page Autoslots. To informed observers there was nothing to suggest that the future development and potential was anything but comfortably assured.

The 25 British-based private owners of January 1927 had grown to 70 by December and the six subsidised clubs had increased to 16, permitting some 3,000 members to receive cheap flying instruction. During the year, 150 new Aviator's Certificates had been issued by the Royal Aero Club.

In December, when reflecting on David Kittel's European tour of September and October, the much matured 'Private Flying' section of *Flight* commented:

'The vogue of purely private flying on any regular and considerable scale can be considered as having been definitely established this year.'

Stag Lane Aerodrome during the summer of 1927 in a view looking west. Further development of the permanent factory site and additional blocks of lock-up aero-garages can be seen near the two bungalows at the centre left of the photograph, which acted as a canteen facility for the workforce. de Havilland

JANUARY TO JULY 1928

IF 1927 HAD been the year for consolidation of the flying club movement and private ownership, led by the Moth, then the year 1928 was to be remarkable for the plethora of design innovations applied to the basic aeroplane, introducing new materials, a new production engine, undercarriage and safety devices. The aeroplane was to set records for speed, height, endurance and reliability, and production reached such a peak of efficiency that a further price reduction of almost 11% was applied. And there were always pilots who wanted to travel great distances or at high speed, feats for which the Moth was eminently adaptable and well suited.

Lady Heath, who had shipped her Avian G-EBUG to South Africa in December 1927, promised to tour the country before flying back to Croydon, two feats she duly achieved. Her ladyship flew a short race against three Moths at Baragwanath Aerodrome, Johannesburg, on 28th January, her competitors being Dick Bentley in G-EBSO; Captain W G Bellin of the Johannesburg Club and Major Allister Miller. Lady Heath proved the winner with Bentley and Bellin next and Miller disqualified. Although it was supposed to be fun, the de Havilland people would not have been pleased. The events at Baragwanath were the culmination of an entire week of civic activities in support of the Johannesburg Light Plane Club which included lectures on the subject of 'British Aviation' attended by an audience of 300, a dinner and official discussions on the siting of a new municipal aerodrome. Saturday's flying meeting was the first of its kind ever held in South Africa and attracted the biggest crowd on record for an event in the city when 6,000 cars needed to be parked.

Early in the New Year another significant overseas sale was recorded when Carlos Bleck accepted DH.60X C-PAAA (477), the first aeroplane to carry Portuguese civil markings. Bleck flew the aircraft from Croydon to Lisbon at the end of January and in February continued on to Portuguese Goa and Cairo. In August 1929, C-PAAA was sold to Colonel George Henderson at Brooklands and registered G-AARM, but in November she crashed at Port Meadow, Oxford, and was written off. Bleck's purchase of his first Moth resulted in his later appointment as de Havilland agent in Portugal and a long and rewarding association with the parent company.

The very severe winter weather experienced in England at the turn of the year and resulting in a white Christmas, curtailed club activities and not for the first time Wally Hope was one of a number of Air Taxis' pilots operating from Stag Lane who parachuted supplies of food, organised by the Salvation Army, into villages cut off by deep snow. In appalling conditions five days before Christmas, Sir Sefton Brancker had flown from Martlesham Heath to inspect the Suffolk Aero Club at Hadleigh. In order to offer a Presidential welcome, Lady Bailey flew there to greet him in her Moth, seemingly impervious to the 'heavy snow and bitterly cold wind'.

Such devotion would have been applauded by the American aviation enthusiast Clifford B Harmon's *International League of Aviators* who had already named Lady Bailey 'Lady Champion Aviator of the World' for 1927, in recognition of her practical enthusiasm.

At Woodford, the Lancashire Club Moth G-EBMQ (201) ran away when being taxied on frost-hardened ground and slid into a pond. Although the pilot was unhurt the passenger in a car which rushed to the rescue broke his nose when the vehicle hit a ridge, and was credited as the first Club member ever to receive an injury.

At the close of 1927, the British Air Attaché in Paris, Group Captain Malcolm Christie, made a bid for one of the semi-redundant CFS Genet Moths, said to be lying at Wittering, and on 7th January the Air Ministry's Contracts Technical Supervision Department (CTS) was asked to investigate the permutation of various loading options. These included the carriage of extra fuel to permit long, non-stop cross-country flights into French North Africa and regions of the Sahara whilst carrying one or possibly two specially designed suitcases capable of hold-

Following the blizzard which struck southern England in December 1927, in the New Year, Moths were employed to drop essential supplies to some villages which were still cut off. Organised by the Salvation Army, Wally Hope waits while sachets of dried milk are loaded into sacks which were to be dropped overboard. LNA

ing full Service dress, probably made of aluminium and tailored for easy removal from the front cockpit. The CTS was reminded that the deployment had been agreed to be effective from February, and arrangements needed to be confirmed as soon as possible to permit contracted work to be completed at Stag Lane. RAE Farnborough analysed a number of options to carry additional fuel but was concerned by the disposition and, possibly, weight of baggage and suggested that provision should be considered for slinging suitcases under the fuselage.

The whole requirement changed during the first week of February when it was decided that DH.60X J9121 (528), allocated to 24 Squadron, would be posted to Paris instead and, apart from a standard 25 gallon long-range fuel tank and additional oil capacity, the only other modification would be the

provision of oversize tyres of the type already carried by the Genet Moths. The scheduled date for delivery to Paris was quoted as 6th April when the Air Attaché was due to leave Paris for official duties in North Africa, but official records indicate that delivery was nearer to 16th April. The matter of the carriage of luggage had been resolved by personal discussions held between Group Captain Christie and de Havilland at Stag Lane, much to the surprise of various departments at the Air Ministry. At the end of Christie's tour in March 1930, J9121 returned to England and was allocated to duties with the Andover Communications Flight.

Two pilots who had learned to fly at Stag Lane during the poor summer of 1927 fled the English winter after the turn of the New Year, taking their Moths with them. Mrs Maia Carberry left England by ship on 6th

January bound for Kenya, accompanied by DH.60X Moth G-EBSQ (421), named *Miss Propaganda*. The aircraft was assembled at Mombasa and flown to Nyeri in February. Shortly after, G-EBSQ was joined by the DH.60X G-EBUL (443), owned by local de Havilland agent Commander Lionel Robinson, to take part in Kenya's first flying meeting in Nairobi. In company with a Fokker Universal and a Klemm Daimler, the Moths indulged in a landing competition, air race and flour bombing exercise during the late afternoon before a 'large and representative crowd' but on 12th March, G-EBSQ spun into the ground from low altitude at Ngong Road landing ground near Nairobi. Mrs Carberry was believed to have been giving instruction to her passenger, but was seen to jump out of the aeroplane before it hit the ground. She was killed instantly and Dudley Cowie died in the crash.

On 10th January, Douglas Mill sailed for home with DH.60X No 500 stowed as cargo. The ship arrived in New Zealand on 17th February when the Moth was registered G-NZAT to Mill's company, Air Survey and Transport Co Ltd at Hobsonville where she made her first flight on 11th March. During his time in England, Douglas Mill had not only acquired 'A' and 'B' pilot's licences, but had also qualified for his Ground Engineer's Certificate. As distributing agent for de Havilland products in New Zealand, his company was preparing to maintain a fleet of taxi Moths and to open a flying school in addition to its recognised role in air survey work for which G-NZAT had been fitted with camera equipment at Stag Lane. However, re-registered ZK-AAB in January 1929, the aeroplane was sold to Hawkes Bay Aero Club the same month, the first operational flying club in New Zealand and established without government support. She survived several major accidents until she failed a technical inspection in 1937 and was reduced to spares early the following year.

One member new to the London Club, Hugh Bergel, recalled that, although underpowered, the Cirrus I Moth, when compared with those with bigger engines that came later, was by far the nicest to fly:

Prior to their Christening with a bottle of local produce, already in position to be shattered on the propeller hub, the two DH.60X Moths delivered to the Royal Aero Club of Spain in the spring of 1928 were blessed by the Bishop of Madrid. BAE Systems

When Douglas Mill sailed for home in January 1928, to become the de Havilland Agent in New Zealand, he took with him DH.60X Moth No 500 which was registered G-NZAT to his company, Air Survey and Transport Co Ltd. The aircraft was later sold to Hawkes Bay Aero Club.
Auckland Weekly News

'Stag Lane was very small and in wet weather dual instruction could not be given as those early Moths could not get off the sodden ground. The aircraft had a simple and bouncy undercarriage which quickly reacted to clumsy landings so that the Club members took pride in the widely accepted saying that anyone who could land a Moth at Stag Lane could land any aeroplane, anywhere!'

In spite of some earlier reservations over the power of the Cirrus engine, the Australian Defence Department announced on 25th January that the DH.60X Moth had been selected as the new basic training machine for the Royal Australian Air Force in preference to the more expensive Avro 504N. The initial contract for 12 aircraft was later increased to 20, all to be delivered from Stag Lane, via Melbourne, at a unit cost of £551.10s each, together with sufficient technical data and drawings to enable a further 14 aircraft to be built in Australia at a later date. The Australian Company's tender for this work was accepted at the end of 1928 and the de Havilland staff in Melbourne was increased to 25 as a consequence.

The 20 aeroplanes of the first contract were supplied in two batches, Nos 540-546 and 549-551 (RAAF serials A7-3 to A7-12 and A7-14, but not in sequence) and 596-603 and 614, (A7-13 and A7-15 to A7-22, but not in sequence).

All the aircraft in the first batch qualified for their Certificates of Airworthiness in England prior to shipment to Melbourne for erection and delivery to the RAAF. None of the aircraft in the second batch qualified in England with the exception of Nos 613 (A7-9) and 614 (A7-13), the latter supplied as a Moth Seaplane.

There is reason to suspect that, at a late stage in production, a decision was made to have all RAAF Moths fitted with slots. Those in the first batch were modified by mid-April with some of the second batch ready from mid-May. When installed, the system increased the tare weight by about 23 lb.

The new Moths were distributed to units at Point Cook, Richmond and Laverton in 1928 and 1929, and most were involved in accidents typical of those sustained at training establishments. A7-15 (596) was written off when it crashed into a hill in December 1928, the same month it was delivered to 3 Squadron at Richmond. Six aircraft were written off the following year, two in 1930 and a further two in 1931.

Cirrus I Moth S-AABN of the Aero Materiel Flying School fitted with skis, receiving fuel pumped from cans on the back of the wagon. Note the pennant attached to the starboard rear interplane strut, possibly signifying a pilot under instruction.
Aero Materiel A-B

Between 1930 and 1932, nine surviving aircraft, all of which had been converted at the earliest opportunity to accept the Gipsy I engine and a split undercarriage, were transferred onto the civil register against government ownership and, of these, four were impressed back into RAAF service in 1940 when each was allocated a new serial: 540/A7-85 (A7-14); 597/A7-101 (A7-16); 549/A7-83 (A7-17) and 613/A7-82 (A7-9). This latter aircraft, registered VH-UAO before and after the war, spent more than 46 years in the private ownership of the Ayling family in Western Australia before sale to a new owner at Bankstown in January 2004, when she was air delivered the 2,000 miles in a flight time of 26 hours. The Seaplane A7-13 (614) was converted to a landplane in 1932 and became VH-UHU with the Civil Aviation Branch for loan to the Tasmanian Aero Club. She retained that identity throughout the war until the letters were cancelled in 1951. The aircraft was acquired by Sydney Technical College from the estate of the last registered owner, H C Mark, and in 1984 she was rebuilt to static condition for display in the city's Powerhouse Museum, painted in the pre-war blue and silver colours of her Tasmanian operators.

Captain Carl Florman of de Havilland's Swedish agent, Aero Materiel AB, ordered three DH.60X Moths for delivery to their new flying school which was opening in February. The AMA School was the first civilian flying training establishment in the country. Based in Stockholm, it was challenged to train pupils to fly on an aircraft fitted with a conventional wheeled undercarriage, floats, or for the entire winter, a ski system designed by them. The three Moths, S-AABM, 'BN and 'BO (480-482), were delivered by sea early in January and the first was towed through the city centre and put on display for three weeks in the entrance hall of the Nordiska Kompaniet warehouse.

On 29th January, all three aircraft made their first public appearance at the Royal Swedish Aero Club's Display held on the frozen surface of Lake Brumsviken, a meeting attended by the Crown Prince of Sweden, members of the Royal Family and 40,000 spectators. Three days later, in the presence of the Chief of the Air Force, senior staff officers and members of the government, the AMA School was declared open. During its first seven weeks of operation, the School trained 22 pilots to licence standard, involving 4,000 flights on skis from the surface of the frozen lake.

In the sunshine of South Africa the Durban Light Aeroplane Club, which was founded in February 1927, finally took delivery of its first aeroplane after DH.60X Moth G-UAAI (479) was registered to them on 2nd February. Funds for purchase of the aeroplane had been raised as the result of much local initiative including the dropping of 10,000 leaflets offering five free flights. The drop had been completed on a windy day and the papers were scattered over a distance of 15 miles. Durban Aerodrome was also the base for African Aerial Travels, a company specialising in commercial passenger work. Their first DH.60X Moth, G-UAAE (439) registered on 2nd November 1927, crashed at Pomeroy on the day after Christmas and G-UAAG (442), crashed at Bloemfontein on 7th February, just as the local club was starting operations. Such a record appears to have had no lasting effects as the club remained loyal to the Moth and were regular customers as new models appeared over the years.

The two major developments to which de Havilland committed themselves during the winter of 1927/1928 were flight trials and demonstrations of Moths fitted with Handley Page Automatic Slots and their own Gipsy I engine. The two works' aircraft, DH.60X prototype G-EBQH (276) and DH.60X G-EBTD (430), were both to create much excitement but not always in a manner the Company had intended. Theirs was to be a continuing story. Meanwhile, in

January the Design Office was taking a serious interest in a DH.60X with a 'metal body'.

Following his return from Canada in December 1927, St Barbe wasted no time in convincing the Company of the importance of an official presence in North America. Bob Loader, his lieutenant in the Business Office, was given the responsibility of setting up another 'overseas branch', and Toronto was chosen to be the centre of operations. Such was the urgency of the mission that Loader arrived in the city during the first week of February 1928, in the middle of the winter, tasked with establishing a facility in which to erect imported aeroplanes and a field from which to fly them. Fortune being what it is, the old de Lesseps Field near Mount Dennis was suggested and, when approached, owner Frank Trethewey admitted to being a member of the newly formed Toronto Flying Club. Fred Hotson wrote in his history of the Canadian Company:

'An old produce shed, also on the Trethewey property, would shortly become available. It had a spur line off the Canadian National Railway and was only a short distance from the flying field … Bob Loader must have been very pleased with the day's work. He had acquired not only a flying field, but a works shed, a business manager (recruited from Trethewey's staff) and an order for another Moth placed on behalf of Brett-Trethewey Mines.'

Loader set up a tiny office in Bay Street, Toronto, while Arthur Robins arrived from Stag Lane at the beginning of March to convert the old wooden canning shed into an aeroplane factory and to oversee construction of a new hangar at the airfield. A corporate structure was arranged by the Company's retained lawyer, William Zimmerman, effective from 5th April 1928, but when the name *The de Havilland Aircraft of Canada* was first painted in large letters on the railway side of Robins' erecting shop, the sign writer stood back to discover he had created a new legend spelled *'de Haviland'*.

Bob Loader was replaced at Stag Lane by W T W Ballantyne who transferred from the Drawing Office, and he was joined by Ronnie Malcolm, owner of DH.60 G-EBNO. Both were officers in the RAF Reserve. In the factory, Bert Groombridge, whose re-organisation of production was largely responsible for the increased manufacturing efficiencies leading to price reductions, was promoted to Production Manager and Harry Povey became Chief Inspector.

G-EBTD, which had been engaged on Gipsy engine flight trials from September 1927, by late January and into February, was being flown at a constant take-off weight of 1,200 lb with an experimental induction system, centrally mounted Zenith carburettor similar to that fitted to the Puma engine, and variations of DH5166 and Leitner-Watts Z64 propellers. A series of fuel consumption tests beginning on 3rd February concluded that the engine burned a little more than the Cirrus II, about 4.375 gallons per hour at a cruising speed of 76mph, rising to 7.5gph 'all-out' at about 90mph. It was mostly the consumption that caused the capacity of the main fuel tank to be increased to 19 gallons, a figure which could be augmented by a number of standard options for auxiliary tanks from 10 to 25 gallons capacity, located within the fuselage.

Obviously nervous about the threat posed by the de Havilland engine and the future prospects for their own Cirrus range, ADC Aircraft Ltd began an advertising campaign in February to remind the world that it was their original Cirrus I engine which had made possible the current light aeroplane. They even published an attractively illustrated booklet telling the story of the Cirrus engine and detailing the pioneering part it had played 'in the commencement and development of private flying, its wide adoption today and the great flights in which it functioned so successfully'.

The de Havilland Company, not wishing to alienate a still important business partner, immediately responded. Presented under the heading 'One a Day', the text read, in part:
'Without referring to the many successes and achievements of the Cirrus-engined Moth during the past three years, and avoiding the use of extravagant adjectives such as supreme, ideal, premier *or* best, *we respectfully invite an appreciation of the significance which lies behind a demand justifying this production rate.'*

The illustration that took up the majority of the space was finished in the style of an etching and featured a swarm of hand drawn Moths flying over what was supposed to be a working day scene at Stag Lane Aerodrome. Unlike most advertisements commissioned by the Company, this example was outstanding only because the artwork was so poor. The artist had compounded his felony by adding the Company name and address to his layout by badly hand drafting the information in which he managed to commit the classic sins of spelling 'Staglane' as a single word and 'Edgeware' with three 'e's.

In September 1927, ADC Aircraft had purchased DH.60X Moth G-EBUF (441) and engaged Neville Stack to fly her as company test pilot. The aeroplane attended flying meetings in the capacity of 'ADC Service Machine' but she was also a valuable PR tool and served the company well for many years as a flying test-bed for continued engine developments.

DH.60X Moth G-EBQH had been fitted with Handley Page automatic slots in November 1927 and the apparatus was installed on G-EBTD at the beginning of March following conclusion of the Gipsy engine fuel consumption test programme. The leading edges of the outer five-eighths

The correctly sign-written wooden hangar erected at Mount Dennis, Toronto, for assembly of dismantled Moths received in crates from Stag Lane. The windsock is inscribed 'MOTH'. The entire structure was later moved to the new aerodrome established at what was to be known as Downsview. LNA

The experimental Mk I 'split type' undercarriage fitted to G-EBTD in March 1928, before the conduct of trials with Handley Page Autoslots and a disastrous demonstration in front of the press. *Flight*

DH.60X G-EBQH following repairs after she was damaged at Stag Lane when Hubert Broad hit a hedge during 'turn-back' demonstrations. Neither the split-type undercarriage nor the tailwheel were replaced and standard top mainplanes, less ailerons, were fitted. *Flight*

of the top mainplanes were notched to allow the wooden 'slats' which, when hinged open, created the 'slot' to maintain an otherwise undisturbed aerofoil section when they were at rest. In flight, as the speed of the machine decreased and the angle of incidence of the wing increased, the greater suction on the top surface forced the hinged slat forward or 'open'. Initially, the slats could not be locked in either the open or closed positions but during trials, any intermediate disposition could be measured against the scale on a quadrant fitted to the under-surface of the leading edge on the starboard upper mainplane.

A disadvantage of the early installations was the need to modify the leading edge of the wing. Later, the slats themselves were developed to provide a thin, rigid structure which sat as flush with the top surface of a standard wing as was physically possible. This eliminated the need for specially adapted wings and created the market for straightforward, retrospective installations.

At the end of January and in preparation for a series of slat trials, G-EBQH had been prepared with ailerons fitted to the top wings interconnected with those on the lower planes and the slots extended in length inboard and fitted with longer hinged links. Additionally, the aircraft acquired an experimental undercarriage, known as the Mk I 'split' type, together with a tailwheel. The new alighting gear was considered essential to the trials and involved a track widened by 9in and possessing an ability to withstand an increase of 30% in landing shock loads. Early references to the new Mk I termed it 'split axle chassis independent type', or 'split undercarriage pylon type', but for everyday use it became known simply as the 'split undercarriage'. At the attachment points, the wooden fuselage was also strengthened. The original 'straight axle' could prove to be a hazard when landing, taking-off or even taxying in long grass, when it was not unknown for vegetation to wrap itself around the axle rod and retard progress, in extreme cases causing the aircraft to tip onto her nose or even flip over.

While wings modified to take slots were being prepared for G-EBTD, a Mk I split undercarriage was fitted together with a tail-skid which could be steered by interaction with an 'experimental' rudder, cut away at the bottom leading edge and resulting in a slightly reduced surface area.

Hubert Broad reported that the additional ailerons made little difference and that the new slot offered only a slight improvement in lateral stability in a stall. He believed the greatest benefits had been achieved by the slight reduction in rudder area and adjustment of the centre of gravity. Demonstrating the effectiveness of the slotted wing when flying G-EBQH at Stag Lane on 21st February, on several occasions after take-off Broad simulated an engine failure at 50ft and deliberately turned back towards the aerodrome. On one flight, momentarily unsighted by the lower planes, the aircraft collided with a hedge causing considerable damage and putting the pilot into hospital for a week. Everybody was pleased when Broad was considered sufficiently recovered

in April to set more world records with the Company's new bomber prototype, the DH.65 Hound.

In March 1928, it was agreed that DH.60 Moth J8030, lying damaged at Martlesham Heath following an undisclosed accident in which she had most likely turned over on the ground, should be repaired on-site in preference to sending her to Stag Lane. The requisition for spare parts placed on de Havilland included a port upper mainplane, interplane strut, fuel tank, rudder and propeller. The Company quoted a total of £60.2s.10d for the parts plus £9 to deliver them to Suffolk. At the same time, the Air Ministry decided that pending conclusions drawn from de Havilland's trials with slots, as an old aeroplane, J8030 should be refurbished, fitted with slots and possibly ailerons on the upper wings, then offered as an experimental machine in support of the

The state of the aerodrome surface can only be imagined if the condition of the hangar floor at Stag Lane in February 1928 is an indicator. To be able to house 12 aeroplanes (of identical type) in such a confined space is testament to the practicality of a folding wing design. Note the crumpled state of the bottom of the rudder at extreme left! de Havilland

slot trials' programme rather than purchasing an entirely new aeroplane for the purpose. Later it was realised that with her early standard of mainplanes, she was unable to accept the slot arrangements currently under investigation, and for the moment, the requirement was dropped. Faced with similar problems amongst civil Moths, at a future date de Havilland devised a range of modification kits suitable for all types of DH.60 mainplanes.

A pre-planned announcement from Stag Lane was published just two days after Broad's landing accident. The Company advised that the price of a DH.60X Landplane, complete with 84hp Cirrus engine and full equipment, painted any colour, registered and with a Certificate of Airworthiness, had been reduced to £650. The cost of a fully-equipped Seaplane, a type now much in demand, was also reduced, to £980.

'We are pleased to be able to announce that, due to the effect of quantity production, meeting a growing demand now reaching one machine a day, the manufacturing costs of the Moth have been reduced and we are able now to revise the price of all models. The steadily increasing output has made possible the gradual organisation of a specially equipped production plant which is directly responsible for a very high standard of workmanship and finish. Three years of worldwide use, covering over two million miles of flying, are reflected in the development of every feature of its design and in the carefully balanced characteristics of the ubiquitous Moth.'

While G-EBQH was undergoing repair, during which she lost her split undercarriage and tailwheel, G-EBTD took on the role of autoslot triallist. Clem Pike flew her on 9th March and with the slats 'screwed down' recorded times and speeds for a stalled descent between 3,000ft and 1,000ft. With an ASI reading of 42mph and occasionally 38mph, the descent time for each 1,000ft graduation was measured at exactly 100 seconds, an equivalent vertical speed of 68mph. An identical set of tests was made three days later with the slats free to operate, but in conditions described as 'cloudy and bumpy'. In two out of three tests, the results indicated the descent time was five or six seconds quicker!

Whilst debating the merits of the slot or otherwise, the Air Ministry was advised by the RAE that '...the fitting of slots would detract from the value of these aircraft as training machines', but suggested that one aircraft from the contract placed in December 1927 should be fitted with slots 'to obtain the opinion of the Services'. Being specific, it was suggested that the DH.60X scheduled for Sir Sefton Brancker, who had requested slots be fitted, would make the perfect military trials aircraft.

DH.60X G-EBSF (415) had been registered in the name of Captain Geoffrey de Havilland at Stag Lane in July 1927 and used as a Company trials and demonstration machine. In November 1927, the aeroplane had been flown to investigate the circumstances under which the main petrol tank became pressurised. At an indicated speed of 80mph, fuel in a U-tube mounted in the front cockpit, connected to the main tank, suddenly blew out. The phenomenon remained under scrutiny at least until April 1929. Lady Mary Bailey had proved to be a remarkable asset for de Havilland publicity, a fact not lost on the Company when she announced her intention to fly a Moth to South Africa On 6th March 1928, G-EBSF was registered in her name while on the same day, ownership of her old Moth, G-EBPU (373), was listed to Geoffrey de Havilland.

Flown mostly by 'The Captain', both G-EBPU and G-EBSF were subjected to rigorous fuel consumption tests during the first week of March. The final test on 7th March established that, with 44 gallons of petrol on board, G-EBSF would cruise at 79mph, burning 4.3 gallons per hour. Two days later, on Friday 9th March, Mary Bailey took off from Stag Lane for Croydon Airport, outward bound for Cape Town, whilst all around the country, flying clubs were hit by another band of foul spring weather which included heavy showers of snow.

The journey of G-EBSF through Europe was occasionally delayed by bad weather but Lady Bailey reached Malta on 16th and the following day was escorted for a time towards the north coast of Africa by a trio of RAF seaplanes. Because her journey was the longest solo flight yet attempted by a woman, there was great public interest and concern for Lady Bailey's safety. The Editor of the *de Havilland Gazette* was anxious to provide his readers with all the facts as they became available:

'Lady Bailey reached the African coast at a point between Khoms and Tripoli, and spent the night at Sirte. On the 19th she arrived at Benghazi and flew to Cairo on the following day. Here she was delayed for five days by the British Residency, who refused permission for her to cross the Sudan alone.

'The Gordian knot was happily cut by The Johannesburg Star. At that time Lieutenant R R Bentley was flying north with his new wife in his Moth G-EBSO which he flew from London to Cape Town in 1927. The Star telegraphed to him asking if he would escort Lady Bailey over the dangerous area. This he agreed to do, and Lady Bailey eventually left Heliopolis Aerodrome on 27th March and, flying via Luxor, Wadi Halfa, and Atbara, reached Khartoum on 1st April. Here she met Lieutenant Bentley, who escorted her to Nimule, and then she continued alone.

'Lady Bailey reached Tabora on 9th April where she met with an unfortunate accident in landing, happily unattended by any personal injuries, although her machine was damaged to such an extent that, in the absence of certain essential spares, repairs were impossible.

'She was flying from Kisumu to Tabora with no map of this stage. She flew to Nzega, but found it impossible to land, so she turned back to Shinyanga, landed to enquire the route, and then flew on to Tabora in Tanganyika. Owing to this delay,

Lady Bailey in her familiar check-pattern
suit taking a quizzical look into the cockpit
of G-EBSF, attended by RAF officers and
men, during a stop in Cairo in March 1928
while on her way to Cape Town.
DH Moth Club Archive

Lady Bailey in her familiar check-pattern
suit taking a quizzical look into the cockpit
of G-EBSF, attended by RAF officers and
men, during a stop in Cairo in March 1928
while on her way to Cape Town.
DH Moth Club Archive

*Tabora was not reached until the hottest
part of the day, and the air was consequently thin and surging; added to this, the
aerodrome on which Lady Bailey had to
land is 4,000ft above sea level. She struck an
air pocket near the ground and the machine
made a heavy landing in which the undercarriage was considerably damaged.*

*'Undaunted by this misfortune, Lady
Bailey at once cabled to her husband in
Cape Town. Sir Abe Bailey arranged to purchase another Moth from Mr J H Veasey, the
de Havilland Agent at Johannesburg, and
this machine was immediately despatched
to Roberts Heights, Pretoria, the South
African Air Force Depot, where it was overhauled and tested. This Moth left Pretoria
on 16th April, piloted by Major Meintjes of
the SAAF, and reached Broken Hill, Northern Rhodesia, on the same day, having covered the distance non-stop in eleven hours.
On 18th April the machine was delivered to
Lady Bailey at Tabora, just nine days after
the accident.'*

Having delivered the replacement (unidentified) Moth from South Africa, a very complicated business situation appears to have
developed. The de Havilland Company
arranged that a DH.60X Moth based in
Nairobi, Kenya, owned by W R Carr, G-EBTG
(469), should be acquired by the local
agent, Commander Lionel Robinson, and
sold to Lady Bailey, taking the newly-arrived
aircraft in exchange. As part of the deal, the
engine from G-EBSF was transferred to
G-EBTG and the wrecked airframe of
G-EBSF was subsequently sent by railway to
Pretoria, presented to the Johannesburg
Light Plane Club and rebuilt by their members to fly again later in the year.

*'On 20th April Lady Bailey left Tabora in
her new Moth G-EBTG. At Broken Hill she
was forced to remain for a few days, as she
had unfortunately contracted influenza,
but even this ailment was not sufficient to
delay her progress long, for she reached
Bulawayo on 24th April. Two days later,
having missed certain landmarks, she had
to land at Nylstroom for petrol, and spent
the night at Warm Baths in the Transvaal.
When she took off from this aerodrome, her
dexterity in avoiding ant-heaps was much
admired. She was escorted from Warm
Baths by nine South African Air Force
machines and was received at Pretoria by
a large gathering of Air Force officers and
civilians. Later in the day her flight was
resumed for Johannesburg. She was again
escorted, this time by six machines. At noon*

*on 28th April, Lady Bailey set out again
and, flying by Beaufort West, arrived at
Cape Town on 30th April.'*

Dick Bentley, who had escorted Lady Bailey's G-EBSF across the Sudan, continued on
to London with his wife and landed at Croydon on 12th May. The de Havilland publicity
machine failed to acknowledge that between
Bulawayo and Khartoum, and from Tunis to
Naples, Bentley's DH.60X Moth G-EBSO had
also provided escort for Lady Heath's Avian
G-EBUG, returning to England after a successful tour of South Africa. He surprised
everybody at Stag Lane by flying in unexpectedly after formalities at Croydon, then
left for a holiday in Norfolk. During a lecture
to the Royal Aeronautical Society in London
on 1st June, Bentley was asked whether he
would change any details of the Moth's construction. He replied that his wife had found
the front seat to be very uncomfortable and
expressed surprise that the wooden fuselage
was not fabric covered prior to painting.
During the hottest parts of his flight the top
layer of the high quality aviation 3-ply used
to construct the fuselage sides, had developed a series of unsightly cracks.

Having achieved the distinction of being
the first woman to fly solo the 8,000 miles
from London to Cape Town, Mary Bailey left
on the return journey to England on the
same day that Dick Bentley arrived at Croydon but, during a forced landing at
Humansdorp, G-EBTG sustained damage
which caused a postponement of the trip
until later in the year.

Wally Hope was commissioned to deliver
DH.60X Moth I-BUBI (559) to Italy on 18th
March, taking with him the new owner, Italian racing driver and motor manufacturer
Count Franco Mazzotti. According to
reports published in the newspapers at the
end of the month, close to 1st April, when
crossing the Alps, Hope was forced to land
the aircraft at 8,000ft, the Moth settling into

a snowdrift, cushioned by the bottom
wings. The two crew were rescued by Alpine
guides who had witnessed the landing,
using ropes, and were taken off the mountain to an overnight shelter.

The following morning, a team of men
dug out the undamaged aircraft and, with
the aid of sledges, hauled her to a plateau at
about 5,000ft where the main wheels were
dropped into boxes fitted with skis. Flying
solo, Hope took off over a precipice when
the temporary undercarriage structure fell
away, allowing him to continue on his journey to Turin. Curiously, Hope's logbook
indicates the delivery was made to Milan,
operating via Le Bourget, Lyons and Nice,
and there is no mention of a forced landing.

On 19th March, the de Havilland Company invited the aviation press to Stag Lane
to witness a demonstration of the effectiveness of the Handley Page 'Autoslot' system
as a means of improving slow-speed handling, and therefore, of increasing safety,
especially for inexperienced pilots. G-EBTD
was flown by Captain de Havilland who
declared his intention to land the aeroplane
from a number of unusual attitudes, including an intentional stall at about 200ft. The
weather was cold and miserable and with
limited visibility, but the demonstration
went ahead although the outcome was not
entirely as planned. Later, Captain de Havilland was pleased for the opportunity to
describe what had happened:

*'In the first test the machine was taken
up to 1,000ft. and the engine shut off on a
turn, I deliberately pulling the stick back in
an attempt to spin. It was found that nothing worse than a steep spiral resulted, well
above the minimum flying speed.*

*'After this the machine was 'landed 10ft
up', a common fault with pupils. On this
occasion it merely 'pancaked' down without losing lateral balance, the experimental undercarriage effectively absorbing the
impact.*

The standard instrument panel of a wooden DH.60 Moth: left to right, oil pressure; air speed indicator with 'MOTH' inscription; aneroid (height indicator); engine speed indicator (tachometer). A curved, bubble-type turn indicator is at the top of the panel. Note the pedestal mounted compass on the floor and in the shadows, a glimpse of the non-parallel motion rudder bar. The externally mounted ignition switches can just be seen at top right; the throttle lever and part of the trimmer quadrant are visible on the port side frame. BAE Systems

G-EBTD with the first flight-test Gipsy I engine installed under Cirrus type cowlings, Handley Page Autoslots which retract into recesses notched into the leading edges of the upper mainplanes, and a split-type undercarriage. Note the indicating quadrant fitted to the starboard slat mechanism for the benefit of the flight-test observer. *The Aeroplane*

'Another form of bad landing was demonstrated by flattening out too late and gliding into the ground. The machine then bounced upwards to a height of between 15ft and 20ft, hovered in the air, and then 'pancaked' down satisfactorily as in the previous test.

'The third test, a very drastic manoeuvre, and one which few pilots would care to attempt, was deliberately to stall the machine at 200ft, allowing it to sink right down to the ground with the stick full back.

'This test, which had also been carried out several times previously, although demonstrating satisfactorily the feasibility

Below left: **The moment of impact. Through the murk of the March day, G-EBTD can be seen stalling heavily into the ground, losing the undercarriage and breaking the fuselage adjacent to the rear cockpit.** BAE Systems

Below right: **The sorry sight of G-EBTD after the accident which was analysed and freely discussed, providing more of a practical demonstration of safety than had been intended.** *The Aeroplane*

DH.60X Seaplane G-CATH was sold to Laurentide Air Services in Canada in May 1928 and named 'Alice' in a ceremony held at Rochester, where the aircraft was flight-tested on her Short floats. Short Bros

of such a manoeuvre, ended on this particular occasion somewhat unfortunately. In order to lighten the machine as far as possible some odd load had been removed from the locker behind the pilot's seat, and this reduced the vertical impact. This had the tendency to move the centre of gravity farther forward, thereby increasing the longitudinal stability. With the increase of stability the machine, so to speak, rebelled against the stalled condition, and tried to put its nose down to recover flying speed. This was checked almost as soon as begun by the elevators being 'up' and although the average condition of the descent was the same, 40mph forward and 7mph vertically, the flight path consisted of a series of gentle undulations accompanied by slight oscillations about the mean.

'Unfortunately it so happened that impact with the ground occurred when the nose had dipped, the speed having temporarily increased.

'The extra load due to this slight increase of speed could, no doubt, have been supported by the undercarriage without any damage to the structure, but when combined with a steeper flight path the 40mph component is not so readily turned into a horizontal run, consequently a greater shock has to be taken on the structure. In this particular case it is interesting to note that it was not the undercarriage, but a cross member in the fuselage which succumbed, with the result that a considerable amount of damage was caused.

'An examination of the machine afterwards showed that the occupants of both the pilot's and passenger's cockpit would be unharmed under such conditions, and on this occasion I was not thrown forward, as usually happens in an accident.'

In addition to the cost of the Autoslot hardware, the Handley Page Company was entitled to a royalty on every installation. This fee, about £35, was added to the price of the aeroplane on delivery and, as a result, Autoslots always remained an optional extra on the de Havilland price lists. The term 'Slotted Moth' was applied by some as frequently as any other description at the time although 'Sloth' was to be a name invented by an aviation correspondent who further suggested that a slotted Moth with the new split undercarriage might be termed a 'Sploth'. In almost every accident report published after the Autoslot became a practical proposition, inspectors would highlight whether the subject aircraft was fitted with slots or not.

The first privately-owned Moth with 'slots' was G-EBWY (584), a DH.60X registered to Sir Nigel Norman in March and qualifying for her C of A on 5th April. On the following day, Good Friday, G-EBWY was one of 13 Moths which assembled at Lympne in support of the first flying meeting of the 1928 British season. It was really a glorified fund-raising event for the Cinque Ports Club with all the aeroplanes and 'B' licensed pilots offered free of charge. The club dispensed fuel and oil and collected the proceeds from about 350 successful five shilling joyrides. Norman Jones arrived in his new maroon and yellow DH.60X Moth G-EBWI (557), named *The Camberwell Beauty*, the trademark of Samuel Jones and Company, the purveyors of specialist *Butterfly Brand* stationery items. Hubert Broad stunted the company demonstrator and soon to be resident Moth G-EBWC, and Squadron Leader Tom England was there with the Handley Page slotted Moth G-EBWS (558), on loan from de Havilland and recently fitted with a split undercarriage. It was a rousing start to another 'open season'. One enthusiastic young visitor to arrive by air was the 18-year-old Geoffrey de Havilland Jnr who flew his father to Lympne from Stag Lane in Lady Bailey's old Moth, G-EBPU.

Many of the visitors to Lympne moved on to Hadleigh on Easter Sunday where the Suffolk Aeroplane Club had organised a varied two-day programme of racing, aerobatics and joyriding. Moths predominated, and, as anticipated, so many had flown up from Lympne that the Air Ministry had made special arrangements to assist their safe passage across the Thames Estuary.

Travelling somewhat further was Lieutenant Commander Henry MacDonald who purchased DH.60X Moth G-EBVX (538) in January. Converted to single-seat configuration and with long-range tanks fitted, the air-

craft was delivered on 22nd March and with only eight hours solo time logged at the de Havilland School, on 2nd April MacDonald set off for India. After a series of adventures and misfortunes, G-EBVX arrived in Baghdad on 28th April only for her pilot to be advised that the monsoon season was about to break. Heeding good advice not to go on, MacDonald arranged for Imperial Airways to overhaul both airframe and engine and on 3rd May he left on the return journey to Stag Lane. Flying over the Bay of Sollum, the engine failed, but a successful forced landing was made on a rough beach. While working on repairs, MacDonald persuaded some local Arabs to deliver a message to the nearest Italian outpost. When attempting to take off, the undercarriage collided with a boulder and the aeroplane was wrecked, but an Italian armoured car arrived at the crucial moment, rescued MacDonald, and helped him on his way to Egypt and a ship to England.

A batch of 12 identical DH.60X Seaplanes was supplied to the Canadian Department of Defence between April and July 1928, and allocated civil registration letters G-CYYH to G-CYYS (485-496 but not in sequence). Nos 485-490 qualified for Cs of A in England between 28th February and 10th March and the remainder between 4th and 18th April. G-CYYR (486), was issued with her C of A at Rochester on 2nd March, but three days earlier, on Leap Year Day, she had been flown with what was described as a 'Short patent propeller', manufactured against drawing CR1718/2. This was a big metal propeller of 6ft 9in diameter which, at cruising revolutions of 1,800rpm, propelled the seaplane at 85mph. Full throttle tests at 1,000ft coaxed the speed up to 100mph at 2,080rpm, but the propeller option appears not to have been taken up by Canada or any other seaplane operator. Induction of the fleet into Canadian military service occurred slowly and sporadically between late April and 7th

Four of 20 DH.60 Cirrus II Moths which
were ordered by the Air Ministry in 1927.
J9113, nearest the camera, was last
reported with No 43 (F) Squadron at
Tangmere in May 1931. de Havilland

July when the last five machines finally were taken on charge.

Of this batch of twelve, five aircraft were written off after accidents which occurred before the end of 1929 and two were converted for use by the military as instructional airframes between 1935 and 1937, after which they were scrapped. The remainder (485, 486, 488, 490 and 494) were all converted to accept the Cirrus III engine and at least three were later rebuilt with metal fuselages. With the exception of G-CYYM (494), which was sold to the de Havilland Company in 1931 and re-registered CF-APM for a private owner, all the others were transferred to Canadian flying clubs and had been written off before the summer of 1940.

DH.60X G-EBWV (566) was retained by de Havilland for test work at Stag Lane and was scheduled to make history in July. No 561 was shipped to Major Shirley Kingsley, the Company agent in Argentina, and was operated by Cia Aerofotos until at least 1937. Others in the same batch, 560, 562-565 and 567-582, were all shipped to de Havilland's Canadian assembly plant at Mount Dennis. With the exception of G-CAJU (560), which was registered to de Havilland Aircraft of Canada for subsequent presentation by Sir Charles Wakefield to Toronto Flying Club, all others were supplied against another order from the Department of National Defence for allocation to the subsidised flying clubs at Calgary, Edmonton, Granby, Halifax, Hamilton, London, Montreal, Moose Jaw, Ottawa, Regina, Saskatoon, Toronto, Vancouver and Winnipeg. Registered almost sequentially G-CAKK to G-CAKZ and G-CALA to G-CALD, the exceptions were that, officially, 576 became G-CALD and 582 was registered G-CAKX, which was probably a mistake.

G-CALC (581) was exhibited at the Montreal Aero Show held in the Craig Street Drill Hall during the second week of July before she was delivered to the London Flying Club in Ontario. None of the batch survived beyond 1937, all but one falling victim to accident damage. Although she was awaiting repairs at the time, G-CAKZ (578) was destroyed in a hangar fire in Ottawa in November 1928.

Bob Loader had hardly signed the lease on the assembly building at Mount Dennis, allowing Arthur Robins time to allocate floor space, when crated aircraft were delivered from Stag Lane. The first Moth to be assembled, G-CAJU (560), was displayed for publicity purposes on Good Friday at their hangar at Weston, as de Lesseps Field became known, and was flown by the company's newly-engaged test pilot, Leigh Capreol, on 18th April. Also on 18th April, Capreol test flew G-CAJW (535), and two days later G-CAJV (554), which was retained as a company demonstrator. G-CAJU was delivered to the Toronto Club on 27th April and on the same day Leigh Sheppard became the first private owner in the country to be supplied from Weston when he accepted G-CAJW.

Working to maximum capacity the Stag Lane factory was at its most efficient, but the business brains were soon made aware that the cost of shipping aircraft parts to Canada was almost 30% more expensive than sending the same components to Australia, an inconsistency of world trade rules and one which could only be reflected in the delivered price quoted to the customer. For the time being, the Canadian company was content to receive aeroplane kits for assembly in Toronto but increased local content was inevitable.

By mid-summer, over 90 Moths were in operation in Canada, 49 of them owned by the Federal Government and mostly loaned to the flying clubs. Joining them was Frank Sparks who had emigrated with his family from London in April. Arguably the world's first light aeroplane club Chief Pilot Instructor, Sparks took all his knowledge and experience from Stag Lane to Montreal where the Club had enrolled 128 members and received applications from 1,700 others. In August, the de Havilland Company at Stag Lane was advertising on behalf of 'a number of new flying schools to be opened in Canada' for British flying instructors with over 1,000 hours' flying experience, to apply for the posts. Salaries for the first year would be approximately $5,000.

The Canadian Company was encouraged
to start a flying school through which
instructors for the flying clubs could be
routed for familiarisation and assessment.
The picture shows from left to right,
W L Sanderson of the London (Ontario)
Club; L H Reid, Halifax; Leigh Capreol,
Chief Pilot for de Havilland Canada, and
L E Maynard from Ottawa. de Havilland

DH.60X Moth Seaplane G-EBUJ on her beaching trolley in the hangar-workshop of the Singapore Flying Club, established near the Yacht Basin in the main harbour. A second Seaplane, less wings, probably G-EBUK, can be seen in the background, seemingly about to have her engine removed. BAE Systems

The Canadian Company had established its own flying school by September at which new owners were offered primary instruction. In addition, at the request of the Department of Defence, the de Havilland school took on the business of refresher training for flying instructors engaged by the Canadian clubs, a task shared with the RCAF at Camp Borden.

Moth operations in Australia continued with great energy and reports filtered back to England of bizarre incidents and accidents, all commensurate with the big increases in utilisation and exposure to owners and club pilots with limited experience. Passengers managed to jam controls with their feet or by dropping packages; aerobatics were flown at too low a level; lack of communication between front and rear seats resulted in neither occupant having control, a predicament resulting in one Moth losing height so rapidly that she hit a fence at 85mph. Another which collided with a hedge was destroyed by fire when a bystander dropped a lighted cigarette. Flying at low level in poor visibility accounted for three aircraft which variously collided with the ground, the only tall tree in a fallowed field, and a cow obscured by a patch of tall thistles.

At Stag Lane, a revised version of the Mk I split undercarriage, the production standard Mk II, was first fitted to G-EBWX (583) at the end of April 1928. The aircraft was sold to Captain Harold Balfour, an ex-RFC pilot who had learned to fly on a Caudron at Hendon, and who was then General Manager of Metal Propellers Ltd of Croydon, the company responsible for the manufacture of Leitner-Watts propellers for high performance aircraft. The design staff was already working on a metal unit with detachable and adjustable blades suitable for use on light aeroplanes.

For some time following introduction of the new-style undercarriage, the straight axle was still available on request and, when G-EBTD was quickly rebuilt following her mishap on 19th March, her experimental split system was replaced with the straight axle type. In addition, her top wings were not fitted with slots. In spite of her return to near-standardisation, when G-EBTD was weighed on St George's Day, her tare weight had increased by 40 lb.

Singapore Flying Club DH.60X Seaplane G-EBUK, in a later colour scheme, about to be cast off in shallow water after completing an engine-run. Richard Riding

It is a popular myth that the DH.60X Moth was so named because of the geometry of the split undercarriage. The 'X' designation was applied by de Havilland to denote an experimental model in 1927 but the Marketing Department liked it and the appellation was retained. About 90 Cirrus II-powered aircraft built with the straight axle undercarriage were sold as DH.60X Moths and some aircraft modified for racing were similarly fitted, using smaller diameter wheels as often as not, as part of an effort to minimise drag.

Reliant on the float undercarriage supplied by Shorts, the Singapore Flying Club's first Moth Seaplane, DH.60X G-EBUJ (450), was test flown from Singapore Harbour on 19th April by Flight Lieutenant D V Carnegie, a member of the RAF's Far East Flight, in transit to Australia. Both G-EBUJ and the Club's second Moth. G-EBUK (451), which joined her sister on the water at the end of April, had received their British certificates in England before shipment to Kallang.

With the aid of a generous government capital grant and its own efforts, the Singapore Club had raised sufficient funds to purchase the two aircraft and establish and fully equip a base near the Yacht Club basin. In addition, a government subsidy was voted to help with annual running expenses and to pay the salary of a full-time flying instructor. The Club was declared 'open' on 28th April when the aircraft were christened *Cherub* and *Humming Bird* at a ceremony attended by all the local dignitaries including His Excellency, the Governor, Sir Hugh

Clifford. Aware of the high cost of insurance, quoted at 17.5% of declared value, the Club decided to cover for Third Party risks only. G-EBUJ suffered the indignity of sinking at her moorings during the night of 3/4 October so the Club took the opportunity to dismantle and overhaul the engine whilst the mainplanes and front fuselage were dried out. The following year, Club aircraft were capsized on touchdown three times and were repaired at their own expense.

An independent engineer asked to inspect the Club's Moth Seaplanes reported in December that the wooden hoop inside the front fuselage decking to which the centre section attached was evidently overstressed and regularly delaminated in spite of local modifications. More robust ash hoops had been substituted with additional wires continuing directly to the brackets on the bottom longerons which took the undercarriage struts. The Company was asked to consider improvements and also to pay much greater attention to the problems of corrosion in addition to strengthening the floats which tended to bulge when the keel bottomed near the shore.

According to Club historian Donald Spiers:

'The airframes were considerably improved in 1930, being fitted with phosphor-bronze in place of aluminium parts which were eaten away in a few weeks, stainless steel bolts, nuts, washers and packing plates, and having the three-ply doubled in thickness to one eighth of an inch. Fuselage deterioration was found to be very rapid when operating in humid, salt water conditions and fuselage timbers had to be renewed every nine months. The wings and tail surfaces were recovered every year and a spare set of wings was held so that these components could be overhauled thoroughly without holding the machine out of service too long.'

The environment in which the Singapore Club operated was always likely to have a profound effect as it did very dramatically on two separate occasions. The aircraft were fitted with metal propellers due to the damage caused to wooden blades by sea spray and on 20th May 1933 one of the Seaplanes suffered an in-flight failure of a propeller blade which broke off at the hub. Due to imbalance, the engine was pulled out of its mounting but the remaining blade, still rotating, tore into a float which prevented the engine from leaving the aircraft altogether. Now nose heavy, the instructor, Flight Lieutenant S H Potter, ordered the pupil to climb up onto the fuselage decking and slide towards the tail until balance and control were restored. After they were, Potter put the aircraft down near the shore-line with no further damage but the punctured float filled with water and the aircraft sank. Later investigation revealed that the propeller boss had become crystalline due to fatigue, a situation resulting from vibration caused by sea spray hitting the propeller whilst taxying in rough water.

Five years later there was an identical incident when a Moth Seaplane was being flown solo towards the centre of the island. The engine again fell onto a float and the pilot, E H Whitely, an instructor with the club, discovered he still had control if he flew at high speed. He managed to touch down on one of the reservoirs after approaching at 120mph then climbed down into the water and swam with the machine to the shore.

By the end of 1928, only one other club in the whole of the British Empire claimed to offer training facilities on seaplanes. In Canada, the Halifax Aero Club was established in July but suffered a dismal record. Their first aircraft allocated by the government, DH.60X G-CALD (576), capsized after a forced landing in July 1929 and G-CAKX (582), overturned on touchdown a month later. Replacement aircraft DH.60M CF-ADX (1301), received in September 1929, capsized at her moorings in October 1930 following the demise of CF-CBH (1326), which had spun out of cloud the previous month!

The de Havilland Company's promotional campaign which for years had focused on the ease of travelling by air when compared with by road, achieved another milestone between 23rd and 30th April when the famous Harrods store in London declared a 'flying week' for which a Moth was imported for display. Twice a day, a short film was shown at the beginning of which a lady driver is seen hardly coping with a flat tyre. Fifteen minutes and 800ft of film later, she is a qualified pilot and owner of a Moth. To back up the film, daily lectures were presented by accomplished Moth pilots including the irrepressible Wally Hope and the usually shy and modest Hubert Broad, for whom public speaking engagements were becoming quite a regular feature of his life.

Broad flew G-EBTD to Bristol for the city's Pageant on 5th May. His passenger, Francis St Barbe, would have been pleased at the general turnout of aeroplanes witnessed by a crowd of 30,000 spectators. Whilst stunting G-EBTD in the afternoon, it was noticed that the top and bottom wings bore the hastily overpainted registration of G-EBWS, the Handley Page slot demonstration aircraft which was also on the aerodrome, flown from Stag Lane by Alan Butler with his wife Lois, whom he was teaching to fly. Clearly, to expedite G-EBTD's return to good health, the de Havilland Service Department had indulged in a degree of discreet component swapping.

On the following Monday morning, G-EBWS was demonstrated to a group of foreign air attaches by Tom England and James Cordes at Handley Page's aerodrome at Cricklewood where a weakness in the attachment of the newly installed Mk II split undercarriage was revealed when the system collapsed after two heavy landings. The problem was quickly resolved by a fuselage stiffening modification proposed by the Design Office which was also incorporated into production models. The demonstra-

Rebuilt without slots after her accident in March, G-EBTD was flown by Hubert Broad at the Bristol Air Pageant on 5th May. Sharp-eyed observers could see that the starboard upper wing had once belonged to G-EBWS whose own top wings were new, requiring leading edge modification to accept the slots she had been enrolled to demonstrate. Richard Riding

Configured as a single seater, DH.60X
G-EBXP was flown by John Carberry at the
International Meeting at Gothenburg in
May. The aircraft accompanied John
Carberry to Canada in November and
eventually to the USA. Richard Riding

tions at Cricklewood were successfully completed after de Havilland loaned another Moth, dutifully delivered by Hubert Broad. The engine and wings from the damaged G-EBWS were transferred to a new fuselage which permitted Tom England to leave London on 11th May for an extended tour of 13 European countries from Poland to Spain, expected to last for up to 12 weeks.

At Stag Lane, interrupted by Broad's delivery flight to Cricklewood, G-EBTD and her Gipsy engine began another intensive series of flight trials. Operating with only three gallons of fuel in the main tank, the aircraft (and engine) were subjected to prolonged left hand and right hand turns with the engine 'on and off' (cruise power and throttled down), together with steep climbs at full throttle. It was noted that when idling, 'at no time was there any sign of the engine either dying or failing to pick up immediately when the throttle was opened…'.

On 8th May, Captain de Havilland and Richard Clarkson in G-EBTD flew a series of simultaneous climbs in company with Cirrus II-powered DH.60X No 574, (scheduled to become G-CAKV), crewed by Broad and Tiltman. Both aircraft were loaded to 1,352 lb and fitted with a Z64, 6ft 4in metal propeller suited to the appropriate rotation of the engine. Four days later, Captain de Havilland and Tiltman flew 'TD with a 6ft 8in diameter DH5166/2 wooden propeller which against the smaller Z64 under the same climatic conditions, provided identical climb speeds at 200rpm less. Trials and consumption tests continued into early June with stub exhausts, a new air intake, another large wooden propeller, DH5174, and a Fairey Reed FR43886/2 with metal blades of 7ft in diameter.

Together with bench running, the six preproduction Gipsy engines collectively had accumulated 1,000 hours by this time, singularly free of mechanical failures. Frank Halford did admit that, owing to seizure of the top piston rings in their grooves due to insufficient clearance, the engine failed its Air Ministry Type Test, but passed with flying colours at the second attempt.

'One feature of the test was very important to us and to all future users of the engine. To the best of my belief, it is the first time this Type Test has been run by any engine on ordinary No 1 petrol. The conditions of the test as we all know are very severe, and although we could have selected aviation spirit or a benzole mixture, we wished to demonstrate under offi-

cial observation how far the standard edition of this engine approximates to that of a standard car engine. Incidentally, for the last hour of the test when the engine must be run at full throttle and maximum speed, 2,100rpm, the power developed was over 97bhp and showed no signs whatsoever of falling off. Throughout the entire test, the oil consumption averaged under a half pint per hour.'

Hubert Broad's weekends were, seemingly, filled with as much promotional flying as could be arranged. He was invited by the Greenford Motorcycle Racing Club to join them during their weekly meeting on Saturday 12th May. While the motorcycles took fast corners in controlled skids, Broad flew overhead, deliberately skidding into his turns which manoeuvres were quickly and aptly dubbed 'broadsides'.

Having witnessed the death of his wife in Nairobi, John Carberry returned to England and took delivery of a new DH.60X Moth, G-EBXP (626), with which he represented de Havilland at the Gothenburg International Flying Meeting between 17th and 20th May. Not only did he arrive from Stag Lane within two minutes of his 'pre-arranged' time but went on to win the Speed Event, Race on Formula and Climbing Competition. A Swedish-registered Moth flown by a local pilot took the honours in the Controllability Event, Aerobatics and Obstacle Race.

Meanwhile, Broad was giving up another Saturday to demonstrate G-EBTD at the Southern Aero Club's meeting at Shoreham where his appearance on 19th May was described, probably prematurely, as the first in public by the new 'G' type Moth. Broad subsequently won first prize in the Wing Folding Competition, Taxying Competition and Height Competition, climbing to 2,000ft in two minutes 35 seconds, an advantage of eleven seconds over the Avro Gosport. He was thrilling crowds at the Midland Air Pageant at Castle Bromwich three weeks later flying DH.60X demonstrator

G-EBXG (615) when 'he exhibited the uncanny control imparted by the automatic slots by remaining in the air for some ten minutes, at times actually drifting backwards, and finally landing 200 yards from his take-off!' The reporter did not mention that the pilot had considered it prudent to land as one of the slats had become jammed in an intermediate position!

Another small but significant cosmetic modification was first applied to DH.60X G-EBWD (552), delivered to her new owner, Mr Hylton Murray-Philipson at Stag Lane on Friday 25th May. The aircraft was fitted with three-piece Triplex windscreens for front and rear cockpits, replacing the miscellany of largely ineffectual mica half-moons which had been standard since the first prototype. Mr Murray-Philipson was said to have been 'flying hard until dark' after acceptance, getting used to his machine prior to flying her, over the Whitsun weekend, to a field specially prepared in the grounds of his Scottish home, Stobo Castle, Peebles-shire. In the Stag Lane workshops, the final touches were being applied to DH.60X G-EBYV (648), sold locally to Major Albert Nathan, the first aircraft to be fitted with a production standard steerable tail skid.

The fact that RAF Moths had been taken on charge against civilian standards of construction and Inspection, and that all Autoslot flight trials had been funded and executed as a private venture by the de Havilland Company, resulted in the Air Ministry requesting clearance for a pilot from RAE Farnborough to be permitted to fly a production-standard slotted Moth and to compare it with an identical aircraft less slots. The Company was pleased to co-operate and, on 1st June, Flight Lieutenant D W Bonham-Carter flew slotted Moth demonstrator G-EBXG (615) at Stag Lane, followed immediately by standard DH.60X G-EBXF (609) provided by the de Havilland School. Meanwhile, on the ground at Stag Lane, an official from the Air Ministry's Contracts Technical Supervision Department (CTS) inspected

After spending many hours familiarising himself with his new aeroplane at Stag Lane, Squadron Leader Hylton Murray-Philipson flew G-EBWD back to his home at Stobo Castle, Peebles-shire, where she lived in a stable-garage behind the Castle, alongside the family Rolls-Royce.
Hylton Murray-Philipson

Inside the Stag Lane Works, a number of engineless wooden fuselages share space with the mainplane construction area and one complete, painted, folded Moth.
BAE Systems

Slotted Moth demonstrator G-EBXG, seen here taking off from an exhibition site, probably in Holland, was flown from Stag Lane in June by a test pilot nominated by RAE Farnborough, in order to compare her behaviour with a standard aircraft, less slots. *Flight*

the construction and installation of the slot mechanism, an item outside the accepted requirements of a Certificate of Airworthiness, but needing to be addressed if future Service use was ever to be considered on a formal basis.

Farnborough was anxious to define the type of slot which Bonham-Carter had experienced and the Chief Superintendent at the RAE was called upon to make a record:

'*These slots are of the plate type, which type of slot has been adopted in preference to the normal type, as requiring less alteration to existing structure when fitted, and does not entail the nosing of the mainplanes being entirely re-constructed in order to adapt them to existing aircraft.*

'*In fitting this plate slot, which consists of an aerofoil constructed of 12swg sheet duralumin following closely the contour of the upper surface of the mainplane nosing, it is only necessary to open up the fabric at the three points in order to fit the three mounting nose ribs and no other alteration to existing structure is necessary. No torque tube is provided for, as the fitting of this would add complications to this mechanism, which has been made as simple as possible for adapting to the civil aircraft, but any tendency on the part of the link to jam, due to uneven opening of the slot, has been catered for by providing sufficient clearance at the pin joints.*'

Following their team success at the 1927 RAF Pageant, the Central Flying School put up a pair of Genet-powered Moths for the Hendon show on 30th June 1928. Flown by Dick Atcherley and Dermot Boyle of the 'Inverted Flying Flight', the two officers had been allowed to devise an inverted fuel system operated from the cockpit by a dope cock and utilising a modified fine-adjustment throttle device scrounged from a Sopwith Snipe worked with what was otherwise the altitude control lever. An auxiliary cylin-

On 25th June 1928, Amelia Earhart flew from Stag Lane in slotted DH.60X Moth G-EBXG with Captain 'Jimmy' White, CFI of the de Havilland School. Miss Earhart had arrived in the country almost by accident. Already an accomplished pilot, she had been a passenger in a Fokker F.VIIb Seaplane which left Newfoundland on 17th June headed for Ireland, but the aircraft alighted at Burry Port in Carmarthen Bay, West Wales, 20 hours later. Amelia Earhart is credited as the first woman in history to fly the Atlantic. LNA

To maintain sociability, in May 1928 Alan Butler bought himself a standard two-seat DH.60X, G-EBUX, operated for the previous six months by Wally Hope's Air Taxis. The aircraft was kept at Stag Lane where she was photographed with the Company Chairman's Rolls-Royce Phantom, YW4232, described as 'the first with a Mulliner body'. Alan Butler

Together with J8820, Genet Moth J8816 is believed to have been the second aircraft modified by CFS Display Team pilots Dick Atcherley and Dermot Boyle to accept a fuel system permitting sustained inverted flight. The unauthorised modifications were inspected by officialdom and improved before the two aircraft were allowed to fly at the RAF Display at Hendon on 30th June. de Havilland

drical tank of about half a gallon capacity was bound by cord to the port undercarriage strut providing a total 'inverted' endurance of about 20min.

News of the modifications which were carried out with the local approval of CFS and no written authority from the Air Ministry, were greeted with some dismay at Farnborough from where an Inspection Party was despatched to Wittering on 11th June to find that only J8820 (383) had been converted, with a second aircraft on standby. The RAE team were moderately satisfied with the system and its installation, in the knowledge that it was temporary. Their several recommendations for physical improvement included the request to undertake a maximum-endurance inverted flight, primarily to check that the plugs would not oil up. A second inspection was scheduled but time was so short that it was agreed that this would only be possible when the aircraft arrived at Hendon on the Wednesday before the Display.

With this crude but effective system the aircraft were capable of completing an outside loop, a manoeuvre never before seen at a public event in Great Britain, and repeated to huge acclaim at the Blackpool Air Pageant a fortnight later.

Blackpool is believed to have been the first occasion when aircraft were attended by 'AA Scouts' from the newly created Aviation Department of the Automobile Association. The whole idea had been proposed by Ivor McClure and Oliver Tapper and

Ludwig Garfunkel of the Berlin based
Opalgraph Duplicator Company registered
an ex-German DH.60X Moth in Switzerland
in June 1928, and the aircraft was displayed
that summer fully rigged, on the back of a
lorry, in the centre of Basel. The Swiss
registration was cancelled in August 1929,
re-registered to her original German owner
in October and cancelled in November after
the aircraft was destroyed by fire.
de Havilland

Skis Canadian style. Originally supplied as
a DH.60X Seaplane, G-CAJZ was delivered
to John Bailes and Sons Ltd in Toronto in
July 1928. She ended her days as a
Seaplane in 1934 when she crashed during
an attempted touchdown on a glassy
surface. BAE Systems

soon to announce that in the 30 days of
June, 39 Moths had been manufactured.

The Company always maintained a close
and active interest in propellers. Although
they designed whole families of wooden
propellers, they never manufactured them,
except that some years in the future the
design and production of metal blades was
to become a significant part of the business.
On 3rd July, what was described as a 'new
DH prop, steel tube', was flight tested on
DH.60X G-EBZF (644), a machine commissioned as a Company demonstrator. Compared with the performance of a standard
DH.60X, G-EBZF was reported to be slower
by about 1mph, a deficiency blamed on her
slots and split undercarriage, although it
was noted that there was 'no vibration'. In
order to best demonstrate her slotted performance as economically as possible,
G-EBZF was fitted with seating for two passengers in the front cockpit.

During an Arctic expedition, the Italian
airship *Italia* had crashed on 25th May and
in miserable weather and over inhospitable
terrain, a rescue operation was launched
involving a mixed fleet of aircraft assembled
by six nations. During an attempt to reach
one party of survivors, a rescue aircraft suffered engine failure during an approach and
turned over on landing. The Swedish Air
Force arranged to charter DH.60X Moth
S-AABN, fitted with skis, from the Aero
Materiel Flying School in Stockholm, considering it the most practical type of aircraft
with which to launch a mission to rescue
the pilot. Flown by Lieutenant Schyberg,
S-AABN located the tiny tent, touched down
safely alongside and was greeted by Captain
Lundborg but the condition of the ice was
considered so dangerous, barely allowing
the Moth to get off, that no further flights
were authorised. Arctic Moth pilot John Grierson later wrote that he believed the rescue
of Captain Lundborg was the first case of a
stranded Arctic rescuer being himself rescued by another aircraft, and of a type
supremely suited to the difficult task.

stemmed from their own experience of the
lack of aviation maps and aerodrome and
route information available to the growing
number of aerial tourists. The new Aviation
Department was ideally placed to prepare
such documentation initially from AA Headquarters at Fanum House in Leicester
Square, London. When the AA published its
General Service flying maps, members were
advised periodically to return their copies to
Headquarters where notified amendments
would be applied by hand on an individual
basis. A squad of Scouts was recruited,
mostly ex-RAF personnel, who would attend
to the needs of the private owners by mar-
shalling, picketing, covering and preparing
for flight as requested.

At Blackpool, a most practical innovation
was a billboard-sized map of the British
Isles covered with weather symbols, kept
up to date by reports called in by AA Patrol-
men around the country. The Department
also published a list of landing grounds.
A copy was issued to every Patrolman, one
of whose duties was to inspect and report
on all such facilities in his sector at least
once a month.

The establishment of this service was
another vital building block in the infra-
structure which was necessary to support
the accelerating growth of light aviation, private ownership and air travel conducted for
both business and pleasure. To emphasise
the fact, the de Havilland Company was

JULY TO DECEMBER 1928

WHILE THE Stag Lane Design Office was becoming more excited in the merits and weights of different gauges of square section Reynolds steel tubing, very much with the immediate future in mind, a lot of attention was also being paid to the clutch of Moths being groomed for the King's Cup Air Race scheduled to start from Hendon on 20th July.

An essential entry, the first designated DH.60G airframe, No 801, was registered G-EBYZ to Air Taxis Ltd at Stag Lane and was fitted with Gipsy engine No 5, one of the pre-production batch which Frank Halford was anxious should be used and abused as much as possible, and which already had accumulated many test-bed hours. The first 'production' Gipsy I engine was delivered to the Erecting Shed on 19th June, and almost certainly installed in de Havilland's other King's Cup hope, DH.60G G-EBYK (825), sponsored by Sir Charles Wakefield and to be flown by Hubert Broad. Incorporating a number of minor changes to fuselage design and construction and to the empennage which would become standard on production models, G-EBYK was cleared to operate at an all-up weight of 1,400 lb and 1,370 lb for aerobatics. Racing modifications included a special engine cowling to cater for the lack of exhaust pipes, a nine gallon gravity tank and 25 gallon 'pressure' tank in the front cockpit, a racing undercarriage with small wheels and a streamlined head fairing. As usual, gaps were sealed and all efforts made to reduce drag. Standard wings were fitted, without slots.

Prior to the installation of the modified fuel system on 21st June, Hubert Broad and Richard Clarkson flew G-EBYK on a series of

trials over the Stag Lane Speed Course, the 3.53 miles between their local pub on the Edgware Road, the Bald Faced Stag, and the steeple of Harrow Church. The trials were to compare a number of different propeller pitches based on the DH5174 design. Four days later the aircraft flew to gather data on the DH5166 and a metal Fairey Reed.

Following her catastrophic accident at Stag Lane in February during her 'turn-back' trials flown by Hubert Broad, DH.60X Moth G-EBQH was sold to Alan Butler and the airframe rebuilt in a racing configuration and fitted with another of the pre-production Gipsy I engines. She had been modified in a similar manner to G-EBYK except that all

A general view of some of the aircraft being prepared at Stag Lane during the afternoon of 19th July 1928, prior to a mass exodus for Hendon, and the start of the King's Cup Air Race the following morning. LNA

The first designated DH.60G airframe, G-EBYZ, was a 1928 King's Cup entry by Air Taxis, flown by Wally Hope. The aircraft was fitted with Gipsy I engine No 5, taken from the pre-production batch, and was modestly streamlined in comparison with other efforts. *Flight*

Hubert Broad flew the heavily streamlined DH.60G Moth G-EBYK in the 1928 King's Cup Air Race, an entry sponsored by Sir Charles Wakefield. A nine-gallon fuel tank was concealed within a faired centre section and special cowlings were designed to cope with the lack of an exhaust pipe.
Michael Stroud Collection

control cables were hidden inside the fuselage, the cockpit coamings were low profile and she carried a new cantilever tailplane. The aeroplane was test flown at Stag Lane by Alan Butler on 6th July and positioned to Hendon on the eve of the King's Cup Race.

To preserve his social flying, Alan Butler purchased a standard DH.60X Cirrus Moth, G-EBUX (476), from Air Taxis in May, possibly as part of a greater business arrangement. The aircraft was registered as a King's Cup competitor, entered by Alan Butler but to be flown by Captain de Havilland with his eldest son, Geoffrey Jnr, as co-pilot. Altogether, 13 Moths were entered in a field of 38 and included Soden's Genet Moth G-EBOU, Morris Jackaman's G-EBRT which had been prepared by the de Havilland Service Department, Major Nathan's newly-delivered G-EBYV; Norman Jones and Winifred Spooner in their own Moths, G-EBWI and G-EBOT, and Neville Stack in the ADC test aircraft, G-EBUF, now fitted with ADC's riposte to the Gipsy engine in the form of the new 85hp Cirrus III.

As the aircraft gathered at Hendon on the eve of the Race, Geoffrey Dorman reported:
'At about five minutes to four, out of a perfectly clear sky, it suddenly started to Moth. There could never have been such a storm of Moths before. There were Mk I Moths, Mk II Moths, G Moths, X Moths, Genet Moths and Cirrus III Moths, Moths with big fuselages and Moths with small fuselages, Slotted Moths, Service Moths, in fact Moths of all kinds and colours.'

Although the success of the DH.60 Moth as a type was assured and many new developments were already taking shape in the fertile and imaginative minds at Stag Lane, it was important for the prestige of the Company that the Moth, and especially a Gipsy engined Moth, was well placed in the 1928 King's Cup Air Race.

The Royal Aero Club changed the Race route every year but the basic rules remained reasonably constant. The 1928 Race was run against a handicap formula over a course of more than 1,000 miles around Great Britain and during two days called at many of the aerodromes where light aeroplane clubs were operational. Much to the Company's relief and delight, for the third year in succession the Race was won by a de Havilland Moth when Wally Hope arrived at Brooklands just before 4 o'clock on the afternoon of Sunday 21st June in his much modified G-EBYZ. But it was a close-run thing. In his exuberance, Hope had not actually crossed the finishing line and had to be encouraged to take off again and fly a quick circuit which was completed just before the second-placed aircraft arrived.

Wally Hope's average speed was 105.5mph, a psychologically important set of figures to be associated with his Gipsy engine in all the post-event publicity. Winifred Spooner was third in her Cirrus II-powered Moth G-EBOT at an average of only 83.5mph. Both the other Gipsy-engined Moths completed the course and, in the provisional results, DH.60 Moths took 1st, 3rd, 4th, 5th, 6th, 7th, 11th and 12th places amongst the 23 finishers. In the new integrated club competition for the Siddeley Trophy, won by Winifred Spooner, it was probably no surprise that Moths should have taken the first five places.

The de Havilland advertising agents and copy writers serving the suppliers of fuel, oil and proprietary parts were quick to pounce on the achievements whilst those for ADC Aircraft very soberly announced that they were now in a position to accept orders for the Cirrus III engine 'which although devel-

oping a greater horsepower than the Mk II, possesses better cooling efficiency with the same reliability, the same consumption, the same weight, the same price and the same experience behind it...'. The engine inherited the family's familiar right hand rotation and the nose cowl was still noticeably rounded, but unlike the long exhaust pipes of the Cirrus I and Cirrus II, that of the Cirrus III followed the Gipsy I routing to the fuselage side via the inside of the most forward cabane strut.

The Stag Lane factory built 28 wooden and 33 metal airframes with Cirrus III engines installed, a minimal production when compared with the Gipsy. In December, three wooden aircraft were supplied: two additional Seaplanes for the Singapore Flying Club (920 and 921) and an aircraft scheduled for de Havilland which eventually went to New Zealand (922). In January No 923 was sold to Mexico as X-BACO. During February and March, 28 Cirrus III- powered Metal Moths were exported to Mount Dennis for final assembly and delivery to the RCAF at Camp Borden (734-739 and 746-752) and Vancouver (740-745) with the remainder (753-761), distributed amongst other RCAF stations and flying clubs. On arrival in Canada it appears that Nos 752-755, all allocated to clubs, had their Cirrus III engines replaced with the Gipsy I. In addition, ADC Aircraft (Cirrus Engines Ltd) did persuade some owners to accept delivery of bare airframes into which they arranged for the installation of their own engine, purchased separately, and more aircraft were converted in the field. In an effort to improve their market share, further development resulted in another more powerful engine, the Hermes, which was to be launched the following year.

Sadly clashing with the King's Cup was the first International Air Meeting at Rotterdam. This gathering, high on socialising, was well attended by British Moths including the slotted demonstration aircraft G-EBXG and Sophie Heath's new Cirrus-engined aeroplane, G-EBZC (678), in which she was placed first in the final classification after taking part in a number of competitions. In the speed test, G-EBZC had averaged 98.8mph over two circuits of a 15 mile triangular course.

Perhaps in recognition of the Moth's recent successes, the Company authorised the manufacture for sale at three shillings and sixpence a pack, a small batch of linen-

Reginald R Green of the Aeronautical Inspection Directorate, handing a sealed barograph to Mrs Louie de Havilland at Stag Lane, prior to an attempt on the World Height Record on 25th July 1928, flying the specially prepared, Cirrus II powered DH.60X, G-EBWV. de Havilland

Captain de Havilland in his high-altitude flying suit and Mrs de Havilland in the front cockpit of the Gipsy I powered DH.60X G-EBWV, after setting a World Height Record on 25th July 1928. Just visible is the faired-in and extended centre section. After installing a fuel tank in the front cockpit, the Works ran out of time to paint over the red dope visible on the front cowl.
BAE Systems

faced playing cards featuring 'an artist's impression in bright colours of a Moth traversing the countryside'. The Sales Department had already been handling the merchandising of painted wooden models but later that summer announced that these were to be discontinued in favour of unpainted, white-metal models, priced at three guineas each, 'beautifully made by a well-known concern specialising in this work (the Birmingham Medal Company). Supplied as a land machine or as seaplane, suitable for attachment to motor car radiator caps as a mascot or for use as paperweights, ornaments or the like…'.

In March, the works had completed construction of DH.60X Moth G-EBWV (566), a Cirrus II powered aircraft used by the Company for test and demonstration purposes. In June this machine was selected for an attempt on the World Height Record for two-seater light aircraft, a laurel once held by Lady Mary Bailey and Mrs Louie de Havilland but taken in October 1927 by a Baumer Monoplane for Germany which achieved 18,700ft. A pre-production Gipsy I engine with stub exhausts was installed together with a Fairey-Reed propeller and every component subsequently fitted to the aircraft was carefully selected including a strut-mounted thermometer, an aneroid and crew oxygen equipment. The straight-axle undercarriage carried small Palmer wheels (450 x 60) and a nine gallon header fuel tank was hidden in the faired-over centre section, plumbed to receive fuel pumped up from a ten gallon tank under the decking of the front cockpit. The centre-section was extended to exclude the normal cut-out of the top plane trailing edges above the rear cockpit, eliminating the facility of folding the wings.

Her third flight after conversion was on 4th July when Captain de Havilland, accompanied by his wife, took off from Stag Lane and climbed steadily at full throttle towards the west. The aircraft weighed 1,314 lb at take-off carrying 12 gallons of petrol. The weather was fine and warm and after almost 52 minutes with the outside air temperature

at -14°C, the observed height was 17,700ft, equating to a corrected aneroid height of 19,500ft.

Five days later another attempt was made, with Richard Clarkson in the passenger seat. Changes embodied since the first climb included a heated induction manifold drawing hot air from a muffler on the exhaust pipe and replacement of the propeller by a metal Z64/4 without a special boss. Taking off into fine conditions at a starting weight of 1,305 lb, the climb was discontinued at 7,000ft.

The third attempt was made by Captain de Havilland and his wife on 25th July, after the King's Cup victory celebrations had died down. The big fuel tank which had been faired into the top planes, was filled with 10 gallons of Benzol mixture 20/80 and at a

take-off weight of 1,249 lb, G-EBWV set course at full throttle on a steady climb towards Reading. After 70min the aircraft had reached an indicated height of 21,300ft over Maidenhead although the engine had started to misfire as 17,000ft was passed. The descent to Stag Lane was accomplished in 15min after which it was found that only six gallons of petrol had been used. Although the Company immediately announced a new world record of 'over 21,000ft', later revised to 'over 4 miles high', corrections to the barograph readings set the actual figure at 19,980ft. The world record was ratified by the Royal Aero Club at a height of 6,054 metres in September and was to stand until 21st February 1930 when a height of 22,245ft (6,782m) was achieved by a Fiat AS1 over Rome.

In Canada, reported only as a matter of passing interest, a member of the Victoria Aero Club climbed his Moth to 15,000ft in 43min and was still climbing when he decided to descend on the grounds that he was 'not properly attired for the freezing temperatures'. Meanwhile, for G-EBWV, more mundane climb trials were continued into August by Hubert Broad before the aeroplane was withdrawn into the premises of the Service Department for modifications in support of yet another prospective Public Relations spectacular.

It was ironic that what was believed to be the first reported in-flight structural failure of a Moth occurred near Stag Lane Aerodrome, close to the spot where the prototype had also met her end. On 3rd August, London Aeroplane Club DH.60X Moth G-EBYD (672), barely a month old and with only 43 hours in her logbook, suffered progressive break-up of her mainplanes after the starboard upper wing disintegrated during an aerobatic routine.

The inconclusive result of the official enquiry was that the cause must be regarded as 'obscure', given no evidence of faulty workmanship or materials, the past history of the type or of the pilot having mishandled G-EBYD during the flight. The accident inspector could take no heed of rumours circulating at Stag Lane which suggested the pilot enjoyed flying at low level and that on the day of the accident, the aeroplane had collided with a tree prior to its final aerobatic routine, possibly sustaining structural damage unknown to him.

The matter was serious enough to be considered at several successive meetings of the Air Ministry's Accident Investigation Sub Committee starting on 9th October 1928. Inspector of Accidents Major J P C Cooper, reported that the first spar failure had

occurred close to the root and that compression creases had been found in the front spars of each top plane. This was the only failure of a top spar to have been reported to date. He added that some signs of splitting on bottom spars could be accounted for by bad landings and he was aware that the de Havilland Company discarded a large number of spars through cracking before they were built into mainplanes. Since July 1928, eleven split spars had been the subject of concession, six were rejected on detailed inspection and a further six discovered in aircraft following unrelated accidents. The Sub Committee subsequently considered changes in moisture content that could set up stresses; the fact that there were horizontal bolt holes near the root where the spar web was thin, and evidence from another Moth accident where the leading edge of a top mainplane had peeled back resulting in twisting of the bottom plane, and cracking of the spars. It was agreed that all the broken wings would be sent from de Havilland custody for examination at Farnborough.

As the British summer of 1928 wore on, the number of flying clubs steadily increased and existing ones managed to survive in spite of a habit of closing down like any other business during public holidays. No longer was the main concern whether set-up funds independent of subsidies could be found, rather than the willingness of a local authority to assist with the establishment of a municipal aerodrome from which to operate. Also, the clubs now had a wider range of aircraft types from which to choose, the latest being the Cirrus-powered Simmonds Spartan which received an excellent press, but which, for all its innovations and advertised price of £620, against the all-powerful enterprise producing, supporting

and promoting the Moth, could have little chance of making any significant impact.

An agency for Simmonds aircraft was taken up by P&P Motors of Reading before the company developed into Phillips and Powis Aircraft (Reading) Ltd, one of whose initiatives resulted in the establishment of the expansive Woodley Aerodrome in 1929 and where a flying school and club were soon thriving. Already an astute motor car business, P&P took the precaution of acquiring an agency for de Havilland aircraft too, and a Moth was on display in the company's showrooms in Oxford Road by September.

Almost every gathering of light aeroplanes somewhere was reported in the aviation press which published details of all the different types attending, and quickly got into the habit of distinguishing between 'Moths' and 'Slotted Moths'. Every opportunity was taken to demonstrate the 'Slotted Moths' with the result that many long-standing owners traded-in older aircraft for the new 'G' model fitted with slots, the Mk II 'pylon type' split undercarriage and the Gipsy engine, any combination of which could be retrofitted to compliant airframes. At the prestigious Berlin International Aircraft Exhibition in October, the Handley Page Company's stand devoted itself entirely to presentation of the 'slot' and displayed a full size Moth wing, supported by a working model and a montage of photographs.

DH.60X Moth No 682 was registered G-EBZL to Handley Page Ltd in July but appears not to have been delivered as the aircraft was sold to George Boyd-Carpenter and shipped to Kano, Nigeria. G-EBZL is the first aircraft to be credited with 'metal slots'. That portion of the 'slot' which lifted off the leading edge of the wing was known variously as an 'Auxiliary Plane' or 'Auxiliary Aerofoil' and continued development and refinement resulted in their manufacture in 12 or 14 gauge plain Dural, 12 gauge plain aluminium or 'wood and double Dural'. Although never a technical definition, the 'auxiliary aerofoil' came to be known most commonly as a 'slat'.

It was essential that an early-production DH.60G Moth was expedited to Canada and aircraft No 813 was despatched to Mount Dennis and immediately put on display at the Toronto Exhibition in August. Later registered G-CAVK she joined the Montreal Light Aeroplane Club in November and later, in private hands, survived until 1940.

On 8th August, de Havilland announced an order for eight DH.60G Moths placed by the New Zealand Air Ministry. Following the examples already set elsewhere, some were

DH.60X G-CALC of the London (Ontario) Flying Club, being towed amongst a procession of new cars making their way from the city centre of London to the new airport, for an inaugural ceremony. Via Gerry Schwam

to be civilian aircraft, despatched to the New Zealand Air Force Base at Wigram for assembly, test flight and certification early in 1929. The first four, 866-869, were registered G-NZAW to G-NZAZ and allocated to the Aero Clubs at Auckland, Marlborough and Canterbury (two). The remaining four were all scheduled for the Air Force, to be based at Wigram, with serial numbers to reflect their build identities, 870-873. Of this quartet, only 871 and 872 survived to become civil aeroplanes later: 871 was registered ZK-ADZ in 1936 but crashed into the sea off Greymouth a year later while 872 was loaned to Marlborough Aero Club in January 1936 as ZK-AEM, but was written off after a heavy landing at Blenheim two weeks before Christmas 1937. Two additional DH.60G Moths, 914 and 915, were later added to the order and registered ZK-AAJ and ZK-AAK. They were loaned to the Marlborough and Auckland Aero Clubs in whose hands they were written off in November 1932 and October 1937 respectively.

The New Zealand order was received at a time when the Stag Lane factory was midway through production of a batch of 24 Cirrus II DH.60X Moths for the Chilean Government, Nos 651-670 and 673-675 (serials G.1 to G.24), acquired through one of the Company's South American agents, Morrison and Co, the last four supplied as seaplanes. No 665 was specified to receive parachute seats and a DH.60G type rudder, while Nos 667-670 all were fitted with larger capacity oil tanks and ten gallon auxiliary fuel tanks. The fleet qualified for Cs of A at Stag Lane or Rochester between 6th July and 16th August and, following acceptance flights by Captain Montecina, were shipped to Santiago.

Early in October, the Chilean Government placed a repeat order, this time for forty DH.60G Moths, Nos 930-969 (serials G.25 to G.64). The first six machines were expected to be shipped at the beginning of November with the contract completed by the end of the year, but aircraft were still being processed at Stag Lane in the middle of March 1929 and the final Cs of A were not issued until April. Twenty aircraft were fitted with long-range tanks and scheduled for

use as 'refresher trainers' and in a communications role which included opening up an extensive and successful aero postal service. Following the leads already set by others, perhaps, some were allocated by their military owners for operation by civilian flying clubs where tuition was offered free of charge.

To prove that military aviation could have its lighter side, the following year the Chilean Army Air Force organised what they called a *Gin-Kana* with their Moths at Los Cerrillos, Santiago. For a first prize of $20,000, contestants had to fly around a 1,000km circuit when time and fuel consumption were measured; descend from 1,000m with the propeller stationary and land and stop within a 50m circle and then enter the *Gin-Kana* against the following rules: tow the Moth 100m, start the engine, take-off, land near a goal, fold the wings, push the machine through the goal-mouth,

spread the wings, start the engine, take-off and make two circuits of the aerodrome, land in the vicinity of a control, sign a book, take off, make a circuit and land over a finishing line.

De Havilland's summer publicity coup began at 5.30pm on Thursday 16th August when, after a roll of 13 seconds, Hubert Broad took off from Stag Lane in G-EBWV. Outwardly, there was little to distinguish the aircraft from its configuration for the attempt on the world height record only three weeks before except that a 25 gallon gravity tank was now evident in the centre section; the rear cockpit was provided with a much wider and taller mica windscreen; navigation lights sprouted from the top wings and conventional wheels were fitted. Not discernable was additional fuel tankage installed in the rear locker which increased the total capacity to 80 gallons, 'equivalent to the weight of four fully grown men',

Wally Hope shaking hands with Hubert Broad at Stag Lane, a little after 5.30pm on Friday, 17th August 1928. Broad had just landed in DH.60X Moth G-EBWV, having been aloft for 24 hours in another publicity venture to draw attention to the reliability of the new Gipsy engine. Richard Riding

DH.60G Moth G-AAAA was used extensively for promotional work on behalf of the Company, urged on by a belief that the registration would be widely recognised and associated with the excellence of the product. A suitcase shaped to fit within the contours of the luggage locker was marketed later. The originators of this pose created licence in the self-belief that both the lady passenger and the golf clubs could be carried together. *Flight*

advised the Company's publicists. To cope with the uplift, the maximum gross take off weight of G-EBWV had been approved at 1,660 lb. At 5.30pm the following day, Hubert Broad landed G-EBWV back at Stag Lane, summoned by the firing of a Very flare to signify the passage of 24 hours since his departure.

At cruising power, the Gipsy engine had consumed less than three gallons of petrol per hour and on return the aircraft still carried sufficient fuel for at least another four hours of flying. Broad himself subsisted on coffee, cocoa, sandwiches and boiled eggs and read his way through three novels in an effort to relieve the monotony. Jimmy White, sent up from Stag Lane in a Moth to check on him, thought he had gone to sleep, but Broad was tucked down inside the rear cockpit, engrossed in one of his books, the titles of which were never revealed.

During the flight, which meandered along a pre-planned route over much of England south of Stamford in Lincolnshire, the aircraft is estimated to have covered more than 1,400 miles, easily beating any distance record had that been the object, rather than proving the efficiency and reliability of the Gipsy engine. Never without a comment, the Sales Department reported that the engine had completed 2.5 million revolutions for which each magneto had provided 10 million sparks.

Absent from Broad's welcoming committee, headed by his old friend Wally Hope, was Geoffrey de Havilland. The Captain had accepted delivery of his own personal DH.60G Moth, G-AAAA (805), and was away touring in Cornwall with his wife, behind Gipsy engine No 5. It was most unlikely that the first of the new series of registration let-

ters was allocated to Captain de Havilland by sheer chance although applications made to the Air Ministry at the time were saturated with Moths. The press picked up the significance of the lettering, reporting that nobody could fail to appreciate that this aeroplane was nothing but special.

The Danish Government signed a contract on 20th August for the supply of eight DH.60G Moths at a basic price of £650 each plus extras. Six aircraft were for the Army Air Corps to replace old German LVG B.IIIs as basic trainers, and two were for the Navy. The Army aircraft (901-906), painted silver overall and with no markings, were shipped to Copenhagen in three deliveries in November and December, assembled during the winter, and taken into the military inventory in March 1929 when they were issued serials S-101 to S-105, although their relationship with the build numbers is not confirmed. Training on the aircraft was undertaken at Lundtofte and confined to the summer months. One aircraft was lost in a crash at Hjarbaek in 1932 and the following year the survivors were traded with de Havilland's agent in Denmark for five new DH.82 Tiger Moths. The two naval aircraft, Nos 899 and 900 were taken on charge on 24th November and received serials 148 and 149. Known as Type LB.III they were used as primary trainers at Avno.

The Nottingham Aero Club suffered two fatalities at Hucknall on 22nd August when DH.60X Moth G-EBSK (417), dived into the ground from about 200ft after what appeared to be a normal take-off. The accident investigators believed that neither the pilot's nor passenger's safety harness were properly locked and that the pilot's control of the aeroplane may have been hampered

by the passenger falling forward against the control column which they suggested should not have been in place for such a flight. But their biggest criticism repeated a previous view in that one of the improvements effected in the design of the DH.60X was the security with which the main fuel tank was held in the centre section. They contended that in the event of a collision with the ground, more often than not the cabane structure collapsed forward onto the hot engine. On earlier aircraft the wire retaining strops invariably broke on impact, permitting the tank to be thrown clear and out of harm's way.

The matter was taken up by the RAE who, together with the Company, agreed that it was impossible to incorporate the old method of attachment into the new design of tank, but other improvements to prevent the risk of fire were agreed. In some accidents the duralumin protection to the Petroflex supply pipe, rigidly attached to the petrol cock, had caused the cock to be torn out of the bottom of the tank, releasing the contents. The cock was subsequently modified by the addition of a flexible coupling

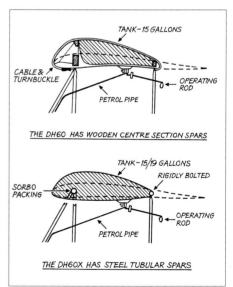

The original 15-gallon tank of pre-DH.60X Moths was buried inside an aerodynamic fairing, sported on wooden cross spars and retained by steel cables. Following redesign in 1927, the increased capacity tank was bolted to steel tube cross spars, adding rigidity to the cabane structure. Clive Abbott

The Air Ministry's Accident Inspectors were critical of the new fuel tank design and installation when it was recognised that after violent contact with the ground, the cabane structure nearly always collapsed forward, allowing fuel from a damaged tank to escape directly onto a hot engine, rather than be flung free as often was the case before. Proof was provided by G-AASZ when she crashed at Hanworth in 1932, although fuel spillage did not result in a fire. Richard Riding

between it and the on/off control rod and the protective duralumin cover was shortened to expose the Petroflex pipe which was left unsupported at the union. The Air Ministry subsequently raised a Technical Order and all Moths in the field were subject to retrospective mandatory modification.

G-EBSK had been gifted to the Nottingham Club by the chairman of the famous local firm of Raleigh Cycles, Sir Harold Bowden, and she was replaced by G-AABA (700), a DH.60X described by the Club as a 'G' Moth with a Cirrus II engine. The new aircraft was delivered on 8th September but on 9th March 1929 she flew into the North Sea about 90 miles off Hull, probably as the result of encountering mist and of having an incorrectly set altimeter.

At the beginning of August, Hubert Broad flew racing DH.60G Moth G-EBYK from Stag Lane to Berlin in a four day trip which, unusually for the time, received no publicity of any kind. One can only speculate that the visit was to demonstrate the Gipsy engine to de Havilland's German agent and to make preliminary arrangements for the company's display at the International Aircraft Exhibition to be held in October. A month later, on 8th September, Broad flew the aeroplane to Paris to take part in the International Light Aeroplane Competition at Orly. The aircraft had been modified to take maximum advantage of the requirements, as far as they were known, for each of the separate elements of the competition, although it proved impossible to satisfy them all and remain faithful to the basic design philosophy.

Perhaps de Havilland put no great weight on the results, for G-EBYK was their only Moth entry. Dick Bentley had entered but failed to arrive in his Moth G-EBSO, recently re-engined with a Cirrus III. Broad flew solo from Stag Lane with a spare propeller strapped to the port side of the front fuselage but no parachute in the front cockpit,

Hubert Broad, in his city suit by the propeller, helps to marshall the high-efficiency DH.60G G-EBYK through a confined space during the Light Aeroplane Competition at Orly in September 1928. The aircraft was penalised for not having a parachute in the front cockpit, or a self-starter, and for employing a cross-axle undercarriage. Richard Riding

which fact immediately lost him marks. He borrowed a passenger when necessary who found that apart from their seat and the flying controls, their cockpit had been stripped out and was noisy as the special engine cowling concealed the fact there were no exhaust pipes.

Fuel was carried in a standard gravity tank but the volume of the luggage locker had been increased by lowering the floor, the increased carrying capacity being an important part of an 'efficiency formula'. However, G-EBYK's racing style undercarriage with cross axle and 600 x 75 thin wheels, traded against improved speed, lost marks in a 'quality assessment' of the aircraft's likely inclination to turn over on the ground. More marks were lost as the Gipsy engine was not fitted with a self starter, but Broad's overall performance in the concluding eight day 'Reliability Trial', which covered 1,500 miles, was such that he achieved third place in a field of 14 com-

petitors, behind a low-powered German Klemm and Edgar Percival flying a Cirrus III-powered Avian. He collected 30,000Frs, about £240, for his efforts. Later in the year, Broad was reported to be using G-EBYK for 'experimental inverted flying', for reasons which would soon become clear.

A casual visitor was DH.60 Genet Moth G-EBOU. The aircraft was on her way back to England after touring in Spain with her owner, Flight Lieutenant Frank Soden and CFS Instructor, Flying Officer Richard Atcherley. A British observer noted:

Flying Officer Atcherley gave another spectacular demonstration on the Genet Moth. He performed his very slow rolls lower than ever commencing it seemed, at the very beginning of a climb from close to the deck. He also circled the aerodrome inverted, both clockwise and anti-clockwise and accomplished the falling leaf whilst inverted. Incidentally, stunting was forbidden at Orly and when Atcherley went

up and commenced with a roll, the gendarmes indicated that he would be arrested, but when he followed up with his inimitable display they were compelled to forget their official attitude and become admiring human beings.'

Another correspondent wrote:

'Atcherley excelled himself. With an engine not quite giving the required revs he took three attempts to describe the outside loop. The first two efforts just failed and resulted in two spectacular tail-slides after an appreciable suspension in mid-air. He succeeded at the third attempt which roused characteristic enthusiasm amongst the French who were professionally impressed.'

The questionable durability of a light wooden aeroplane structure in daily use as a trainer or commercial seaplane had exercised minds in the Stag Lane Design Office for some time. Serious investigations into the prospect of radical changes to the DH.60X Moth fuselage were begun late in 1927 following receipt of a letter from the Canadian Company dated 3rd October, which detailed incidents of wooden engine bearers shrinking and many difficulties with rigging. The wide acceptance of the Moth in its many roles in Canada, a massive country with a range of demanding environmental situations, and the prospect of many further sales, prompted Stag Lane to accelerate work on a fuselage structure manufactured from steel tubing.

What resulted was a DH.60X with a 'metal body' and a full technical description was carried as guest editorial in *The Automobile Engineer*:

'There has, in the past, been some prejudice against oxy-acetylene welding as applied to steel tubing, but in the last two years intensive research both in England and America, has located the trouble. New alloy steels having low carbon content, have been developed which now give a degree of reliability when welded which is beyond reproach.

'The fuselage structure of the DH.60M is built up of a number of tubular units with welded joints, but retains the three-ply type of top cowling, flooring etc. Steel gusset plates are welded on to all joints, thus reinforcing what would otherwise have been simple butt-welds.

'Considerable thought has been given to the question of the facility with which repair work can be carried out in the event of a crash, and the structure of the fuselage has been sub-divided into a number of convenient units, giving ease of replacement and economy of packing space for export abroad where the machines may quite easily be assembled. These units are all made to fine limits on jigs, giving strict interchangeability. The various units are as follows:

- *'Engine mounting sides complete with rubber blocks and housings.*
- *'Centre section of fuselage and side frame, the bottom longeron of which has been made detachable since it is often found in minor crashes that this is the only fuselage member to sustain any damage.*
- *'Rear fuselage side frame.*
- *'Rearmost bay of fuselage with joints to take tailplane, fin and tailskid gear (known as the knife-edge). This is welded into one complete unit which can be detached.*
- *'All cross frames and struts are bolted to side frames, the rear fuselage being braced with duplicated high-tensile wire.*
- *'The longerons are of square section tubing and of 22G in all cases with the exception of the forward portion of the lower longeron, in way of the cockpits, which is of 17G. This tubing of ⅞in face, lends itself extremely well to either welded or bolted construction, the joints being very easy to effect in either case. The web members of the centre section side frames are of round section tubing in most cases, ⅞in diameter, and of 22G. Where the concentrated load from the undercarriage is applied these are of square section. All web members and cross struts in the rear fuselage are ⅝in diameter tubes of 22G except the cross strut where the tailplane stay struts occur which is of square section. The plywood floor and the cockpit cowling are bolted direct to the longerons at a number of points, but the front centre section bracing wires, which in the machine with wooden fuselage are attached to a fitting on the cowling, are now carried to the forward top joints of the fuselage itself.'*

Four fuselages were laid down, 339 to 342, the first three incorporating 24 gauge Reynolds tubing for the rear frame but changed to the heavier 22 gauge for No 342 and all production models.

There were few visual clues externally to the nature of the new structure. A pair of fore and aft wooden stringers beneath the side fuselage fabric, both running parallel with the top longerons, distanced the covering from the frame and created tell-tale edges along their entire length. Aft of the rear cockpit, the ply turtledeck, replaced by fabric-covered wooden stringers supported by two steel tube hoops, provided the most obvious evidence of a difference. The surfaces of the wooden structure of the 'metal bodied' Moth hidden under the fabric covering were treated in a manner similar to all other de Havilland products, receiving a generous coating of varnish, while the tube fuselage was painted with black enamel to an allowance of 2 lb per frame externally and treated internally with an anti-corrosion agent.

In 1931 the Company had received a sufficient number of complaints about varnished wood absorbing moisture that they changed their internal protection policy and

wooden structures received a coating of specially formulated dope.

Following earlier experiments in which the tailskid was steered by cables connected to the rudder bar, the new arrangement was much simpler. The bottom forward edge of the rudder was cut away, reinforced and fitted with ears on both lower edges that at some reasonable degree of rudder application (on the ground), reacted against the face of a lever attached to a swivel tube. It was a safe and almost entirely foolproof system that greatly facilitated ground manoeuvring.

A concession to aerobatically inclined pilots was the facility to lock the automatic slots, but this could only be achieved on the ground after climbing up a stepladder, by turning three spring loaded catches which projected through each 'auxiliary plane'.

The new design was designated DH.60M and instantly became the 'Metal Moth'. The first prototype, G-AAAR (339), was completed in mid-August and flown by Hubert Broad on a 15 minute test on 6th September. The aircraft qualified for a C of A on 29th October and such was the urgency to test her in winter conditions that she was almost immediately despatched to Canada where she was registered G-CAVX to the de Havilland Company on 30th November and evaluated by the RCAF on wheels, skis and floats. She later survived as a Club aeroplane until 1937 when she stalled in gusty conditions and crashed when landing on Wolfe Island.

The new structure was welcomed by all in Canada and the fifth and sixth bare frames extracted from the jigs, Nos 349 and 350, were sent to the Dominion and exchanged for wooden fuselages. They were to be the first of a continuous stream of bare frames and split undercarriages supplied from Stag Lane which, together with Gipsy engines sent to replace the old Cirrus, provided years of extended life for almost all the earliest imports and many airframes undergoing major repairs. The fashion was followed in other countries too and several wooden Moths operated by the subsidised clubs in New Zealand were granted life extensions by the implant of steel tube fuselages. The second flight-capable aircraft, G-AACD (340), qualified for her C of A on 30th October and was retained by her maker for a multiplicity of tasks concerned with future development.

When operated in conditions of heat and from high-altitude airfields, the performance of the DH.60M with a Gipsy I engine was described as 'lumpen' when compared with the wooden DH.60G, often barely making a 100fpm rate of climb. And unlike Canada with its sophisticated aviation facilities, the DH.60M proved far more difficult to repair in places like Africa where, according to Shell Aviation historian Hugh Scanlan: '...every township had its Indian *fundi*, who could fashion almost anything from wood...'.

Canadian-designed skis were tested by the Royal Canadian Air Force at Camp Borden on the prototype DH.60M Metal Moth, G-CAVX, which had been received from Stag Lane late in 1928 and retained by the Company as a demonstrator. The Air Force was subsequently supplied with 30 sets of skis which were said to have given 'perfect satisfaction'. de Havilland

John Carberry took his DH.60X G-EBXP to Canada with him in July, and in September flew her in a race from New York to Los Angeles where he was placed first in a local Speed and Efficiency Contest. The aircraft was later registered in the USA and eventually sold to Mexico. BAE Systems

Engineers from the de Havilland Service Department, aided by Vicomte de Sibour, tinker with the engine of DH.60G G-EBZR, before the Vicomte and his wife left on a world tour, sent-off by a large party of well-wishers who gathered at Stag Lane on 14th September. BAE Systems

Sixteen Canadian clubs provided aircraft for their first big air race at Border Cities, Essex County in September, flying around a 100 mile course and it surprised few that DH.60 Moths took the first three places. DH.60X Moth G-CAUE (637), was bought by two members of the Hamilton Aero Club, Kenneth Whyte and Harry Campbell, specially to take part in the 2,145 mile International Race from Windsor, Ontario, to Los Angeles, and in taking three and a half days, came second to an aircraft with double their engine power. Already in Los Angeles for the National Races was John Carberry and his DH.60X Moth G-CAXP, the previously registered G-EBXP (626), now resident in Toronto. Carberry had been a contestant in the Transcontinental Race starting from New York and achieved 18th place amongst the 22 finishers, and, much to the surprise and consternation of American designers, subsequently winning the Speed and Efficiency Contest by completing the 50 mile circuit at a speed of 95mph, reportedly carrying 560 lb of ballast. G-CAXP was sold to the Ryan Aeronautical Corporation of San Diego the following March and registered NC9305, following which she passed through a number of different local ownerships until 1934 when she was sold to Mexico.

Moths had little to prove where the subject of long-distance flying was concerned and many names, reputations and feats of staggering audacity were yet to unfold. One of the most fulfilling journeys by Moth was begun in a blare of publicity at Stag Lane on 14th September when the Vicomte de Sibour and his wife Violette, daughter of department store magnate Gordon Self-ridge, left in their blue and silver DH.60G Moth G-EBZR (844) on nothing less than a tour of the world. No records or stunts were

sought and there was no fixed schedule. The trip was estimated to last about nine months during which time they would see as much as possible travelling between 6.00am and noon, and then only on fine days.

From Stag Lane the de Sibour's route was first to Paris then Lyons, through Spain to North Africa and via Tunis along the well-trodden route to India. From there they flew over 'extremely dangerous country' via Burma and Indo-China into Siam and on to Japan where the Moth was dismantled and sent by ship to Seattle. So began a flight across the USA during which they were received by President Hoover, ending in New York. G-EBZR was shipped to France to allow the crew to spend time at their home in Paris before they flew back to Stag Lane, there to be greeted by Captain de Havilland on Friday 19th July 1929.

During the ten month tour the de Sibours had covered 33,000 miles and all appeared to have been nothing less than routine, except for an extraordinary episode in Iraq recalled by the Vicomte. Fearing an Arab attack on a British adventurer, an RAF punitive expedition was sent out, accompanied by an officer with the Vicomte in G-EBZR, armed with smoke bombs. The Moth ran very short of fuel and after landing in the desert, taxied for 35 miles before the petrol finally ran out. The crew started to walk and were spotted by another aircraft when transport was sent out with supplies.

Following the apparent overnight success of the Handley Page 'slot' and its heavy promotion as a safety device, some pilots seemed to misunderstand the philosophy behind the system. The Air Ministry was moved to issue a Notice on 24th September 1928:

The attention of all pilots is drawn to the fact that the object of the Handley Page Automatic Slot is to improve the safety factor of flying by giving increased control to aircraft when brought below the flying speed either through inadvertence on the part of the pilot or in cases of real emergency.

'Unless, therefore, all slotted aircraft are normally flown exactly as if they were not fitted with slots, the additional margin of safety given by the slots is entirely destroyed.

'Consequently it is particularly emphasised that the criterion of good pilotage in normal flying should be that the slots are never in use for the purpose of giving control below stalling speed, except in the emergencies for which they were originally fitted.'

The second safety matter was a patent granted on 27th September 1928 in the joint names of Hubert Stanford Broad and the de Havilland Aircraft Company Ltd, for an improved safety harness: '...relating to harness for airmen and refers particularly to harness intended to be worn by a passenger, for example, the pilot, as a safety device when performing evolutions such as looping and the like, and when other movements of the machine are effected which would otherwise tend to place the passenger in danger of falling from the craft...'.

Until the de Havilland harness was designed (the patent application was made in July 1927) the standard restraint consisted only of a broad chord lap-strap or a de Havilland designed four-point shoulder harness. The new design featured shoulder straps connecting by means of a steel pin to a single floor-mounted crutch strap, although even this advance proved to be but an interim step. The Air Ministry had previously decided it did not like the three-point harness as no other Service type was fitted with it, and issued instructions for the four-strap Sutton Mk IV to be fitted as standard for all current and future contracts. In addition, arrangements should be made for drawings and fittings kits to be supplied for retrospective conversion of Moths already delivered. It was appreciated that installation in the rear cockpits of Genet Moths would be different from the Cirrus, entailing a variation on the type of anchorage to be employed.

The de Havilland Company refused to comply with this request on the grounds that the Sutton Mk IV was entirely unsuitable for installation in a Moth cockpit. The matter rumbled on from May until September when it was agreed that the Company's own four-point harness was acceptable after all and the necessary Technical Order was published. A stock of harness sets had been created at Stag Lane, each of the four individual straps stamped with a numerical indication of the sequence of attachment to the central pin. These were rejected on the grounds that the sequence was not in accordance with current Service practice (left arm; right leg; left leg; right arm), and although it was agreed they could be released for civil use, they were banned from installation in any Service aircraft contracted for construction or reconditioning.

The frailty of the old system had been revealed on 13th September by a bizarre accident at Lympne. Having been instructed in aerobatics in the morning, Guy Skinner, described as a 'large man weighing over 15 stone' was practising solo in the late afternoon flying DH.60X Moth G-EBSS (423). After several well-executed manoeuvres the aircraft entered a spin from which she made a sharp recovery at about 800ft when the pilot was thrown out of the rear cockpit. Examination of the wreckage revealed that his seat belt had broken at the port anchorage and that the leather restraint in the front cockpit was badly torn in the same area.

A month later, on 14th October, David Tennant, a BBC wireless announcer, arrived at Lympne en-route from Stag Lane to France in his DH.60X G-EBZP (681), with his wife sitting on the lap of a friend in the front cockpit, presumably restrained by no seat belt at all. The authorities at Lympne prohibited further progress and David Tennant flew to St Inglevert first with his friend, returning to Lympne to collect his wife, after which the threesome continued their interrupted journey to Paris. Tennant made the headlines again in November when it was reported that he had inherited £90,000 following the death of his mother.

Those stationed along the route between England and Africa were becoming accustomed to the regular passage of itinerant Moths. Flying red and silver DH.60G

A rare shot of a DH.60X Moth with the engine cowlings removed, revealing how far forward in the wooden bearers it was necessary to locate the main unit, to allow auxiliaries, such as the magnetos, to be accommodated ahead of the bulkhead. The presence of the test gantry would indicate that G-EBZZ was almost certainly undergoing final checks at Stag Lane before leaving on her delivery flight to Accra.
Richard Riding

Captain Robert Rattray's arrival in Accra on 15th January 1929 was greeted with considerable interest from officials and members of the local population.
DH Moth Club Archive

Lieutenant R R 'Dick' Bentley and his much travelled DH.60X G-EBSO, in two-seat configuration, complete with a Mk II split undercarriage and a Cirrus III engine for which the cowlings and spinner had been specially designed by Neville Stack.
Richard Riding

G-AAAH (804) in a single-seat, long-range configuration, Wally Hope left Stag Lane on 11th September bound for Kenya where he was to collect photographs of a Royal Visit to the colony on behalf of the *Daily Mirror*. The outward trip was delayed when Hope suffered sunstroke after leaving Cairo, and just managed to land at Wadi Halfa where he was committed to bed for a fortnight. On the return journey he shipped the Moth from Alexandria to Brindisi which saved time, but plans for a direct flight from there to London were thwarted by strong *mistral* winds. When approaching Paris at low level and in poor visibility, the propeller was shattered after hitting a bird and Hope was forced to charter an aircraft for London where he arrived on 17th October with his precious consignment of plates.

Stanley Halse and his wife left Croydon on 19th September in their new DH.60G Moth G-EBYS (829), bound for Johannesburg, where following their safe arrival the aircraft was registered ZS-ABO in November. Flying in the opposite direction was Lady Mary Bailey in DH.60X G-EBTG (469), repaired following an abortive start from South Africa in May. She had finally left for England on 21st September, though a series of delays caused by illness, bad weather and official obstructionism, meant she did not reach a snow-covered Croydon Airport until 16th January 1929. At Mogodor on Boxing Day, she had met Captain Robert Rattray, a Provincial Commissioner on the Gold Coast, who had left Croydon on 5th December in his new DH.60X G-EBZZ (691), bound for Accra. Mary Bailey's much praised achievement was completely unostentatious and flown against no pre-conceived timetable. Captain de Havilland flew G-EBTG back to Stag Lane from Croydon, anxious to see how the aeroplane had sur-

Repainted since her record-breaking achievements earlier in the summer, DH.60G G-EBWV looking very travel-stained when photographed at Stag Lane prior to shipment to Canada, from where she took off on 17th October 1928 and was last seen 600 miles east of Newfoundland. *Flight*

vived practically no attention at all for almost four months in a variety of different environments.

Dick Bentley, who had already flown his DH.60X Moth G-EBSO from London to Cape Town and back again, left Croydon with his wife on 19th October for another flight to South Africa. The aircraft carried a silver plaque, a gift to Bentley from members of the Liverpool and District Aero Club where he had spent most of his summer months instructing. Changes to G-EBSO since her previous trip included the fitting of a Mk II split undercarriage and a Cirrus III engine, this provided by ADC Aircraft together with a new cowling and spinner designed by company test pilot Neville Stack. The Bentleys arrived in Pretoria three days before Christmas, but England had not seen the last of them.

Sadly, nothing more was seen of Henry MacDonald and DH.60G Moth G-EBWV after she was spotted by the Dutch steamer *Hardenburg*, 600 miles east of Newfoundland at about 0300 GMT on 17th October, steering a course that would have taken them to Iceland. MacDonald had purchased the aircraft following Hubert Broad's 24 hour endurance test in August and, following modifications which were completed by mid September, had shipped her from Liverpool to St Johns with a view to flying her back across the Atlantic directly to Stag Lane. By utilising the front cockpit, fuel capacity had been increased to 100 gallons which MacDonald believed would equate to a 35 hour endurance. Other informed opinion estimated that at the most economical cruising speed, fuel would be exhausted after a maximum of 26 hours, probably insufficient for the 2,000 mile crossing to Ireland even with a following wind forecast at 30mph. It was hoped that MacDonald had, perhaps, actually landed in Iceland or ditched in the sea near a ship, but no trace of him or the record-breaking aeroplane was ever found.

The last production DH.60X Cirrus Moth to be completed at Stag Lane was No 702, purchased by the British Aviation Insurance Group and registered G-AABL she was delivered as a replacement aircraft to the London Aeroplane Club on 22nd September. It was not to be a happy association. Thirty-six days later she was badly damaged in a heavy landing, then the following June she collided on landing with Frederick Guest's DH.60X G-EBUS (444). In October 1930 she crashed at nearby Kingsbury and was written off.

The de Havilland Company had recognised the importance of establishing a foothold in the United States either through an agent supplied solely from Stag Lane, or preferably from a local production facility which would require heavy investment. During the summer of 1928, the Company identified a site at Buffalo, New York, at which they proposed to erect a factory to build both Moth airframes and Gipsy engines and arrangements were put in place for local provision of the $2 million considered necessary. The scheme was not proceeded with following an approach by Mr Minton M Warren of the Aero Supply Manufacturing Company Inc, and Richard F Hoyt of Hayden Stone and Company, to establish a new company quite independent of de Havilland, to import an agreed quota of DH.60G and DH.60M Moths from England before commencing to build both types under licence. These were to be fitted with British-built Gipsy engines until plans to manufacture units in the USA had come to fruition.

Following a visit to Stag Lane by Minton Warren during which he placed the first of an ultimate order for 16 DH.60G Moths to be delivered before the end of February 1929, the Moth Aircraft Corporation was constituted under the laws of the State of Delaware on 17th October 1928. A brick-built factory with floor space of 100,000ft^2, occupied during the First World War by the Cartridge Company, was acquired almost

immediately at Lowell Airport, Massachusetts, and plans were laid for the reception of disassembled aeroplanes shipped from Stag Lane with local manufacturing to begin as soon as equipment and labour could be organised. This proved not to be until the spring of 1929 and after American production of Gipsy engines had been licensed to the Wright Aeronautical Corporation of Paterson, New Jersey.

The first British-built DH.60G Seaplanes were Nos 839 and 840, ordered for the Sarawak Government in Borneo. They were never registered but rather operated against the authority of a State badge applied to the front fuselage sides. Hubert Broad flew both aircraft from the Medway at Rochester where they had been fitted with Short floats, qualifying for their Cs of A on 26th October. The following year, 840 was written off when she flew into telegraph wires and in November 1929, after a year of successful operations between flooded mines which dotted the interior of the country, 839 was sold to Malayan Air Services at Port Swettenham, with whom she was registered G-AASN. Late in 1934 the aircraft joined the Royal Singapore Flying Club, ironically as a landplane.

Catching a ship in England on 2nd November to travel to the USA was the plan of Clarence Chamberlain. He left Stag Lane in a Moth flown by Clem Pike only an hour before the *Leviathan* was due to sail from Southampton. The 72 miles to Hamble were covered in 42 minutes leaving 18 minutes to reach the docks by car, but it was insufficient. The ship had just sailed so Chamberlain chartered a motor launch and overtook the liner which allowed him to board. Who should be a fellow passenger but Lady Sophie Heath, lecturing on her South African adventures while travelling to attend a conference in Washington?

Flying solo from Croydon with a borrowed Cirrus III engine fitted to her DH.60X Moth G-EBZC (676), Lady Heath had claimed a new single seat world height record of 23,000ft on 4th October. Castrol Oil, the Cirrus Engine Company and ADC Aircraft immediately placed substantial advertising in the national newspapers acknowledging the achievement. The Royal Aero Club later failed to ratify the claim on the grounds that not only had the aircraft not been weighed prior to the attempt as required by International Regulations, but corrections applied to recorded barograph

At the end of a filming session in Tanganyika, Genet Moth D-1651 was hit by a storm, blown away and badly damaged. She was repaired by two German carpenters who happened to be touring the area at the time of the incident.
Jan den Das

values reduced the achieved height to 18,800ft, well below the existing record.

In the USA, the irrepressible Lady Heath subsequently failed in another world altitude record attempt at Curtiss Field on 3rd December but ten days later was presented to the House of Representatives in Washington, the only woman delegate at the International Air Conference being held in the city.

Two DH.60G Moths arrived at Lowell from Stag Lane in November: No 886 was registered NC9718 to George Washington Jnr of Mendham, New Jersey; the other, No 885, became NC9720 with the Heyer Products Co Inc, for use partly as a flying laboratory for development of magnetos and electrical test equipment for the aircraft industry. In later life this aircraft achieved fame when she was modified as a single-seat racer for American aviatrice Laura Ingalls who subsequently flew 980 continuous loops in a flight which lasted for 3hr 40min, and who later completed 714 continuous barrel rolls over St Louis. King White of the Cleveland Tractor Company paid a personal visit to Stag Lane before Christmas and sailed home with his DH.60G Moth No 924, NC9749. Between 1st January and 15th February 1929, 49 additional aircraft were sold by the new Corporation.

Under pressure from British business interests, Avro had been granted a licence to deliver 50 Avians into the USA. The Moth Aircraft Corporation was stung and were advised that the issue of a permit for another British-built type was very unlikely. By working through contacts in Washington, approval for the import of up to 20 aircraft was obtained although the hope had been for at least 40. While engines could be procured from Stag Lane, it was vital that airframe production in the USA was started as soon as practicable if the new company was to have a product to market.

The day after Clarence Chamberlain had almost missed his boat, Captain Malcolm Campbell and Flight Lieutenant David Don left Croydon in DH.60G G-AAAJ (803) for an aerial survey of parts of the North African desert, searching for a suitable location for an attempt by Campbell on the world land speed record. During their return flight to England, G-AAAJ successfully forced landed on a beach near Ouaouizert, Spanish Morocco, but ran into the sea. The aircraft was salvaged by the Spanish authorities and returned to Stag Lane for repairs after which

she was shipped to South Africa where Campbell resumed his search. In 1934, Campbell took DH.60III Moth Major G-ACMY (5055) to the Kalahari Desert on a similar mission.

Early in 1929, Sir Malcolm Campbell established an agency for the sale of new and second-hand Moths, opening a depot at Heston and a London shop at Byron House in St James' Street. By June the company claimed to be selling a new Moth every day. As an indication of how the Moth had become an accepted part of society, Sir Malcolm Campbell (1927) Ltd, advertised Moths for sale in the *Daily Telegraph*. In a leader, *The Shooting Times* suggested that 'many young fellows of wealth prefer a Moth plane to a pair of best guns' and an advertisement for a seven-roomed stone-built house in Kent proclaimed that at £1,000 the property was situated in a natural aerodrome and the garage provided accommodation for a car and a Moth.

Geoffrey de Havilland and his wife flying DH.60G G-AAAA, and accompanied by Alan and Lois Butler in their DH.60X G-EBUX, flew to Tempelhof Airport, Berlin from Stag Lane on 19th October 1928, to visit the Berlin Aero Show. The Captain took the opportunity to demonstrate the Gipsy Moth to the popular German stunt pilot Ernst Udet and others, and engage in friendly competition against locally based aircraft. Udet was impressed by the Moth although Captain de Havilland later expressed his dislike for the man as a person.

Following the acquisition of Genet Moth G-EBOU by Sir Malcolm Campbell's sales agency in May 1929, the aircraft was overhauled at Stag Lane and sold to Udet to be

flown by him and Leni Riefenstahl. Udet collected the aircraft on 11th June and immediately took part in an aerobatic competition at Essen, claiming the Moth was the only aircraft which could be put up against his arch-rival Gerhard Fieseler's special machine. The Genet Moth was registered D-1651 and subsequently appeared at many displays in Germany and in a film made in the Alps, *Weisse Holle am Piz Palu*, in which, equipped with skis, the aeroplane is used to rescue the damsel in distress. Between October 1930 and March 1931 she appeared in a film shot in Tanganyika, *Strange Birds over Africa*. At the end of production, the set was hit by a sudden storm and D-1651 was blown about 100ft across the ground and wrecked. Two German carpenters who happened to be in the area and who had never seen a light aeroplane close up, were enrolled to rebuild her. This they did, lacking only silver dope to complete the job.

During the flight home to Germany, the aircraft was forced landed in the scudd country of the Upper Nile near Malakal in the Sudan. The news that Udet was missing reached Tom Campbell Black in Khartoum, where he had stopped to refuel during the delivery flight of his Puss Moth to Nairobi. By great good fortune whilst en-route to Juba, Campbell Black spotted the aircraft and landed alongside to offer Udet much-needed supplies of food and water before flying on to report his position.

Another film appearance was in *SOS Eisberg* shot in Greenland in 1932 in which Ernst Udet played himself. Following a series of low-level manoeuvres on 13th August, the Genet Moth was flown straight into an ice-strewn sea. Before the scene ends the pilot is

Captain de Havilland taking his seat in the rear cockpit of his DH.60G Moth G-AAAA, equipped with a coupé top, in October 1928. The moving parts of the arrangement can be easily identified, and on this first model there are no deflector plates for the rear cockpit's open sides. The style of hat worn by the occupant of the front seat leads to the supposition that it is Arthur Hagg, who may have had a hand in the design of the coupé arrangement. LNA

The coupé top as a unit was available at £25.0s.0d when supplied separately, or £34.15s.0d when fitted by the works. At 8ft 9in long, a standard weight of 15 lb was quoted for the transparencies, spruce frame, fixings and the plywood extension which faired into the rear decking, a figure by which the baggage allowance consequently was reduced. The rounded, single piece, front windscreen moulding was made from 1.5mm thick Cellon, as were the top covers to front and rear cockpits, the 'decking' which separated them and the internal transparent bulkhead behind the front seat. The cross-over rigging wires for the rear cabane struts passed through eyelets let into the centre decking at positions that could only be determined after the aircraft had been erected. A fixed ³⁄₁₆in thick Triplex glass panel was fitted on the port side of the enclosure at the front cockpit position only and although there were no side panels at all for the rear seat, a slipstream deflector was mounted vertically to both sides of the coupé frame. Each seat had its own roof cover which was hinged along its left edge and when open allowed access through the narrow drop-down doors on the starboard side. The first aircraft manufactured with a coupé top was DH.60G G-AADC (917), delivered to Captain W R (Bill) Bailey at Stag Lane three days before Christmas.

seen to climb out of the cockpit and along the rear decking until the tail swings down to the water. It is believed that if D-1651 had been fitted with floats she would have been saved for another day but was instead allowed to sink, and was officially cancelled in February 1933 as 'destroyed'.

It has been suggested that it was Mrs de Havilland who proposed more or better protection for passengers in open cockpits as the result of sitting in the front seat of G-EBWV during the world height record flight with her husband in July. As a seasoned aviatrice since 1910, it seems unlikely, but, shortly after the de Havillands returned to Stag Lane following their touring holiday to the West Country in DH.60G Moth G-AAAA in August, The Captain did admit that he

started to set out basic plans for what was to materialise in September the following year as the DH.80 Moth Three. Perhaps it was as an interim measure that G-AAAA was fitted with a coupé top, photographed from all angles and heavily promoted from the beginning of November 1928?

'...the new coupé top, which can be supplied permanently fixed or as a separate unit for permanent attachment to a standard Moth, affords complete protection to both cockpits. Warm, draught-proof, and noise reducing, the Moth coupé provides limousine comfort at low cost. With eyes protected from the rush of air, goggles and helmet are unnecessary in fact, no special flying kit is required. The view in all directions is comfortable and unrestricted...'

Early Moth Seaplanes were generally fitted with a front cockpit door on the starboard side of the fuselage only permitting the passenger egress onto the starboard wing root and subsequently via the leading edge, down onto the float to assist with mooring. The long exhaust pipe mounted on the fuselage side prevented an exit to port until a door was placed on that side in which case the exhaust pipe was removed and replaced with stubs or the long pipe

A side view illustrating the clean lines of the coupé version of the DH.60G, with Oscar Handley Cooke, Editor of the *de Havilland Gazette*, standing by the rudder. The decking behind the rear seat incorporated a wider than standard locker door, although maximum stowed weight was limited due to the additional mass of the coupé top. *The Aeroplane*

JULY TO DECEMBER 1928

Although DH.60G CH-205 was registered to the Basel Section of the Swiss Aero Club, the aircraft was housed initially at Stag Lane before moving to Switzerland, where she suffered major damage in April 1930. de Havilland

had a 'U' bend built in, wide and deep enough to accept the door when flapped down. Such was the case when a coupé top was specified for a Moth Seaplane. The door was on the port side; the top cover of the front cockpit only was hinged to open to starboard and the Triplex side screen was moved to that side too.

Shell's continued operation of G-EBQE throughout the European winters of 1927 and 1928 convinced the company that for serious business use an aircraft with a closed and heated cockpit was probably essential. Britain's first recognised business aircraft came to a bizarre end. Following sale to Heston in June 1929 she was owned by a miscellany of different names until 1931 when she was acquired by Lauro de Bosis, an Italian anti-Fascist exiled to France. The new owner took off from Cannes and headed in the general direction of Italy with the front cockpit loaded with propaganda leaflets, but he soon became disorientated and crash landed at Bastia, Corsica, where the lightly damaged aircraft appears to have been abandoned.

G-EBQE had been traded-in by Shell for DH.60X G-AAIM (1153), furnished with a coupé top, but in spite of a continuing programme of modifications the canopied Moth was never a success. G-AAIM, *Arom II,* was re-converted to open cockpit configuration fitted with a new Cirrus engine, the 105hp Hermes, and continued in service with Shell until replaced by the elegant and efficient DH.80 Puss Moth in 1930. The expansion of the Shell fleet began in 1929 with acquisition of a DH.60M, R135 (1429), for use in Argentina, then with additional DH.60Ms in Australia, South Africa, India and Kenya.

Apart from pictures showing Captain de Havilland flying in a lounge suit and trademark trilby hat, supporting the coupé top publicists, most other aviators appear to have maintained their traditional mode of dress. In spite of an increase in cruising speed of about 6mph few aircraft were fitted with the coupé top which owners more

used to open cockpits soon found was limiting their view and creating a mild degree of claustrophobia. In nearly all cases, factory-fitted tops later were removed and the Moths returned to standard configuration. When first installed it was suggested that the coupé top on G-AAAA was a temporary arrangement, but not until 1st April 1930 was the top removed and three days later the aircraft was sold to Ivor McClure of the Automobile Association to whom the registration letters were all important.

Following the 1928 King's Cup Air Race, Alan Butler's nominal DH.60X Moth G-EBQH remained at Stag Lane, unflown but certainly not neglected. During the autumn she received a racing Gipsy engine identical with that fitted in DH.71 Tiger Moth G-EBQU, and there is some evidence to suppose it might have been the same engine. Alan Butler flew her around the local area on two short circuits on 14th October followed by two longer sessions during the first week of

November. It was the Chairman's intention to make an attempt on the World Speed Record for two-seat light aircraft and, in an effort to achieve the maximum weight of 883 lb, some lightening measures were necessary. The sole petrol tank of 9 gallons capacity was faired into the centre section and the tank in the front cockpit, with its pump and piping, was removed, as was the front control column and its socket. The pilot and passenger were obliged to sit in lightened seats without cushions and, in addition to general streamlining, the front cockpit was to be totally enclosed. As presented, G-EBQH weighed 879 lb.

The aircraft was flown on the Stag Lane speed course on 1st December and with a DH5180/4 propeller of 5ft 11in diameter, at 2,600rpm achieved an indicated speed of 127mph. More local testing followed during the next few days. On the morning of Friday 7th December, Alan Butler flew his conventional DH.60X G-EBUX on the well-known

In conditions of poor visibility and low cloud, Alan and Lois Butler took off from Stag Lane at 3.35pm on Friday, 7th December in their racing-configuration DH.60, G-EBQH, and landed back in near-darkness half an hour later, having created a new World Speed Record for a 100km closed circuit. The news was broken to those attending the Works' Dinner that same evening. British Aerospace

Cirrus Moth J9109 in a single-seat configuration and sporting patterned wheel discs, with another aircraft painted in a similar fashion standing behind, probably J9115, photographed during a winter detachment to 22 Squadron based at A&AEE Martlesham Heath. DH Moth Club Archive

route towards Reading, familiarising himself with the landmarks in conditions of poor visibility and low cloud. Following a local flight in G-EBQH, at 3.35pm, with his wife Lois as passenger, snuggled down inside the closed front cockpit, hidden from view, he took off again in G-EBQH and 30min later landed back at Stag Lane in conditions of near-darkness. Using the turning point at Twyford, just beyond Maidenhead, a closed circuit of 100km had been flown at an average speed of 119.84mph to secure a new world record for the class. It was widely suspected that a higher speed could have been achieved under better conditions, but 7th December was the date of the de Havilland Works' Dinner, and there can be little doubt that a record set on that day was too much of a temptation. The aeroplane was flown again before and after Christmas and on 29th December is credited with a speed of 124mph on the Reading course, flying outbound at 400ft and returning at 1,200ft, possibly as a plum for the Company's AGM which was to be held two days later.

Following Hubert Broad's public endurance test of both man and the Gipsy engine in August, the Company decided to embark on another practical adventure with their new engine. Early in December, the redoubtable G-EBTD was reclaimed from duties with the de Havilland School of Flying and fitted with a Gipsy I engine taken at random from the production line. After forty seals were applied by officials from the Aeronautical Inspection Directorate (AID), so that only routine maintenance such as cleaning of sparking plugs and filters and the adjustment of tappet and contact breaker clearances was still achievable, the aircraft was released to fly a target figure of 600 hours. Pilots were selected, mostly, from amongst the instructional staff of the de Havilland School, and their brief was to achieve the 600 hours as soon as practicable, cruising at a speed of 85mph. A log of

achieved flying hours and distance flown was maintained as usual but, welcoming another opportunity for publicity, the updated figures were sign-written on the fuselage sides on a daily basis. The 'Sealed Engine Tour' as the venture became known, clocked the first figures on 29th December and was to continue for another nine months.

Bob Loader had moved the Canadian Company into new city offices in Bay Street, Toronto, on 1st November and doubled the size of the assembly plant at Mount Dennis, where the workforce had been increased from three to 30. Three weeks later the Canadian Government announced that the following year it would be spending £80,000 on new aircraft for the Royal Canadian Air Force and the flying clubs but before the end of 1928 de Havilland had received an order for 100 DH.60M Moths, 34 of which were to be utilised by the RCAF for primary training at Camp Borden. By February 1930, 119 Metal Moths had been delivered to Canada, the 1929 build positions 713-800 being reserved exclusively for the commitment which continued to receive top-up orders. By modern standards, the attrition rate was extraordinarily high: 70 aircraft were written off within ten years and 25 were lost in anything but combative situations during the war with another 18 in the early days of peace.

One observer noted that at Stag Lane Aerodrome on a Friday morning late in the year, Moths for Denmark, Belgium and Spain had all left together in formation to clear customs at Lympne, leaving others for the USA, Czechoslovakia, Finland, Portuguese East Africa and Chile to await export. Moth production was averaging eleven airframes per week together with 20 Gipsy engines, a number soon to be increased to 16 airframes and 30 engines with all production sold until April 1929. In order to raise £120,000 to fund expansion,

during the year the Company had offered shares to the public. At the next Annual General Meeting, investors were advised that in 1927, 117 machines had been delivered against 336 for the current year and that the workforce had grown during the same period from 400 to 1,560.

The Royal Australian Air Force opted for the DH.60 as their standard primary training aircraft too and in December, de Havilland's agent in China, Arnhold and Company in Shanghai, secured an order against fierce German and American competition, to supply four Moths to be operated commercially. But the South African Air Force stood back and after evaluating the DH.60G Moth, a Spartan and an Avian, both powered by Hermes engines, during trials held in Pretoria, ordered the Avro aeroplane to be fitted with a Genet Major engine, in preference.

The loss of the 20 aircraft order to their competitor stung de Havilland, and the blame was laid firmly at the feet of the Company's local agent, John Veasey, who, as the result of other business matters, had been declared 'insolvent'. St Barbe was interested to receive subsequent reports that the SAAF pilots did not like the Avian and following arrival of the first two machines, deliveries had been suspended until after the Genet engines had been boosted and persuaded to provide more power which, in the South African environment, created the potential for unreliability. The Business Manager was left with a feeling of growing optimism that a Gipsy II-powered Moth still might be 'got in'.

The Air Ministry were in a quandary about the future of the six Genet Moths still on charge. Although the provision of slots for the older design of wings had been achieved, a plan to convert the aircraft to accept Cirrus engines was abandoned in November and the aircraft were routed through the Stag Lane factory for refurbishment, mostly in the spring of 1929, in the certain knowledge that they would be allowed to go obsolete.

A bad fire in the Stag Lane Dope Shop was brought under control with minimal loss of material and no interruption to supply or to the expansive building works which were evident everywhere. According to Alan Butler, these were the key to the future:

'...the facilities that are now at our disposal through the extensions to our works, coupled with our overseas connections, has, we believe, put us in a position second to none to meet a demand that is soon to rank in the first line of England's trades...'

JANUARY TO DECEMBER 1929

ALAN BUTLER and Frank Hearle arrived in New York on 16th January 1929 to meet the principal shareholders in the Moth Aircraft Corporation (MAC) and to discuss the serious matters of finance and business. The English visitors were conducted around the site of the aircraft factory at Lowell where progress in fitting-out was noted to be very slow, and they met executives of Curtiss-Wright at Paterson where they learned that the Gipsy engine was be built at a new factory in the mid-West, beginning in May and until which time they probably would take ten engines a month from Stag Lane. The directors of the Corporation already controlled other aircraft businesses, some of which would be groomed to act as distributors and agents. Their interest in the Moth's sales potential was linked to what was planned to be exclusive provision of Wright-built Gipsy engines. Richard Hoyt, a New York banker, Chairman of the Moth Aircraft Corporation, also held the position of Chairman of the Curtiss-Wright company.

A British-built engine delivered to the USA was already being dismantled for the purposes of inspection and education. Alan Butler was assured that, apart from American specification screws and threads and dimensions quoted in decimal inches rather than metric detail, the engine would not be altered apart from the possible application of Scintilla magnetos when a suitable model became available. In March, Wright announced that production was likely to start in July at St Louis, Missouri, in a new small-engine factory offering production capacity of 200 units per month. They also confirmed that in order to conform to American standards dictated by the Department of Commerce, they were being forced to change the direction of rotation from left to right hand. It was the same Department that decreed that a wire-braced rear fuselage was unacceptable and that the entire structure should embrace welded joints. They also insisted on more substantial wing spars and ribs for which drawings and a stress analysis were submitted in March.

The change in engine rotation was to have a knock-on effect in that cylinder inlets and exhausts, manifolds and carburettor, were all changed to the right hand side of the engine. This necessitated a reversal of

cowling orientation and the long exhaust pipe, now fixed to the fuselage right side unless exchanged for stubs, meant that doors were necessary on the left. Engine production was eventually centred on the Curtiss-Robertson Company plant at St Louis where the 50 hour Type Test, required by the Department of Commerce, ended successfully with only a 0.04 per cent drop in horsepower and no mechanical deficiencies.

The first DH.60G Moth to be exported to the Moth Aircraft Corporation at Lowell was No 814. Registered G-AAAM to Gerald Maxwell of Chrysler Motors in London, she was re-registered NC9704 to the Moth Aircraft Corporation in October 1928. In January, Lady Heath was commissioned to fly her from New York to Florida to take part in an air race meeting. For much of the 1,500 mile journey, achieved in 18 flying hours over several days, the weather was cold and miserable and short of fuel on arrival in Florida, the aircraft was put down without incident on Daytona Beach.

During the races, believing the engine was running hot, Sophie Heath, a licensed engineer, removed the top cowling and all the cooling baffles under the misapprehension that this would improve matters instead of which the engine was cooked. She called the Moth Aircraft Corporation's New York office to claim that Gipsy engines were unsuitable for American conditions and that she should be provided with a Cirrus II. Later, when the Corporation made an approach to a major US dealer offering distribution rights in the south, the business was rejected, it is believed as a direct result of this incident.

On 29th January, Sophie Heath took the oath to become an American citizen and in February, after a dispute with the Department of Commerce, was issued with a Commercial licence. On 29th August in Cleveland, following an extensive tour of the USA promoting the American-built Cirrus engine fitted to an Avian, she was invited to sample the new Cirrus-powered Great Lakes Trainer. The engine was not functioning correctly and the aircraft stalled during an acute sideslipping manoeuvre and crashed through the roof of the Mills Company factory, Lady Heath sustaining serious

head and spinal injuries which many believed had brought an end to her short but epic aviation career.

Following their meetings in New York, Butler and Hearle boarded a train to Toronto. A number of urgent business matters required their attention at the Canadian Company which in 1928 had made a public issue of stock. The majority of the shares were held by directors on behalf of the parent company at Stag Lane and Alan Butler had been elected President. One important issue concerned the financing of a new Company factory and aerodrome at a remote 70 acre site already selected at Dufferin Street. Butler was not convinced it was the correct location but upon reflection changed his opinion and in April 1929 the site was purchased to become the Canadian Company's permanent home.

After Frank Hearle left for England, in February Alan Butler returned to continue business discussions in the USA and to visit the New York Aero Show where the third production DH.60M (341), shipped from Stag Lane in January, was on display wearing '9731' on her rudder. The aircraft was painted in what became trade-mark colours of American Moths, a very attractive scheme of yellow and black, causing Butler to write that 'the Corporation people had got the Moth up very nicely but the rest of the show was in my opinion, rather poor'. This same aircraft was later registered in the name of Richard F Hoyt at Hayden Stone and Co of New York.

The first British aircraft to be sold to China for seven years, DH.60G G-AABM (816), left Stag Lane on 2nd January bound for Shanghai where she was to be flown as a demonstrator by Captain William Jones, Manager of the Aviation Department of de Havilland agent Arnhold and Company. The four aircraft already ordered, Nos 1023-1026, were all shipped at the end of the month, purchased by the Chinese Commercial Aviation Company of Loyang. By the end of the year a further 20 DH.60Gs had been despatched for military use as trainers and communications machines. Frank Swoffer later joined Arnhold as a test pilot, flying an increasing number of new Moths as they were received and erected and converting Marshal Chang Hsueh-Liang, Provincial

DH.60X Moth Seaplane A17-26, one of the batch built for the Royal Australian Air Force by the Larkin Aircraft Supply Company, and taken on charge in July 1930. RAAF Museum

Larkin issued build numbers 1-32 for their aircraft (A7-23 to A7-54), the first of which was not delivered until June 1930, four months behind schedule. Thereafter, deliveries flowed until the last aircraft was taken on charge in March 1931. Although the order was successfully completed within the contracted schedule, the RAAF showed reluctance to accept the last aircraft on the grounds that they were too early and had not been allocated a role.

At Stag Lane, Francis St Barbe was furious with Hereward de Havilland and his fellow directors and the manner in which the Larkin Company had been allowed to take the business. That the Australian Company was not in a position to undertake construction of the 32 Moths was due to Major de Havilland's refusal to install sufficient production equipment at Melbourne on the grounds that after the RAAF order, it might never be required again. Through his contacts, St Barbe subsequently learned that the order had been a government attempt to encourage the total manufacture of the Moth aircraft by the de Havilland Company in Australia, and the contract had deliberately called for a delivery schedule extended over three years to allow for the installation of equipment and the recruitment and training of a core labour force.

Ever anxious to economise, at Stag Lane the Company decided that rather than continue to pay the freelance Hubert Broad a fixed fee for every new Moth he flew, in addition to Flying School instructors called in for occasional testing, a simple option

Ruler of Manchuria, onto his luxuriously-appointed Puss Moth.

The Chinese order was fulfilled at a time when de Havilland was able to claim completion of a Moth on average 'once every five hours', with 60 aeroplanes in total manufactured in January. Far from creating an aura of wonderment, some flying club members wanted to know why the price remained obstinately high and still out of reach of most. That situation was worsened when the Australian Government announced on 15th April that it had contracted for the supply of 32 DH.60X Moths for the Defence Department at a price of £448 each. The position was clarified after the successful bidder, the Larkin Aircraft Supply Company (Australian agents for the Avro Avian and Cirrus engines) of Coode Island, Melbourne, confirmed it was to build the airframe rather than de Havilland Australia who themselves had no facilities to cope with production. Larkin were to be supplied with engines, instruments and other miscellaneous equipment by the Australian Government, equipment which was not included in the quoted price. The royalty to be paid to de Havilland by the government was £1,300.

The RAAF never was convinced about the suitability of the Cirrus engine to military requirements, with the possible exception of initial training, and the contract was changed for the aircraft to be supplied as DH.60G Moths. Seven of them were to be seaplanes for the Seaplane Training Flight at Point Cook. During the period the RAAF

operated seaplanes it is likely that never more than two were ever operational concurrently, a situation governed by the fact that only two sets of floats were ever in commission. By June 1931 these had begun to show signs of corrosion and the decision was made that all Moths should be configured only as landplanes.

From the beginning, production ran behind schedule as Larkin claimed they had not been supplied with a full set of drawings while there were inaccuracies in some of those they had, delaying the design and construction of jigs and special tooling. As a contingency, the Australian Air Board placed an order with de Havilland to supply eight DH.60M Moths (1354-1361) which were built in England, assembled by de Havilland in Melbourne and delivered on 23rd January 1930 with assigned serials A7-61 to A7-68.

DH.60G Moth VT-AAB was operated by the Karachi Aero Club from February 1929 and in 1933 was loaned to the Houston Mount Everest Expedition after their own Moth was damaged. VT-AAB was impressed into military service in 1942 but did not survive beyond 1944. DH Moth Club Archive

Wooden Moth fuselages and welded frames in black enamel finish, side by side in the Stag Lane Works in May 1929. DH Moth Club Archive

DH.60M CF-CAD of the Hamilton Aero Club and Sam Foley on the Penny Farthing, who dressed up like 'Uncle Henry' for the Club's 'Air Meet' in 1929. Via Gerry Schwam

Aerodrome builder Morris Jackaman with his sister, a Riley Nine and 'boneshaker' bicycle at the family aerodrome at Slough. DH Moth Club Archive

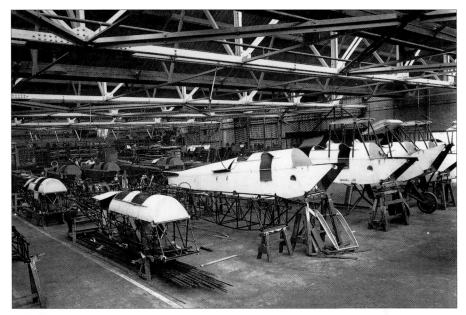

would be to engage a dedicated production test pilot recruited from within the Company ranks and available 'as required'. The spotlight fell on Jack Tyler, the Company's Chief Ground Engineer who had learned to fly with the School in 1927 and who was quickly groomed for his new career.

Early in November 1928, the London Aeroplane Club gave notice that it would be raffling a DH.60 Moth at Christmas. Tickets were available in books of ten at ten shillings each. The aircraft was the old Cirrus I Moth G-EBMF (194), which had been badly damaged in October after she had run into a fence when landing in a field off the aerodrome. Now fully restored, she was offered with a new C of A. The draw was made on 19th January 1929 and the winning ticket holder, Tony Gee, an engineer with the Iraq Petroleum Company, was cabled with the news at his home in Baghdad. According to a Club news item, G-EBMF was almost immediately packed for despatch to Iraq but it is doubtful whether she ever left England. She was used extensively for joyriding around the country by Gee's friend and part-time London Club instructor, Gordon Store, building experience as a stepping stone on the path towards his illustrious position as a senior airline captain which lasted well into the jet age. The aeroplane survived many subsequent adventures until she was scrapped at Gatwick in 1947.

When the first DH.60G Moths were introduced into the Club in April as the old Cirrus-engined aircraft were gradually phased out, all members were required to fly a check-circuit with an instructor to acquaint themselves with the differences imposed by the left hand rotation of the Gipsy I, and what that meant in handling the aeroplane.

Regular monitoring of aircraft weight was carried out by the Stag Lane Design Department in an early effort to identify trends. With DH.60M production now established, at the end of January a randomly-selected wooden DH.60X fuselage (reference No 14705) was weighed after removal from the jig (78 lb), after primer coat painting (84 lb), and as a fitted-out unit, less engine (154 lb). These figures then were compared with a more critical analysis of a metal frame (reference No 1441A), again selected at random. Assembled in the Fitting Shop on 14th January the bare unit weighed 89 lb. The following day the structure was sprayed with black enamel (91 lb) and was fitted out in the Moth Shop on 21st January, less engine, (174 lb). Progressing through the Fabric Shop the next day the frame was treated with dope resistant paint and covered (179 lb). The final weighing was after a visit to the Dope Shop on 24th January where a coat of sprayed aluminium took the total to 182 lb.

The sample fuselage was allocated to work's No 729, and as a complete aircraft was weighed on 28th January, tipping the scales at 943 lb less finishing coats (allowance 3 lb) and removable equipment. At this still early stage in development, the average weight of a standard DH.60M was booked at 948.4 lb. Sold to the Canadian Government and registered CF-CAA, No 729 qualified for her C of A on 29th January and was operated by the Toronto Flying Club until she was written off after a heavy landing in October 1940.

Following a visit to England by Hereward de Havilland during which discussions were held on the prospects of moving the Australian Company factory from Melbourne to new premises at Mascot Aerodrome, Sydney, Captain de Havilland and his wife left Stag Lane on 3rd March in their coupé Moth G-AAAA. They arrived back a little over three weeks later having flown 4,600 miles in easy stages down through France and Spain to Rabat in Morocco, staying locally for a week and making flying visits to remote parts of the coastline where the Moth was landed on deserted beaches.

The Design Department's interest in metal-sparred flying surfaces resulted in DH.60M G-AACU (342) being fitted with what were described as 'metal top planes supplied by Boulton-Paul' on 19th March.

Two weeks later, standard wooden-sparred wings were fitted, proving to be some 15 lb heavier. A new DH.60M, G-AAHY (1362), was delivered to Gloster Aircraft at Brockworth on 11th June for further involvement in the 'metal wing' programme. The Company's second experimental DH.60M G-AACD (340) acquired longer rudder levers and on 23rd March received 'old DH.60 wings' in preparation for a series of spinning tests. Flown by Jimmy White and Richard Clarkson, the aeroplane was clocked at 107mph at low level on the speed course, fitted with a fabric-covered DH5180 propeller in preference to a 'thick edge' type.

The Air Ministry was anxious that propellers with a Cerric finish, a proprietary cellulose lacquer manufactured by the Cellon Company and used extensively on quality motor cars to provide a durable, high gloss finish, should replace fabric-covered blades, but at the expense of a thickened trailing edge. De Havilland had opposed the proposal on the grounds that the revised finish had not been trialled to establish performance, in particular engine rpm. At the time, the Company was ordering propellers in minimum batch quantities of 100 and had no wish to take commercial risks. Their argument was accepted by the RAE who agreed on 14th February to issue a concession.

Initially three, and later twelve, of the DH.60X Moths supplied to the Chilean Government in July and August 1928 were earmarked for a mail and passenger service to be operated by a new officially sponsored organisation, Linea Aeropostal Santiago-Arica, later to become Linea Aerea Nacional (LAN Chile). By 21st January 1929, 36 exploratory flights had been completed from Santiago during which one Moth had been wrecked when she was forced landed on the El Palque station. The first recognised mail service flown by the organisation

was on 5th March when Moth G9 left El Bosque Aerodrome for Ovalle flown by Lieutenant Arturo Maneses Kinsley and from where the service continued in stages to the northern border city of Arica.

A night mail and freight service was opened in Sweden by Aero Materiel using DH.60M Seaplane SE-ABY (1333), delivered by Jimmy White who stayed on to fly some of the first schedules, operating successfully between Gothenburg and Oslo and later Gothenburg to Malmo and Copenhagen. Norwegian DH.60M N-30 (1345), delivered to the shipping line Halle and Peterson in June 1929, operated a night mail service between Kjeller Aerodrome, Oslo, and Gothenburg, flown by Lieutenant Alf Gunnestad and other Army pilots. Returning to Kjeller early in the morning of 2nd August 1931 in DH.60M N-45 (1435), Gunnestad crashed on landing causing slight injury to himself but writing off the Moth. His place was taken by Lieutenant Schyberg and DH.60M N46 (1442), which only two weeks previously had been rammed on the ground by another Moth, causing the starboard upper wing to collapse.

Following analysis of the service by Captain Munthe-Dahl who had conducted some of the early trials, he concluded that a seaplane service would be more reliable, and the following year, Halle and Peterson, de Havilland's Norwegian agent, acquired a DH.60M Seaplane, N-20 (1534), for night services from Oslo to Gothenburg whence the mails were carried on to Malmo or Copenhagen by the landplane N-30. A flare system, installed under the lower mainplanes, could be ignited to assist with night landings. The Seaplane was later loaned to the Norwegian Navy for evaluation.

In South Africa, Union Airways was formed, based at Fairview Aerodrome, Port Elizabeth, from where they operated a fleet of five DH.60G Moths (ZS-ABH to ZS-ABL) on subsidised mail services to Maitland and the Transvaal, three of the aircraft having a special compartment fitted in place of the front seat. The operation had grown to such an extent that after the first six months the Moths were withdrawn in favour of larger aircraft.

The Mozambique Aero Club's first DH.60G Moth, C-PMAA (1001), delivered in May, was immediately pressed into service carrying mails by the coastal route to Inhambane. In South America, a DH.60G (1018), supplied by de Havilland's Berlin agent Alfred Friedrich, to German national Peter von Bauer, was the first of at least five Moths to equip his new Colombia-based airline SCADTA, in the summer of 1929. The air-

DH.60M N-30 was delivered to Norwegian shipping line, Halle and Peterson, for operation on the night airmail service between Oslo and Gothenburg.
Colonel Knut Kinne

The Mozambique Aero Club took delivery of their first DH.60G, C-PMAA, in May 1929, which was persuaded into flying mail along the coastal route. The aircraft was re-registered CR-MAA in 1930. Vasco d'Avillez

DH.60G Moth Coupé C-PMAB was supplied via South African agent John Veasey and delivered to private owner Armando Torre do Valle in Lourenco Marques on Christmas Morning, 1929. By the afternoon, the aircraft had been crashed and broken in two, but was repaired and survived until 1938. Vasco d'Avillez

DH.60X K-SILC on what appear to be broad-chord, short skis. She was the tenth aircraft to be built by the State Aircraft Factory at Suomenlinna, and is currently preserved in the Central Finland Aviation Museum.
Via Eino Ritaranta

craft opened an experimental mail service by flying across the Andes from Buena-Ventura to Bogota in advance of a proposal to link all the country's principal cities with the capital.

An early and unexpected thaw in March turned the Canadian Company's aerodrome at Mount Dennis into a quagmire with the result that 20 assembled Moths could not be flight delivered although some for more distant destinations were packed into crates. Two nights of frost over a weekend at the end of the month permitted Leigh Capreol and an RCAF officer to complete test flights from soon after dawn to late morning when the sun melted the frozen surface. As soon as the aerodrome dried out, Moths were collected by private owners and pilots sent from flying clubs. Five DH.60M Moths delivered to the RCAF for forestry patrol work in Alberta and Manitoba were fitted with batteries and wireless equipment which occupied much of the front cockpit but which could be stripped out quickly when necessary.

In Finland, the winter weather appears not to have hampered delivery in February and March of eight DH.60X Moths with Cirrus I engines, from the State Aircraft Factory at Suomenlinna, near Helsinki, to the Finnish Air Force. The aircraft, built under the licence agreement signed in March 1928 and allocated build numbers 1-8, were taken on charge as MO-96 to MO-103. Capable of operating on wheels, skis or floats, the aircraft were allocated as trainers to the Air Schools at Kauhava and Santahamina or to various Detached Maritime and Land Squadrons for liaison duties.

Due to lack of funds, MO-103 (8), delivered to the Air Force in March, was decommissioned in June and transferred to the Finnish Air Defence League in Helsinki to whom civil registration K-SILD was allocated in March 1930. Similar financial constraints forced the next two production aircraft, 9 and 10, also to be re-allocated. No 9 was registered K-SILB to Mikkeli Flying

Club although she flew in the colours of the Air Defence League. She was sold during the Depression and re-registered OH-ILB to the Karhumaki Brothers at Keljo in July 1931 where she was used for training, joy-riding and aerial photography in support of map-making until 1934. The last DH.60X Moth from the first production batch at Suomen-linna, 10, became K-SILC (later OH-ILC) with the air defence company Viipurin Ilma-puolustusyhdistys. In other hands the air-craft worked continuously until 1957 when she was withdrawn from active use and pre-served as a museum exhibit.

When the Air Defence League's OH-ILA, the former K-SILA (447), was badly dam-aged, the Karhumaki Brothers bought her in August 1931 Having rebuilt her, they sold her back to the League in December 1933. The brothers were allowed to operate her on the understanding that she would even-tually be retired to a museum.

During ownership by Pauli Massinen at Viipuri in 1937, OH-ILB (9) was badly dam-aged and the wreckage was acquired by the Karhumaki brothers. She was rebuilt by 1940 and test flown with the markings OH-VKG although never formally registered as such. In December 1940 the aircraft was sold to the Air Force who allocated the ser-ial MO-103, originally reserved for Finnish built aircraft No 8 in March 1929. The Moth remained in service until July 1942 when she crashed after engine failure.

This gathered expertise eventually resulted in the establishment of a small pro-duction facility through which, from 1934, the Finnish Air Force routed its Moths for servicing and repair and in which three 'new' Moths were built, disguised as repaired aircraft to avoid any dispute with de Havilland over licence fees. The first, OH-VKD (1/VK), was registered in July 1936, sold to the Air Force as MO-93 in January 1940, and destroyed in a hangar fire at Hir-vas in April 1944. The second aircraft, OH-VKE (2/VK), was sold to Lars Nylund in Helsinki in June 1937 and in October 1939

was donated to the Air Force and received serial MO-94. She suffered engine failure on take off from Naarajarvi Aerodrome in June 1941. The last of the trio, OH-VKM (4/VK), was built from spares as late as 1949 and was fitted with a Gipsy Major engine and enclosed cockpit. The aircraft was sold to Sweden in 1956, eventually finding her way to a museum in Malmo.

Mrs Adelaide Cleaver bought DH.60G G-AAEA (1030), in February 1929 and on 8th March, a week after receiving a C of A, and piloted by Captain Donald Drew of Imperial Airways, the trio left Heston for a leisurely tour to North Africa which was later extended through the Middle East to Karachi. Mrs Cleaver proved that the Moth was the ideal transport of delight, available at an instant to follow any whim, or not, as the mood dictated. With nothing but aerial sight-seeing as the aim, G-AAEA eventually meandered back to England where she arrived on 23rd May, having covered 12,000 miles without incident. In much the same orbit and with similar ambitions, Baron Bernard de Skorzewski and his wife had left England on 1st December 1928 in DH.60G G-AACM (991) and, after some months in North Africa, returned to their home in Poland on 30th April, with practical experi-ence which could be exploited in the admin-istration of their de Havilland agency.

In spite of generally adverse weather Hubert Broad headed towards Greece after taking off from Stag Lane on 24th March in DH.60G G-AAAK (807). The aircraft was demonstrated in Athens and Salonika to Ministers of Marine and Communications until 19th April when Broad left for home by train, having sold the aeroplane to the Greek Naval Air Service, but no follow-up orders were received.

Although the Handley Page automatic slot was well established by reputation and practical application, they were not univer-sally appreciated as the auxiliary planes (slats), could stick in or out, and not always together, which proved distracting for a novice pilot. A complementary device unveiled to the press at Handley Page's Cricklewood Aerodrome on 8th April was the 'Interceptor', and test pilot James Cordes demonstrated the equipment fitted to DH.60X G-EBXG. The Director of Scientific Research at the Air Ministry published a description of the system:

'The Interceptor is a flat plate 75% of the slat span long and a little over 2in wide, hinged along its longer edge on the upper surface of the upper wing and 4in back from the leading edge. It lies under the slat when the slot is closed and behind the slat when open. The port interceptor is made to rotate about its hinge as the port aileron is rotated from 10° up to its full-up position and the starboard interceptor is similarly rotated by upward rotation of the starboard aileron. The chord of the slat is 7in thus, when the control column is within the lateral range represented by port aileron up 10° to starboard aileron up 10°, both interceptors are lying flat between the slat and the upper surface of the wing when the slat is closed on the wing. The gearing between the aileron and the interceptor is such that for maximum upward rotation of the aileron the interceptor is normal to the upper surface of the wing at the line of attachment.

'At stalling incidence the application of the conventional aileron is generally ineffective in rolling the aeroplane and gives an adverse yawing moment which takes charge and yaws the aeroplane in the direction of the downward aileron. The interceptor is a device mechanically operated by the control column, for increasing the drag and decreasing the lift of the wing to be depressed, so that the additional rolling moment due to the interceptor has the same sign as that due to the aileron and the yawing moment due to the interceptor is of opposite sign to that of the ailerons.'

DH.60X G-EBXG had been modified to accept the interceptors on the top planes, which also were fitted with ailerons. The interceptor plates were connected to the top trailing edge of the aileron by three actuating rods. The bottom ailerons were locked in neutral and the top ailerons were connected to the control column by push-rods inside the lower mainplanes, via an actuating rod situated vertically behind the interplane struts, from a hinged joint at about the mid-chord position. Apart from G-EBXG, Handley Page experimented with a number of aircraft of differing configurations and at Farnborough the RAE modified a Siskin fighter, but the system was cumbersome

and complicated. Although experiments continued in different forms for several more years, it was never taken up, leaving the relative simplicity of the slot gear to speak for itself.

Since before the First World War, a London scientist, Dr A P Thurston, had been conducting experiments with a new form of auxiliary plane based on the behaviour of birds. Called a 'rotary thumb' the device was shaped like a small airscrew and was centred on a spindle recessed into the leading edge. At high angles of incidence the 'rotary thumb' was designed to lift on its spindle and rotate when it was said to produce a much more intense effect than the slot. Although wind tunnel tests were carried out, the nearest the device got to installation on a Moth was an artist's sketch.

Other hopeful inventions were tested too: the Savage-Bramson Anti-Stall Gear of 1927 featured a vane on a horizontal arm in the manner of a strut-mounted pitot. At a total weight of 8 lb it was claimed that its simple signalling impulse could not be disregarded. The Wynn anti-stall siren was worked by two vanes designed to rotate at different speeds which when nearly coincident, indicating the approach of the stall, produced a loud screeching noise audible in the cockpit and, from a height of 1,500ft, by observers on the ground. A working model was attached to the front interplane strut of a Moth at Leicester during the summer of 1929. In 1932, two New Zealanders, Messrs Roberts and Young, set up a business in London to market the Roberts Stabiliser, a fairly basic apparatus weighing over 18 lb, attached to the control column, to permit the aircraft to be flown 'hands-off' in turbulent conditions. The device was fitted to DH.60G G-AAVY (1230), based at Heston and used for demonstration purposes on the Continent early in 1932, following which the French and Italians were said to be very interested.

While G-EBXG was demonstrating to the press, the de Havilland Sealed Gipsy Engine

tourist, G-EBTD, was earning her keep by flying a series of trials with a new design of vent pipe on the top of the fuel tank in an effort to establish the best shape and position for the maintenance of high pressure within the tank. Some pilots had experienced mysterious 'engine failure' causing forced landings, but reported that after inspection, no problem with the engine could be found. Suspicion had fallen on the fuel supply from the centre section tank and in particular the influence of the vent pipe in determining the degree of pressure, or lack of it, within the tank.

The trials with G-EBTD confirmed an improved situation with a new design of vent pipe, now standing some 4in above the top of the tank. In the front cockpit, Richard Clarkson connected the pressure tube for his test ASI to an open copper tube mounted on the end of a stick which he could move about for exploratory purposes. He discovered that there was 'negative pressure' (suction) within the cockpit but also a boundary layer effect on the underside of the tank, quite sharply defined, which was thicker at higher cruising speeds. He also established that, outside the boundary layer, pressure remained high underneath the tank right down to the neighbourhood of the front windscreen.

Prompted by the American requirements, de Havilland received formal Air Ministry approval in April for construction of an 'all-welded metal fuselage' in which the wire bracing in the rear bays was replaced by steel tubing, and the previously detachable rear 'knife edge' structure became an integral part of a one-piece rear pylon. The same clearance covered modifications to the structure of the wing ribs, a reinforcement at the front spar and attachment of the top rib boom to the rear spar by pen steel clips. On the same date the Directorate of Technical Development issued a concession to raise the permitted aerobatic weight to 1,570 lb, reminding the Company not to ask

An artist's impression of Dr A P Thurston's 'rotary thumb' applied to a Moth. The 'thumb' was one of many devices which the inventors believed offered enhanced performance or greater efficiency, but only the simple slot proved both effective and enduring. DH Moth Club Archive

DH.60M CF-ADA spent much of her early life in Montreal following arrival at Mount Dennis in April 1929. In this picture, the well-dressed gentleman standing on the port float is Leigh Capreol, Chief Pilot of de Havilland Aircraft of Canada. Bombardier Regional Aircraft

Canadian flying clubs were keen to promote themselves and their names on the hangar in large letters ensured exposure. The staff of the Regina Flying Club pose with their fleet of two Cirrus Moths and a DH.60M, CF-CAE, delivered to the Club in May 1929. Via Gerry Schwam

hand pump for a long-range tank. The rear cockpit was enlarged by cutting away part of the decking and installing a new bulkhead at the luggage locker position. The aircraft were delivered in May using ferry markings MW-113 to MW-116, but little is known of their subsequent operations.

Rear cockpit modifications made to DH.60G G-AAGA (1058), also in May, included lowering the seat and moving the rudder bar forward by more than 4in at the request of the customer, who was reported to be very tall and with only one leg. In July, Northern Newspapers took delivery of DH.60G G-AAJS (1139), in which the front seat was re-shaped and moved forward to allow a camera to be operated from the rear cockpit, for which purpose a hole was cut in each fuselage side and furnished with a sliding shutter.

The RAE report on tests it had conducted on dummy wooden mainspars following the accident to G-EBYD in August 1928 was published in May and centred on moisture content, wood shrinkage and the manufacture of spars in respect of the position of the annual growth rings. The findings were disputed by de Havilland as probably having no connection with the cause of the accident as implied in the report. Another department at Farnborough also queried the paper and suggested that redesign of the root-end joint and closer inspection as a matter of routine, possible when the wings were folded, would be of more immediate and practical value.

The first British-built Moth with an all-welded fuselage frame was G-AAKB (1365), the landplane coupé DH.60M displayed without markings at the Olympia Aero Show from 16th July. The aircraft was mounted on top of a specially constructed pedestal within which were displayed over 100 cups and trophies won by de Havilland aeroplanes, mostly Moths, and loaned by winners from all over the world. G-AAKB was fitted with a 15 gallon auxiliary petrol tank, modified wing and tailplane spars, a slot locking device operated from the cockpit and was presented in a special high gloss finish of gold and white. In spite of being described by an American visitor as a flying

for further increases which under prevailing conditions, would not be granted.

The many hours of testing completed on the early Gipsy I engines before production was authorised ensured that its introduction to service was as trouble-free as could have been hoped. Development of the DH.60 airframe and its inevitable rise in both tare and maximum authorised weights led directly to the 120hp Gipsy II on which Frank Halford started design work on 1st July 1929. The new engine differed little from its forebear but incorporated larger bearing surfaces, a longer stroke and a higher compression ratio. The cylinder was redesigned as a carbon steel forging, machined all over, which enabled the cooling fins to be more closely spaced to increase the cooling area. In a dry condition the unit weighed 298lb. The increase in horsepower and running speed of the engine together with its application to a metal airframe caused a review of vibration

insulation with the result that the engine mounting feet were redesigned as trunnions surrounded by thick rubber bushes. Other differences of note were a change of carburettor from Zenith to Claudel-Hobson and the enclosure of the push-rods inside metal tubes with the valve gear encased in pressed metal boxes.

The prototype engine, No 2000, was not test flown in a new DH.60M G-AASL (1430), until November. The Gipsy II was not intended to replace the Gipsy I and although there was a deliberately imposed price differential; either type was chosen by Stag Lane's customers in almost equal proportion.

Four DH.60Gs supplied to a Spanish air-survey company in Madrid, (1013-1016), were modified to carry a Zeiss camera in the rear cockpit. To accommodate the operator who sat facing the tail, all controls were removed and the pilot, operating from the front seat, was additionally furnished with a tail trimmer, a full set of instruments and

Captain Roy Maxwell, director of the Ontario Provincial Air Service, and champion of the Moth in Canada, paddling a DH.60M from her mooring to the slipway, prior to loading for a flight to Remi Lake with the Minister of Lands and Forests, Mr W C Cain. Via Gerry Schwam

The Company displayed two Moths at the 1929 Olympia Aero Show in London. Without markings, DH.60M Coupé G-AAKB was mounted on a specially constructed pedestal, within which were exhibited over 100 cups and trophies won by Moth aircraft, and borrowed from willing owners around the world. Alan Butler

Short Bros designed and built a special amphibious undercarriage for the owner of DH.60G G-AADV, John Scott-Taggart. One central float carried a lateral shaft fitted with a wheel suspension system at each end. The shaft could be rotated to raise or lower the wheels according to choice. Short Bros

chocolate box, de Havilland announced that the aeroplane had been sold during the show to André Jomain in Paris and was subsequently registered in France as F-AJOA.

During the course of the show and as an added attraction, de Havilland conducted a public demonstration of the processes involved in building a metal fuselage frame and at the end of the year when presenting the Company's Annual Report, Chairman Alan Butler said that he believed the Aero Show was of such significance that results would continue to be reflected in the Company's accounts for the next two years.

The second of the two aircraft displayed on the de Havilland stand, yellow and white DH.60M Seaplane No 1339, was sold to the Norwegian Kosmos Whaling Company and, registered N-42, was flown to Oslo as a landplane by Leif Lier, leaving Stag Lane on 3rd August. Fitted with floats, the Moth was carried as deck cargo on board the whaling fleet's new flagship, the 32,000 ton *Kosmos,* which sailed for Antarctic waters on 10th August. The adventure was to end in tragedy the day after Christmas when with Leif Lier and observer Dr Ingvald Schreiner on board, N-42 disappeared without trace during a routine reconnaissance flight to the Balleny Islands.

Displayed by Short Bros at Olympia was DH.60G G-AADV (998), mounted on a central float straddled by a pair of main wheels which could be winched down into position, or up, as appropriate. The water rudder at the tail of the float acted as a skid when the aircraft was operated off land. John Scott-Taggart had presented DH.60G Moth G-AAEX (997), to the London Aeroplane Club in April following his return from an air-touring holiday in Switzerland with his landplane G-AADV, after which that aircraft had been delivered to Rochester for conversion.

Moth Amphibian G-AADV with the wheels rotated to the down position, clearly illustrating the wide central float and two light outriggers. *The Aeroplane*

Short's test pilot, John Lankester Parker, taking off in G-AADV at Lympne Aerodrome. On the ground, the water rudder fixed to the back of the central float was designed to act as a tailskid. Short Bros

At the same time that Short Bros were supplying floats for the two British Moth Amphibians, the Moth Aircraft Corporation was investigating an identical configuration for a DH.60GM. NC829H was fitted with what were termed 'experimental floats', and in the photograph the aircraft is seen standing on her own wheels in July 1929 at Omaha, Nebraska. Via Gerry Schwam

The amphibian was widely demonstrated during the summer and the weather at the Marine Aircraft Experimental Establishment (MAEE) at Felixstowe in October was ideal for her general testing in support of de Havilland's application for a civil Certificate of Airworthiness. The test pilot assigned to the task flew the aircraft at various CG positions and was enthusiastic about handling and performance both on the water and in the air, but was fiercely critical of the spring loading device designed to provide fore and aft trim on all marques of Moth, believing it was a 'definite handicap'. Don Brown who learned to fly at Shoreham on DH.60X G-EBZG (676), and later became Chief Test Pilot for the Miles Aircraft Company, said his only criticism of the Moth was the trim system which largely marred the fore and aft 'feel' of the aircraft because one was pulling or pushing against the spring. He also admitted that he preferred the Avian which initially had no tail trim and did not need it, and later was fitted with an adjustable tailplane.

G-AADV capsized when touching down in rough seas off the Kent coast on Christmas Eve 1929 but following salvage she was not repaired. A second Moth Amphibian, the Hermes engined wooden DH.60X, G-AAVC (1238), was prepared for Ernest Guinness in March 1930, to be based at Phoenix Park, Dublin. The aircraft was displayed at Croydon in June prior to delivery but the registration was cancelled in November 1930 after the aircraft was declared to have been written off.

The first two aircraft with the production standard 'new fuselage' were G-AALX (1410), delivered to Airwork at Heston in September with what might have been a reconditioned engine, probably supplied by the customer, and G-AARB (1412), sold to Frank Soden, now promoted Squadron Leader and posted to Amman.

Following extensive testing on a structural test specimen, the certificated weights of the DH.60M landplane were increased to 1,800 lb, and to 1,550 lb for aerobatics, with or without modifications to the structure of the luggage locker which, as an option, was offered with increased capacity.

In the USA, the Moth Aircraft Corporation (MAC) reported that since production began at Lowell in March, manufacturing rates had reached four Moths per week and the company had received orders for 134 aircraft, all for delivery by the end of the year. The first American-assembled aircraft is thought to have been a DH.60G created from materials, as opposed to sub-assemblies or component parts, supplied from Stag Lane. This was allocated local build number 1A or X-A, an identity advised by the MAC on 8th April 1929 when registration N589E was issued. However, analysis of Company correspondence casts doubt on whether this aircraft was ever built although the factory certainly celebrated production of its 'first' aircraft by naming a Moth *City of Lowell* and christening her in ginger ale due to the Prohibition Laws. Another theory is that it may have been X-A which crashed on Saturday 11th May when the Company's English test pilot, Ronald Smith, was killed and quickly replaced by Al Krapish.

An application for registration of an aircraft, initially quoting build number 1 and later and consistently 1A, was first made on 15th March and the identity N9797 was issued on 30th March although all subsequent register records for N9797 refer to her as 1-A. Officially, this aircraft took the place of N589E as the first to be completed using imported raw materials. Aircraft 2A, NC894E, was a whole aircraft imported in a dismantled condition to act as a pattern and, having never flown under the rules pertaining to British certification, became the subject of special attention by the bureaucrats. Four further DH.60G Moths (3A to 6A), were constructed in the same manner as 1A. A letter from MAC says, '6A completes all the imported planes or planes of the British type and materials which we propose to licence. Hereafter, all planes will be built to the plans filed in the Department of Commerce under Aeronautics Branch, which were figured for a gross weight of 1,650 lb without the extra fuselage gas tank and 1,700 lb with the extra fuselage gas tank'.

The first aircraft wholly built from locally-sourced supplies, the wooden Moth NC809E, was defined as a DH.60GM against a revised identity system, curiously beginning at 1-B, which specifically introduced a hyphen between numeral and letter. Sixteen more DH.60GM wooden fuselage Moths (1-C to 1-R) were built using Stag Lane-supplied Gipsy engines before Lowell switched production entirely to Metal Moths, also referred to as model DH.60GM, in the early summer of 1929, when the 'G' indicated installation of a de Havilland built Gipsy engine. By November about 120 additional aircraft had been completed.

DH.60M G-AALX was the first aircraft to be built with the production-standard all-welded fuselage, and was delivered to Airwork at Heston fitted with a Gipsy I engine from an early batch, possibly supplied by the customer. Richard Riding

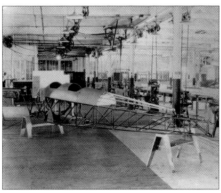

An early wire-braced fuselage frame posed for the camera at the Moth Aircraft Corporation plant at Lowell, Mass, a single storey factory used to make explosives during the First World War. The two vertical templates ahead of the front cockpit appear to be checking the contours of the top cowl. Milton Shepperd via David Watson

The next aircraft built after 1-R was NC229K for W T Backus of Beach Hill, New Hampshire. This aircraft was allocated builder's reference '41', for which American Moth historian Vincent J Berinati has another theory:

'There were six aircraft in the series 1A to 6A, all DH.60Gs; 18 DH.60GMs in the series 1-A to 1-R plus another 18 in the prospective series 7A to 23A which never materialised, totalling 41. This means the new series should have started at 42, but perhaps this can be accounted for if the company never did or never admitted to building N589E, in which case starting at 41 would be correct.'

To add further confusion, the Department of Commerce later issued an Airworthiness Directive mandating the attachment of streamlined wires to brace the fin to the tailplane. 'It is imperative that this equipment be applied to all Moths of serial numbers 1-50 inclusive. However, beyond No 50 the above equipment is purely optional.'

On 31st May 1929, technical approval to fit EDO Type N floats to a Moth was signed and in July the MAC contracted with the Edo Aircraft Corporation for the supply of floats which were fitted to DH.60G NC9720 (885) for demonstration purposes. Edo's Vice President George Post described the Moth as 'the slickest little seaplane I have ever flown in!'. On 27th January the following year, EDO Type I floats were approved.

DH.60GM 1-R, first registered X829H in 1929 probably due to her configuration as a test vehicle for a Loening three-float amphibious undercarriage, was referred to as a 'Curtiss Moth Sport' and appears to have begun her career with a Cirrus engine, later replaced by a Gipsy I.

The MAC received yet another intervention from the Department of Commerce who wanted the Moth to carry an adjustable tailplane. The requirement, eventually, was fought off and in August 1929 MAC was issued with Approved Type Certificate No 197.

Delivered to Kenneth M Lane's Air Associates in New York in April 1928, DH.60X Cirrus Moth NC5359 (547) had been intended as an entrant in the Guggenheim 'Safe Aircraft Competition' but could not meet the required speed range and was withdrawn. The British entry was left to Handley Page with their much-slotted H.P.39 Gugnunc, a design that they said included many of the best features of the DH.60 Moth, including the undercarriage. NC5359 was sold to the Loening Aeronautical Engineering Corp. of New York in June 1928 and was the test vehicle used to gain approval for the Cirrus II engine in the USA in November 1929, although local production was to concentrate solely on the Cirrus III. When Alan Cobham arrived in the USA

NC9720, a DH.60G manufactured at Stag Lane, was used as a demonstrator by the Moth Aircraft Corporation until sold to the Heyer Company as a test vehicle for items of aviation electrical equipment. Has the Nation-Wide grocery sign been specially positioned? Via Gerry Schwam

with his demonstrator Moth in December 1926, Albert and Grover Loening had been guests invited to his welcoming dinner.

Some American-built Moths were fitted with corrugated skin fuel tanks, probably supplied from Stag Lane, and with vertical sight gauges on the top surface, while others featured a round contents gauge, angled down from the under-surface for convenient reference from the rear cockpit, and of a type never fitted to aircraft built outside the USA. Tanks were later manufactured for American Moths to the same basic aerodynamic shape and with the round gauge, but from flat sheeting which proved easier to fabricate and repair, and was cheaper.

According to Company brochures, the MAC-supplied Moth was available at a fly-away price of $4,500 but only with a green or silver fuselage and silver wings, although many were delivered in a scheme of yellow and black. Also available was a 'de luxe' Moth, custom built, finished in a high lustre colour scheme of the owner's choice together with, amongst other things, a chromium-plated finish on all exposed metal parts, white-walled tyres, instrumentation in both cockpits, special upholstery, navigation lights and a coupé top with cockpit heater. Included under 'accessories' were Goodyear air wheels and brakes which could be supplied at an extra $150. Strangely, parallel-motion rudder pedals were not adopted.

The idea of a parallel-motion rudder bar was first suggested to the Design Department by Bob Hardingham in his capacity as Chief Engineer of the de Havilland School of Flying. He reported an occasion when a Moth had taxied with difficulty through the Stag Lane mud and one of the pilot's feet had slipped off the bar and punched a hole through the fuselage side. The new system became a standard fit from July although the Chief Engineer never received acknowledgement for this or a number of other ideas taken up by the Design Office following his suggestions.

Published by the Sales Office at Stag Lane in July, the Company's price list quoted £700 for a DH.60M landplane and £960 for a Seaplane against £675 and £910 as appropriate for the DH.60G. It was noticeable that de Havilland and their arch-rival Avro had stopped quoting prices on their regular advertisements, which instead asked anyone with an interest to contact the manufacturer for details. The lists carried prices for the increasing number of optional extras, items of loose equipment and services available. The inflexibility of the slot locking system had been recognised by the Design and Sales Departments, and a new locking device was offered as an option, activated from the cockpit. When Mary Bailey flew to Ireland it was reported that she had carried an inflated inner tube in the locker as her sole emergency equipment. Now, owners were encouraged to purchase the 'Auliffe belt, complete with cylinder'. The price list was keen to advise that although slots were available at £17.17s.6d per set, the royalty due to Handley Page was an additional £20.13s.6d for a wooden landplane rising to £36.19s.10d for a metal seaplane. The royalty payment was the reason that few if any of de Havilland's flight development aircraft ever were fitted with slots until redeployed to their School or sold.

In March, the Royal Aircraft Establishment had called for urgent provision of a Moth to take part in fog landing trials at Farnborough. The Director of Technical Development discovered that his Department owned only one Moth, J8030 (233), based at Martlesham Heath, where the aircraft was used for flying practice. RAE insisted that their trials' aircraft must be equipped with slots and a split undercarriage but, apart from Sir Sefton Brancker's personal aircraft, no Service machine was yet fitted with the new alighting gear. With no alternative aircraft available and de Havilland unable to supply a new Moth for many months, Martlesham Heath reluctantly delivered J8030 to Farnborough in July where RAE was anticipating the tasks of

The scene near the Central Garage, High Street, Broadstairs, Kent, in May 1929 when, during the General Election campaign, Captain Harold Balfour, Parliamentary Candidate for the Conservative Party, toured the Thanet Constituency in DH.60X G-EBWX. Captain Balfour noted on the picture: 'After landing at St Peters, the aircraft stayed the night in this garage and I took it off next day in a field between the station and sea'. John Mayer

For the 1929 King's Cup Air Race, Nigel Norman entered his DH.60G G-AAHI. The aircraft had been converted into a Coupé but was reconfigured to provide a small streamlined cabin for the rear seat with the front cockpit faired over. BAE Systems

Alan Butler and his new green and black Coupé Moth G-AACL were competitors in events flown during the Northampton Air Pageant, held at Sywell Aerodrome on Whit Monday 1929. DH Moth Club Archive

overhauling the airframe and fitting slots and undercarriage purchased separately from Stag Lane.

Apart from being 'an old aircraft' credited with 'extremely poor performance', RAE discovered that the existing fuselage would not easily accept the new undercarriage and alternative wings were required for the fitting of slots. By August it was recognised that the aircraft was entirely unsuitable and J8030 was struck off charge. The fog landing trials were not commenced until 18th June 1930 when at 4.45am Farnborough Aerodrome was blanketed by fog to a height of 90ft and 'a standard Avro aeroplane' took off and landed five times with an exceedingly brave RAF pilot and Air Ministry Scientific Officer as crew.

A British General Election was held in May and Captain Harold Balfour flew his DH.60X G-EBWX (583) 'on the hustings' when he toured parts of Kent and south east England in support of his campaign to become the elected Conservative Member of Parliament for Thanet. Not only did he win the seat to champion the cause of aviation from the Opposition benches, but subsequently rose to high office and a Peerage, never losing his interest in aviation and becoming a specialist in airline safety matters. Several other Parliamentary candidates also are known to have harnessed the convenience of air travel to dash from one meeting to another, especially in areas where difficult geographical features had to be overcome. The Marquis of Douglas and Clydeside flew his DH.60G G-AAEB (1003), around Argyllshire aided by his sister, Lady Mary, also a pilot; Hylton Murray-Philipson flew his DH.60X G-EBWD (552), throughout the division of Peebles-shire and South Midlothian, convening meetings near to the few convenient landing grounds; W E Allan, Unionist candidate for West Belfast, was chauffered by Sir Osmond Esmonde in his DH.60G EI-AAC (1000), having never flown before. Captain Frederick Guest fought for the Liberal Party in Bristol North using DH.60X G-EBUS (444), whilst another Liberal candidate, Major F M Dougall, toured Hereford with his friend Captain Harry Yeatman in Cirrus Moth G-EBVD (247), the aircraft previously evaluated as J8031 by the RAF's Central Flying School at Wittering.

The 1929 King's Cup Air Race started at Heston on 5th July, stopping at Blackpool that evening before racing back to Heston via Scotland the following day. Of 60 entrants the 41 starters included 20 Moths of which four were listed as Coupé Moths and a dozen others as Gipsy Moths.

DH.60G G-AAHI (1082), delivered to the very tall Nigel Norman at Heston in May as a standard Coupé Moth, had the front part of the canopy removed to provide semi-streamlined accommodation over the rear cockpit only and from where Nigel Norman was able to indulge in his interest of taking oblique photographs with a cumbersome hand-held camera, in comparative comfort. DH.60X Cirrus Moth G-EBVK (467) was modified by

the addition of a streamlined headrest, but this resulted in removal of the hinge for the locker door which had to be sprung carefully into place when closed. Sold to new owners at Broxbourne soon after the King's Cup, the door flapped open in flight causing the recently qualified pilot to put down for a precautionary landing but, during a late adjustment to face into wind, a wing tip touched the ground and the aircraft cartwheeled. The pilot was unhurt although he had been ejected from the cockpit as a result of not being strapped in.

Following his return from North America, Alan Butler re-acquainted himself with his beige and red racing DH.60G G-EBQH. On 18th April he made the first flight of the new

Painted cream and green, the racing DH.60G Moth G-AAHR was prepared by the Company as the 1929 King's Cup Air Race entry made by Sir Charles Wakefield, to be flown by Hubert Broad. Due to bad weather in Scotland, a precautionary landing cost any hope of a top placing. *The Aeroplane*

dark blue and green family Moth Coupé G-AACL (887), which was to be regularly exercised by Alan and Lois Butler as a team, Mrs Butler later receiving instruction in the aircraft with Bob Reeve at Stag Lane. Both Moths were entered in the King's Cup.

The Company effort for 1929 was directed towards a special racing Moth entered by Sir Charles Wakefield to be flown by Hubert Broad, the cream and green DH.60G G-AAHR (1068), named 'Pullover' or 'Turkish Bath' by local hacks. The aircraft was built as a special coupé flown from the front seat position. The apex of the canopy was only slightly higher than the line of the engine top cowling with a raised turtle deck running from the pilot's headrest to the tail. Fully streamlined, G-AAHR was unveiled with a racing undercarriage, faired centre section containing a nine gallon fuel tank with modified sump and no slots, tightly cowled engine and no exhaust pipes.

Fuel from the centre section was gravity fed via a faired pipe into a fuselage tank behind the front cockpit, but unlike other racing Moths, the centre section was not extended to create a continuous trailing edge. To compensate for solo pilot operation from the front seat, lead counter-weights were carried on brackets fitted to the underside of the tailplane.

Considerable interest was shown in the configuration of the front cockpit which was described by C G Grey:

'The cockpit was covered over by a little cap, or lid, the top of which was within an inch of the top of Mr Broad's skull. The front windows were so close to his face that he said they were just like looking through a large pair of spectacles. The two side windows were made to slide back so that the cockpit was quite well ventilated and although from the outside there appeared no possibility of the pilot having any view at all, Mr Broad said that it gave him just as good a view as any machine with an open cockpit. In effect, closing the lid was almost exactly the same thing as putting on a flying cap with goggles.'

Although the Race was won by a two-seat trainer version of the Gloster Grebe crewed by an RAF pilot and navigator, second place went to Lieutenant Llewellyn Richardson RN in his old DH.60X Moth G-EBPQ (357), now fitted with a Cirrus III and easily recognised in her black and white paint scheme. Third was Wally Hope in the scarlet-painted G-AAHP (1067), the DH.60X/G hybrid in single seat racing configuration registered to Air Taxis and powered by a pre-production example of the new Gipsy II engine. It was this aircraft de Havilland had put up on 29th April for certification of the new engine in a wooden airframe.

The great hope of achieving a third consecutive Moth victory had rested on the three 'speed machines' and in particular the Sir Charles Wakefield entry, but Hubert Broad, who was in eighth place at the end of the first day, could only achieve 20th position overall. On the second morning he had run into a fierce storm south of the Cheviot Hills and, faced with no forward visibility and high ground ahead, chose to land when he was met by a friendly farmer who entertained him to lunch.

De Havilland would have been disappointed that the highest placed Moth was not fitted with a Gipsy engine. But for a problem due to loss of oil which caused an unscheduled landing at Bicester in search of new supplies, Neville Stack might easily have won the Race in his Avian IVM G-AAHJ, fitted with the new Hermes engine making its first public appearance. The Company's follow-up advertising concentrated on the fact that 16 Gipsy-engined Moths had started and 14 had finished, and that neither of the two retirements was due to mechanical failure. It was also a convenient time to report that the 'Sealed Gipsy' had now achieved 485 flying hours and covered 42,000 miles, some of which had been accumulated by Jack Tyler who flew G-EBTD around the King's Cup course in the wake of the competing machines, carrying an assortment of spare parts. The Company had made a very special effort to support all Moths and Gipsy engines during the 1929 Race, arrangements which included not only G-EBTD but per-

Wally Hope was third in the 1929 Kings Cup Air Race flying his all-scarlet DH.60X/G hybrid, G-AAHP, powered by a pre-production model of the new Gipsy II engine. The aircraft was heavily streamlined, fitted with small diameter wheels, a low capacity fuel tank hidden within the thin centre section, and a high decking with special doors which enclosed all but the pilot's head. *Flight*

A view of the inside of the erecting shop at the new de Havilland Aircraft of Canada site at Downsview. Note the racks of floats against the windows on the left, and nine fuselages in a row behind DH.60M CF-ADH, an aircraft retained as a Company demonstrator. DH Moth Club Archive

sonnel and service equipment at every control point and the de Havilland School's old DH.9J, G-EAAC, which flew every leg of the Race packed with equipment.

Dick Bentley left Johannesburg on 10th July in his DH.60X G-EBSO with an American businessman, Ernest B Filsinger, bound for Berlin. After delivering his passenger, Bentley continued on to Croydon where he arrived on 26th August, uniquely completing the fourth journey between England and South Africa. The following year he sold the aeroplane and in 1932 she crashed on take-off at Brooklands following a GAPAN air display.

Bentley the pilot was recognised to be energetic and resourceful when Shell decided to expand its business aircraft operations around the world early in 1930. He was selected by 'Jerry' Shaw for the European Office where he was described as being 'as indifferent to the weather as to the day of the week, joining in the harum scarum adventures of customers, welcome everywhere'.

By the time of the tenth annual RAF Display at Hendon on 13th July 1929, the Air Ministry was able to confirm that all six Genet Moths on charge had been modified to permit sustained inverted flight under power. The revelation had come in answer to a question about modification of existing Cirrus and Gipsy-engined Moths in the Service to permit inverted flight, this following a number of forced landings following engine stoppages during such manoeuvres. The de Havilland Company indicated it was willing to prepare fuel system modifications to both Cirrus and Gipsy-powered aircraft to permit inverted gliding with the engine off, but it doubted whether the Air Ministry really wanted fully operational inverted systems fitted to all Moths, which, they were later informed, was a correct assumption.

Following much debate, the RAF's Genet Moths were modified at Stag Lane in a programme begun in November 1928, to accept auto-slots. The Air Ministry then decided that a system for locking the slots in the closed position was necessary prior to further inverted display flying and requested de Havilland to prepare a scheme which

DH.60M Seaplane N-35 was acquired for the purpose of locating shoals of fish, close to the Arctic Circle, off the coast of Norway. The exercise was probably the first of its kind and proved to be highly successful. Arne Butteberg via Bjornar Noras

would be circulated for incorporation by the various Commands holding Genet Moths on charge. When it was realised in May 1929 that de Havilland already had a standard locking system, four aircraft, J8816, J8819, J8820 and J8821, then in position at Stag Lane for reconditioning in preparation for July's RAF Display, were fitted with locks although the Company installed an old version, not acceptable to the Air Ministry, who insisted the job be done again at de Havilland's own expense.

DH.60M Seaplane N-35 (1373) was delivered to her Norwegian base at Harsted, 400 miles north of the Arctic Circle, on 25th July, having been flown from Rochester by Lieutenant Wicklund-Hansen. She was to be used by her owners, Harsted Lufttrafikk, to

locate herring shoals on behalf of local fishermen which she did, successfully, from 5th August. The following summer, just after take off in gusty conditions from Stamsund, a small community in the Lofoten Islands, the engine stopped and from a height of about 100ft N-35 fell, semi-controlled, into the sea. The aircraft was wrecked and her operators closed down the business, but their experiment had proved the concept.

DH.60G Moth Seaplane No 1128 joined Sir Douglas Mawson's British, Australian and New Zealand Antarctic Expedition which sailed from London in early August in the barque *Discovery*. The Expedition was largely backed by Australian confectionery magnate Sir McPherson Robertson who in 1934 was to fund and lend his name to

DH.60G G-AACY owned by Airwork, was fitted out as a trials aeroplane for the Amplion Wireless Receiving Installation, a system which would allow private owners to receive weather information broadcast from Heston. Aerial masts can be seen on the upper wings with leads to the top of the fin. Richard Riding

perhaps the greatest Air Race in history, 'The MacRobertson International Air Races' from London to Melbourne.

While DH.60G G-AACY (841), was working with the Airwork School of Flying at Heston, trialling Amplion wireless apparatus, shortly to be installed as operational equipment in Walter Runciman's DH.60X G-EBWT (590), at Cramlington, Mawson's seaplane had been fitted with a Marconi 'wireless receiving set' in the front cockpit, together with aerial mast and wires, aerial winch mounted on the outside of the fuselage and a generator fixed to the starboard lower mainplane. Supplied with both a float and ski undercarriage and painted bright yellow, she was carried as deck cargo packed into crates. Two RAAF pilots, Flight Lieutenant Stuart Campbell and Air Pilot Eric Douglas, joined the ship in Cape Town.

Once the ship was well in amongst the ice, where the water was reasonably calm, the crew broke open the packing cases and started to assemble the Moth. Here they discovered that getting the incidence right was a problem as the ship never stayed still for long and they could only make a rough guess as to the average position of the bubble in the inclinometer. They decided that if the rigging wires were screwed up the same number of turns each side until they felt tight enough, that should work. The job took three days after which the erected aeroplane remained on deck, lashed into a cradle.

As soon as conditions allowed, the aircraft was used for aerial survey and photographic missions, her first being on the last day of 1929. Apart from the wireless which was 'not very satisfactory' her only navigational aid was a P4 compass which the crew discovered had not been corrected for dip in the southern hemisphere so that they had to fly 'nose up or nose down or roll' whenever they wanted to get a decent reading. Although the Moth was not painted with any obvious marks of identity prior to embarkation, she was registered VH-ULD in April 1930 and the lettering seems to have been applied when *Discovery* put into Hobart for a pre-planned winter re-fit.

By contrast, the first Moth to operate in the humidity of the Dutch East Indies was

DH.60G VH-ULD on board the *Discovery* during Sir Douglas Mawson's Antarctic Expedition in 1930. She was said to carry wireless that was 'not very satisfactory'. Via John Grierson

DH.60G G-EBYK was, perhaps, the sleekest looking of all the prepared racing Moths, and achieved over 108mph on the Stag Lane Speed Course. Richard Riding

DH.60G PK-SAD (1046), sold to the Djok-jasche Automobile Company in July and registered to R de Bruyn in October. The wooden aircraft suffered a number of accidents until 1936 when the wooden fuselage was replaced by a DH.60M frame built locally at Bandoeng using parts salvaged from another aircraft.

The reason for Hubert Broad spending so much inverted time in DH.60G G-EBYK earlier in the year became evident on 20th July when the pair won an International Aerobatic Contest staged by the Royal Aero Club at Heston. The Gipsy engine had been tuned to achieve 2,320rpm and the aircraft had been clocked at 108.75mph on the Stag Lane Speed Course.

'Jimmy' White, Chief Flying Instructor at the School and a popular demonstration pilot, was killed together with his passenger F L Knight on 29th July when flying DH.60G G-AAKL (1129), at Stag Lane. Unaccountably, G-AAKL flew a right hand circuit to land and was struck from beneath by the single seat DH.60G G-AAJU (1103), which was flying the normal left hand pattern. Captain George Boyle, who had accepted delivery of his new aeroplane only a fortnight previously, was also killed.

Flying a left hand circuit was normal procedure at all RAF aerodromes and although it may have been coincidental, at the time of this accident, the RAF instructed that the de Havilland strut-mounted 'windy' air speed indicator should be moved from the starboard side where DH had placed it next to the pitot head, to the front interplane strut on the port side where it could more easily be seen by a pilot flying a standard circuit.

Following the substantial Canadian order for Cirrus III-powered DH.60Ms which had been satisfied by late March, and a single aircraft supplied against an in-house order, G-AAFB (1336), sold to Germany as D-1600 in April, only two wooden aircraft fitted with the Cirrus III were registered during the summer: G-AAIM (1153), a coupé Moth named *Arom II* for Shell-Mex in June, and G-AAKJ (1162), for the Anglo-American Oil Company, named *Sam,* in July. G-AAKJ was sold to National Flying Services (NFS), in August 1931 to join a fleet of 22 new Cirrus

Three of the four orange and black Cirrus III powered DH.60X Moths of the National Flying Services Aerobatic Circus, awaiting delivery from Stag Lane in August 1929. Flown by instructors, the team toured the expanding empire of aerodromes and clubs situated around Great Britain.
DH Moth Club Archive

III-powered wooden Moths and four Metal Moths delivered between July 1929 and July 1930 and distributed amongst the growing number of NFS-owned flying clubs. But there were no further customers for the aeroplane with the Cirrus III. Had the NFS experiment not foundered (the intention was to establish an eventual association of 71 British based flying clubs and almost as many aerodromes), many more aircraft fitted with the Mk III and even Hermes engines, might have been constructed.

On 2nd August Hubert Broad flew DH.60G Coupé Moth G-AAHS (1011) to Orly Aerodrome, Paris, to take part in the 1929 'Challenge International de Tourisme'. Of the 45 starters, only two entrants were British, the other being Winifred Spooner in her own DH.60G G-AAAL (809). Lady Mary Bailey arrived too late in her DH.60X G-EBTG (469), now upgraded to Cirrus III power, but flew the 4,000km route around Europe anyway, leaving Paris on 7th August following the usual round of preliminaries and

eliminations suffered by the other entrants.

Especially for the Challenge, G-AAHS had been fitted with a full coupé head but of lower profile for the benefit of aerodynamic efficiency rather than pilot comfort. Broad was placed second overall but first in his class, the Heavy Category, which C G Grey described as the Class best suited for general use all over the world, and effectively proclaimed the Gipsy Moth the champion light aeroplane of its time. Winifred Spooner was the only woman pilot in the competition and her self-supported entry in the well-used G-AAAL was awarded tenth place. Partly as a result of this achievement, in March 1930 she was awarded the Women's Trophy by Clifford Harmon's Paris-based International League of Aviators.

G-AAHS was entered by de Havilland into a similar 'Challenge' held at Evère Aerodrome, Brussels, in September. The Gipsy engine was fitted with heads designed for the new Ghost engine and trials on Stag Lane's High-Speed Course during the morn-

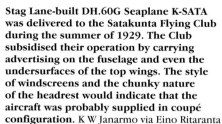

Stag Lane-built DH.60G Seaplane K-SATA
was delivered to the Satakunta Flying Club
during the summer of 1929. The Club
subsidised their operation by carrying
advertising on the fuselage and even the
undersurfaces of the top wings. The style
of windscreens and the chunky nature
of the headrest would indicate that the
aircraft was probably supplied in coupé
configuration. K W Janarmo via Eino Ritaranta

ing of 25th September indicated a speed of 115mph. As a result of these tests, Broad arrived in Belgium four hours after the deadline for entries had expired but, eager to accept him, the authorities conducted a secret ballot amongst the other competitors who voted to exclude him! With only seven legitimate entries, including Edgar Percival in a Hermes-Avian, the contest was barely reported.

The Prince of Wales was flown from Stag Lane to Windsor Park on 30th August in de Havilland demonstrator DH.60M G-AAKM (1369). The occasion was a visit to the de Havilland factory to view progress on construction of DH.60M No 1411, soon to be painted in the colours of the Brigade of Guards, and registered G-AALG in the name of Squadron Leader David Don as nominee for the Prince. The Company was not per-mitted to disclose details of the sale, which bestowed Royal approval on the Moth, until just before the Prince returned from a tour of Africa and took up residence at his Windsor home, Fort Belvedere, alongside which a private landing ground had been prepared.

G-AALG was equipped with all the standard 'extras' available including the deepened baggage locker enabling acceptance of several suitcases and a hat box and, with the assistance of a 'tunnel' into the rear fuselage, golf clubs and walking sticks. For ease of access, in addition to the normal locker door which hinged up on the starboard side, G-AALG was fitted with a secondary door almost 8in deep which hinged down along the line of the locker floor. Special 'arrangements' were made for the Prince's accommodation in the rear cockpit with the aircraft 'commander' sitting in front although both cockpits were fully fitted with luminous dialled instruments and a set of flying controls. In an interview some years after the Second World War the Prince, then Duke of Windsor, admitted that, contrary to many rumours, he had indeed flown G-AALG solo, sent off by David Don to complete two circuits in late December.

In partnership with his two brothers, the Princes George and Henry, DH.60M G-ABDB (1557) was acquired in July 1930 and was operated until June 1933 when she was part-exchanged with de Havilland for a new DH.84 Dragon, G-ACGG.

On 24th September, the familiar blue and silver DH.60G G-EBTD touched down at Stag Lane to complete the 600th flying hour logged by her Gipsy engine, during which time the combination had covered 51,000 miles. After achieving 500 hours in July, the engine temporarily had been removed for exhibition at the Olympia Aero Show and de Havilland had taken the opportunity to run the unit on a hydraulic brake at Stag Lane which indicated practically no reduction in performance. So encouraged was the Company that serious thought was given to the prospect of extending the Tour to 1,000 hours, but 600 hours was already a formidable and well publicised target and within their grasp; any failure during the proposed extension would negate all that had been achieved, so the idea was abandoned.

Subsequent strip examination of the engine revealed very little wear and no damage apart from a broken land on a piston, and the parts were laid out at Stag Lane for scrutiny by members of the Press, who were provided with all the relevant facts and figures gleaned as a result of the exercise. The Tour was considered a resounding success and the integrity of the Gipsy engine provided clear evidence that maintenance and overhaul periods were due to reach almost unimagined values by the standards of the day. The de Havilland Company was so convinced of the engine's reliability that immediately after analysis of the Trial engine, they issued the following pledge:

HRH the Prince of Wales arriving for an
engagement in his dark red and dark blue
DH.60M G-AALG. The luggage locker was
expanded in order to accommodate,
amongst other things, a hat box, obviously
necessary on this occasion. de Havilland

'To all manufacturers, owners and operators of light aircraft.

'The unbroken reliability provided by the standard Gipsy engine throughout the 600 Hour Reliability Tour, recently completed under government seals, has confirmed the manufacturer in their belief that risk of mechanical failure with the Gipsy engine is negligible.

'The de Havilland Aircraft Company Limited now, therefore, pledges itself to undertake, subject to certain reasonable conditions, the cost of repairs to an aircraft delivered to its owner, new and unused, on or after December 1st 1929, which suffers a forced landing from the failure of a Gipsy engine.

'Full particulars of conditions will be supplied on application.'

And those enquiring would have been advised that the undertaking was limited to flying in Europe, although it was hoped to extend the operation to other parts of the world. In addition the Company stated that:

'The engine must have been maintained according to our printed instructions.

'Only the original owner of the aircraft qualifies for protection, unless this Company approves a transfer.

'Damage by failure of proprietary components is excluded, such in most cases being subject to their own manufacturers' guarantees.

'Repairs must be executed to our instructions.

'Disputes to be settled in accordance with the terms of the Arbitration Act, 1889.'

Not operating under such duress was the white-painted Gipsy-engined DH.60M CF-AAA (1302), which was registered to the Aviation League of Canada at Ottawa in June 1929. Flown by the League's President, Major General Sir James H MacBrien, and sponsored by Imperial Oil Ltd, during the next four and a half years the aircraft travelled 100,000 miles in Canada and the USA, visiting clubs and organisations at 154 airfields. In 1932 she was assigned under Sir James' Presidency to the Canadian Flying Clubs Association and was operated by the

Cape Breton Flying Club in Nova Scotia from June 1934, surviving until at least 1941 with other owners.

Geoffrey de Havilland's plans for a fast, cabin monoplane tourer, first outlined in March 1929, assumed an uncluttered forward view for the pilot, previously achieved by sinking the upright engine further into the fuselage, a device limited in practice by the preservation of adequate propeller ground clearance or the avoidance of ungainly undercarriages. The most obvious solution was to invert the engine, an idea originally proposed in France as long ago as 1910, which improved the thrust line and offered a more convenient exhaust disposal.

Before the Gipsy II reached production, Frank Halford was engaged on development of the Gipsy III, essentially a Gipsy II modified to operate inverted. To avoid an accumulation of oil in the cylinders the cylinder skirts were simply extended into the crankcase. A separate oil tank and pump feed, oil return pipes and a gravity scavenge system to return oil to the tank all worked efficiently. Not considering there to be a risk, the prototype flight engine, largely cre-

ated by Eric Mitchell, carried the first DH.80 Moth Three, later named Puss Moth, aloft for a 15 minute test flight from Stag Lane on 9th September in the hands of The Captain. Production engines were released on 6th May 1930, one day after the Gipsy II.

It may have been coincidence that at the time of the first flight of the Gipsy III, ADC Aircraft re-organised their light aircraft engine production and mounted an assault on its own mass production efficiency. In the spring of 1930 the test-bed Moth G-EBUF was sold to Smith's Aircraft Instruments at Heston in whose employ she was joined by her regular pilot, Neville Stack. By the end of 1930, the ADC Company had commenced flight testing of an inverted version of their Hermes engine, dubbed a 'hanging Hermes', and in 1931 they changed their name again to the Cirrus-Hermes Engineering Company.

Taking delivery before the European engine 'guarantee' came into effect were five more military establishments. The Yugoslav Ministry of War and Marine accepted four DH.60G Seaplanes in September (1181, 1182, 1183 and 1189),

although five were shown on the inventory, allocated serials 73-77, painted light grey overall with Kosovo Cross roundels on top and bottom mainplanes and horizontal colour bands on the rudder. The following month four more DH.60G Seaplanes (1191-1194), were delivered to Sao Jacinto on behalf of the Naval Section of the Portuguese Air Ministry. The Norwegian Army received DH.60M 101 (1435), in a packing case on 30th December and 103 and 105 (1436 and 1442), arrived on January 1st 1930, all of which were duly assembled at the State Aircraft Factory at Kjeller. Known as 'Standard' Moths, they were operated from the site by the Army Flying School, Haerens Flyveskole. Two further DH.60M Moths (1445 and 1446) were delivered to the Danish Army at the end of December and taken on charge in January as S-106 and S-107, (later S-356 and S-357), supplementing the six DH.60Gs already in service. Three DH.60G Moths (1212-1214), ordered by the Romanian Air Ministry were registered CV-HAR, CV-HOR and CV-HAZ for operation in the training role by the Air Force.

DH.60X G-EBNO (261), de Havilland's flying test-bed for the first Cirrus II engine in 1926, was sold to Sweden in September 1928 and registered S-AABS, later SE-ABS, to Captain Gosta Andree in Gothenburg, the country's first private owner of a Moth. In September the following year Andree left Sweden for a flight to Cape Town where he arrived in October after a trip of 26 days. During the return flight he crashed in Libya on 13th December and following lengthy repairs undertaken by the Italian Air Force he crashed again on 5th April 1930. Repairs were even more protracted but the aeroplane was eventually returned to her owner

in Rome in December and found her way back to a busy life in Sweden.

Following their disappointment in the 1929 King's Cup de Havilland set their sights on *La Coupe Zenith*, a challenge trophy presented by the French Zenith Carburettor Company for competition by aircraft up to a tare weight of 400kg. This was a pure speed event and the winner was the aircraft which, during the period 1st May to 30th September, completed in the shortest time, the circuit Paris, Tours, Bordeaux, Toulouse, Marseilles, Lyons and back to Paris, at all of which locations it was compulsory to stop and refuel. To satisfy the Regulations, the King's Cup DH.60G G-AAHR, now referred to as a Super Coupé, capable of a top speed of 124mph when fitted with a DH5180/6 propeller, was further modified to accept a minimal seat in the space behind the pilot, and narrow oblong windows which were let into the otherwise blank decking.

Sid Weedon, of the same slight stature as Hubert Broad, was chosen to occupy the space in his capacity as travelling engineer and the team left Stag Lane on 12th September for their base at Orly. The speed attempt was made four days later when they took off from Paris at 7.30am and arrived back just before 5.00pm, having covered 1,150 miles in a flying time of 9hr 23min at an average speed of 112.5mph, some 30mph faster than their nearest rival.

While Broad was creating a speed record in Europe, the Canadian Company was moving into its new premises which it now referred to as Sheppard Avenue in the township of North York, later to be known as Downsview. Due to contractor's delays the facilities were occupied in an unfinished

state, but the original wooden hangar from Mount Dennis had been re-erected at the new site and improved.

DH.60G VP-KAC (1004) was shipped to Wilson Airways in Kenya in July 1929, but had been flown back to England with an American passenger, H A Field of Chicago Field Museum, by the airline's chief pilot and joint-founder, Tom Campbell-Black. Frank Swoffer left Stag Lane with a new passenger on 21st September to re-deliver the aeroplane to Nairobi. On arrival at Le Bourget Airport, Paris, VP-KAC suffered damage on the ground when de Havilland demonstration pilot Hugh Buckingham taxied another Moth into her, resulting in a delay of eight days. Swoffer's passenger disembarked at Naples leaving him to complete the journey solo. Landing at Atbara in the Sudan, nobody could be found at the aerodrome so Swoffer took off and circled the town. This had little effect so he landed close by and taxied up the main street, a dramatic appearance demanding of attention!

The aircraft was safely delivered to her base on 12th October having covered 6,000 miles in 77 hours on 14 flying days. That the trip was made without fuss was of particular interest to some elements of the aviation press which were becoming irritated by the growth in what they perceived as the wrong type of publicity:

'What a relief it is when someone who has flown more than a dozen hours solo, plans a long flight, makes no song about beating someone else's record, badgers no newspapers to photograph him or her in 14 different positions, sets out without arguing with the insurance people or trying to humbug the petrol and oil companies to give them the machine if they get over the Channel, and actually arrives intact at the destination, without breaking something when landing 200 miles from Stag Lane and 300 miles off their course.'

Ensbury Park Racecourse, Bournemouth, abandoned by the Royal Aero Club as a venue for organised racing, became a centre for joyriding during the months of June to September 1929, when 3,000 holidaymakers were flown in a trio of DH.60Gs piloted by a relay of pilots, mostly from Stag Lane. G-AAIW (1081) was adapted to carry two passengers in the front cockpit, a similar arrangement enjoyed by DH.60G VH-UKJ (975), after she was sold to Mrs M L Hider in Melbourne in 1931, both aircraft operating on special concessions. Bournemouth's

DH.60G G-AAHR, now referred to as a Super Coupé, was modified to carry a passenger in the void behind the pilot and, crewed by Hubert Broad and Sid Weedon, took the Zenith Cup in September, averaging 30mph faster than their closest rival. de Havilland

second Moth, G-AAFL (1005), flown by de
Havilland Apprentice John Hoare, hit the
sea on 11th August when reviewing the
Bournemouth Regatta at close quarters and
a relief aircraft had to be chartered until the
end of the season.

To celebrate the Centenary of Western
Australia, the Australian Aero Clubs and the
military pooled resources to organise an
East-West Air Race over about 2,400 miles,
from Sydney to Perth, flying between 12
checkpoints and taking six days. The scheduled start from Mascot Aerodrome on Saturday 28th September was postponed for
two days due to storms, flooded airfields
and strong winds, but got away on the Monday morning into the teeth of a westerly
gale. Of 27 entries, 15 were Moths of which
ten started and nine finished, DH.60G
VH-UKX (1073), colliding with a tree when
flying at low level in fog near Baandee on
the last day.

The de Havilland entry was DH.60G
VH-UIQ (893), *Black Hawk*, flown by Major
Hereward de Havilland. The aircraft had
been specially modified in Melbourne to
conform to the configuration now well
established for most of the works' racing
Moths: covered front cockpit which carried
the main fuel supply; faired centre section
with an extension to allow a continuous
upper-wing trailing edge; racing undercarriage; pilot's headrest; no external exhaust

pipe and maximum effort in streamlining,
which even included fairing of the filler neck
to the front fuel tank. The Gipsy I engine, fitted with special heads, carburettor and
induction manifold, was tuned to run continuously at between 2,300rpm and
2,400rpm. VH-UIQ was flown to Sydney for
the start and then achieved the fastest average speed of 107.8mph for a flight time of
22hr 50min to Perth, placing Major de Havilland in second place on handicap and
£300 better off. After the Race, he flew
VH-UIQ back to Melbourne, operating at full
throttle all the way.

Another contestant, Andrew Cunningham, flew DH.60G VH-UID (819), normally
based on his station near Canberra. Cunningham told how wild dogs had been
attacking his sheep and the solution was to
land the Moth close to the trouble spots
where every hour during the stillness of the
night, he started the engine and ran it up at
full throttle for a few minutes, the noise
from which appears to have frightened away
every dog for miles around.

DH.60G No 996 was delivered to Flying
Officer Lee Murray RAF, at Peshawar and
locally registered VT-AAR in March 1929.
The following month, Murray and his wife
flew the aeroplane to Sourabaya in the
Netherlands East Indies and from there travelled by ship to Darwin. The aircraft was re-
registered VH-ULB, first to Australian-born

Murray and from August 1929 to the Victorian Section of the Australian Aero Club
under whose name the Moth was entered in
the East-West Race with Murray as pilot. By
the early Thirties, Lee Murray had been
appointed General Manager of the de Havilland Aircraft Company based at Hatfield
and, in 1933, he was posted to Canada
where in the interests of economy he took
on a similar role combined with that of aeronautical engineer and Company test pilot.

During the Canadian summer a series of
Air Races was organised to coincide with the
National Exhibition. A race from Toronto to
Cleveland for club machines resulted in
Moths taking the first four places. Spon-
sored by private enterprise, the most inter-
esting event involved a qualifying trial of 550
miles, of which 300 miles were flown at full
throttle, followed by a 65 mile dash from St
Catherines to Toronto against a handicap

DH.60M J9922 was the aircraft chosen to participate in handling and spinning trials at A&AEE Martlesham Heath from May 1929, where she was criticised by pilots and engineers on a number of issues, most of which, over time, were addressed.
British Aerospace

formula decided upon by a committee of all the competing pilots, presided over by an independent chairman. First place went to a Company-entered DH.60G flown by Leigh Capreol with other DH.60Gs in second, third and fifth positions. Later in the year, DH.60Gs took the first two places in Mexico's first-ever air race, a 30 mile sprint to and from Mexico City.

In April 1929 a contract for eleven DH.60Ms was signed by the Air Ministry (912850/29), ordering ten aircraft, J9931 and J9932 (1382-1383) and J9923-J9930 (1385-1392), initially to be issued to the RAF's No 5 Flying Training School (FTS) at Sealand, mostly in October and November. De Havilland revealed the news under the heading 'The Moth as an Elementary Trainer' but were reprimanded by the Ministry who believed that in their opinion, the statement was misleading and implied that the Moth finally had been selected as the standard training machine for the Royal Air Force, whereas it was only one of several types used for the purpose. Whilst engaged in their evaluation, at least three aircraft were written off, J9931 (1382) spinning off an approach to land within days of delivery in November 1929. The survivors were progressively withdrawn during the next two years.

The Company paid particular attention to the weight of the Service DH.60M which was fitted with a modified wing section referred to equally as a 'Special RAF section' or a 'Training section'. After previous flight tests conducted at Martlesham Heath, the spinning characteristics of Moths fitted with the production standard Mk II wings had been described as 'objectionable'. The Mk I wing did not exhibit the same tendencies and its properties were regarded as being superior for military training purposes. To achieve the best results, wings and a tail unit of 'modified strength and construction' which would become standard on all Moths following civil flight trials on a new Company

development aircraft, DH.60G G-AARE (1176), in September, were fitted to a test aircraft in March 1930. The aerofoil section was similar to that of the 'original DH.60 Moth' except that the structure and attachment of the ribs was of the latest standard.

The first DH.60M to undertake military trials was the eleventh aircraft of the April contract. J9922 (1384) was delivered to Martlesham Heath in May 1929 to participate in handling and spinning tests and there to receive criticism that not only were the fixed seats considered to be set too low, preventing a pilot of short stature from reaching the fuel cock when strapped in, but they were very difficult for a pilot to vacate when wearing a parachute, particularly due to the total absence of doors for the rear cockpit. Possibly as a result of this report, after more than four years of operation, the edges of the decking surrounding the cockpits were re-designed and slim, oblong doors were included on the starboard side for both front and rear seats. RAF engineers also believed that the main fuel supply line from the tank should be changed from a rigid to a flexible pipe, and more inspection panels should be provided in the rear fuselage.

In general, the report was positive and carried a statement which must have brought a glow to the Sales Director's face: 'It is considered that this aircraft would be good as a light training aeroplane'.

Following a summer of mostly unsuitable weather permitting only minimal flying, J9922 was returned to Stag Lane for installation of a Gipsy II engine and to undertake a series of maximum weight trials to compare stalling speeds, in parallel with other similar DH.60Ms fitted with Mk II wings. As specified in the contract, the aircraft was not fitted with Handley Page slots and on completion was posted to 5 FTS at Sealand.

Ten additional DH.60Ms, serial batch K1103-K1112 (1450-1459), were ordered

against contract 932183/29 in October for delivery in December and January 1930. All were supplied less engines, which were installed by the RAF at the Home Aircraft Depot at Henlow. The Air Ministry was requested by de Havilland to confirm that unlike the previous batch of DH.60Ms, these aircraft would be acceptable with the all-welded fuselage which could be delivered sooner than the wire-braced type, now superseded as the production standard. The aircraft were later dispersed to Squadrons, Stations and Defence Area Headquarters around the country where they served in the communications role. In September, K1112 was modified to carry navigation lights and Holt Flares at a total weight penalty of 93 lb.

In November the Company announced that with the end of the 'Competition Season', they were offering for sale 'some notable Gipsy Moths'. These included the Chairman's racing DH.60X G-EBQH (276), which had been advertised privately at £600, fitted with a standard Gipsy engine with only two hours after overhaul, and Broad's Super Coupé G-AAHR (1068), both at £575; the Reliability Tour Moth G-EBTD (430), completely reconditioned, at £425, and two development aircraft, DH.60G G-AALJ (1087) at £700 and DH.60G G-AARE (1176) at £665.

G-EBQH was sold to Alan Muntz at Heston who entered her for the 1930 King's Cup Air Race starting from Hanworth in July, but she was a non-starter. Thereafter she was listed to a succession of owners until the aircraft was scrapped following a decision not to renew her C of A in September 1937. In January 1930, G-EBTD set off for a trip via Egypt to India flown by Sir Ahmed Hassanein Bey, Chamberlain to King Fuad of Egypt. The aircraft was damaged when landing at Pisa and returned to Stag Lane for repair after which she became part of the NFS fleet spending time at Hanworth and Lympne. The venerable aeroplane was impressed into military service in 1940 and did not survive. The highly modified G-AAHR was expected to be a difficult sale as proved to be the case, and was retained by the Company for a further year. G-AALJ was converted to a seaplane and delivered to Major Albert Nathan at Port of Spain, Trinidad. The aircraft eventually was returned to Hanworth as a landplane, in which configuration she crashed near West Malling in 1934. G-AARE had logged only four hours when offered for sale. She remained unsold and early the following

Two DH.60M Seaplanes of the Halifax Aero
Club at anchor on 20th October 1929.
CF-CBH was written off in September 1930
and CF-ADX, nearer the camera, capsized at
her mooring the following month.
Via Gerry Schwam

Two DH.60M Seaplanes of the Halifax Aero
Club at anchor on 20th October 1929.
CF-CBH was written off in September 1930
and CF-ADX, nearer the camera, capsized at
her mooring the following month.
Via Gerry Schwam

year was also converted to a seaplane with a revised chassis, and used to test experimental floats not fitted with water rudders, when operating on behalf of Saunders Roe from Cowes.

Roy Tuckett was making an attempt on the London to Cape Town record when he took off from Croydon on 9th November in DH.60G G-AARW (1109), fuelled with 60 gallons of petrol and hopeful of a ten day trip. The flight, which was sponsored by Norman Anstey and Company who owned department stores in Johannesburg and Durban, was soon in trouble. G-AARW was nursed into Aboukir after an oil pipe split over the Mediterranean and temporary repairs had to be made following a precautionary landing on a North African beach. A misunderstanding between RAF engineers during maintenance work at Aboukir caused the engine to start and G-AARW to run away. During his efforts to stop her, Tuckett was knocked unconscious and the aircraft's progress was halted only when she struck a hangar. Following local repair the aircraft flew on to Assiut where she collided with a Fairey IIIF. The Moth remained unairworthy for many weeks and, with all hopes of record times dismissed, Tuckett continued south, damaging the undercarriage on take off from an airfield in Central Uganda on 26th January 1930 which caused the aircraft to overturn on landing at Tororo, a town on the southern border. Repairs were effected in Nairobi but Cape Town was not reached until June where the aircraft took up residence as ZS-ABX. In August, she was written off at Baragwanath.

The Chinese interest in Moths continued with a further eight DH.60Gs ordered in December, each to be supplied with wheeled or float undercarriages, taking the total orders received from Shanghai to 35. One further order was placed by the London Aeroplane Club who had organised another raffle, this time for a DH.60M to be provided in any colour of the winner's choice. All 1,500 tickets were sold at ten shillings each and the draw was made at Stag Lane during the afternoon of Sunday, 23rd March 1930. The winning number belonged to Lieutenant Craig of Totland Bay, although the aircraft was never officially registered in his name and probably was sold prior to delivery.

Making a Christmas present to himself was Sir Hugh Clifford, Governor of the Straits Settlements who had presided over the opening of the Singapore Flying Club in 1928. Sir Hugh had seen a Moth displayed in the window of the Army and Navy stores in London's Victoria Street, where it had been placed on a 'sale or return' basis. The aircraft was registered G-AASZ (1434), to Sir Hugh although it ventured no further east than Brooklands and was sold to the flying club there in March.

Alan Butler and Nigel Norman had agreed to take their wives to Paris on 7th December to watch the Carnera-Stribling fight, but they discovered their boat-train had been cancelled due to gales in the English Channel and also that Imperial Airways had suspended operations. They decided to travel in their own Moths and the necessary paperwork was provided by the Royal Aero Club at no notice and in 15 minutes. Alan and Lois Butler arranged to fly their coupé Moth G-AACL from Stag Lane to Heston where they would rendezvous with the Normans, flying in company from there to St Inglevert and thence to Paris by train. Alan Butler later recalled the occasion:

'When we arrived at Stag Lane the Moth was out on the aerodrome, the engine ticking over, and was held down by five men, two on each wing and one on the tail, but even though every effort was being made to hold the Moth steady it was lurching about in a most alarming manner. One more man was put on each wing and this served to hold the machine steady in a wind blowing west-south-west at 40-50mph on the ground. As I considered it safe to fly we got into our machine and opened the throttle, the men releasing the aeroplane at the same moment. Although I had on board 29 gallons of fuel, a passenger and luggage, the Moth left the ground in ten yards and proceeded to ascend almost vertically above the ground as it met the full force of the wind.

'After 16min we were circling Heston, and people came running out to catch the machine as we landed. When they were about 20 yards in front of me I shut off the engine and flattened out at about 10ft. Then for a long time, or so it seemed, we were suspended in the air, but after pushing the stick backwards and forwards a few times a safe landing was made and the machine secured by three men on each wing.'

Butler and Norman flew their aircraft to Lympne to clear Customs, covering the 70 miles at an average ground speed of 168mph, and landed with assistance in the lee of the hangars. The Channel crossing of 27 miles was achieved in a little over eight minutes and the travellers slipped into their ringside seats twenty minutes before the fight, the only arrivals in Paris that day from England. On 28th February 1931, Charles Job travelled to Le Bourget to collect G-AACL on behalf of her then owner, George Mallinson, but during the return flight to Croydon on 1st March, the aircraft disappeared during a snowstorm over the English Channel.

A young businessman from New Zealand, Francis Chichester, took his first flying lessons at Stag Lane during the summer of 1929 but decided the place was too crowded to make adequate progress and transferred to Brooklands where he completed training for his 'A' licence, purchased DH.60G G-AAKK (1093), and immediately started to plan a record attempt to Sydney. Had he remained at Stag Lane he might have witnessed an experiment by the London Aeroplane Club which required all pupil pilots flying solo under instruction to display an identifying streamer attached to the rudder.

G-AAKK was modified to carry a total of 59 gallons of fuel, about ten hours endurance, and Chichester logged 200 hours in a 12 week period during which he completed a

Roy Tuckett taking off from Croydon on 9th November 1929 in his DH.60G G-AARW, at the start of his planned ten-day journey to Cape Town, although he did not arrive there until June 1930. LNA

'Whereas six months ago we were importing from England machines in a semi completed stage, erecting, finishing and testing them here, we are now building the machines up from the small components which we import from England and approaching 50 per cent of the labour content is of Canadian origin.'

At Stag Lane the parent Company was able to announce that capitalisation had risen to £400,000, that all mortgages had been paid off and the value of the aerodrome and facilities had greatly appreciated. As the light aeroplane movement continued to surge forward, 85 per cent of all British-registered privately owned aircraft were Moths. Sales to the Continent of Europe had increased by 300 per cent, manufacturing licences had recently been agreed with Norway and France, and an Indian branch of the Company had been opened in Karachi to satisfy an increasing demand for spares and service.

But there were dark clouds on the financial horizon too. Business in the USA had been slow to develop but having achieved modest success was hit by the economic downturn. Against a cash payment, the licence agreement had been cancelled, leaving the parent Company free to trade within the USA, and the previously independent Moth Aircraft Corporation to become a fully integrated part of the Curtiss-Wright Group. At home, the Company Chairman expressed concern that restrictive legislation and regulation imposed by the government might negate their modest contribution towards the solution of the unemployment problem which was of growing concern.

European tour, unusually devoid of any press comment.

'On 19th December I worked hard all day then flew over to Stag Lane to have a cover fitted to the front cockpit which was both streamlined and easy to open, so that I could get out my rubber boat in a hurry. Also, I had a hole cut in the back of the front seat so that I could extract food from where I sat at the controls. I collected and stowed all my food and gear. I made telephone calls about last minute permits. Not until after dark did I take off from Brooklands to fly to Croydon Airport where I had to clear Customs. An Air Ministry official immediately pounced on me to know why I was flying without navigation lights.'

Chichester took off at 2.30am the following day and on 25th January 1930 he reached Darwin, only the second England-Australia solo flight in history and the first in a Moth. Five days later he was in Sydney. The journey had taken 180.5 flying hours over a period of 42 days, 30 days longer than anticipated, mostly due to damage inflicted during a night landing on the salt lake at Tripoli which he had mistaken for the aerodrome in the absence of promised lighting. The aeroplane was repaired by the Italian Air Force over a period of 17 days and with all chance of a record gone, Chichester reverted to his stand-by plan 'to discontinue fast flying and go slowly, enjoying the

journey'. In post-arrival publicity originated by KLG Spark Plugs, Chichester was referred to over-familiarly as 'Frank', but it was for the only time.

At the end of the year which also closed a decade of significant progress, the Canadian Company reported delivery in 1929 of 130 Moths, a considerable number of which were Seaplanes, 95 per cent of them fitted with slots. The Company emphasised how the Canadian prospecting business had been entirely altered, the prospectors flying by seaplane in the summer and ski-plane in the winter, achieving more in a single season than had been possible previously in three or four years.

The new factory near Toronto was geared towards taking on a greater proportion of parts manufactured locally and Bob Loader's end of term message was clear:

On arrival in New Zealand with his DH.60G G-AAKK, Francis Chichester's flight between London and Sydney was well publicised by Shell who were pleased to provide transport and, in this shot, to display the aircraft at Rongotai Aerodrome. Shell

JANUARY TO DECEMBER 1930

THE DECADE began with publication of the New Year's Honours, in which Lady Mary Bailey was appointed Dame and Sir Charles Wakefield, who had already gifted seven Moths to flying clubs in Australia, Canada, Great Britain, India and South Africa, was created a Baron: Lord Wakefield of Hythe.

As part of the continuing programme of improvements, often dictated by conditions encountered worldwide, a new option for the 1930 DH.60 Moth was the choice of Dunlop low pressure wheels with tyres inflated to only 8psi rather than the standard thin, high pressure units operating at up to 40psi. Demonstrator DH.60M G-AAKV (1369), fitted with the new 'doughnut' wheels, was flown on 6th January at full throttle around the Stag Lane Speed Course, now extended to Denham, a distance of 9.4 miles from the Bald Faced Stag, to gauge any appreciable difference in performance.

Added to the list of new options for the civil DH.60M was a parachute seat, 'lower, slightly larger and curved and flanged', which was designed to accommodate the 18 lb Irving Seat Pack which a number of private owners were specifying. When not utilised for a parachute, the seat pan could be filled with a specially-designed air cushion.

But not everybody at first enjoyed what the Moth had to offer. Novelist David Garnett wrote a book about his efforts in learning to fly under the title *A Rabbit in the Air*. Of his first lesson in a DH.60 with Arthur Marshall at Cambridge he wrote:

'Moths are quite different. First, there is the tiresome bother of earphones. My old helmet does not fit and the 'phones come in the wrong places. Secondly, I felt buried in the cockpit. I was always dissatisfied with the radius of vision from the Bluebird, but one could see a great deal forward because the Genet radial engine sloped down to the nose. With the Gipsy engine one is almost blind forward, and the wretched little windscreen is quite opaque. One can see nothing unless one cranes one's neck out and round over the side.'

In October 1929, Captain Frederick Guest arranged for three DH.60Gs (G-AABK/811, G-AALK/1174 and G-AALU/1178), to be shipped to Nairobi for an African Tour. In the

Sir Charles Wakefield presented a DH.60G Moth, VT-ABB, to the Bombay Flying Club and the aircraft was handed over by the Governor, Sir Frederick Sykes, on Tuesday, 3rd December 1929. The ceremony took place at Juhu Air Park and in attendance were Mr J A Brown of C C Wakefield Ltd, in the flying helmet, and the Bombay Club's Chief Engineer, Mr W Scott King. There is some suspicion that the aircraft at the ceremony was mispainted as VT-ABB as the letters were allocated to a DH.60M delivered to a private owner in Bombay at about the same time. DH Moth Club Archive

Major Hereward de Havilland with Mr H Henrikson of the Shell Company of Australia, examining DH.60M VH-UNQ during assembly at the Melbourne factory in January 1930. The aircraft was fitted with long-range tanks, increasing fuel capacity to 35 gallons. Shell

New Year and with four pilots, Guest, Winifred Spooner, Flight Lieutenant Rupert Preston and Flying Officer Hordern, each aircraft flew about 200 hours and covered 11,000 miles, operating from high-altitude aerodromes, almost always at maximum weight. Guest, a principal in National Flying Services, was exuberant in his praise for the performance of the aircraft: 'the whole tour went according to schedule, no alteration of plans being necessary'. Following the adventure, Miss Spooner, Preston and Hordern flew the three aircraft back to England where they were returned to normal service by April without any unscheduled attention. 'On the return journey, no mechanic was carried and no need was found for his services.'

Glen Kidston's new DH.60G G-AAJV (1108) was shipped to the RAF station at Aboukir in Iraq in January from where the owner flew her to Kenya for his own three month tour involving shooting and photography. The aircraft was fitted with an Eagle camera and 'a special silencer to deaden the sound of the engine so that the animals may not be prematurely startled', but whether the precaution was before they were photographed or shot was not clarified. The aircraft remained in Kenya where she was acquired by Wilson Airways as VP-KAL. Joining her in October was DH.60M G-ABCZ (1555), soon to be VP-KAO, flown from Heston to Nairobi by Mrs Helen Silver and Captain Cameron who had been her instructor.

C W T Wood left Stag Lane on 11th February in DH.60G Coupé G-AALD (1137). Following safe arrival in Nairobi, the aircraft was registered VP-KAG as the personal aircraft for Mrs F K Wilson, later helping to expand still further the Wilson Airways fleet.

Starting in February, the Finnish State Aircraft Factory manufactured a further eleven licence-built aircraft (11-21), with Finnish Air Force serials MO-106 to MO-116. Known as the *Harka Motti* in Finland (Bull Moth), all were powered by 115hp Cirrus Hermes II engines distinguished by their 'Arctic' cowlings which enclosed the cylinders completely, permitting the cooling air, drawn through the front intake, to escape from a series of louvres in the side panels. Like their predecessors, between February and April 1930 the new aircraft were distributed amongst a variety of military units acting as trainers and communications machines, operating on wheels, floats and skis. Following the Winter War and the Continuation War, a total of seven Moths remained on charge. The last, MO-112 (17), was withdrawn on 7th November 1944 and flown into storage pending disposal.

Francis St Barbe travelled to Johannesburg in February 1930, a trip which lasted nine weeks, providing a first-hand opportunity to analyse the business climate. He persuaded Aeros (Pty) Ltd, an associated company of the Johannesburg Light Plane Club, and somewhat reluctant agent for Avro, to take on the vacant de Havilland agency instead. Within six months the business had grown to such an extent that Aeros was taken into the ownership of the de Havilland Company together with the Club workshops at Baragwanath. The de Havilland Aircraft Company of South Africa (Pty) Ltd was established there as a sales and service centre under the Chairmanship of Major G S Haggie, the fourth overseas company.

St Barbe's general view was that, apart from the efficiently run Johannesburg Club with about 350 members, nearly all the other

In a Canadian winter, even the protection offered by a coupé top was not considered adequate, and W G Holden, Chief Instructor, engineer and secretary to the Moose Jaw Flying Club, designed and installed a hot-air supply tapped from the exhaust system of DH.60M CF-CAG.
Via Gerry Schwam

flying clubs which had been started with such optimism were in a poor condition owing to low membership, no funds, amateurish management and lack of state subsidy due to a minimal awareness of the national benefits of aviation. St Barbe suggested that aircraft manufacturers were to blame in equal measure, providing a poor spares service, no organised repair facilities which otherwise were provided with some reluctance by the Air Force and then only at Roberts Heights, and no regular circulation of propaganda.

DH.60X J9119 (526) suffered failure of the entire leading edge of the port upper mainplane during aerobatics at Andover in November 1929. It was the fourth report of in-flight damage received within a few weeks, one aircraft suffering simultaneous failure on all four wings. Examination and subsequent testing at Farnborough resulted in a revised method of attaching ribs to the leading edges and by pen steel clips to the front spar, a modification which was mandated by the Air Ministry who called for it to be incorporated on all Moths, civil and military, at the earliest opportunity. Aircraft owners and Ground Engineers were notified by Air Ministry Notice No 2 of 1930, dated 21st January, which advised them that not only was the modification drawing M1226 available without charge from de Havilland, but a free supply of attachment clips was also being offered.

Martlesham Heath was advised in mid-February that the Air Ministry had contracted for de Havilland to carry out the modification work in respect of DH.60X J9922 at no charge to the Crown, and that the Establishment should make suitable arrangements, but Farnborough responded to similar notification in respect of DH.60X J9115 by assuring the Ministry that the Notice issued three weeks previously had already been complied with using local resources. A previous Notice published in December 1929 had imposed a mandatory increase in bolt diameter at the top front spar outer joint on all Moths listed as 'Types DH.60X, G and N' fitted with Autoslots. Under the terms of both Notices, addressees were threatened that Certificates of Airwor-

thiness would not be renewed unless the modifications were embodied.

Rumours were circulating within the London Aeroplane Club that due to increasing congestion at Stag Lane, a change of location was inevitable and imminent. The hot gossip in February laid short odds on the new Handley Page airfield at Radlett, near St Albans, which was due to be opened by Prince George on 7th July (and to which Frederick Handley Page was to invite Alan Butler and Hubert Broad to 'come across in a couple of slotted Moths'). Later in the year, members were advised that the Committee was negotiating with de Havilland for 'more commodious accommodation' at Stag Lane to include lock-up facilities where a certain number of members' own aircraft could be housed. Meanwhile in May, de Havilland opened a new aerodrome of their own near Hatfield on farmland owned by Lord Salisbury and to which as first priority, the School of Flying was to be moved. The Company invited members of the public to suggest a name for the new site by 31st May

after which the person whose submission was adopted would be offered a 15 minute flight in a Moth with Hubert Broad. There is no surviving record of who suggested the name 'Hatfield Aerodrome'.

Only a few weeks previously on 4th April, and without any fanfare, the Australian Company moved into new premises at Mascot Aerodrome, Sydney, a city considered to be very much the centre for business in preference to the location of their original works in the tin-roofed warehouse in the centre of Melbourne.

While the new DH.80 Moth Three and her Gipsy III engine were still involved in an intensive flight test programme, largely conducted by Captain de Havilland, it seemed expedient to compare the properties of standard wooden propellers against a new design which had been promised for light aeroplanes by Leitner Watts, using a company demonstrator DH.60G, G-AARI, fitted with a Gipsy I engine. The tests were conducted at Stag Lane on 27th March using first a DH5180/1 manufactured by the Airscrew

DH.60M Coupé F-AJLV was delivered to Baron de Précourt in Paris in February 1930 but was re-sold in April and withdrawn from use in unknown circumstances in October 1931.
Via Peter Gould

Company from Honduras mahogany, followed by an adjustable hollow blade referred to simply as a series 3143-4 and, combined with a series 448 boss, more than 5 lb heavier than her wooden counterpart. The trials involved three take-offs, a speed run 'all-out' at 2,000ft and a climb to 10,000ft, although on the appointed day, the cloud-base prevented operations above 8,500ft. Observer Richard Clarkson noted:

'It was intended to set the pitch of the Leitner Watts to give the same rpm as the wood propeller when flying all-out at 2,000ft, this being deemed to be a sound basis for comparison. The metal propeller, however, when adjusted as above, was found to be giving slightly more rpm than the wood propeller all-out, but the same static rpm, and owing to the limited time available it was decided to do tests with this pitch setting which should be strictly comparable from the point of view of 'take-off' whilst slightly favourable to the metal propeller when climbing and all-out.'

The results proved that, in almost all circumstances, the wooden propeller was more efficient. Richard Clarkson summarised: 'The running of the metal propeller was generally good. It was slightly rough all-out but quite smooth on the ground and when climbing'. There was no great rush to buy metal propellers in spite of their rapid and easy ground adjustment for a different pitch and the suggestion that a private owner might carry only one blade as a spare. When metal blades were specified as a result of genuine improvements in performance, most owners seemed to favour fixed-pitch propellers supplied by the Fairey Company.

Following her experimental flying at Cowes, DH.60G Seaplane G-AARE was delivered to the Marine Aircraft Experimental Establishment (MAEE) at Felixstowe in March, where she was listed as a DH.60X, for trials in support of the Company's application for a Certificate of Airworthiness at an all-up weight of 1,750 lb, following modifications to the wing structure and tail unit. Flight Lieutenant A R Wardle, who conducted the exercise during the second week of March, reported that the ailerons had been badly rigged and were well outside the normal settings but having rectified the situation, lateral control had become satisfactory.

Like many of his contemporaries, Wardle did not like the spring loading device used for trimming the elevator on the grounds that it destroyed the pilot's sense of feel, especially on landing. He was also critical of the take-off run which he considered too long for a light floatplane, but his main complaint concerned the lack of water rudders:

'While the control on the water is satisfactory in calm conditions, it is necessary to use a considerable amount of engine to turn out of a wind of the order of 10mph. The aircraft would be greatly improved for manoeuvring on the water by the addition of water rudders. This would have the advantage of saving the engine and airscrew when taxying on choppy water.'

On 31st March, Selfridges opened their London-based Aviation Department which was situated in Avonmore Road near Olympia. The showroom displayed a Moth, a Desoutter, Bluebird and Klemm, together with a range of engines, and included a specialist bookshop. The previous week, on 24th March, all the aviation interests of de Havilland's British agent, Malcolm Campbell (London) 1927 Ltd, were acquired by Brian Lewis and C D Barnard Ltd. The Hon Brian Lewis, later Lord Essendon, had been a director with Malcolm Campbell and, fol-

lowing further investment by Gordon Selfridge Jnr, the Barnard attachment to the new Company was dropped. An early recruit to their Heston depot, Philip Gordon Marshall, explained that de Havilland was so busy making Moths that they preferred an outside agency to look after home sales, particularly as improved de Havilland aeroplanes were introduced and so many part-exchange deals were involved, none of which included cars.

From 1st March 1932, the de Havilland Company announced that Brian Lewis and Company, Phillips and Powis Aircraft (Reading) Ltd and Brooklands Aviation Ltd, had been granted exclusive distribution rights within allocated English and Welsh counties, each being responsible for the organisation of sales throughout their own particular areas. Marshall's Flying School was later added to cover some of the Eastern Counties. Brian Lewis also established depots at Hooton Park and Renfrew in Scotland, but closed down in 1935 as the manufacturer became more self-sufficient in handling sales, and due to continuing shifts in policy which permitted flying clubs and other concerns to become local agents and dealers.

The diary entry made by Her Grace, the Duchess of Bedford, for Tuesday 8th April 1930 reads:

'I did a very good take-off and approach, a little bound on the first landing but not a serious one, and was mightily pleased that I had done it, and so I think was my instructor as he was very keen to teach me.'

These few words describe the Duchess' first solo flight in her DH.60G G-AAAO (808), after 30 hours' dual instruction. Her regular instructor, Charles Barnard, had been on the point of sending her solo from Lewsey Farm Airfield between Luton and Dunstable, which they used for flying practice, before business in connection with the Duchess' imminent flight to Cape Town in her Fokker F.VIIA G-EBTS, took him away to Bristol. Her Grace temporarily engaged freelance instructor Sydney St Barbe, brother of de Havilland's Business Manager, who had little hesitation in presenting his pupil

Only on rare occasions did the de Havilland publicists look outside the Company when people were required for a project, a tradition that was carried through to the final days at Hatfield Aerodrome. In the times when many departmental heads were allowed their own secretaries, these personable and intelligent ladies could be called upon to support the cause as in this exercise, shot during the summer of 1930, to promote the world-wide use of the Gipsy Moth. Left to right: Miss Clare, Miss Williams, Miss Chaplin and Miss Stone. The latter met and married the architect of the new buildings at Hatfield Aerodrome, and became Mrs Winnie Monro. de Havilland

with the solo opportunity at the age of 64.

Wholly owned from 4th January 1930, the Curtiss-Wright Corporation boosted advertising for the former Moth Aircraft Corporation's products, bracketing them with the miscellany of other types for which the Company held rights. In April the 'Special Sport Edition' was offered at $5,500 with a note to confirm that the Standard Model 'was changed very little in appearance but the fuselage has been strengthened by the use of stronger tubing and additional heat treatment'. With a Gipsy engine, the model was available at $3,900, flyaway St Louis. By August the quoted price had been increased by $60 and from September the Company was proposing the Curtiss-Wright Flying Club under whose administrative umbrella, Moths could be provided at $4,000 each together with all that was necessary to set up in business as a local flying club.

An analysis of Moths licensed in the USA early in 1930 indicated that at least one was fitted with a Wright Whirlwind engine, a near-inevitability given the parentage, although the type was never promoted as a commercially available option. The American owner of a British-built DH.60M, Ralph Kenyon, wrote to de Havilland to explain how, having 'streamlined-up' he could cruise at 120mph or fly at a top speed of 134mph: 'I built a false bottom to the fuselage and faired all strut fittings, all landing gear fittings, the petrol tank into the wings, the wings into the fuselage, the headrest into the fin, bridged the gap in the ailerons, elevators and rudder and constructed a detachable front cockpit cover and windshield'.

Garland E Peed Jnr. of the Curtiss Flying Service in St Louis, wrote to *Flight*, advising in detail how he had flown a series of inverted aerobatic manoeuvres, including inverted loops, in a standard American-built Gipsy Moth, 'not only the first strictly commercial airplane but the first ship under 200hp and 1,600lb to complete these manoeuvres in the United States', adding that the flights had taken place before a number of competent observers and could very easily be certified. At the time of the first British demonstrations of the inverted loop by the RAF Genet Moth at Hendon in 1928, the de Havilland Company had very specifically warned private owners not to attempt such manoeuvres as the RAF aircraft had been specially modified.

London's Dominion Theatre staged a musical comedy called *Silver Wings* which opened in the spring but found no great

favour from audiences. The theme hung on the non-stop flight of a Moth from England to Mexico with what was described as 'wireless transmitting gear and a stowaway on board'. The aircraft, a DH.60X supplied by the Brooklands School of Flying, was required to start its engine on stage and was provided with a wick carburettor with a container for the fuel. An aviation-minded critic was compelled to report:

'The whole of the fuel content has to be absorbed in cotton wool, and to further comply with the London County Council regulations, the carburettor has to be detachable. It speaks well for the Brooklands' people and the Cirrus engine that since the show has been running the engine has only twice failed to start at the critical moment.'

In Australia, the Vacuum Oil Company took delivery of their DH.60M VH-UVO (1496) in May, painted in the colours of the Australian kingfisher (blue, black, buff and white), and named her *Plume*. Shortly after, the aircraft was exhibited on the stage of Melbourne's Regent Theatre for three performances a day 'for one week only' while Vacuum Oil showed a short film covering the construction and first test-flight of the aircraft. During the performance, *Plume's* Gipsy engine was hand-swung into life and never failed to start on the first pull.

Having decided she wanted to learn to fly, Amy Johnson had written blind to Stag Lane Aerodrome from where her enquiry was answered by the de Havilland School of Flying offering her tuition at £5 per hour, well outside her modest budget. It was only later that Amy discovered the London Aeroplane Club and their heavily subsidised rates. After an unpromising start to her flying training, she was sent solo on 9th June 1929 and on

6th July was issued with her pilot's 'A' licence. To improve her practical knowledge, she worked voluntarily in the London Club's workshops and qualified for her Ground Engineer's 'C' licence on 10th December 1929 and her 'A' licence on 10th March 1930.

The 26-year-old Amy Johnson left Croydon Airport early in the morning of 5th May 1930, determined to be the first woman to fly solo from England to Australia. Her second-hand DH.60G G-AAAH (804), painted green and silver and named *Jason*, had been funded jointly by her father and Lord Wakefield, who divided Wally Hope's asking price of £700 between them. At first, nobody paid a great deal of attention. With 80 hours' solo flying time and little cross-country experience she was regarded as just another madcap young woman but as news of her progress became known, the newspapers grew alert. Her time to Karachi shaved two days off the record and when she finally reached Darwin on Empire Day, 24th May, she was already an international celebrity, welcomed by congratulatory telegrams from HM The King, the British Prime Minister, Secretary of State for Air and other notables from around the world. Her achievement was later described as having the same impact and significance as putting a man on the moon.

Of all the long-distance Moth pilots, the name of Amy Johnson is probably the one best known. Although her later flights did not attract as much attention as her very public married life, the British people always warmed to her. Unknown to Amy, her faithful *Jason* had been acquired by the *Daily Mail* as part of a wider contract agreed with her father even before the aeroplane's return to England. One of the first tangible displays of public affection came on 16th August

Following her crash at Brisbane, Amy Johnson's DH.60G G-AAAH was quickly repaired, but to static condition only, by the de Havilland Company at Mascot, before arrangements were made to ship the aeroplane back to England.
Via David Walters

The readers of the Daily Sketch and Sunday Graphic subscribed towards a new Moth for Amy Johnson which they voted should be called *Johnnie*. DH.60G G-ABDV was presented by Sir Sefton Brancker in Hyde Park and afterwards the aeroplane was displayed in an Oxford Street window of Selfridge's department store. de Havilland

when, subscribed for by readers of the *Daily Sketch* and *Sunday Graphic*, no doubt as part of a *Daily Mail*-baiting campaign, Amy Johnson was presented with a new DH.60G, G-ABDV (1291). The ceremony took place in front of a huge crowd in Hyde Park and was conducted by Sir Sefton Brancker. Named *Johnnie* by her benefactors, and displayed as such in the window of Selfridge's Oxford Street store until mid-September, G-ABDV was later re-named *Jason III*.

The continued popularity of the Moth in all circles of Canadian aviation plus the high costs of importing parts from England, led inevitably to the decision fully to utilise the additional floor space at the Canadian Company's new facilities at Downsview, and to manufacture all the parts necessary for a complete aircraft, buying in proprietary

equipment as required and importing Gipsy engines from Stag Lane. The decision meant that a separate royalty agreement be negotiated for the continued use of Autoslots, although this was not finally signed until 3rd December, with the company representing Handley Page's North American interests, the Aircraft Slotted Wing Corporation.

To manufacture aircraft in Canada was a political decision as much as any and the first contract, not surprisingly, was to supply 18 DH.60Ms to the Royal Canadian Air Force. As was becoming more usual in the supposed interests of security, the allocated serial blocks were deliberately disjointed: RCAF 151-156 (DHC107-112); RCAF 157-162 (DHC101-106), and RCAF 163-168 (DHC113-118). All the aircraft were taken on charge between March and May and

although there are no confirmatory records, it is probable that most served initially at Camp Borden before dispersal amongst other military units. In July and August 1939, eight surviving aircraft were transferred to the civil register for operation by the flying clubs.

Nine further civil DH.60M Moths, DHC119-127, were manufactured before the end of 1930, when DH.80A Puss Moth kits started to arrive from England for assembly. Eight more were built between April and June 1931 (DHC128-135), of which DHC130 was allocated to rebuild DH.60X Seaplane G-CAPC (508), and DHC132-134 were put into store until 1934/1935 when they were completed and sold. Four airframes constructed late in 1930, DHC136-139, were all used to rebuild RCAF DH.60Ms previously taken on charge in 1929. In a report sent back to Stag Lane, one of the Canadian Directors assessed that the Company was making more profit on the steady stream of reconditioning work that was being channelled through the new factory, than from the sale of a new machine.

The Ontario Provincial Air Service, early supporters of the Moth, reported that May and June 1930 were particularly bad months for forest fires and that during a six week period, their fleet of 14 Moths had flown a total of 2,008hr, four aircraft achieving almost 200 hours each during this period. Star performer was George Delahaye operating DH.60M Seaplane CF-APB (1321) from Twin Lakes, who, between 1st and 7th June, flew 61hr 15min, representing a cruising distance of about 4,600 miles. During the same week, DH.60M Seaplane CF-AOC flew almost 58 hours from her base at Orient Bay.

In July 1928, the Australian General Aircraft Company (Genairco), rebuilt the damaged DH.60X G-AUHA (426) at Mascot and re-registered the aircraft VH-ULH with builder's reference '7'. The aircraft was sold to private owners in Sydney who had wrecked her by December. Following agreement with de Havilland in November 1929, Genairco completed a new DH.60X Seaplane Coupé, VH-UMS (8), and a Cirrus Hermes-powered DH.60X, VH-UMK (9), both of which were sold to local residents,

On 25th April 1930, de Havilland Aircraft of Canada displayed some of the latest batch of 35 DH.60M Moths built entirely at Downsview, ordered for service by the RCAF. de Havilland Canada

but in December unveiled the first of a batch of 'improved' Moths each powered by a Hermes engine and known officially as 'Genairco Moths' or more usually as 'Genaircos'.

VH-UNC (10) was registered to Rockhampton Aerial Services in December 1929 and was followed between April and July 1930 by Nos 11-16, excluding No 13 which was not allocated. The aircraft were distinctive due to a widened fuselage to allow two passengers to sit side by side in the heavily sculpted front cockpit, devoid of doors. The opportunity was taken to fill the wider centre section with a larger fuel tank of 27 gallons capacity behind which the normal trailing edge gap in the wings was filled with an extended aerofoil which could be hinged upwards to permit the wings to be folded. Equally distinctive was the rudder, necessarily increased in area but re-designed to be broader and rounder.

Genairco VH-UOF (15) left Sydney on 31st July, flown by owner Andrew Cunningham, on an attempted solo flight to England but, following a series of mishaps in the Far East, the flight was abandoned in Calcutta in October and the aircraft returned to Australia. VH-UOG (16) was used to flight test an Australian in-line engine, the Harkness Hornet, a project which succumbed to the Depression and in VH-UOG was replaced by a Gipsy II. The last two aircraft built in 1930, 17 and 18, were designated Genairco Cabin Moth, similar in configuration to the DH.83 Fox Moth, and both were operated as seaplanes. The last aircraft, No 19, was not completed until June 1931 following which the company closed down. The assets were acquired by Tugan Aircraft Ltd at Mascot who built a further Genairco Seaplane from remaining parts, registered VH-URH against builder's reference No 1, in April 1934.

The Commonwealth Trade Board imposed a 25 per cent tariff on British aircraft imported into Australia from 1st November, previously free, and a 35 per cent tariff on foreign aircraft, previously 10 per cent, in an effort to add stimulus to the creation of a home-based industry. Both Genairo and the Larkin Aircraft Supply Company appealed against the rates, suggesting they should be increased to 30 per cent and 50 per cent respectively, but Hudson Fysh from Qantas argued against any imposition on the grounds that the new tariff would simply increase the cost of aviation in Australia where, he said, it was not yet possible to build aircraft with the same facility available in Europe and the USA.

An order for 30 DH.60M aircraft was placed by the British Air Ministry against contract 5785/30 in February. Mindful of their brush with authority over previous announcements, the Company's 'Press Matter' dated 13th February 1930, drew attention to the RAF Moth as a type exactly similar to that owned by the Prince of Wales, which in addition to its simple-to-maintain and cheap-to-run air-cooled engine, had certain characteristics underlying its success as a training type:

'...despite its speed being only two-thirds that of the modern single seat scout, it handles in just the same way as a high powered type, thus pupils who learn to fly a Moth will have only to accustom themselves to the higher performance to become proficient Service pilots. Because of the simplicity of the Moth, its selection in this instance should materially assist in keeping down the expense of training pilots.'

All the aircraft in the serial batch K1218-K1227 (1500-1509) were delivered less engines to Kenley between April and June,

A fairly relaxed view of life being taken by members of staff of the Ontario Provincial Air Service, when five of the Service's DH.60M Seaplanes were presented to the camera at their base at Sault Sainte Marie. CF-OAG, built at Downsview in 1930 and fitted with a Gipsy II engine in 1934, remained in service until she was sold to a private owner in 1944. Bombardier Regional Aircraft

with the exception of K1227 (1509), which was diverted for the use of the Director of Technical Development on 20th July and was retained by de Havilland for fitment and further testing of the 'training type wing'. The remaining 20 aircraft from the contract, K1198-K1217 (1510-1529), had been distributed amongst a miscellany of home-based RAF units by the end of May with the further exception of K1198 and K1199 which were posted to Malta, K1200 and K1201 to Iraq and K1211 and K1212 to Aden, each directed initially to Sealand where they were packed for overseas despatch by surface.

K1227 was delivered to A&AEE Martlesham Heath to take part in an intensive programme of handling and spinning trials. It was considered these would be more meaningful if they could be flown against a previous triallist, and J9922 was recalled from duties with No 5 FTS at Sealand for the purpose and flown to Martlesham on 31st July. After a thorough inspection, the only difference between the two aircraft was believed to be the 'plaster type' slots fitted to K1227 which, for the purpose of the flights, were first allowed to operate as intended then locked shut and covered with doped fabric. The conclusion of the three trials' pilots was that where K1227 would spin normally, J9922 had to be persuaded with coarse use

DH.60M K1206 in the standard all-silver
scheme of the day, was posted to Station
Flight at RAF Upavon. Note the navigation
light on the starboard upper wing.
Richard Riding

of the controls at the stall. 'K1227 behaves
like a Mk II Moth', they said, 'and in case the
behaviour of K1227 is out of the ordinary for
this type of aircraft it may be useful to fit slots
to J9922 in order to investigate further'.

On 6th August, K1227 was returned to Stag
Lane where low-pressure Dunlop wheels and
tyres were fitted, adopting an earlier suggestion made by the Establishment, and in January 1931 her axles were modified to accept
the new Goodyear air wheel. Later she was
relegated to communications duties and
occasional armament trials at Martlesham
until 1937 when she was struck off charge as
'not worth the cost of repair'. Sold to Squadron Leader Allen Wheeler at Andover, she
was registered G-AFKM in 1938 and sold to
India in 1940, where she crashed in 1942
when operating as part of the Madras-based
Coastal Defence Flight. J9922 was returned
to Sealand from where she was sold to the de
Havilland Aircraft Company in June 1931 and

registered G-ABNE. As a civil-registered
aeroplane she was operated in a military
environment by the Reserve School where
her progress could be best monitored by
her manufacturer.

With an economy showing signs of distress, a growing range of more competitive
aircraft becoming available from rival manufacturers and a determined effort by makers
of the Cirrus engine not to lose too much
ground to the Gipsy, de Havilland chose
April 1930 to announce a further round of
price reductions. The cost of a wooden
DH.60G, termed the 'Standard Model' with
a Gipsy I engine, was reduced from £675 to
£595, complete with the usual instruments
and loose equipment, yet provided with only
one set of ignition switches and no compass
which was extra. The colour scheme was
restricted to silver for all covered surfaces
and Azure Blue for fuselage, struts and
undercarriage, with black lettering although

variations could be provided for an extra
charge. An aerobatic harness, autoslots with
a locking device, a range of sizes of auxiliary
petrol tank and a steel or duralumin airscrew
with adjustable blades were all available as
options. The Moth Seaplane was offered to
the same specification at £880, reduced from
£950, in a flyaway condition from the Seaplane Station at Rochester.

Described under the heading 'Special
Moth' was the DH.60M, clearly defined as
having a welded steel fuselage with wooden
wings and empennage. The Azure Blue of
the Standard Model could be exchanged for
any colour, as could the black lettering. A
landplane fitted with the Gipsy I engine was
reduced in price from £700 to £675 and a
Seaplane from £995 to £960. For the first
time, prices for the aircraft fitted with a
Gipsy II engine were announced: £750 for a
Landplane and £1,035 for a Seaplane collected from Rochester. The list of optional
extras also offered slightly more variation:

*'As for the standard model with the addi-
tion of coupé head, cockpit heating device,
streamlined headrest, compass in either or
both cockpits, all standard instruments
duplicated in the front cockpit, oil temperature gauge, revolution indicator mounted on
the fuselage and visible from both cockpits,
oversize wheels and tyres, spade grip on control column, detachable cover for front cockpit with quick release windscreen, three-ply
around the leading edge of the bottom mainplanes, float-on-air cushions, rubber floor
mats, fescolised exhaust pipe and silencer
and a range of auxiliary petrol tanks of
between 10 and 25 gallons capacity.'*

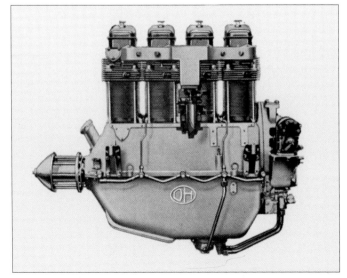

**The port side view of the Gipsy II engine gives the appearance of a tidy and compact unit, while the view from the starboard side
illustrates how the rocker gear is now fully enclosed in pressed steel boxes.** de Havilland

The Gipsy II engine passed its Category Type Test at a rating of 105hp at 2,000rpm in February and DH.60M G-AASL (1430), which had been flight testing the prototype engine since November, was prepared for her C of A on 21st May. The aircraft was presented in standard configuration fitted with a DH5208/A/1 wooden propeller and unofficially labelled the 'DH.60M Mk II'. The certificate was issued on 6th June and, almost immediately, the mainplanes were exchanged for what were identified as 'metal wings' less slots, supplied by the Gloster Aircraft Company, in addition to a 'metal empennage' of de Havilland origin.

The Company had received a full set of uncovered 'metal wings' from Gloster in April and on check-weighing noted that at 164 lb less ailerons, they were 30 lb heavier than the latest standard wooden mainplanes, confirming estimates of some three years previously. The metal empennage weighed 25 lb against 23 lb for a wooden construction. A further set of 'metal wings' was delivered at the end of May from Boulton and Paul and proved to be 15 lb lighter than those from Gloster. Both companies advertised extensively their capabilities, having developed sophisticated techniques for the manufacture and supply of rolled, drawn or fabricated metal spars including metal ribs with patented methods of attachment. To enhance their own aircraft-manufacturing activities, the Gloster Company had absorbed the Steel Wing Company Ltd, a business dating from 1915, and established major engineering bases at Hucclecote and Brockworth. It was their intention to capitalise on contracts awarded following the Air Ministry's announcement that their

On a visit to Jersey with DH.60G G-AAYL, Flying Officer D V Ivan landed on the beach in St Aubin's Bay, between First Tower and Millbrook, then had the aeroplane towed into town where she was refuelled at the garage in the main street. Richard Riding

The Stag Lane Works in May 1930, developed almost to the full potential of the site. The four-bay hangar at top centre is the Service Department with the London Aeroplane Club relocated to a pavilion and hangar adjacent to the right hand bay. Gipsy engines were manufactured in the building with the light-coloured north-light roof at top right, nearest the entrance from Stag Lane. de Havilland

The prototype Gipsy II engine was flight tested in DH.60M G-AASL which was later fitted with 'metal wings' manufactured by Gloster, although no evidence survives to indicate how much flight time they accumulated, when they were removed, and why metal wings were not proceeded with. Note how the exhaust pipe is routed down between the engine and firewall to continue under the fuselage, between the undercarriage legs. *The Aeroplane*

Five DH.60M aircraft, K1213 to K1217, delivered to the RAF but not allocated, were returned to Stag Lane to be modified for use by the CFS Display Team at the 1931 Hendon Display in late June. The aircraft are configured as single-seaters with stub exhausts and all had full inverted systems. The Prince of Wales' DH.60M G-AALG, can be seen on the right.
The Aeroplane

future policy would be to buy only metal air-craft, a decision taken after realisation that in time of war it would be impossible to guarantee delivery of adequate supplies of woods of sufficient quality.

There is no evidence to disclose how long G-AASL flew with metal wings and neither Captain de Havilland nor Hubert Broad claimed any specific 'metal wing' time in her. The Drawing Office had issued paper-work to cover the new wing in March and on 26th June, in a single-seat configuration with an additional ten gallon tank in the front cockpit and no exhaust pipes, G-AASL was re-weighed in preparation for her entry in the King's Cup Air Race starting at Han-worth on 5th July. Approval was granted for the fitting of Autoslots to the metal wing on 5th September making it appear that the air-craft was being flown with her new wings throughout the summer without any form of publicity.

When evaluated by Christopher Clarkson the following year, he reported that, unlike the Mk I, G-AASL was fitted with the revised 'RAF Training Type' wing section, new three-piece Triplex windscreens, parachute seats, Sutton harness, a turn indicator on the instrument board and an exhaust pipe that was routed down the front of the fire-proof bulkhead and out below the floor of the fuselage. There was no mention of the 'training type' wing section being of any-thing but standard construction. What he looked for and found surprisingly absent was an adjustable seat:

'As the DH.60M is fast becoming a stan-dard military training aircraft all over the world, the argument in favour of this fit-ment is more convincing. In any case, it has great advantages both as regards comfort and the ability to obtain a better view if cir-cumstances suddenly require it.'

Having flown both a slotted Mk I and unslot-ted Mk II Moth on the same day, Christo-pher Clarkson was able to offer a positive comparison of performance:

Take-off: *The Mk II shows a great improvement over the Mk I and has a remarkably quick take-off.*

Landing: *The Mk II is more pleasant to land than the Mk I. It appears to float farther as one flattens out, there is less tendency for it to sink suddenly onto the ground and it shows no ten-dency to drop a wing. The landing speed and ensuing run appear to be the same on both machines. The angle of glide is flat with plenty of control in both.*

Controls: *On both machines the controls are well balanced and are moderately light and efficient at all speeds. The ailerons show the approaching stall as well as on any other modern machine of this type, and remain the most efficient of the controls at very slow speeds. All are satisfacto-rily progressive as the speed increases. There was a tendency for the lateral control on the new type to be slightly heavy during aerobatics, but this was due to the adjustment of the differential on that particular machine.*

Stalling and spinning: *The Mk I Moth with auto-matic slots was very efficient at slow speeds and the lateral control remained even when the machine was sinking rapidly. When this new machine was properly stalled on a turn the ensuing drop and 'whip' was rather pro-nounced, and some height was lost before com-plete control was regained. The machine could be spun both ways if forced in. On the new type, which was not fitted with slots, the ailerons remained efficient at low speeds and there was far less tendency for the machine to 'whip' when stalled. It sank gently and it was possible to regain control almost immediately without undue loss of height. It could be spun both ways, and a quick recovery to level flight could be made. Even without slots this machine appeared to be the more satisfactory of the two types. On both machines aileron drag was scarcely perceptible.*

Aerobatics: *Both types are suitable for aerobat-ics. The new type was particularly good for more advanced aerobatics and the increased power, Sutton harness and the different wing-section makes it effective for inverted manoeu-vres. This type was easy to slow-roll and handled well in inverted flying.*

The first production aircraft to be fitted with a standard Gipsy II was DH.60M G-AAYY

(1251), registered to the Stag Lane-based John Chalmers and issued with her C of A on 26th June 1930. The following year on 9th May, Chalmers and his wife flew the aero-plane to Iraq, visiting Baghdad and Basra, before returning to Heston on the last day of the month.

During the first week of June, five of the RAF DH.60M Moths which had been deliv-ered to Kenley but not assigned, K1213-K1217 (1525-1529), were selected to represent the Central Flying School at the eleventh annual RAF Display held at Hendon on Saturday 28th June. The choice of Moths was a late decision as CFS was anticipating Hawker Tomtits but their delivery was delayed, allowing insufficient time for team training. The five DH.60Ms were returned to Stag Lane where inverted fuel systems were installed. This time, the conversion was of greater sophistication than anything consid-ered previously and introduced an indepen-dent fuel system based on an auxiliary petrol tank of three and three quarter gallons capac-ity fitted in the front cockpit, an oil screen for the engine sump, Rotherham windmill pump, Le Rhône needle valve which regu-lated petrol under air pressure delivered to a jet fixed in the air intake of the carburettor, a pair of Jones air relief valves, air pressure gauge and an air cock. The system had been devised in January and was fitted and test flown on DH.60G G-AACO (874) in March.

Flown by instructors, none of whom had been part of the previous Genet teams, the display routine included a lot of inverted fly-ing and precision formation aerobatics, but the extreme evolutions of previous years were missing. After the Display the aircraft were returned to standard configuration and dispersed amongst other units within the Service with the exception of K1217, which was delivered to RAE Farnborough and issued with a new serial, K2235. Con-verted to an experimental seaplane, the air-craft was fitted with a 25ft long central float representing a scale model of the hull of the Short Singapore flying boat and was posted to the MAEE at Felixstowe.

For the 1930 King's Cup Air Race, a one day, 750 mile circuit of Great Britain starting and finishing at Hanworth on 5th July, the rules had been changed to exclude aircraft designed specifically for anything except civil purposes and as a probable result the event attracted a record 101 entries, 39 of which were DH.60 Moths.

The CFS Display Team had little time to practice their 1931 routines due to the late decision to provide them with DH.60M Moths rather than Tomtits. The essence of their performance was inverted flying as a team. The top of the rear fuselage and the arrow design on the top wings, including the tank, were bright red.
DH Moth Club Archive

Aware that such a situation was likely, and that as a result of aircraft continually changing hands they could not notify owners individually 'by direct circularisation', the Company enlisted the aid of press notices to draw the attention of '…those Moth owners who wish to enter for the King's Cup Air Race to the necessity of communicating immediately with the Company in the event of their requiring special work done or equipment supplied. Immediate notice is especially necessary in the case of special airscrews to prevent the engine of a cleaned-up machine "over-revving", these taking a fortnight to manufacture'.

The Works' main effort was centred on the new DH.80A Puss Moth of which nine were entered by pilots including Captain de Havilland, Hubert Broad, Mrs Lois Butler and Wally Hope. Geoffrey de Havilland Jnr was the nominated pilot for the Gipsy II-powered demonstrator G-AASL, but all were faced with competing against the Company Chairman's new DH.60M, the much-modified 'Moth Special' G-AAXG (1542).

The aircraft was essentially a DH.60M built specially for high speed with a Gipsy II engine installation lowered by 2in and cowled within a specially designed close-fitting unit that blended into the fuselage. The front cockpit was faired over with a transparent cover when carrying a 20 gallon fuel tank and a slim gravity tank of nine gallons capacity occupied the cabane structure, built to conform exactly to the profile of the wing section and hardly noticeable. For the King's Cup the aircraft was fitted with a streamline racing undercarriage with continuous axle and small diameter, thin wheels. Only the rear parts of the elevator control cables were exposed, all other cables were run internally. Rudder cables were routed from a shortened rudder bar to reduced length levers repositioned to the lower hinge position on an enlarged section rudder spar. The leading edge of the tailplane was modified by running the fair-

ing strip all round with the fabric covering carried over and the unit was supported by streamline section stay tubes. The tailskid tube was streamlined and fitted with a new type of shoe and even the pitot head was miniaturised. The root end rib of each lower mainplane was swept up to make a seal with the fuselage and the trailing portion of the upper mainplanes adjacent to the centre section was built to be square, and not angled as would be required for wing folding, with a fairing between the revised line and the rear cross-spar of the centre section. The most obvious deviation from standard was the cabane in which the normal structure was replaced with an entirely original and unique system, three sets of 'V' struts, all braced with streamline wires running vertically from the cross spars to the top longerons.

G-AAXG tipped the scales at 976 lb empty when weighed on 26th June after which Alan Butler completed a 40 minute maiden flight to qualify for a C of A. He logged a further nine hours before 4th July when the aircraft was positioned to Hanworth for inspection by the scrutineers.

Captain John Irving's Cramlington-based DH.60G G-AADA (1019) was also modified to accept a shallow gravity tank in the centre section and, flown as a single-seater, had a high sculpted rear cockpit surround, long sloping windscreen and headrest. The wing roots were faired into the fuselage and all other excrescences meticulously attended to. The improvements resulted in an average speed of 111.67mph and were indicative of the interest being shown by genuine private entrants, but they were still only good enough for G-AADA to achieve 38th place.

Alan Butler's Moth Special G-AAXG, entered in the 1930 King's Cup Air Race, illustrating the revised cabane structure, thin centre section with minimum cut-out at the trailing edge, faired strut ends, revised engine cowlings, racing undercarriage with small diameter, thin wheels, high rear fuselage, and transparent cover and doors at the front cockpit. BAE Systems

Major Charles Pickthorn's entry for the 1930 King's Cup Air Race was DH.60G G-AAWR, in which the front seat passenger sat low down in a substantially glazed, faired-over cockpit, and the pilot was similarly encased, the top of his head just protruding and protected by a minuscule windscreen. DH Moth Club Archive

It would have been necessary for John Irving to arrange a mandatory inspection of the front engine supporting brackets on his DH.60G before taking part in the Race and to replace them with a new design available from the manufacturer. Cracks had been detected in the brackets on wooden fuselage Moths fitted with Gipsy, Cirrus III and Hermes engines and the matter was considered serious enough for the Air Ministry to insist on replacement brackets being fitted by the end of June and to deny renewal of a Certificate of Airworthiness for unmodified aircraft.

Donald Marendaz, a well known designer and driver of racing cars, had been experimenting for some time with a car exhaust silencer fitted to DH.60X Moth G-EBOT (272), which he entered in the King's Cup to be flown by W H Sutcliffe. A company, Vortex Silencers Ltd, had been formed with Major Frank Halford as a board member, to exploit the idea whose working principle was to utilise the inertia of the exhaust gas to create vortices. Although successful in motor-boating and car racing, the full potential of the system was not realised during the King's Cup as Sutcliffe failed to round a turning point beyond Manchester and was disqualified.

Much to de Havilland's undoubted chagrin, the Race was won by an Avian III flown by Winifred Brown at an average speed of 102.75mph, but Alan Butler was second at 129.7mph, the fastest official speed, just beating his wife in DH.80A Puss Moth G-AAXL who achieved fourth place at 129.56mph. In the usual post-event promotion, the Company was quick to capitalise on what it had achieved and made much of the fact that 52 Gipsy engines had started in the Race, only one of which failed to finish due to a mechanical problem.

For a man who made consistently generous contributions to the Royal Aero Club's prize fund, Alan Butler might have been amused, after the Race, to receive a clutch of cheques: £100 for his second place; £100 for achieving the fastest speed and £50 for beating his handicap, all presented by C C Wakefield on behalf of Castrol Oil. In addition, there was £50 from Shell for what they termed 'publicity value' and £30 from the Newcastle *Evening World* newspaper for the fastest time between Hanworth and their city. There was even a trophy, presented by the Bristol *Evening Times*, for securing second place.

Signor Savino, an Italian pilot, attempted to fly a Moth Seaplane from Rome to Australia in July. He reached Karachi safely where the onward flight was abandoned in favour of an attempt to fly back to Rome within five days, but whether he did has never been publicly recorded.

The International Touring Competition of 1930, starting from Berlin's Tempelhof Airfield on the morning of Sunday 20th July and organized by the German Aero Club as a consequence of their win in France the previous year, attracted 97 entries of which 60 were starters, 30 from the host country. The British element of seven aircraft included four DH.60Gs with two more amongst the three entrants from Spain.

The 4,700 mile route round Europe passed through nine countries and including the 'technical tests' similar to those conducted in Paris the previous year which were due to be completed by the survivors on their return to Berlin, the Tour was scheduled for 16 days. Almost inevitably, bad weather on some sectors caused delays and the stragglers were allowed an additional two days to complete the circuit. Of the two Spanish Moths, DH.60G M-CKAA (1133), achieved 30th place of the 35 finishers amongst which DH.60G Coupé M-CGAA (1098), was not listed. Lady Mary Bailey, the only competitor who attempted, and failed, to fly over the Pyrenees rather than round them in her DH.60G Coupé G-AAEE (981) was placed 31st.

Hubert Broad, flying the Company-entered DH.60G Super Coupé G-AAHR (1068), was eighth. Since her French adventures the previous year, the aircraft had been fitted with a Gipsy II engine and a

The Company entry in the 1930 International Touring Competition was the Super Coupé G-AAHR flown by Hubert Broad, now fitted with a Gipsy II engine and a variation of the Puss Moth undercarriage. Alan Butler

modified, shorter version of the Puss Moth undercarriage which utilised streamline section rather than round rubber blocks. A DH.60X undercarriage radius rod was fitted, also reduced in length but otherwise standard. It is probable that these modifications were introduced ahead of the 1930 King's Cup Air Race but the aircraft was withdrawn in favour of an additional Puss Moth entry. Frederick Guest's DH.60G Coupé G-AALK (1174), recently returned from adventures in Africa, was certainly modified specifically for the Tour with the addition of Bendix two-shoe servo brake units fitted to Dunlop wheels, cable operated from a quadrant-mounted lever in the rear cockpit. Pilot Winifred Spooner was the highest-placed British entrant at fourth and collected total prize monies of 16,500Frs against Broad's 10,500Frs paid to the Company account.

For Alan Butler, there was nothing. His Moth Special G-AAXG had tipped forward landing on soft ground at Posen, breaking the propeller. He was disqualified from the Competition on the grounds that he had not carried the replacement propeller on board the aircraft with him. In spite of a consistently high standard achieved throughout the Tour and against popular opinion, Alan Butler lost his appeal and was excluded from the technical tests, But there was still something for the Company to cheer and post-Competition publicity centred on the reliability of all the Gipsy engines which were run at full throttle throughout the event, and the fact that not only had Winifred Spooner achieved first place in the 'Heavier Class' of light aircraft, but Hubert Broad was first in the 'Speed and Reliability' section.

Both as a keen sportsman and Company Chairman, Alan Butler would have been disappointed at his result and flew home to Stag Lane on 2nd August. Having acquired a new Puss Moth in June (G-AAXL/2020), which was as fast as his Moth Special, in August, after some modifications which included the fitment of a split undercarriage, he sold G-AAXG to his friend Edouard Bret in Cannes and on 21st August flew to France in the Puss Moth to ensure all was well. Bret subsequently put up the fastest time of 8hr 46min, equivalent to a record 122mph, for flying the 1,036 mile route laid down for the 1930 Zenith Cup, choosing to start and finish at Bordeaux on 27th September. The aircraft was registered in France as F-AJZB in October and the following year won the Zenith Cup for a second time but, in 1933, the Moth Special returned to England, exchanged for a new Puss Moth.

To supplement the three DH.60M aircraft ordered from Stag Lane at the end of 1929, early in 1930 the Norwegian Army Aircraft Factory at Kjeller geared up for production of ten licence-built DH.60Ms to be listed on the inventory as 'Standard Moths'. These were to be constructed against works' iden-

tities 137-146 and allocated in sequence, military serials 107-125, using the odd numbers only. The agreement with de Havilland permitted Kjeller to build every part themselves except for the Gipsy I engines which were to be supplied from England.

Kjeller spent the first half of the year adapting the drawings to ensure that the resultant parts could be easily manufactured using the factory's existing facilities and two engineers, Arne Andersen and Erling Eckhoff, were sent to Stag Lane to study the construction processes. A major difficulty experienced at Kjeller was that during preparation, de Havilland issued amendments to 240 of the 402 published drawings which often included small errors or inconsistencies and were frequently supplied with incomplete or no materials lists.

Production began in July but the first aircraft was not handed over until June 1931 and the last by April 1932, all of which were flight tested by Ore Reistad. At the end of the programme it was estimated that the ten aircraft had cost a total of 169,244NKr, a figure which included 82,700NKr for jigs and tools and 6,330NKr spent on drawings. The total was about 2,000NKr more than if the aircraft had been purchased outright from Stag Lane. An official explanation was that any financial advantage would be carried forward in the utilisation of jigs and tools, especially if major repairs should become necessary, and certainly when a subsequent batch of Moths was ordered, which, with the introduction of the DH.82 Tiger Moth, it never was.

In support of an investigation into the prospects of establishing a regular air route between Great Britain and North America, elements of The British Arctic Air Route Expedition, led by H G 'Gino' Watkins, left London on board the SS *Quest* on 6th July and arrived off their Base Camp at Niarunak in East Greenland three weeks later. On board their ship the Expedition carried the dismantled dark red and silver DH.60G Coupé G-AAUR (1245), which was to be joined later by a second DH.60G Coupé, G-AAZR (1275), acquired only after additional late funding had been secured, and delivered on board the Danish Government steamer *Gustav Holm*.

G-AAUR, described in her log book as a DH.60X, had been test flown at Stag Lane by production test pilot Jack Tyler on 13th May when two short trips were made. The aircraft had been modified to carry a P14 plate camera in the reduced length front cockpit, capable of both vertical and oblique shots, and incorporated a special locker for the stowage of rifles, skis and other emergency equipment. Emphasis had been placed on the need for an efficient cockpit heating system and this was installed in both aircraft together with long-range petrol tanks increasing endurance to seven hours.

Hubert Broad and Super Coupé G-AAHR making light work of the take-off trials which were part of the technical tests completed at Berlin following arrival from the tour of Europe. Alan Butler

Wilfred Hampton learned to fly with the Cambridge University Air Squadron and flew Moths with the Reserve at Bristol before his recruitment by the Expedition to supervise the aircraft and act as relief to the two pilots seconded from the RAF. During his time as a trainee engineer with de Havilland at Stag Lane and with experience on Moths, he had been one of the team involved in accumulating 200 hours on DH.60M G-AASL in support of the Gipsy II engine test programme. On 3rd June, Hampton, 'Ham' to his friends, flew G-AAUR at Stag Lane and the following day positioned her to the Short Bros' works at Rochester where a float chassis had been prepared. This was to carry specially-strengthened floats to allow for emergency landings on both snow and ice and, although funding prevented more than one chassis being ordered to be shared between the two aircraft, each had a pair of Canadian-designed skis. Again restrained by finance, the spares package carefully selected by 'Ham' included only a single float.

Following arrival off Greenland, the fuselage of G-AAZR was erected on deck between 31st July and 2nd August, then hoisted over the side and floated to the only convenient flat area of beach for the aircraft to be fully rigged and the engine test-run. 'Ham' later constructed a small hangar capable of accepting both aircraft, utilising the discarded packing cases, and following several successful operations with G-AAZR in October, with uncertain weather prospects, both aircraft were fitted with skis and the opportunity seized to improve the cockpit

The first of the two DH.60G Coupé Moths used by the British Arctic Air Route Expedition in Greenland during the summer of 1930 was G-AAUR. The aircraft was painted bright red and operated on both floats and skis. Mrs Joan Hampton

The second DH.60 Moth Coupé which travelled to Greenland with the British Arctic Air Route Expedition was G-AAZR, erected on dry land in September 1930. A small hangar was later constructed from the aircrafts' packing cases. Mrs Joan Hampton

ferred back to G-AAZR which 'Ham' test flew on 30th April.

The Expedition's plans had included a flight by both Moths across the interior of Greenland to Godhavn, then via Cumberland Peninsula, Hudson Bay, Port Nelson and on to Winnipeg, but the adventure was abandoned. With G-AAZR serviceable and back on floats, senior pilot Flight Lieutenant Narborough D'Aeth considered flying her home to Great Britain along part of the intended air route. The Seaplane was meticulously inspected and fitted with a number of additional instruments to aid navigation but the London-based Expedition Committee advised against the plan which was reluctantly cancelled. Both aircraft were returned to England by ship, overhauled to standard configuration and sold to new owners.

Wilfred Hampton reported to de Havilland that few problems had been encountered with the Moths during their operation but he believed two points were worthy of note. The wooden Canadian skis had coped with snow conditions but on ice had become very considerably worn and hardly lasted the winter. It was recommended that skis be metal shod in future. The other concern was over the rubber-in-compression suspension in the main undercarriage legs. After the aircraft had been subjected to temperatures of 0°F for some time, the legs froze solid at their acquired level of compression. This reduced the choice of landing places to those which were known to be absolutely smooth and placed unwelcome limitations on the flexibility of the operation.

Italy had not been included in the route of July's International Touring Competition, possibly because the Italian Aero Club had organised its own *Giro Aereo d'Italia,* beginning in Rome on 25th August. The competition was a handicap speed race covering 2,115 miles around Italy in stages over four days, and attracted 66 entrants of which 53 were involved in the usual round of technical tests before the race as an aid to calculating the handicap values. Of these, 47 were Italian, but the one British entrant was Winifred Spooner, again flying DH.60G Coupé G-AALK which, amidst much acclaim, she grittily steered into a most creditable fourth place.

heating which was already considered inadequate.

On New Year's Day 1931, RAF pilot Iliffe Cozens flew G-AAUR to Tassiussak to collect provisions but with daylight fading had been forced to stay overnight. A severe gale developed which blew continuously for 30 hours, and in spite of gallant efforts by all available hands to restrain G-AAUR at her pickets, she was blown away and all but wrecked. 'Ham' believed he could repair the aeroplane in time to complete the planned winter programme. Starting on 19th January with the Expedition's second civilian relief pilot, John Rymill, and some natives offering assistance, over an eight week period, working ten hour days in sub-zero temperatures in the field, he did so.

During the re-building programme, on 26th February, G-AAZR was damaged when she hit a well-camouflaged ice hummock on touch down at Angmagssalik. The aircraft's centre section and mainplanes were temporarily transferred to G-AAUR to accelerate the recovery process which was completed on 18th March when she was test flown by 'Ham'. It must have been heart-breaking for all concerned when G-AAUR was hit by another gale on 3rd April while picketed at Base Camp, when both starboard wings were broken, the Fairey metal propeller bent and a float cracked. With the end of the Expedition in sight, G-AAUR was dismantled and made ready for the voyage home. Her loaned centre section and port wings were trans-

In spite of cabin heating, which proved to be inadequate and was improved by engineer Wilfred Hampton, the crew were wise to wear full Arctic protective clothing. Snow shoes and other bulky equipment were carried externally, lashed to the fuselage side. Mrs Joan Hampton

The Air Ministry signed another contract, 27847/30, with de Havilland during the autumn of 1930 for the supply of a further 83 Gipsy I-powered DH.60M Moths: K1825-K1829 (1658-1662), K1830-K1849 (1580-1599), K1850-K1859 (1624-1633), K1860-K1883 (1600-1623) and K1884-K1907 (1634-1657). Following established practice, Nos 1580-1623 were supplied in flying condition and Nos 1624-1662 were basic airframes into which engines were installed by the Royal Air Force. None was allocated for initial flying training duties and deliveries, which commenced in October and were completed in March 1931, were to a miscellany of RAF Home Units with the exception of K1893 and K1895 which were despatched to Aden via Sealand.

K1876 (1616) was allocated to the Refresher Flight at RAE Farnborough where she arrived on 28th January 1931 and from August was based with Handley Page at Radlett or at Farnborough engaged on further experimental work involving slots and interceptors. This programme continued until the late summer of 1936 when flight tests of a flat spoiler were undertaken to find a means of reducing the lag in the response of its operation which effected a powerful lateral control. For the tests the spoiler, a plain rectangular plate the same width as the aileron, just over 9ft long but only 4in wide, was fitted to the front spar of the starboard upper mainplane only, hinged to open forward and upward. Measurements were made of the roll produced by the ailerons and by the spoiler, and different arrangements of the spoiler plate were tried with growing success. Flying with spoilers of various chords and with perforated and serrated lower edges was planned but results have not survived. At the end of the trials, K1876 was posted to Martlesham Heath for communications duties in September 1937.

Having become the owners of a considerable fleet of Moths, the Air Ministry embarked upon production of the necessary Air Publication and AP 1422 Volume 1, *The Moth Two-Seater Light Aeroplane, Gipsy Mark I Engine*, was published in October 1931 and available for public sale at two shillings per copy. 'This descriptive handbook is issued for the information and guidance of all concerned' was the simple message it bore on the cover.

Like its competitors, de Havilland closely monitored its products; each aircraft was carefully weighed and the results recorded and plotted in an effort to establish any adverse trends. The Design Department at Stag Lane were at pains to identify an average 'standard weight' for RAF Moths against which to gauge aircraft manufactured under the terms of the new contract. Their simple specification for all Moths supplied to the RAF was metal fuselage, Gipsy I engine and the 'Training Wing Section'. Aircraft notified for communications duties only would be fitted with slots but no locking device and at a 'standard' tare weight of 1,008 lb would be heavier than those allocated to training by the difference in the slot weight, listed at only 15 lb.

The enterprising Airwork Company had installed airfield floodlighting at its new Heston Air Park to allow night operations, and they wired two DH.60Gs to permit legitimate night flying instruction. The initiative was demonstrated to club members, friends and the press on 10th September when the Chief Instructor, Val Baker, flew a night aerobatic sequence whose progress could only be followed by constant sight of the aircraft's navigation lights. Private owners were encouraged to have their aircraft modified too, at an individual cost estimated at less than £20.

Company DH.60G demonstrator G-AAYG (1546), was fitted with a Rotax lighting system in February 1931, an installation that conformed to the requirements for night flying equipment in that the dash lamp 'adequately illuminated all instruments simultaneously', and was subsequently put into service with the de Havilland School at Stag Lane. The RAF contracted de Havilland to fit night flying equipment to 24 Squadron's K1839 (1589), but not until January 1932 after which she was detached for the summer to No 3 Squadron operating Bristol Bulldogs from Upavon. She was modified at Stag Lane to accept special wing-tip flares weighing almost 9 lb, three times the weight of a standard Holt unit, in addition to recognition lights which she continued to trial on return to Northolt, and later at North Weald, until she returned to normal duties with 24 Squadron in March 1933.

Airwork supplied one of its night flying DH.60G Moths, G-AACY (841), for a demonstration of the American Driggs-Faber flare system conducted at Hanworth on 31st August 1932. The aircraft was landed with the aid of flares held in the manner of torches by ground personnel, when they provided not only illumination, but also copious quantities of smoke, enrolled as a ready aid to wind direction. G-AACY also flew with a battery of flares strapped to the side of the fuselage although observers were assured this was a temporary measure for demonstration purposes only, which illustrated how large commercial aircraft could benefit from a permanent installation.

An early casualty of night flying was Sir Philip Sassoon's DH.60M G-AARD (1414), which crashed on 29th October after taking off from a private field near Oxford to return to Croydon. The pilot, an RAF officer, inadvertently descended during a turn started at 400ft and collided with trees which took off the wings, allowing the fuselage to fall to the ground relatively undamaged. The Accident Inspector was fiercely critical of the cockpit lighting which was capable of illuminating only one instrument at a time. Thus, while concentrating on the compass, the pilot had been unable to read the unwinding altimeter.

Sir Sefton Brancker, Director General of Civil Aviation, and Lord Thompson, Secretary of State for Air, were amongst 48 passengers and crew killed when the airship R101 crashed in France on Sunday 5th Octo-

An impressive line-up of RCAF DH.60 Moths from the Training Squadrons at Camp Borden during the Canadian National Exhibition held in Toronto in September 1930. Richard Riding

Airwork's DH.60G G-AACY was used to demonstrate the Driggs-Faber flare system at Hanworth when a battery of flares was strapped to the side of the wooden rear fuselage in what observers were assured was a temporary measure.
DH Moth Club Archive

Sir Philip Sassoon's DH.60M G-AARD crashed during a night take-off from a private airfield near Oxford because the cockpit lighting was inadequate, and did not permit all instruments to be read at the same time. Jack Meaden

the load into the trees from a height of 10ft. For best results the atmosphere needed to be calm and humid which caused the programme to extend from 31st October to 18th November, with some additional sorties required in December, achieving a high rate of success.

As a result of the licence granted to the Paris-based Morane-Saulnier Company in November 1929, de Havilland supplied the Company with DH.60M No 1468 in February 1930. The aircraft was painted as F-AJLQ for summer display purposes when it was described as a Morane-built Moth, although it was not officially registered as such until December. The bare airframe of DH.60M No 1475 was delivered from England in April 1930 to be used as an educational pattern. It is almost certain that this was completed by Morane-Saulnier at their factory at Puteaux, north of Paris, as No 1, the first of 48 DH.60Ms constructed by March 1932, and was registered F-AJOE to Mlle Maryse Hilsz in May 1930.

An unidentified Morane Moth was displayed on the Morane-Saulnier stand at the 12th International Aero Show held in the Grand Palais, Paris, from 28th November. There it was supported by a DH.80A Puss Moth loaned by de Havilland and accompanied by Hubert Broad acting in a new capacity as technical salesman. A survey by a British journalist resulted in a critique of the

ber, during her maiden voyage to India. It was Brancker's drive, personal interest and enthusiasm that had steered the earliest days of the British flying club movement from which, by choosing the Moth as standard equipment, had been established a base for the further successful development of the light aeroplane.

What is believed to be the first attempt in Australia at arboricultural dusting from the air was achieved with considerable success in October. In August it was reported that the Yarrowee State Forest in Victoria was suffering an infestation of the harmful case

moth. RAAF DH.60G A17-39 (39), held at No 1 Air Depot at Laverton, was modified for the attack by removing the front seat and fitting a simple hopper which exhausted through a hole cut in the floor, regulated by a sliding door controlled by cables. Trials proved this arrangement not to be effective or efficient and an air-intake system was devised which pressurised the hopper, exhausting its contents through a controllable vent.

The aircraft could lift 200 lb of calcium arsenate dust and the operations were conducted by No 1 Squadron which distributed

Although DH.60M F-AJLQ was described as a Morane Moth when first displayed in France, she was built at Stag Lane and sold to the Morane-Saulnier Company in February 1930, not taking up her French registration until December. Via Peter Gould

DH.60: '…the workmanship seems to be good but the finish is poor, judged by our standard…'. A French Levasseur propeller was fitted to a Gipsy I engine imported from Stag Lane and the type was offered for sale at a brochure price of 95,000Frs.

Under the somewhat complicated terms of a Decree Law, in the near future the French Government were to pay subsidies of up to about forty percent of the purchase price when French citizens bought new aeroplanes that had been designed within the previous six years, and built in France. Against the Morane Moth's price tag, a Gipsy-engined Caudron C.270 Luciole was available at only 54,250Frs.

Eager to learn more about the C.270, Robert Morane arranged to fly one and in a confidential memo addressed to his business partner Raymond Saulnier, wrote:

'The aeroplane is classic Caudron construction with a wooden rudder bar and concealed rudder controls. The stick pressure is compensated by a tensioning device on the elevator controls, similar to that of the Moth… The cockpit floor is in wood, the trimming is imitation leather, the ignition contacts the two-strap system that we have abandoned, and the engine controls are very rustic: in brief the whole thing is of typical Caudron construction… Altogether I consider that this aeroplane could be put into any hands and that it is more agreeable to fly than a Moth.'

Although, on account of its range, speed and relative comfort, the Puss Moth was to be used for some spectacular flights which pushed human endurance and courage to their very limits, throughout 1930 long-distance flights in DH.60 Moths were still approached with a high degree of optimism.

Salim Sassoon Daniel acquired DH.60M G-AASD (1440) from Brooklands Aviation in January and flew her to Baghdad to become the first privately-owned aircraft in Iraq where, with the minimum application of paint, she took up national markings YI-ASD in May 1932. Mr Daniel, an oil-mining engineer who had qualified for his 'B' commercial pilot's licence in England, gave notice of his intention to start a Moth taxi service and

This anonymous DH.60M was built by Morane-Saulnier and exhibited on the Company's stand at the Paris Aero Show which opened in November 1930. A British journalist believed that, in comparison with a Stag Lane product, its finish was poor.
DH Moth Club Archive

later confirmed that in the first year since arrival, his aeroplane had travelled across the Syrian desert eleven times on trips to Egypt and Syria and had taken hundreds of joyriders on their first flights.

An Indian student at Bristol University, Man Mohan Singh, left Stag Lane on 11th January in DH.60M G-AAHF (1051) in an attempt to fly solo to Karachi. During his fourth forced landing before reaching Paris the aircraft was damaged and repaired at Le Bourget before she was flown back to England on 25th January. On the same day, re-united with his aeroplane, Singh left Lympne but on 3rd February out of Naples, he crashed near Cosenza in Calabria and the Moth was returned to Stag Lane for further repairs. Singh eventually departed from Croydon on 8th April in another aircraft, DH.60M G-AASF (1439), and reached Karachi on 10th May, just two days outside the time limit of one month necessary to qualify for a £500 prize offered by the Aga Khan to the first solo flight by an Indian national between the two countries.

New Zealander Charles Parkerson took off from Lympne in his DH.60G G-AALM

(1160) on 20th January bound for Australia but, due to fog, forced landed near Paris. The damaged aircraft was returned to England and following repairs Parkerson left Croydon on 21st April but again encountered fog in France. The aircraft was destroyed by fire after she hit a tree and crashed at Arquel near Poix.

Also on 20th January, Sir Ahmed Hassanein Bey, first chamberlain to King Fuad of Egypt, set off from Heston in the hard-worked old DH.60G G-EBTD (430) to fly to Cairo. During the take-off run a tyre burst, causing the aircraft to tip onto her nose, breaking the propeller. The replacement was fitted without delay and Bey left immediately for Lympne, only to become fog-bound. G-EBTD reached Pisa on 28th January but was damaged on landing and shipped back to Stag Lane when plans for a further attempt were abandoned.

In September 1929, Stag Lane-based Peter Hoare sold DH.60G G-EBZY (806) to his friend Nathaniel Chalmers, a Fiji-based barrister, and the aeroplane was shipped to Suva. Following erection at Albert Park, the first flight took place on 3rd February, but

Man Mohan Singh leaving Stag Lane on 11th January in DH.60G G-AAHF, in an attempt to claim the Aga Khan's prize of £500 for the first Indian to fly between England and India. Although that attempt failed, in spite of numerous difficulties, Singh did complete a flight in May, but was disqualified as his time was two days over the limit set by the rules. Fox

on landing the aircraft collided with telephone cables and was badly damaged. Shipped to New Zealand she was repaired and registered ZK-ABV, but was badly damaged and repaired on a number of occasions until December 1937 when she crashed on take off, having been fitted with an inverted Gipsy III engine at the time.

Leaving Eagle Farm Aerodrome, Brisbane, at 4.30am on 13th February in two separate aircraft as far as Sydney, Julian Moxon and Charles Scott flew on together in DH.60G VH-ULR (977) to Melbourne, a total distance of more than 1,000 miles, and arrived at Essendon at 6.40pm that day. The purpose of the trip was explained by Moxon as demonstrating the suitability of light aeroplanes for quick and safe transport in Australia and to promote the fact that his Company, Moxon Motors of Brisbane, was to take an agency for de Havilland products.

DH.60G VT-AAZ (1161) was loaned by the owner to the 17-year-old Aspy Engineer who, with Ram Chawla, left Karachi for England on 3rd March. The flight was uneventful but on arrival on 20th March, Croydon Airport was obscured by fog. Uncertain of

his position, Chowla overflew London and landed at Thetford in Norfolk. VT-AAZ was positioned to Croydon the following day and prepared for a solo return flight. Aspy Engineer left Croydon on 25th April and arrived back in Karachi on 11th May to win the Aga Khan's £500 prize. Jehangir Tata, the first Indian pilot to be trained in his native country, took off from Karachi on 3rd May in his DH.60G G-AAGI (1010), arriving at Croydon ten days later, anticipating a return flight in further pursuit of the £500 prize, but it was already too late. Some consolation for Mr Tata was that he was from a wealthy industrial family and at home founded his own airline with a Puss Moth, carrying mail from Madras and Bombay to the terminus for European flights at Karachi.

When, at the end of 1931, the Ministry of Posts and Telegraphs ran out of funding for continuation of the service previously contracted to Imperial Airways to fly mail from Karachi to Delhi, the task was taken over on a daily basis by a Delhi Flying Club Moth 'which is known for safety and will offer real possibilities of economic operation'. The Delhi Club bought a new DH.60G, VT-ABN

(1089), expressly for the service and Club-trained member P D Sharma, who had qualified for his 'B' commercial licence, flew the first schedule on time on 3rd January 1932, and all but two of all the trips until the contract ended on 4th July 1933. On only four occasions did the mail miss the connecting flights from Karachi, twice due to weather and twice through engine problems. One return flight was not completed after VT-ABN collided with a vulture in mid-air, the Moth suffering a cracked front spar.

In Great Britain the Postmaster General sanctioned the carriage of mail between the north Scottish mainland and the Orkneys at a surcharge of one half penny per letter, having contracted with the North British Aviation Company. The service was due to start in May 1932, complementing the existing passenger and freight services operated out of Inverness by Captain Ted Fresson and his DH.60G G-AAWO (1235), but the mails were not carried until 29th May 1934 in a DH.84 Dragon, G-ACCE, flown by the same pilot, but now operating as the already legendary Highland Airways.

In New Zealand, James Hewett flew his Falcon Airways' DH.60G ZK-AAR (1102) non-stop from Dunedin to Auckland on 15th March, covering a distance of 740 miles in a flight time of ten hours, non-stop. Vicomte Jacques de Sibour replaced his faithful 'world tourist' DH.60G G-EBZB (844) in February when he purchased DH.60M 1443, registered to him in Paris as F-AJKT. The following month he flew to Addis Ababa where he arrived on 27th March and sold the aeroplane to the Regent of Abyssinia for his personal use. During the Italian occupation in 1936 the aircraft was found abandoned at Akaki.

In May and June 1929, Hugh Grosvenor flew a 32 day clockwise circuit of Australia in DH.60X VH-UGS (604), starting and finishing at Adelaide. Three amateur pilots, Frank Bardsley, Reg Annabel and K Wedgwood, left Mascot Aerodrome, Sydney, on 2nd April 1930 in DH.60Gs VH-UIF (821) and VH-UJK (984), and DH.60M VH-UMZ (1371). They flew the same 8,000 mile cir-

DH.60 Moth Coupé VT-AAZ passed through Malta twice, in March and May 1930, when flying India-England-India in an attempt on the Aga Khan's prize. The return trip, flown solo by the 17-year-old Aspy Engineer, qualified for the £500 prize.
Malta Aviation Museum

Ted Fresson and his DH.60G G-AAWO during a proving flight to Kirkwall, prior to beginning a regular mail and passenger service. Note the jury strut between the folded starboard wings. The aircraft is being towed to shelter in a local coal merchant's shed. Jack Meaden

DH.60M VH-UMZ was one of a trio of Moths that flew the 8,000 mile clockwise circumnavigation of Australia in 25 days in April 1930. BAE Systems

cuit, returning 25 days later. 'There was no forced landing during the whole trip, and the engines behaved splendidly'. On 28th February 1931, Reg Annabel in VH-UJK was the first pilot to fly under Sydney Harbour Bridge. In 1932, under licence from the Australian Company, a single DH.60G VH-UQN (1 MC), was built in Sydney by J H McConnell for Reg Annebel. In July 1934 Annabel was killed in the aircraft when he failed to pull out of a loop started at too low a height at Mascot.

In April, DH.60M No 1472 was allocated to Harrods and may have been displayed in their Knightsbridge store although she was registered G-ABAI to the de Havilland Company in May and sold to Dudley Watt at Ford in July. Selfridges in Oxford Street certainly displayed DH.60M G-AAWV (1478), also in April, which they sold to Eric Hook at Heston. On 20th June, Hook and James Matthews left Lympne bound for Australia, but after leaving Akyab for Rangoon on 3rd July, the aircraft crashed into the jungle during a rainstorm and was wrecked.

DH.60G CV-TUR (1269), was built to the order of Prince Jean Ghica of Romania for an attempted long-distance flight from his home country. The aircraft was modified to carry both a 35 gallon and a 27 gallon fuel tank in the front cockpit plus a 20 gallon tank in the luggage locker and as a consequence was issued with a special C of A at an increased all-up weight of 1,900 lb. The prince left Bicester to deliver the aeroplane on 9th July but crashed in Bulgaria the next day. A replacement aircraft was ordered, DH.60G No 1805, which carried the same registration letters, and was delivered in September. Nothing further was heard apart from a report that the new aircraft crashed on 1st May 1931 and was a total loss.

Pat Fairbairn and Kenneth Shenstone departed Croydon on 17th September in DH.60G G-AAJO (1101) heading for Nairobi, but the flight was terminated at Cairo on the last day of the month after a landing accident. In March 1931, Mrs Venetia Montagu and Rupert Belville took off from Heston in DH.60G G-ABFW (1820), on an eight-week tour of Eastern Europe, Persia and Russia. G-ABFW was destroyed by fire after an accident in Persia on 2nd May 1931 and arrangements were made for the purchase and refurbishment of G-AAJO

which was then located in Amman. The 'tour' recommenced in mid-May from Tehran and ended when G-AAJO arrived back at Heston on 15th June.

Flight Lieutenant Cedric Hill took off from Lympne on 5th October in DH.60G G-ABEN (1812) on a record attempt to Australia, firmly believing he could shave several days off Hinkler's standing record of just over 15 days. He reached Timor in 12 days having flown several sectors at night to make up time lost through bad weather but he crashed on take-off for Darwin on 17th October. The aircraft was not serviceable until 9th December and G-ABEN reached Darwin the following day, 67 days after leaving England.

Hill sold his aeroplane in Brisbane where she was registered VH-UPV. Harry Bonney bought her for his wife 'Lores' (her real name was Maude Rose), who flew her from Archerfield to Wangaratta on 26th December, unwittingly setting a new Australian women's record by flying 947 miles in one day in a total airborne time of 14hr 30min. In August 1932, Lores Bonney circumnavigated Australia flying anti-clockwise from

Brisbane in 44 days, during which a camera aircraft got too close and collided with her port wingtip, fortunately without serious consequences. Starting in April 1933, she set out to fly to England. The journey was interrupted by two major accidents before VH-UPV reached India, but Mrs Bonney touched down at Croydon on 21st June to become the first woman to fly solo from Australia to England.

A 27-year-old Scot domiciled in New Zealand, Oscar Garden, who learned to fly at the Norfolk and Norwich Aero Club whilst on holiday in England, purchased DH.60M G-AASA (1438), after part-exchanging his car for the aircraft at Selfridge's Aviation Department. G-AASA was modified to accept a 20 gallon long-range tank in the luggage locker whose contents were banished to the front cockpit to share space with another 20 gallon tank. Garden left Croydon on 17th October for a flight to Australia but due to poor weather his first forced landing was in a field near Folkestone before he had even reached Lympne. He returned to Croydon, started again and landed at Wyndham in North Western Australia on 4th November, but

Mrs Lores Bonney in flight over Essendon Aerodrome, Melbourne, in her DH.60G VH-UPV, during her anti-clockwise circumnavigation of Australia in August 1932. The following year she flew the aeroplane to Croydon, the first woman to fly from Australia to England.
DH Moth Club Archive

due to bad luck along the route narrowly failed to improve on Hinkler's record. The flight was a remarkable achievement in view of Garden's experience but was completely over-shadowed by Amy Johnson's triumph only five months previously, a flight which had put the name 'Moth' firmly into almost every household's vocabulary.

On 12th November 1930, Mlle Maryse Hilsz left the Morane-Saulnier's test facility at Villacoublay, near Paris, in F-AJOE on a solo flight to Saigon, French Indo-China, where she arrived on 4th December. Apart from the usual frustration of delays caused by weather, eight days were lost in Rangoon due to a leak in the fuel tank, probably the long-range example fitted in the front cockpit of what was otherwise a near-standard aircraft. The return flight begun on 11th December went less smoothly and F-AJOE crashed at Istanbul on Christmas Day. Paris was not reached until 7th December the following year as one biographer noted: 'only after using three propellers, two fuel tanks and eight lives!'

In spite of April's significant price reductions, by November, the general effect of the recessional slow-down in world business was being experienced at Stag Lane. Taking an optimistic view together with an unwillingness to impose anything but unavoidable lay-offs in the workforce which none the less, were inevitable and considerable, the Company decided to build aircraft for stock.

Rather than see capital tied up and unproductive, as part of a new initiative, St Barbe's office contacted all light aeroplane clubs to explain how they understood that the clubs could not always afford to buy and run additional aircraft, and that the lack of equipment was often the major obstacle to expanded operations, increased cash-flow and financial security.

The de Havilland proposal which they themselves described as 'experimental' was to offer from stock, brand new Gipsy I-powered, wooden DH.60G Moths, each equipped with telephones, autoslots and a compass, fully insured against all risks including Third Party risks, for a fee of £60 per month, reducing to £50 per month after a six month continuous period of hire. Numerous practical conditions were outlined identifying who was responsible for what, none of which was either surprising or unreasonable:

'It is expected that this scheme will be welcomed by new clubs in districts in which local support is not yet assured, where it will be advantageous to experiment with the temporary use of a machine in order to experience what support is forthcoming and to gauge the probable success of the enterprise.'

Individual aircraft in the steady flow of Moths which continued to be registered after November's announcement were, with few exceptions, listed against the identities of their first users rather than the Company, making it impossible to separate obvious leases from sales and to estimate just how successful the initiative proved to be.

It was the general condition of business, strictly enforced by St Barbe, that de Havilland agents paid the Company for any aircraft delivered for use for local demonstration purposes. It was widely publicised that Captain de Havilland had been required to pay the list price, less an agent's commission, when he took delivery of his DH.60G G-AAAA. As sales of the DH.80A Puss Moth began to accelerate, agents declined to take new DH.60s into stock, often relying on part-exchanging a Puss Moth for a good condition Moth which could be maintained until re-sold.

Shareholders in the Canadian branch of the Company were advised in the Chairman's report published in December that DH.60 sales had certainly been hit by the introduction of the Puss Moth, and that a number of sales had been held up waiting for deliveries of the new type which were running late.

DH.60M G-AASA at the de Havilland factory at Mascot after Oscar Garden had flown her from England with no fuss or publicity in October 1930, narrowly failing to beat the record held by Bert Hinkler.
Via David Walters

JANUARY TO DECEMBER 1931

I N A CONFIDENTIAL letter received at Stag Lane in January 1931, an American correspondent confirmed that he was convinced that the worst of the Depression was over and business and general employment were showing an 'upward trend'. However, he reported that four Moths built at Lowell and fitted with British-built Gipsy I engines remained with Curtiss Wright at St Louis, unsold. Another four locally-built DH.60GMW aircraft with Wright Gipsy engines (176-179) were then being assembled, less slots, having been sold at a price of $3,750 each. Records show that these four, (NC613V-NC617V), may not have been registered in the names of their new owners until January 1932. Of greater concern to de Havilland was the news that although a further 70 to 80 Moths of the current specification probably could have been sold in 1931 at a price of about $4,000 each, Curtiss Wright had, according to the informant, already made a different decision:

'The Travel Air Trainer has been produced and flight tested in St Louis in competition with the Moth. The Travel Air proved to be considerably faster but the Moth beat it in take-off, climb and landing speed. The Travel Air has been returned to Wichita for such modifications as to enable it to beat the Moth in every respect. When, if and as, they get it in this shape, they propose to abandon Moth production entirely.'

It proved to be an accurate piece of intelligence for after the four Moths reported as being assembled, no others were built in the USA. Just exactly how many were built remains a matter of conjecture but the most likely numbers were supplied by a one-time Inspector at Lowell, transferred to St Louis, who suggested that British-built wooden DH.60Gs assembled at Lowell numbered 14 (although it might have been 17!) followed by 18 DH.60Gs possibly built entirely on the

premises. One British-built DH.60M was assembled for educational purposes with four others, which might have been shipped in from Canada, and possibly were the four airframes reportedly of British manufacture lying unsold at St Louis. British-built Gipsy I engines were installed in 150 metal fuselages constructed under the designation DH.60GM with a further 29 fitted with Wright-built Gipsy engines and designated DH.60GMW.

Not heeding the advice of those with the appropriate experience, Amy Johnson had planned a flight in her new DH.60G from London to Peking, operating via Poland and Siberia in the midst of the winter. Flying G-ABDV, *Jason III*, she took off from Stag Lane on New Year's Day, and after a number of forced landings, the aircraft was damaged landing in fog north of Warsaw where Amy made the decision to abandon the onward flight. Following local repairs, she flew the aeroplane back to England, operating via Switzerland where she enjoyed a few days rest, arriving at Lympne on 11th February.

The fragility of the Moth Seaplane when dependent on ship-board accommodation

was illustrated by two incidents early in the year. The DH.60G operating in the Antarctic with Sir Douglas Mawson, VH-ULD (1128), was damaged during retrieval on 27th January after landing in a rough sea. In a letter to Arctic Moth pilot John Grierson, Flight Lieutenant Stuart Campbell described the nature of their problems:

'On the first flight we had found it rather hazardous hoisting the aircraft aboard as we had only manpower on the lifting tackle and it took rather a long while to lift her out of the water and above the bulwarks. If the ship was rolling (and she was always rolling) the aircraft got up a swing like a pendulum and the wingtips were in constant danger of being crumpled against the ship's side. We had had the same trouble in aircraft tenders in the RAAF and found it generally preferable to have the ship steam slowly into the swell and hook on under weigh. We decided to try the same tactic and steamed into the swell at about 3-4 knots, Eric Douglas came in right under the hook and Sir Douglas Mawson who was passenger, hooked neatly on; we gave the signal to haul away and Eric cut the motor.

DH.60G Seaplane A7-55, built by the Cockatoo Island Dockyard and Engineering Company, travelled in a fully rigged condition, lashed to the roof of the hospital on board the survey vessel *Discovery II*, to assist with the search for an American airman lost in the Antarctic in 1933.
RAAF Museum

Francis Chichester, pipe in mouth, standing on the port float of his DH.60G Seaplane ZK-AAK, prior to his attempted flight across the Tasman Sea to Australia. Via Jack Meaden

But the lifting was too slow and before all the slack and the spring in the derrick had been taken up, the aircraft weather-cocked into the light breeze and swung at right angles to the line of advance of the ship which was still moving ahead. The port float being dragged side-on through the water buckled the booms holding the two floats in position and moved in under the fuselage. The port wingtip dropped and became submerged and finally the drag tore the slings out, ripping a couple of great gashes in the petrol tank, and she drifted away astern with the port wingtip still dragging in the water. The ship stopped, we got out the dinghy and towed the aircraft back and with some difficulty rigged two rope strops around the fuselage and eventually tipped her back on board.'

Using all their inventiveness and initiative, the aircraft was repaired on board *Discovery* and was airworthy again for flights on 10th and 11th February, the last, as it transpired, of the Expedition's flying programme.

The New Zealand Permanent Air Force loaned DH.60G Moth Seaplane '995' for operations against the rebellious Mau organisation in Western Samoa. The aircraft was embarked in HMS *Dunedin* on 8th January and stowed with the wings folded on an extension to 'X' gun-deck. The expedition arrived at Apia on 12th January and a shore base was selected. The Moth was hoisted out with wings folded but these were spread while still suspended and the aircraft was dropped into the crest of the swell and towed in. Her 90 hours of operational flying covered communications, reconnaissance, and distribution of propaganda leaflets. Equipped with wireless and

an operator in the front cockpit, the combined weight could not be lifted off the water and it was impractical for transmissions to be made by the pilot flying solo. The wireless was removed and donated to an army unit on shore. During re-embarkation in HMS *Dunedin* on 11th March, the aircraft was dropped onto the deck from 20ft and suffered damage estimated to be beyond economical repair.

At home in New Zealand, Air Force Moths were enlisted to fly mail between Gisborne and Hastings when road and rail communications were severed by an earthquake which hit the Hawkes Bay area of North Island early in February, the size of each letter being controlled to permit maximum uplift.

As part of a world tour that included New Zealand and Canada, Francis St Barbe stepped off his ship in Perth, Western Australia, on 3rd February, anxious to visit the new Company facilities at Mascot Aerodrome in Sydney. He was dismayed to learn, as his trip progressed through Melbourne, of the low esteem in which the Australian Company was held, particularly in respect to inattention to correspondence, delayed deliveries of supplies and slack business methods generally, added to which the RAAF expressed their disappointment over the award of the contract to the Larkin Company. In Sydney, St Barbe immediately instituted a number of major changes in an effort to improve efficiency and reduce costs, convinced that nothing except new management at a senior level would restore the reputation. St Barbe was introduced to Major Alan Murray Jones, an experienced pilot and ambitious young man then in charge of the country's Civil Flying Operations in the office of the Controller of Civil

Aviation who, after considerable thought, accepted St Barbe's offer to join the business. Under Murray Jones' leadership there was to be no rush into full-scale production of the DH.60, rather, a positive attempt to recover the Company's reputation by offering a good service in the supply of spares, maintenance and repair.

The Cockatoo Island Dockyard and Engineering Company of Sydney were granted a licence to build one DH.60G against a government order, which they did in 1933. The aircraft was constructed under the supervision of designer Lawrence Wackett in another attempt to encourage local manufacturing but the experiment is reported to have cost over £1,000, almost twice the price of an off-the-shelf aeroplane. Wackett's aeroplane was taken on charge by the RAAF as A7-55 in April 1933, converted to a Seaplane and painted bright yellow, was posted to the Antarctic Flight at Point Cook for immediate use in the search for a missing aircraft. She was carried fully rigged, facing the bows, lashed onto the flat roof of the hospital accommodation of the survey vessel *Discovery II*, and during the mission flew five sorties totalling less than five hours. The pilot was Eric Douglas, veteran of the Mawson Expedition, now commissioned and promoted Flight Lieutenant. In addition to the difficulties associated with operating light biplanes in Antarctic conditions already related by Stuart Campbell, Eric Douglas added notes of his own:

'When the air temperature was below 1°C, it was necessary to pre-heat the engine and lubricating oil prior to starting. This required an asbestos lined engine cover having some form of flue for receiving hot air from a kerosene burner. It was found necessary to continue this process from 20 to 30 minutes. Benzoline was used to prime the cylinders. It was found necessary to enrich the carburation mixture, especially at medium revolutions, by fitting a larger compensation jet. All exposed oil pipe lines were lagged with asbestos. The induction elbow was also lagged. To reduce excessive cooling, approximately half the normal open engine cowling was closed. Before taking off, the engine was thoroughly warmed up by steady taxying at medium revolutions. In flight, the engine behaved normally, but when gliding in prior to alighting, it was advisable to run the engine at at least half the normal full revolutions to keep the engine warm should it be required in a hurry.'

Having learned much from his earlier experiences, Douglas was able to recommend

An unidentified DH.60G Seaplane of the New Zealand Air Force at Hobsonville. Note the kink in the exhaust pipe which permitted doors to be installed on the port side, expediting the transit of a crewman from the cockpit to port float when required for mooring purposes. Via Jack Meaden

Three Morane Moths and several other aircraft types in the hangar of the Aero Club Roland Garros at Orly Aerodrome, Paris. The Morane-Saulnier badge can be clearly seen on the fuselage side, just ahead of the footstep position. Via Peter Gould

that, as the ship's derrick boom was sufficiently long, the aircraft should be swung out with the engine already running, and lowered nose-first towards the water. It was necessary to achieve a take-off quickly to reduce the risk of spray freezing on the floats and under-surfaces of the wings. He was also positive in dictating the best position of the ship when the aircraft was taking off or landing and during the recovery operation: 'the machine to come aboard on the lee side with the ship stationary, or nearly so'.

Possibly as a result of their experience gained at Cockatoo Island and to capitalise on it, in March 1934, in yet another effort to aid industry, the Australian Government ordered a batch of six DH.60M fuselages to be built by the Aircraft Construction Branch of the Munitions Supply Board Ordnance Factory in Melbourne, at a contracted price of £430 each. Allocated serials A7-69 to A7-74, the fuselage frames complete with empennage were all delivered after what has been described as 'three acrimonious years' to No 1 Air Depot at Laverton, between October 1935 and June 1936, where the RAAF fitted sets of wings already held in reserve.

The London Aeroplane Club drew the winning tickets for its annual raffle at Stag Lane on 17th February. More adventurous than ever, the first prize was a brand new DH.80A Puss Moth, but second and third were the well-used DH.60X G-EBWY (584) and G-EBXS (593). The first aircraft was won by Captain Leighton-Davies who had bought a ticket during a visit from Singapore and had no use for the prize, which he sold to LAC member Reginald Presland for £250. G-EBXS was won by Brian Lewis, the de Havilland agent at Heston, and was sold in March to newly-qualified Stag Lane pilot Laurie Lipton, soon to make his mark as a most enthusiastic air racing competitor.

After his arrival in Australia in January 1930, Francis Chichester immediately travelled onwards by ship with his DH.60G G-AAKK to a hero's welcome in Wellington, New Zealand, where the following year the aircraft was appropriately registered ZK-AKK. Chichester planned a flight in the Moth back across the Tasman Sea but, with no land aerodromes between New Zealand

and Australia, it was necessary to convert ZK-AKK to a seaplane and Chichester fortuitously acquired the salvaged floats that had been attached to the Air Force DH.60G Seaplane 995 when she was accidentally dumped onto the deck of HMS *Dunedin*. Starting from Auckland, Chichester left Parenyarenga Harbour, North Island, on 28th March 1931 bound for Norfolk Island, a vital stepping stone in his attempt to be the first to fly solo, east-west to Australia. His plan was to continue from there back to England via Japan and Russia, Canada and the Northern Route to Scotland. Demonstrating phenomenally accurate navigation, ZK-AKK touched down in Cascade Bay, Norfolk Island, after a flight of 5hr 50min over nothing but sea. Chichester reached Lord Howe Island after a 7hr 40min flight on 1st April but whilst anchored in the harbour overnight the Moth was hit by a squall and capsized at her moorings.

There was no alternative but to salvage the aircraft and attempt to rebuild her, a Herculean task which, with the assistance of some skilled islanders, occupied the next nine weeks. Essential spare parts and drawings were ordered from the de Havilland Company at Mascot and just managed to catch the next regular steamer service from Sydney. ZK-AKK took off on the final 480 mile leg of her Tasman crossing on 10th June and touched down alongside warships anchored in Jervis Bay, about 80 miles south of Sydney, after nursing a faltering engine through storms and squalls encountered near the Australian coast.

Following engineering assistance provided by the Royal Australian Navy, Chichester left again on 3rd July and transited New Guinea, The Philippines and Shanghai, moving on to Kitsugara Bay in Japan from where he took off for Tokyo on 14th August. On arrival, due to concerns about the prox-

When shipping Moths from Stag Lane, the Export Packing Department was able to locate two fuselages, with engines installed, into one crate without the whole becoming totally unmanageable. Wings were packed separately. This photograph was taken at the Chinese aerodrome at Mukden, where a fleet of Moths arrived in crates, imported by the de Havilland agent in Shanghai, Arnhold and Company. DH Moth Club Archive

imity of some welcoming boats, he failed to notice telephone wires stretched across the harbour entrance and ZK-AKK crashed into them, falling to the base of the harbour wall as a complete wreck. The pilot spent several weeks in a Tokyo hospital and what remained of the aircraft was given to a local school.

When the idea of an Air Corps or Independent Air Force for Iraq was first mooted in 1930, the Iraqi Government ordered five Gipsy II-powered DH.60Ms for delivery in April 1931. The first aircraft, No 1 (1675), was to be supplied against a standard specification for general training and communications duties but the other four, Nos 2-5 (1676-1679), were required for serious military intent. These aircraft, cleared to an all-up weight of 1,820 lb, were configured for the pilot to fly from the front seat while the rear cockpit was occupied by an operator responsible for the wireless, batteries and trailing aerial, a P14 camera let into the floor, release mechanism for four 20 lb bombs carried on an underfloor rack and various items of safety and signalling equipment. The rear cockpit was otherwise devoid of flying controls and the decision was made not to fit Autoslots. Both cockpits were provided with sealed containers of emergency rations and a two gallon tank for drinking water was situated on the cockpit side of the front bulkhead.

The first of the militarised Moths, No 1676, was flown on 4th October 1930 by Jack Tyler, in a series of tests associated with the wind-driven electrical generator, and during which a full complement of four 20 lb dummy bombs (which actually weighed 98 lb) was carried. In March 1931, No 1676 was the subject of maximum weight performance trials at Martlesham

Heath, resulting in minor criticisms including the Establishment's recommendation that the generator, mounted on the port lower mainplane 24in from the root, should be moved inboard by about 6in to take maximum advantage of the propeller slipstream. The report also suggested that the positioning of various electrical switches, dials and connectors might be improved, as could earthing and bonding; that the aerial winch would be better placed if repositioned within the rear cockpit and particular care be taken when retrieving the last few feet of aerial to prevent the swinging lead weight from damaging the fuselage.

The Iraqi aircraft were built at Stag Lane and qualified for their Cs of A in February and March but, in addition to a DH.80A Puss Moth supplied for the personal use of King Feisal, they were handed over to Iraqi crews on 8th April at Hatfield, one being positioned there that day by Hubert Broad. The aircraft left immediately for a formation delivery flight to Baghdad, arriving there two weeks later having completed the journey in 'easy stages,' to form No 1 Squadron, Royal Iraqi Air Force. The initial order was

A DH.60M of the Iraqi Air Force. The aircraft was intended for offensive operations more than mere training and slots were not fitted. The generator on the port lower wing was required to power wireless and other equipment carried in the rear cockpit. *Flight*

The DH.60T Moth Trainer was aimed at the more discerning and multi-requirement military market, where the carriage of extra equipment and external stores was necessary as part of the training programme for a military pilot. Prototype G-ABKM first flew in May 1931 and the following month was part of a consignment sold to the Swedish Air Force. *Flight*

The exhaust system of a DH.60T was routed forward and down to expel under the nose cowling, thus allowing doors to be situated on both sides of both cockpits, an essential aid to escape by parachute. BAE Systems

followed by a second for an additional four aircraft built to the same specifications. These, probably serialled 6-9 (1776-1779), were delivered by air to Aboukir in January 1932, during which flight No 1776 forced landed on a road near Jerusalem and was written off. Within a year they were all involved in offensive operations against a Kurdish uprising.

The Air Ministry was persuaded that RAF flying instructors, sitting in the front seat of open-cockpit biplanes, surrounded by struts, wires and minimally sized doors or hatches, or no doors at all, deserved better if ever they had to consider a speedy escape wearing a parachute. As a result of this policy and the interest being shown in the DH.60M as a cheap introduction to the art and craft of combative military operations, de Havilland built in November 1930 what they described during initial planning as a DHT (Training) Moth and later as a 'Special RAF Machine'. Essentially a DH.60M, powered by a Gipsy II engine provided with an inverted fuel system of the type first used by the RAF display team at Hendon the previous July, aircraft No 1672 was complete by 5th December. The most obvious visual change was the appearance of a deep drop-down door on the starboard side of the front cockpit, which necessitated changes to the geometry and construction of the fuselage side frame, especially to the line of the top longeron.

Following review, the Company decided that the specification could be further improved. The deep front door was applied to the port side also, a modification which increased the total weight of the revised side frames by 7 lb, and standard-depth doors were provided for both sides of the rear cockpit, enabled by routing the exhaust pipe vertically down the port side of the front cowling. Numerous other minor modifications were incorporated in the structure of the wings and tailplane, and there was a revision of the interplane strut attachment and the diameter and positioning of some rigging wires. The front and rear lift wires now converged to locate at a common point, the lower wing root-end fitting just ahead of the front cockpit, allowing unhin-

dered access from the front seat onto the walkway. Handley Page Autoslots, not included at the first rigging, were considered but not fitted, probably in an effort to save weight and expense. Possibly for the same reason, the luggage locker was reduced in depth to discourage excessive use. The root-ends of the upper mainplanes were cut away at 45° to permit a better upward view from the rear cockpit and for the instructor, a mirror was let into the top of the engine cowling, positioned to allow a view of the sky immediately above. Another was fixed at the side of the front windscreen, angled towards the rear cockpit, which the salesmen claimed was 'to give a feeling of closer contact'.

The revised No 1672 was fitted with air wheels on 23rd February 1931 and re-weighed to record a tare weight of 1,063 lb, well within the limits for certificated weights of 1,820 lb in the Normal Category and

1,640 lb for Aerobatics. She was flown on the Harrow Speed Course on 23rd March when the result of 101.83mph was described as 'very poor' due to 'the rpm being down'. The aircraft was registered G-ABKU to the Company on 1st April and was despatched to Martlesham Heath under de Havilland's recyclable test identification E.3. Upon return to Stag Lane, she was issued with a Certificate of Airworthiness on 13th May and in July was demonstrated at Heston, by Geoffrey de Havilland Jnr, to representatives from the Portuguese military before being dismantled, or as the Company recorded: 'reduced to redundant stock'.

The marketable version of the aircraft was unveiled as the DH.60T Moth Trainer carrying a basic price tag of £995, offered against the military requirements of instruction in the roles of air fighting using camera guns, bombing, wireless and photography. An initial batch of six airframes was laid down in

DH.60T 5110 in her delivery colours, one of the many schemes adopted by the Swedish Air Force during the type's service career. *Flight*

the early spring, G-ABKM to G-ABKS (1700–1705), excluding the letter 'Q,' each of which was registered to the Company on 4th April, all except G-ABKS qualifying for their Cs of A in May and June. G-ABKN (1701) was loaned to the RAF at Northolt from where Geoffrey de Havilland Jnr collected her on 1st June.

In Sweden, the Air Force was still using the Heinkel HD36, designated Sk.6/6A in the Swedish inventory, for initial training. These became so unreliable that in the spring of 1931 the Air Board imposed restrictions which effectively rendered them

unsuitable for training purposes. With a summer course in prospect the Air Force urgently needed a replacement aircraft type and the de Havilland Company unveiled their DH.60T at the critical moment. The Swedish Air Board sanctioned the immediate acquisition of the first five aircraft, which were taken on charge in July and August as Fv5103-Fv5107, for operation by the Central Flying School at Ljunbyhed under the Sk.9 designation. The Air Force subsequently ordered five additional aircraft, Fv5108-Fv5112 (1718-1722), which were taken on charge at Ljunbyhed in August where the

summer training course began after a delay of only three weeks.

As delivered, the Sk.9s were painted silver bronze overall with black crowns on a white circle in six positions and blue and yellow rudder stripes. The colours, markings and serial numbers were changed in 1932, 1933, 1935 and again in 1937 when the drab 'panzer grey' scheme was applied to the survivors, for it had not been an altogether happy association. Within weeks of delivery, Fv5106 and Fv5112 had collided during formation aerobatics over Bonarp and in November, Fv5103 and Fv5104 also collided. Hooked together, the two aircraft descended in a gentle turn to port until they both hit the ground and were wrecked.

Following Iraqi evaluation of the DH.60T Moth Trainer, two aircraft, '13' and '14' (3031 and 3032), were delivered in July 1932 after which, believing it more economical to train pilots locally rather than send candidates to England, the Iraqi Air Force established its own Flying Training School at Hinaidi in June 1933 and in preparation, took delivery there in April of a further three DH.60T aircraft, 25-27 (3050-3052). The passing-out parade of the first 14 pupils was on 13th May 1934, an occasion attended by King Ghazi, members of the

Above: **What is Squadron Leader Hylton Murray-Philipson doing at Stag Lane on 22nd May 1931? Answer: he is writing a cheque in favour of the de Havilland Aircraft Company Ltd before taking delivery of his new DH.60G, G-ABMA, which, as soon as the ink on the cheque was dry and safely in the hands of Francis St Barbe, he was to fly home to Stobo Castle, Peebles-shire.** Hylton Murray-Philipson

Left: **The new Dunlop 'air wheel' and doughnut tyre introduced during the autumn of 1931, reduced the propeller tip ground-clearance by about two inches. A warning was issued to owners of straight-type undercarriages not to attempt a conversion. Note the mix of windscreens, with a 'Triplex' unit fitted to the rear cockpit.** *Flight*

In Canada, the St Catherines' Flying Club fitted outsize 'air-wheels' to the undercarriage of their DH.60M CF-CAW, in order to cope with very wet aerodrome surfaces, particularly evident during the spring thaw. Via Gerry Schwam

Iraqi Government and senior officials from the British Military Mission.

Introduction of the DH.60T Moth Trainer was timely but it was recognised that the specification would need further refinement. Somewhat prematurely, six fuselages built to the original 'E.3' standard with a deep door on the starboard side only, were shipped to Canada where initially they were not accepted due to the fact that no civil version of the type had either been anticipated or approved by the British authorities. It was not until 24th April that the British Air Ministry was advised of the problem when a request was made for transmission of clearance documentation through the London-based Canadian Liaison Officer.

Following his visits to Australia and New Zealand, Francis St Barbe arrived in Ottawa on 12th May to learn that the Company had lost an order for 20 initial training aircraft to the Fleet, an American-designed biplane assembled in Canada, and had been advised by the RCAF that no more Moths would be ordered unless egress and view from the front cockpit were greatly improved.

The appearance of the new 'air wheel' prompted some owners to enquire whether they could be fitted to older aircraft with the straight-through axle, but the Company advised against as with a smaller diameter, the new wheels brought the propeller tips 2in closer to the ground. Owners with air-wheels fitted to their aircraft were recommended to check hub discs after several were reported to have come loose and fallen off in the air. The replacement was described as 'springy quality vulcanite' which could be screwed on. The Company also warned owners in some countries of the danger of punctures caused by taxying over 'camel thorns and other similar objects'. Dunlop could supply a new inner tube ready filled with a special puncture-sealing compound at an additional cost of five shillings. And while the Company was in communicative mood it advised that after many years of protecting internal wooden surfaces with varnish, a sufficient number of complaints had been received to initiate a change, with Air Ministry approval, to the use of dope.

For his England-Australia record attempt which began on 1st April 1931, Charles Scott carried 103 gallons of petrol and three gallons of oil on board his DH.60M G-ABHY. The aircraft was cleared to operate at an all-up weight of 2,050 lb. DH Moth Club Archive

During the year there was to be the usual round of long-distance touring and, with a growing confidence, more record attempts. Following 1930's International Tour and the slim prospect of further honours, DH.60G Racing Moth G-AAHR (1068) was finally retired and in November 1930 she was sold via Phillips and Powis to Theodore Sanders at Broxbourne. As a standard two-seater in March 1931, Sanders flew her from Heston to Cairo and back to England where she stalled off a loop and crashed in 1933. DH.60G G-AADW (988) was acquired by the Asiatic Petroleum Company in January 1931 and on 22nd March left Lympne for a tour of the Far East and China flown by the Company's Aviation Manager, John Ford. The aircraft had reached Greece the following day where she was damaged after being forced down in a snowstorm. There was further trouble along the route and G-AADW eventually reached

Hong Kong by sea, only to be destroyed in a hangar fire at Kai Tak in May 1932.

Whilst Francis Chichester was engaged in epic adventures over the Tasman Sea, Charles Scott, a British pilot working as an instructor in Brisbane, was asked if he would travel to England, buy an aeroplane and fly it back to Australia for a local customer. Scott ordered a Puss Moth from Stag Lane but after flying one in Brisbane was not impressed by its performance in high temperatures when fully loaded so changed his order to a DH.60M which was to be fitted up for very long range. Scott took passage to England and in February 1931 was introduced to his aircraft, DH.60M G-ABHY (1685), which had been configured to uplift more than three gallons of oil and 103 gallons of petrol distributed between the normal gravity tank, two separate tanks of 55 gallons and 27 gallons capacity in the front

cockpit and the first installation of a 20 gallon tank in the luggage locker. G-ABHY was cleared to operate at an all-up weight of 2,050 lb at which the de Havilland Design Office suggested that 'the strength and performance are considered sufficient for a special flight if the aircraft is carefully handled by an experienced pilot'. It was estimated that at maximum weight the aircraft would take 285 yards to unstick and 820 yards to reach 120ft.

To gain experience with the aircraft and appreciate her 16 hour endurance, Scott proposed a trial start along his planned route by flying from London to Frankfurt and on to Vienna before returning to Lympne, but the practice flight was hampered by strong winds which limited his range and he landed at Frankfurt, returning to England the following day. The late delivery of a permit allowing him to fly through Syria, coupled with uncooperative winds for the first part of the flight, delayed the departure of G-ABHY until the early hours of Wednesday 1st April, when Scott flew non-stop to Belgrade.

The remainder of the trip was often made to the limit of the fuel endurance and involved several landings after dark fol-

lowed by departures before daybreak. With few minor deviations from the plan, Scott arrived at Darwin on 10th April having established a new record time of 9 days 3hrs 40min. He was greeted with a shower of congratulatory messages including those from The King, British Prime Minister, Secretary of State for Air and the de Havilland Company. The aeroplane was the first overseas flight to land at Brisbane's new municipal airport and was duly delivered to her owner, R S White, to whom she was registered VH-UQH on 7th September.

Scott flew the aircraft on to Sydney where at Mascot the long-range fuel and oil systems were removed. Shortly after, while relaxing at a party in Melbourne, Scott was asked if he would consider a return flight to England and, being tired, he fobbed off his interrogator by saying of course he would, but the next day discovered that his reply had been taken seriously and he was being offered a new Moth courtesy of Lord Wakefield. To claim an out-and-return record and to miss the monsoon, it was essential that the earliest possible start should be made. De Havilland confirmed they could fit an engine to a stock fuselage, build a set of wings and empennage and install the petrol

tanks and other equipment removed from G-ABHY, all within three weeks. The result was DH.60M VH-UQA (1566), registered in the name of C W A Scott on 16th May 1931. With no time to fly consumption tests, Scott decided to rely on his experience of the outward flight together with data collected during the positioning flight to his point of departure on the northwest coast.

The record attempt began at Wyndham on 26th May and was completed in what Scott described as 'easy stages', initially through very poor weather conditions and a delay at Lambok due to a recurring problem with the long-range oil system. The final sector from Brindisi to Lympne on 5th June, a distance of 1,350 miles, was flown non-stop in thirteen and a half hours. The time was another record at 10 days 13hr 25min, taking two whole days off Kingsford Smith's previous time. There was more: it was the first solo return flight between England and Australia, the first out-and-back crossing of the Timor Sea and had created record times for out-and-return flights between England and India. In Great Britain, Scott toured the country with his Moth during the summer, sponsored by the *Daily Herald*.

While de Havilland Australia had been completing VH-UQA at Mascot in May 1931, in the adjacent hangar they were fitting a Gipsy II engine into a second-hand DH.60G, VH-UFT (363), which they had traded-in and re-sold to a young Scot, James Mollison, a pilot flying commercially with Australian National Airways, and who was anxious to fly in record time to England.

Always short of money, the persuasive Mollison had contacted Lord Wakefield to ask for assistance, a plea that was rapidly answered by the Wakefield Company's organisation in Australia with the presentation of VH-UFT. The aircraft was converted in a similar manner to Scott's G-ABHY which, by coincidence, Mollison had flown without authority at Brisbane whilst the aircraft was waiting to be ferried to Mascot, but at Mollison's insistence the fuel capacity was further increased to 119 gallons, sufficient for a still air range of 2,000 miles.

A fleet of DH.60 Moths all delivered in crates and erected at Mukden, China, where they were test flown by Frank Swoffer acting for the de Havilland importing agent, Arnhold and Company of Shanghai. Frank Swoffer

Amongst the several shipments of Moths to China was at least one DH.60G Moth Coupé which was intended as the personal transport of a senior Army officer and on which he learned to fly. BAE Systems

Taking off in darkness on 6th June from the absurdly inadequate 500 yard runway at Darwin, an aerodrome Scott had advised him not to use, the Moth collided with specially lighted telegraph wires and a pole when crossing the boundary fence in a semi-stalled condition. Following the agreement of his benefactor, Mollison had the aircraft returned to Mascot for repair and a second attempt was made, starting at 1.00am on 29th July, from the larger airfield at Wyndham. Within the first day, Mollison had flown 1,730 miles to Batavia, the greatest distance ever flown in a single day by a light aircraft. On 6th August, utterly exhausted, he landed on the beach at Pevensey Bay, on the south coast of England, and telephoned Lympne Aerodrome to confirm his safe arrival and to report that he was going to take a short rest before going on to a reception at Croydon. His time was yet another record: 8 days 19hr 25min, cutting Scott's short-lived record by an incredible 50 hours.

It was estimated that Mollison earned £7,000 in fees for product endorsement and promotion following his trip after which he sensed great prospects for future record attempts providing that public interest could be retained and nurtured by flights of an increasingly daring nature. His first adventure began on 6th November flying VH-UFT, when he took off from Lympne in an attempt on the record to The Cape recently established by Gordon Store and Peggy Salaman in a Puss Moth. VH-UFT had been modified since her arrival in England to accept a Marconi AD6 Wireless Receiver in the luggage locker but this was of little assistance as poor visibility closed in around him, forcing Mollison to grope his way back to the aerodrome to wait for an improvement.

He left again on Friday 13th November, dismissing superstition, making good progress until he reached Egypt, where he experienced difficulty in transferring fuel to the gravity tank which he estimated would shortly run dry. Before the engine stopped, Mollison decided to land in the dark but the field he chose was covered in maize reeds up to 5ft tall, growing in thick mud, and after touching down VH-UFT turned over. He was at El Minya, 150 miles short of Cairo. The Moth was repaired in Alexandria after which Mollison chose to fly her back to England in

easy stages via the Eastern Route through Turkey to Vienna. The journey proved to be a complete nightmare, plagued by appalling weather, bureaucratic and military intervention, and lasted for 53 days.

A specially modified DH.60M, No 1717, was delivered to Hendon in July for the exclusive use of the Belgian Air Attaché, and the aircraft was painted in a military scheme, less serial. The Air Attaché, Captain Chevalier Willy Coppens, had lost a leg during the First World War and the aircraft was configured to permit rudder operation from the rear cockpit through a wheel fitted to the top of a revised control column. The handwheel was connected by chains and cables to a modified front cockpit rudder bar from which control cables led to the rudder horns. To compensate for the restricted lateral movement of the control column within the cockpit, the aileron chain sprockets in the wings were reduced in diameter. The aircraft remained in use until October 1942 when she was absorbed into 510 Squadron, an RAF unit formed from 24 Squadron, to handle a miscellany of inherited aircraft

types. The Squadron was renamed the Metropolitan Communications Squadron in 1944 and the DH.60M is believed to have been transferred to the military in Belgium in 1947.

On 10th July, an aircraft identified as a 'DH Training Moth T1' fitted with a Gipsy II engine was weighed at Stag Lane. In most respects she was identical with the final specification of another aircraft which had been tested using identity E.3, DH.60T G-ABNY (1724), one of three destined for China, fitted out with bomb racks and provision for wireless, electrical generation and camera guns. The exception was that Training Moth T1 was fitted with swept mainplanes, the top set staggered forward of the lower wings. Her centre of gravity in this configuration was closely compared with No 1724 and found to be further forward, the difference noted as being due to an increased tare weight and '*the forward shift of petrol*'.

The increase in tare weight was accounted for by the addition of 'a controlled slot locking device' and 'a drop door

The port side view of a Gipsy III engine, essentially a Gipsy II with a redesigned oil system to allow the unit to run inverted. Sitting lower in the bearers and with a sloping top to the crankcase, the new engine made a radical difference to the design of the nose of the aircraft and to the view forward from the cockpits. The starboard side view shows the carburettor, induction manifold, and some of the baffling designed to direct cooling air between the rearmost cylinders. de Havilland

(four) fuselage'. The petrol tap was described as being 'cockpit controlled' rather than positioned on the cabane where it could not have been reached from the rear cockpit. With the addition of petrol, oil and crew the Training Moth T1 was 11 lb over the maximum permitted aerobatic weight, a detail in need of attention. According to Richard Clarkson, the solution adopted in the case of three similarly afflicted DH.60Ms supplied to the Royal Danish Navy in February as Type L B III, 1682-1684, was simply to select the lightest components, a practicality which resulted in a saving of 18 lb per machine.

The T1 Moth had been configured by moving the whole of the cabane structure forward of the front cockpit, removing the petrol tank from immediately above the occupant's head, thus satisfying both the views of the Canadian authorities and interpretation of the Air Ministry's latest trainer specification 15/31. It had been necessary to

sweep the wings as the most practical method of regaining some of the loss of balance. It is probable that the T1 Moth was in fact No 1705 (G-ABKS), which carried the test marks E.4 and was flown by Jack Tyler on 21st July and by Hubert Broad in August. E.4 never qualified for a C of A before she was declared redundant and dismantled.

To comply with another Air Ministry requirement, a prospective training aeroplane had to be given a name, one beginning with the letter 'T' (for Trainer), and de Havilland chose *Tiger Moth*. The first aircraft with swept wings to be designated a DH.60T Tiger Moth was No 1726, fitted with an inverted Gipsy III engine and registered G-ABNI to the Company on 25th June 1931.

St Barbe was concerned about the views he had received in Canada, a country still suffering from the effects of the Depression, and in August G-ABNI was despatched with haste to Toronto where her arrival was greeted with anything but enthusiasm. The

second DH.60T Tiger Moth, G-ABNJ (1727), was delivered by Hubert Broad to Martlesham Heath on 18th August wearing identity E.5, where the general impression gained from the trials which began four days later was favourable, except that, in the opinion of her test pilots, landing in a crosswind put her into-wind wing tip perilously close to the ground and that when taxying across uneven territory any down-aileron was liable to make contact with the surface.

At Stag Lane, DH.60T Tiger Moth G-ABPH (1732) was re-rigged to accept additional dihedral on the lower wings only, adequately solving the problem. Hubert Broad flew her to Martlesham Heath on 3rd September from where it was reported that the change in rigging had created no adverse effect on handling. In this new configuration the A&AEE's report cleared the aircraft as a military trainer of a type which would be acceptable to the Air Ministry. In support of a prospective order from the Portuguese Government, in December, Hubert Broad delivered G-ABPH to Carlos Bleck, the Company's agent in Lisbon, where she was sold and absorbed into the military.

The Design Department at Stag Lane decided that a sufficient number of major alterations had now been embodied in the basic DH.60 for a new Type Number to be applied to the Tiger Moth. This was not a hasty decision, for all design and stress calculations, modification summaries and flight test reports collectively formed the aircraft Type Record held by the Design

The result of installing a Gipsy III engine in a DH.60T airframe produced a very clean nose and improved the forward view of the pilot. The wings of the aircraft were swept back to compensate for the move of the cabane structure forward of the front cockpit. In this configuration the type was known as the DH.60T Tiger Moth.
British Aerospace

DH.60X Cirrus Moth G-AAPA was modified in order to tow Herr Krause's Lyons Tea sponsored Falke glider in the Cross-Channel Gliding Competition on Saturday, 20th June 1931. The cumbersome arrangement was attached to the cabane structure and passed through a loop designed to keep the cable clear of the tail. DH Moth Club Archive

Authority. A change of Type Number usually signalled an entirely new design of aircraft requiring a new Type Record to be established, a time-consuming and expensive exercise. By October 1931 the inevitability of a change of Type Number was accepted within the Company and the next available was DH.82. However, to avoid cost and excessive administrative effort, the Type Record for the DH.82 Tiger Moth continued to be referenced to the key type, the DH.60X, under whose protection it remained.

The efforts involved in establishing and developing the new aerodrome at Hatfield in addition to progressing the work at Stag Lane, all under the influence of the deteriorated business climate, left little space for official Company involvement in flying competitions, although many changes to rules and regulations worked to exclude them anyway. The French Tour which started at Orly Airport, Paris, on 25th April, was limited to French competitors. Of the 41 starters, six were Moths, five of these built by Morane-Saulnier. Similarly, the Dunlop Cup Tour of France in August was restricted to French-built aircraft entered and flown by French owners and pilots, a ruling later adjusted to allow the use of foreign engines. This relaxation permitted nine Morane Moths to enter, one of which, flown by the Count de Rouvre, was declared the winner just ahead of a Farman 234 but well ahead of the rest of the field. Moths were excluded in 1932 after the decision on engines was reversed and the person making the competition entry, the pilot, the airframe and the engine, all had to be French. The German Tour in July 1931 was confined to what were termed 'modern sports machines' and the rules stipulated only German-built engines.

Following the cavalcade of the 1930 King's Cup Air Race, the Royal Aero Club too changed the rules for 1931, stipulating a minimum handicap speed of 100mph and pilots of amateur status. There were 41 entries of which 40 started from Heston on 25th July and the field included a dozen DH.60Gs and five Puss Moths, but none with Company backing and they must have felt disappointed that first place went to a Bluebird, second to a Spartan and only third to Peggy Salaman's Puss Moth.

During the working week which followed the King's Cup, Stag Lane received six RAF DH.60Ms, K1878-K1883 (1618-1623). With one as reserve, they had formed the Central

Flying School's Display Team at the 1931 RAF Display held at Hendon on 27th June. They were at the works for conversion back to standard training configuration having been taken on charge in February and March by the Display Flight of the CFS at Wittering. Although fully modified for sustained inverted flight, which had become an established and integral part of the team's routine, new regulations introduced by the Air Ministry prohibited display pilots from remaining inverted for longer than five minutes at a time. Under the command of Flight Lieutenant Basil Embry, the five-aircraft team had performed a series of polished formation manoeuvres, mostly inverted, which revealed that the top wings were liberally painted with areas of red to help the crowd to distinguish orientation. It was to be the last display by the CFS Team using DH.60 Moths for in 1932 they appeared in their new DH.82 Tiger Moths, sporting even more distinctive colours.

Pilot Officer John Grierson bought second-hand DH.60G G-AAJP (1123), in August 1930 and flew her to Karachi to join his RAF bomber squadron. The aircraft was painted black on one side and red on the other and carried the name *Rouge et Noir*. In May 1931, Grierson flew the aeroplane back to Lympne in the record time of just under four and a half days. In September 1932, *Rouge et Noir* was flown on an 8,800 mile tour to Russia and Samarkand and the following year Grierson contemplated a flight around the world, an ambition which ended when Moscow rejected his application to fly across Siberia. G-AAJP was overhauled by the Blackburn Aircraft Company which fitted floats designed for their own Bluebird, considered by Grierson to be more robust than the usual Short floats. With a frame aerial installed in the wings feeding a Marconi-Robinson 'homing receiver' and a fuel capacity of nearly 70 gallons, including two auxiliary tanks in the front cockpit designed, constructed and installed by Blackburn, she left Brough Aerodrome on 4th August heading for New York via Iceland and Greenland. She was damaged when touching down at

Reykjavik on 7th August and following repairs capsized during an attempted take-off 13 days later. Dismayed, John Grierson returned to England to re-plan the flight which he later completed in a DH.83 Fox Moth, although not without incident.

Denys Finch-Hatton flew DH.60G G-ABAK (1265), from London to Kenya in May 1931, intending to land at Nairobi, but on 14th May the aircraft overturned on take-off from the Kenyan town of Voi and Finch-Hatton was killed. The accident became a pivotal off-screen moment in the film *Out of Africa*, shot in 1985, in which the starring role was taken by DH.60GM G-AAMY (US86), chosen from several possible contenders by the production's Art Director who enthused over her black and yellow colour scheme.

Miss Aline Barton purchased DH.60G G-ABGY (1807) in the spring of 1931 and on 24th May the aircraft was damaged at Reims. Aline Barton was reportedly attempting a flight to Australia from where her aeroplane was to be shipped to her native New Zealand. In the event, G-ABGY was returned to England for repairs, and in October, Miss Barton and Frank Richards left Heston for Nairobi where the aircraft took up residence as VP-KAQ. In April 1932 she was sold to a new owner in Nyeri who wrote her off in July.

Count Laszlo de Almasy discovered six of the oases on the old slave route through the Sahara early in 1931 and in August acquired DH.60G G-AADP (1022), with a view to mounting an aerial expedition to find the seventh. With Count Theodore Zichy as second pilot, G-AADP set off on a European tour in preparation for the desert adventure, but crashed at Alexandretta in Turkey on 25th August, from where the aeroplane was returned to Woodley for repair and sale. In April 1932, Count Almasy and Sir Robert Clayton East flew to a base camp at Kharga in the Libyan Desert in DH.60G G-ABDK (1804), to resume the search for the lost oasis of Zarzura. The expedition believed they had located the site. However, with only days before they were due to leave the country, and as supplies were not in place

Five DH.60T Moth Trainers for the Egyptian Air Force were handed over at Stag Lane Aerodrome on 3rd November 1931 and afterwards were dismantled, packed into crates and sent by sea. When the ship reached Gibraltar, the aircraft were unloaded and returned to England where they were reassembled at Hatfield and left on an airborne delivery flight on 23rd May 1932.
British Aerospace

to cover any addition to the 30 hours' flying achieved, they were unable to confirm it.

By October 1931 the veteran DH.60 G-EBLV (188) had been acquired by speedway riders Stan Lupton and Stuart 'Stiffy' Aston, who prepared her at Broxbourne for a flight to Stan's native Australia. The press took an interest and published details on 29th October indicating that the trip had already begun. Sadly, left in the open at Broxbourne Aerodrome the previous night in anticipation of an early start, a gale had blown G-EBLV out of her pickets, inflicting severe damage and causing the trip to be abandoned.

A Military Air Service for Egypt, moulded on the model set by Iraq a year before, was established in the late summer of 1931 and a £7,000 order was placed with de Havilland to supply five DH.60T Moth Trainers configured to 'the E.3 Type'. These were issued with serial numbers E-105 to E-101 in descending order (1734-1738) and later supplemented with a single DH.60M E-100 (1799), almost certainly as a communications and training machine.

There were many similarities with the standard and emergency equipment carried by the Iraqi DH.60Ms and, although the aircraft were wired and bonded for an electrical generation system, no generator was actually fitted on production. Wireless equipment was carried in the fully instrumented rear cockpit, a camera in the front, and the aircraft had two full sets of controls. The rudder cables were routed to the front cockpit which allowed a flexible configuration for the rear. Bomb racks were fixed under the floor and, unlike the Iraqi aircraft, Autoslots and locking devices were fitted together with doughnut wheels and tyres.

The first aircraft was ready on 22nd October 1931 and all five DH.60Ts qualified for Cs of A in preparation for the handover ceremony arranged at Stag Lane for 3rd November, following which it was expected that the aircraft would be flown to Egypt by RAF pilots. This proposal later was changed to include three Egyptian pilots just completing their training in England.

The Director of the new Air Service, Air Commodore A G Board, seconded from the RAF, was mindful of winter weather in Europe and the limited experience of his new crews. He returned to Cairo to await the arrival of his aircraft having arranged for them to be crated and despatched by sea. The Egyptian Government queried the decision when it was known that the Iraqi Moths had all flown from England in formation and as national pride was at stake, a decision was made that the crated aircraft were to be unloaded when their ship called at Gibraltar, and returned to Stag Lane. The position of the Director became untenable and Board resigned from his post. The fleet was subsequently re-assembled at Hatfield and embarked upon its journey on 23rd May 1932, led by Flight Lieutenant S J Stocks, RAF, Director of Flying Training, Egyptian Air Force. The aircraft arrived at the new Almaza Aerodrome, Heliopolis, on 2nd June where they were greeted by King Fuad, the Crown Prince, members of the Egyptian Government and the Diplomatic Corps.

In November 1931, two former Danish military pilots, Bjorn Andersen and Niels Egebjerg, bought two second-hand DH.60Ms from England, No 1337, previously used by the American Air Attaché in London without markings and recently registered G-ABSF, and G-AALF (1402). They flew the aircraft home to Copenhagen on 5th December where as OY-DAG and OY-DEG respectively and joined by a Klemm L.26, they formed a travelling air circus under the name of Dansk Flyvestaevne Tourne. The show toured the country the following summer, often including the added attraction of Danish parachutist John Tranum, but on 2nd October near Sonderborg, Andersen's OY-DEG refused to come out of a spin. The aircraft landed amongst a group of trees and was completely demolished but the pilot was only slightly hurt. In England, as a safety precaution, Leslie Irvin's DH.60M G-AAKN (1380) was modified to carry a 'dummy man' for parachute trials, for which a 'quick release gear' was fitted in the rear cockpit.

At the end of a difficult trading year, Company Chairman Alan Butler had to report a reduction in business of 10 per cent although the Company had remained in profit. He said that he felt that quicker transportation of personnel, mails and merchandise would be a big factor in hastening the return of assurance and prosperity and made particular reference to the number of notable flights that had taken place during the year. The sector showing the largest downturn was, not surprisingly, that of the British private owner but sales of Moths for military training purposes was steady both at home and overseas and the Company now had a new type 'being thoroughly tried out by the Royal Air Force' for which it was hoped that further orders would materialise.

JANUARY TO DECEMBER 1932

I N THE CLOSING days of 1931, the Brazilian Ministry of War placed an order for 15 DH.60T Moth Trainers for early delivery to Rio de Janeiro. It was a significant breakthrough for de Havilland: the first British aircraft ever to enter service with the Brazilian military and chosen after comparison with seven other types offered by manufacturers in four countries. The aircraft were to be configured in the role of the modern, multi-task, economical military trainer, to include a capability for inverted, night and blind flying on metric instrumentation, wireless operation, gunnery, bombing and photography.

Laid down at Stag Lane at the beginning of a new block of builder's identification numbers, 3000-3014, the aircraft were allocated serials K-141 to K-153 in sequence. Jack Tyler initiated the production test flying programme at the end of January 1932 and all 15 aircraft were cleared for Certificates of Airworthiness by 17th March. Both 3003 and 3010 are known to have been written off shortly after delivery, seemingly before they received formal Army identification.

The first of three shipments of five aircraft left the London Docks on 20th February accompanied by W T W Ballantyne, taking up his new appointment as de Havilland's General Representative in South America, and Hubert Broad, scheduled to spend March and April test flying the aircraft as they arrived at their base at Campo dos Afonsos near Rio, helping with training and also sampling as much of the opposition's hardware as seemed decent.

On completion of the contract the Brazilian Government placed an order for a further 12 DH.60T Moth Trainers to the same specification, but for use by the Naval Air Service, and to which markings I1H-21 to I1H-32 were allocated, (3015-3026). These aircraft were delivered in two batches of six to the Training Squadron at Ilha do Governador, commencing at the beginning of May. There is a suspicion that one of the original 12 airframes was damaged before delivery as the Stag Lane works allocated a replacement fuselage, No 3030, which was substituted during what might have been extensive repairs.

During a formal inspection in September when all 12 Navy Moths flew together in a formation choreographed by wireless commands issued by the Minister of Marine, the government announced a repeat order for 12 more DH.60Ts for the Navy, I1H-75 to I1H-86 (3036-3047), for delivery by January 1933.

Students of the de Havilland Aeronautical Technical School spent part of their training working in the production shops and late in 1931 it was agreed that they should be allowed to construct a DH.60G Moth to the latest standards in their own premises. Consequently, build number 1900 was allocated to the School in November 1931, and a

The Brazilian Navy was pleased with its fleet of DH.60T Moth Trainers, and the service supplied by the Company, and in 1932 ordered a further 12 aircraft. The officers responsible were probably those inspecting the Training Squadron at Ilha do Governador in the Bay of Rio de Janeiro. DH Moth Club Archive

It was almost inevitable that the students of the de Havilland Aeronautical Technical School at Stag Lane would be allowed to construct a complete Moth, and the first of several, G-ABTS, was issued with a C of A in February 1932. The students operated their own flying club at Stag Lane, and later Hatfield, with Geoffrey de Havilland Jnr as their instructor. Via Michael Benaki

Ownership of this extremely smart
DH.60GM, NC139M, first registered in
1930, was transferred to Inez du Val
Crosman of Sea Island Beach, California, in
1932. Flown as a two-seater, the
streamlining of the wheels rather than a
full enclosure as a 'spat' or 'pant', is a
feature not seen on any of the racing Moths
based in Europe. This shot was taken at
Floyd Bennett Field in 1934. Vincent Berinati

DH.60G, built by the students, was registered G-ABTS to the Company on their behalf in February 1932. Completely standard apart from a change in the length of the Autoslot's rear links, made at the suggestion of Handley Page, which increased the gap when the slot was open, and the choice of metal interplane struts which were fitted in May, the aircraft qualified for her C of A on 23rd February and was closely followed by a second aircraft, DH.60G G-ABXT (1901), in July. Both aircraft were allocated to the School's own Flying Club based at Stag Lane and were operated for the cost of the petrol, the students maintaining the aircraft themselves. Instruction was given by staff pilots drawn from the de Havilland School of Flying until Geoffrey de Havilland Jnr qualified as an instructor and took over the task on a full-time basis in May.

Just after lunch on Thursday 22nd September 1932, G-ABTS suffered a restriction to her aileron controls and spiralled down onto the roof of a house in Whitchurch Gardens, Edgware. The pilot, Peter Wright, was uninjured but the aircraft was badly damaged. The control restriction had been caused by a slide rule which was discovered on the cockpit floor and re-united with its owner. The aircraft was used as a repair specimen and returned to service in June 1933. A third DH.60G, G-ACAM (1915), was completed in January 1933 at which time G-ABXT was sold to two South African students, Stanley Pearce and Thomas Fisher, who left Stag Lane on 20th March and flew her home to Cape Town.

The construction of two further DH.60G airframes was started in 1934 but, following a period of storage, they were not completed until 1938 and then sold by the Company as standard commercial transactions. No 1924 was registered G-AFDZ on behalf of the Newcastle upon Tyne Aero Club and No 1925 went to the Canterbury Aero Club in New Zealand as ZK-AGU.

The appetite for globe-trotting by Moth continued unabated during the year. Arthur Lewin flew to Nairobi from Heston in DH.60G G-ABGN (1814) in January, but

during the return flight in May 1933 his aeroplane was blown out of her pickets at Malakal and wrecked. Henry Sears flew eleven hours solo at Reading in September 1930 before returning to his home in Nairobi by ship, taking DH.60G G-ABFD (1800) with him. He logged 300 hours in Africa before flying back to England in February 1932. Miss Irene Sewell started on a solo flight from Gatwick purely to visit friends in Transjordan on 23rd February in DH.60M G-AACD (340), and was weatherbound in Naples for nearly a fortnight, but she completed the 3,500 mile trip without incident arriving in Amman on 19th March.

Rab Richards and Lady Isabel Chaytor left Lympne on 5th March in DH.60G G-ABSD (1883) on a leisurely trip to Australia where

DH.60G CH-325 was delivered to her owner in Zurich in November 1931 and in March 1932 collided with trees at Waldenburg. She was repaired at Dubendorf and collided with power cables at Liestal in March 1933. Via Chris Tucker

'Bee' Chaytor had arranged to deliver lectures on British fashion. The flight was interrupted in Bulgaria when G-ABSD stood on her nose and broke her propeller when landing on the snow-covered aerodrome at Sofia which, prior to arrival overhead, had been signalled as clear. Due to illness she left the aircraft in Calcutta and Richards carried on alone, reaching Australia on 25th April. By October, Richards had accumulated 200 hours in the aeroplane, but running short of funds was forced to sell her. During the delivery flight from Melbourne to Sydney, the uninsured aircraft crashed into a hillside during an attempt at a forced landing near Bungendore, NSW, on 13th October. The wrecked airframe together with the engine from DH.60G VH-UJL (985), destroyed by a storm in 1931, were acquired by Nancy Bird and rebuilt by Nancy and Wally Kuhl. Registered VH-UTN in April 1935, at the end of the year the aircraft was traded against a new Leopard Moth supplied by the de Havilland Company at Mascot.

Charles Scott, one-time holder of both out and return records between England and Australia, had lost both by November 1931 but believed he still had the mental and physical capacity to recapture one or the other using the DH.60M VH-UQA (1566) gifted to him by Lord Wakefield. Retaining her Australian markings, Scott had toured Great Britain with the aeroplane following his arrival from Wyndham on 5th June 1931, and he made arrangements to have her overhauled at Brooklands during the winter, planning to leave for Australia on 19th March 1932.

The day before the intended start, Scott flew his DH.60 from Stag Lane to Lympne in company with Jim Mollison in Puss Moth G-ABKG. Mollison also was planning to leave early the next morning for another attempt on the Cape record. The two pilots had once been good friends, but intense rivalry gradually developed into jealousy, and, by the time of the MacRobertson Races in 1934, verged on hatred.

The foggy morning of 19th March proved totally unsuitable for flying and both pilots returned to their hotel to discover the newspapers were full of stories of Mollison's romance with Amy Johnson. Mollison took cover for several days and eventually left Lympne on 24th March to break Gordon Store's record. Scott needed better condi-

The Company designed the DH.60GIII principally for Club training and the sporting pilot who enjoyed open cockpit flying, and the prototype, G-ABUI, first flew in March 1932. Essentially, the aircraft was a wooden Moth fuselage with all the benefits of an inverted Gipsy III engine, and was an attempt to hold off competition from rival manufacturers, especially Avro. de Havilland

tions and delayed his departure until the next full moon on 19th April. His flight was plagued with strong headwinds and the last sector from Koepang was flown mostly above cloud so that when he made his descent he was well off track, eventually landing at Litchfield to regain his record by a little under six hours. Scott and VH-UQA returned to England by sea and continued a round of what Scott considered to be a most boring season of touring and joyriding. The aircraft was re-registered G-ACOA, but not until April 1934, when she was listed to the professional display business, Air Pageants Ltd, at Croydon.

A requirement to improve the structure and attachment of wing ribs had been mandated by the Air Ministry in January 1930 when some rib slats were doubled and a pen steel clip introduced for attachment of the top rib boom to the front spar. With the gradual increase in maximum all-up weights, the Air Ministry saw fit in May 1932 to issue Ground Engineer's Notice No 22 which required that in addition to a similar clip, now introduced for attachment of the top boom to the rear spar, the bottom flanges and webs were to be bound with waxed, braided cord at the rib booms adjacent to the inner faces of both spars. In addition, the wing fabric was to be bound to the top booms over the whole length between the same spar faces. The modification was mandated for all DH.60X, 60G and 60M types whose Certificates of Airworthiness permitted operation in the Normal Category at 1,750 lb or at 1,550 lb for Aerobatics. The work could only be achieved with the wings removed and at a considerable cost in time and effort and disruption to the surface finish.

Hereward de Havilland had raced DH.60X G-AUGX (425) as a single-seater in the Australian Aerial Derby in 1928 and, now registered VH-UGX, she was acquired by James Weir of Sydney in August 1931. On 6th June 1932, Weir left Darwin en-route to England but he was taken ill in Karachi where the flight was abandoned. VH-UGX was returned to Australia and sold to Derick Rawnsley who left Darwin on 7th February 1934 and flew her to Lympne over a period of 7¾ days. In England the aircraft took up residence as G-ACXF but during the war she was broken up for spares.

In June the RAAF donated six Cirrus-engined Moths to civilian aero clubs, having first taken on charge new DH.60Gs as replacements, an aeroplane type that was well liked and 'completely aerobatic and viceless' in the primary training role. At the Richmond Air Pageant in 1934 the RAAF demonstrated a method of retrieving a stranded aircraft by towing one into the air behind a Wapiti. With its propeller removed, the Moth cast off at a suitable height and performed a series of 'evolutions' before touching down safely. Liking the aeroplane too, the Royal Air Force established its own Flying Club at Hatfield in 1933, and in 1935 was gifted two ex-Service DH.60M Moths from Cardington on 4th July, K1202 (1514) and K1828 (1661), which were civilianised as G-ADLJ and G-ADLK respectively.

The 13 British light aeroplane clubs which enjoyed subsidies under the Air Ministry's scheme, last revised in July 1927, were subject to further review in 1932 when again emphasis was placed on the number of pilots trained. The next review on 1st April 1937 was anticipated to last for five years but, due to the European political situation, was actually revised in 1938 with the introduction of the Civil Air Guard (CAG). Thousands of enthusiastic members were charged from as little as two shillings and six pence an hour, and the last of the Moth family, the DH.94 Moth Minor, was ordered in hundreds.

It was inevitable that the inverted Gipsy III engine should have been installed in a DH.60 Moth and no great surprise that the metal training type was chosen to be the first recipient in June 1931. This line of development was carefully and deliberately pursued in compliance with changing military specifications and the prospect of substantial orders. There was little further potential in the basic civilian DH.60G and DH.60M models and, although plans for a Metal Moth with a fuselage similar to the Tiger Moth, straight wings and a Gipsy III engine were drawn up under the designation DH.60MIII, there is no evidence to suppose an example was ever built. However, the DH.60MIII was included in the list of types to be approved when Demec navigation lamps were investigated in January 1933.

Following the successful launch of the DH.82 Tiger Moth in October 1931, and with growing threats to the DH.60 from competitors for the private owner market, not least from the Company's own DH.80A Puss Moth, de Havilland chose to offer a new sporting DH.60 model for those who enjoyed open cockpit flying, choosing to combine the well-proven, and cheaper, wooden airframe with the Gipsy III engine. The result was what the Company first called the Mk III Gipsy Moth but which was marketed as the DH.60GIII (for Gipsy III engine). The prototype aircraft, G-ABUI (5000), first flew in March 1932. The pilot may have been either Jack Tyler or John Rae as Hubert Broad was still in South America and Captain de Havilland was flying a Puss Moth in Africa. The Captain's first flight in the new model was not until 21st April, after his return to Stag Lane.

Tragedy struck the following week when Jack Tyler was killed. He was making a routine test flight on a Moth on 28th April when the wings on one side folded back due to an imperfectly fitted locking pin. His place was taken by Bob Waight who had joined the Company as an apprentice in 1928 and qualified for A and C Ground Engineers' licences in March 1931. He learned to fly that year and gained his A licence within a month of starting. When Hubert Broad left the Company in the autumn of 1935 following differences of opinion about the DH.87

Arthur Marshall's family business was motor cars but he bought a second-hand Moth, Wally Hope's 1928 King's Cup-winning DH.60G G-EBYZ, and started a flying school at his home at Fen Ditton, Cambridge. The business grew to become one of the biggest privately-owned aerospace companies in the world.
Marshall Aerospace

Hornet Moth, Bob Waight took over the position of Chief Test Pilot at Hatfield.

Following resumed flight trials with G-ABUI on 5th May the new Moth was certificated at 1,750 lb in the Normal Category and 1,550 lb for Aerobatics, the same authorisation as the basic DH.60G and DH.60M. But there were many subtle changes to the structure. The bottom front spar root fittings used on standard Moth wings were modified and new wing locking bolts introduced. The centre section bracing wires, front and rear, were extended through the fuselage cowl to anchor points at the top longerons. In all other respects the cabane structure was standard DH.60. The Gipsy III engine was mounted in a pair of steel tube bearer frames, identical with those of the DH.82 Tiger Moth, which projected forward from the fireproof bulkhead where the fuselage was described as being 'cut off' when compared with the normal wooden structure. Oil and petrol systems were the same as the Tiger Moth and Moth, with the fuel control

cock mounted within easy reach on the centre section, where it could be clearly seen.

The greatest basic changes were in the structure of the fuselage, with the bottom cross members and some fittings in the area of the cockpits being re-designed or replaced by parts carried across from the DH.60M. The 3-ply tray in the luggage locker was replaced by an aluminium unit and the front parachute-type seat was modified to suit the position of the control box in relation to the seat bulkhead. The tail end of the wooden fuselage, described previously as 'knife edge' was boxed with ply and carried a steerable skid built up from mainly Puss Moth parts, while the entire tail unit was different only in minor respects from the Tiger Moth, which also donated undercarriage and control system. The trademark star, which mostly had been applied to a front or centre fuselage position on DH.60 Moths, was, on the DH.60GIII model, placed, as a distinguishing feature, squarely in the middle of the fin.

The position of the exhaust manifold removed all limitations on the arrangement for cockpit doors and the DH.60GIII was fitted with four doors of equal size, hinged on the top longeron. Surprisingly, after so much historical evidence to support its worth, a full harness was not included in either cockpit, only a lap-strap which, in view of the promoted aerobatic potential of the aeroplane, was an arrangement greeted with some reservations.

The Company's backing for the 1932 King's Cup Air Race, run over two days from Brooklands on 8th and 9th July, was partly directed at Wally Hope's DH.83 Fox Moth G-ABUT. For publicity and trial as much as racing purposes, the aircraft had been fitted with the third production model of a new engine. Known initially as the Gipsy IIIA, by comparison with its forebear the unit had been increased in capacity from 5.7 litres to 6.12 litres and the maximum power output from 120hp to 130hp. The engine was first offered with an overhaul life of 450hr rising to 750hr the following year and eventually to double that, figures quite unprecedented for the time. In view of the potential military business it was considered that a name rather than a number should be adopted. To call it Gipsy Major was both logical and appropriate and future engines with names beginning with 'G' became traditional within the Company. Wally Hope's Fox Moth came home in first place to complete a historic trio of King's Cup wins, all in Moths.

Eight DH.80A Puss Moths took part in the 1932 Race and the highest placed, Peggy Salaman's G-ABLG, was third. Unlike previous occasions, only five of the 42 starters were DH.60G Moths, including the Company's other interest, Hubert Broad's entry sponsored by Lord Wakefield. The fourth DH.60GIII, G-ABVW (5003), was fitted with an experimental Gipsy III EX engine producing 133hp, with stub exhausts and Fairey Reed metal propeller of 5.3ft pitch and 7ft diameter. The aircraft had been subjected to the usual cleaning-up operations, fitted with a streamlined headrest and a

DH.60GIII G-ABVW was fitted with a Gipsy IIIA engine (prototype Gipsy Major) and flown by Hubert Broad in the 1932 King's Cup Air Race. The aircraft was later sold to Amy Johnson and then to Laurie Lipton, who raced her with great success until 1936 when she was sold. Richard Riding

DH.60G G-AAJO was flown from England to Australia by Stan White, who arrived at Darwin in October 1934 amidst a situation of high alert for the receipt of aircraft taking part in the MacRobertson International Air Races. Having reached Sydney, G-AAJO was towed to the city docks from where she was shipped to Stan White's native New Zealand. Via Jerry Chisum

Having qualified as a doctor in England, Cyril Payne acquired a second-hand DH.60G, G-EBZR, the aircraft used by the de Sibours for their world tour in 1928, and flew her back to his home in Bulawayo, Southern Rhodesia, where she became **VP-YAM.** DH Moth Club Archive

straight-axle racing undercarriage which, due to the tyre pressure factor of the 3in by 17in wheels, was limited to an all-up weight of 1,480 lb. She carried a nine gallon centre section tank and with the front cockpit faired over, a 27 gallon tank in place of a seat, both tanks supplying fuel directly to the engine via twin pumps. G-ABVW was fifth home at an average speed of 133mph. There was satisfaction at Stag Lane to learn that 22 starters were powered by Gipsy engines, that none had retired through mechanical failure, and Gipsy-powered aircraft filled the first nine positions.

Immediately following the King's Cup, G-ABVW was fitted with a standard Gipsy III engine and flown twice by Captain de Havilland on 12th July in preparation for sale to Amy Johnson who named her *Jason 4.* In May 1933 the aircraft was acquired by Laurie Lipton who flew her in a successful racing career over the next three seasons.

Richard Allen bought DH.60M G-AAUS (1477) from the Brian Lewis organisation in July and on 3rd August left Heston for Australia, arriving at Wyndham on 19th September where the letters, almost appropriate to a new Australian resident, were changed to VH-UQT. Following their successful flight to Amman in 1931, Mrs Venetia Montagu and Rupert Belville abandoned a trip to China in DH.60G G-AAJO (1101) in August 1932, after starting from Heston, when permission to over-fly Russia was refused. They opted for an October tour of Indo-China instead. In August 1934 G-AAJO was sold to Stanley White who took off from Heston on 18th September and arrived in Darwin on 27th October, unwittingly becoming enveloped in arrangements for the reception of MacRobertson Races aircraft on their way from Mildenhall to Melbourne. G-AAJO was shipped on to Stan White's native New Zealand and registered ZK-ADT in December. Following general overhaul, the metal propeller used during the flight, now showing signs of stress, was discarded and an attempt made to fit the wooden propeller carried as a spare from England to Australia, lashed to the side of the fuselage, but it was found to have an incompatibility of mounting holes and if needed along the route would have proved quite useless.

The first long-distance flight in a DH.60GIII began from Woodley Aerodrome, Reading, on 31st August when Henry Sear left in VP-KAR (5004), heading for Nairobi. Only a few weeks before, Dr Cyril Payne had flown home from Woodley to Bulawayo in Southern Rhodesia, in his newly acquired DH.60G VP-YAM (844), previously G-EBZR, the de Sibour's 'world-tour' Moth of 1928. Previously, Cyril Payne had been forced to sell his DH.60X Moth VP-YAA (608) in Rhodesia in order to fund studies in London. He bought his new aeroplane to fly home after qualifying as a doctor.

Charles Winters Scott was employed at the School of Forestry in Burma and learned to fly with Phillips and Powis at Woodley where he took delivery of DH.60G G-ABPT (1874) in March 1932. In mid-September, with Mr Aung Baw as passenger, travelling to join the Forestry Service, Scott took off from Woodley and arrived in Rangoon on 10th October having covered 6,815 miles without any problems, travelling against a pre-determined schedule of about six hours flying per day.

During the course of the summer, several DH.60M rear fuselages, particularly those with a high accumulation of hours, were found on inspection to be developing cracks in the lower longerons, close to where the square tubes came together at the rear of the fuselage and were welded to a gusset plate. At first it was believed that individual cases of cracking, suspected to have been caused by fatigue, should be subject to local repair, but in September de Havilland warned that a scheme of modification was to

be mandated whether cracks were evident or not, which required replacement of the entire section of longeron from the tailplane stay tube bracket to the sternpost, a length of about 27in, together with the welding of a new gusset and sternpost brackets, a major exercise.

The Company was anxious to substantiate DH.60GIII data supplied for the use of the Sales Office's 1933 catalogue and on 4th and 5th October, a series of 'full-scale' flight trials were undertaken with DH.60GIII No 5013, loaded up to the maximum 1,750 lb with the aid of 280 lb of lead shot ballast. The aircraft appears not to have achieved much else until December when she qualified for her C of A, and was shipped to India to become VT-ADY with the Kathiawar Flying Club.

DH.60M Seaplane CF-ADC (783) was erected at Mount Dennis for new owner Dougal Cushing of Montreal in May 1929, but in June 1932 she was converted to a landplane, sold to Jacques Hibert and shipped back to England, from where the owner intended to set out on a flight to Australia as part of a world sight-seeing tour. Additional fuel was carried in a 15 gallon tank forward in the front cockpit, an additional 13 gallon tank in the front cockpit and a 7 gallon tank in the rear luggage locker. In an unusual arrangement, fuel from the centre section tank and the rear and middle auxiliary supplies was hand-pumped to the forward tank and gravity-fed directly to the engine from there. With full fuel, a 10 stone pilot and no baggage, the aircraft was 49 lb over the maximum certificated weight.

Hibert left Heston on 12th October and arrived in Darwin on 6th December but four days later, when landing at Cloncurry on the way to Sydney, CF-ADC collided

with goats loose on the airfield. The aircraft was damaged badly enough for the world tour to be abandoned and, having sold the wreck to Qantas, Hibert returned to Canada by ship.

Thomas Guthrie purchased DH.60G Moth Seaplane G-ABJT (1244) in October and the aircraft was delivered by Rex Stocken to his home on the Gare Loch where a hangar and slipway had been constructed. The journey up the east coast of England and Scotland proved to Stocken how few facilities there were to cope with the passage of a privately-owned seaplane and he also expressed his opinion after the experience that, ideally, a light seaplane should be a pusher with a self-starter, water rudders, special protection from corrosion and be so designed that picking up moorings was an easy job. Thomas Guthrie may have shared the opinion as G-ABJT was converted to a landplane and sold to Brooklands Flying Club only seven months later.

The 19-year-old Victor Smith left Cape Town at midnight on 12th November in DH.60G ZS-ADB (1849) and arrived in England 12 days later, only to overturn during a forced landing in Kent on arrival. The aircraft was sold and registered G-ACBU for use by Iona National Airways in Ireland, a company formed by Lady Sophie Heath. Fully recovered from her catastrophic accident in the USA, she retained her title and American citizenship but was now married to George Williams. In May 1934, the aircraft was registered EI-AAW in the name of Lady Heath in Ireland, but crashed in England in November 1935 whilst on service between Dublin and Croydon. Following such a glittering early career, in May 1939, having taken up again her best-known aviation name, Sophie Eliott Lynn fell down the stairs of a London tramcar, fractured her skull and died in a Shoreditch hospital.

The Company closed its 1932 account in profit in spite of a further reduction in business of 25 per cent and a cut in the workforce of almost half. Development of the DH.81 Swallow Moth had been abandoned together with its new 80hp Gipsy IV engine, but the Puss Moth continued to sell and there were growing signs of success for the Tiger Moth, the Fox Moth and the new twin-engined transport aircraft, the DH.84 Dragon Moth.

A scene which says much about London in the early Thirties: Father Christmas, making his way to Selfridges in DH.60G G-AAIV, an aircraft owned by the London Stock Exchange Flying Club, is waylaid by a group of polite young children and what appears to be a huge dog. The carter's horse clip-clops on. Not a car in sight.
Sport and General

The
COLOURFUL WORLD OF DH.60 MOTHS

DH.60G G-AAWO was supplied in June 1930 via de Havilland agent Brian Lewis and C D Barnard of Heston. The aeroplane was used for commercial services in Scotland pre-war and was stored at Inverness between 1939 and 1945. As part of the government's re-organisation of Scottish air services post-war, the aircraft was at one time registered to British European Airways. Currently owned and flown by Nigel and Louise Reid, 'Ah-wo' is based at Lee-on-Solent in company with the family's other DH.60G, G-AAHI. Gordon Bain

DH.60G CH-217 was sold to Switzerland in 1930 and acquired as a rebuildable project from Grenchen by Cliff Lovell in 1976. Registered G-ABEV, she was completed by Ron Souch at Hamble in March 1980. Sold to Brian Woodford's Wessex Aviation and Transport collection in 1985, G-ABEV was photographed on the lawn at Chalmington Manor in Dorset with one of the Collection's Rolls-Royce cars. Gordon Bain

DH.60X Seaplane K-SALF was delivered to Finland by ship in 1927 and demonstrated in the Baltic countries by Hubert Broad. She was registered K-SILA and later OH-ILA to the Air Defence League of Finland. Stored at Tampere during the war she was restored to static condition in 1970 and was later moved to the Central Finland Aviation Museum at Tikkakoski.

DH.60X 503 was delivered to the RCAF in 1928, allocated the 'military' identification G-CYYG in May and issued to the Post Office Department. The aeroplane was transferred into civilian ownership in 1929 and appears to have remained active until 1942. Donated to the Reynolds Pioneer Museum at Wetaskiwin, Alberta, G-CYYG was restored to static condition in 1989 and to full airworthiness in 1993.

DH.60X G-EBWD was purchased new by Hylton Murray-Philipson in 1928 and operated from a field alongside his home at Stobo Castle, Peebles-shire until she was exchanged for DH.60G G-ABMA in 1931. In 1932, G-EBWD was sold by Brooklands Aviation to Richard Shuttleworth for £300 (…one secondhand Cirrus II Aircraft G-EBWD as seen, tried, approved and agreed…) plus a registration fee of one guinea. This photograph was taken on the lawn at the Shuttleworth Mansion, Old Warden Park, on 14 February 1992, 60 years to the day after the Moth was first delivered there. Stuart McKay

DH.60X G-CAUA was registered to International Airways of Canada Ltd at Hamilton in 1928 and remained active until 1941. Following a long period in storage, she was presented to the National Aeronautical Collection at Ottawa and, in 1963, rebuilt to static display condition by employees of the de Havilland Aircraft of Canada plant at Downsview. David Reader

DH.60G Moth No 940 was one of the large batch of aircraft supplied to the Chilean Government in 1929, following a delivery of DH.60X Moths the previous year. She served with the Chilean Air Force as G35 and is currently preserved in a non-flying condition in Santiago. David Reader

Supplied to the RAAF as a DH.60X Seaplane in 1928 and operated by the Training Flight at Point Cook until 1932, A7-13 was converted to a landplane and registered VH-UAU for use by the Civil Aviation Branch. Withdrawn from use in 1951 and stored, the aeroplane was acquired by Sydney Technical College as an instructional airframe and later restored for static display at the city's Power House Museum.

DH.60M CF-AAJ was rebuilt to airworthy condition by Watt Martin at Milton, Ontario, between 1980 and 1989. Originally G-CYXE with the RCAF at High River in 1929, the aircraft is believed to have remained active until 1943. In the summer of 1993, Watt Martin fitted floats and operated CF-AAJ from Lake St John Airport near Toronto. Gordon Bain

DH60X VH-UAO in basic civil markings was caught at The Oaks in New South Wales in October 1988 in company with her younger sister, DH.60M VH-UQV. It was one of VH-UAO's rare visits to the eastern side of the country, having lived in Western Australia exclusively since 1932. Almost exactly a year after this photograph was taken, VH-UQV was badly damaged when she struck power lines near Rutherford but is under active restoration at Mount Waverley. Bruce Winley

Owned by the Aylmore family in Western Australia between 1957 and 2004, VH-UAO had begun life in 1928 as A7-9, a Cirrus-engined DH.60X which served with the RAAF at Laverton, Richmond and Point Cook. She was rebuilt with a Gipsy II engine in 1956 and repainted in her former RAAF colours in 1991.

DH.60X Moth No 627 was supplied as a Seaplane to The Aircraft Operating Company and registered G-EBXU to them in 1928 for aerial survey duties in Brazil. The remains of the aircraft were discovered in 1992 by David Cooper-Maguire, who was largely responsible for rebuilding all the major component parts. Erected by Aero Antiques at Durley and flown in 1998 powered by a Gipsy II engine, the Moth was based at Goodwood, later Findon, and currently is owned by Dr Gilbert Pugh at Stapleford.

The remains of DH.60G Moth EC-AAO were discovered in an olive grove near Lerida in Spain from where they were rescued by Jose Villar and exchanged in 1983 for other Moth structures with John Pothecary in England. EC-AAO was rebuilt at Shoreham, and painted in Spanish Civil War colours as EM-01 flew again in 1986. In 1989 the aircraft was repainted in Spanish military colours as 30-76. Upper photo D M Stroud; Lower photo Gordon Bain

Built by de Havilland Aircraft of Canada in 1930, DH.60M CF-AGX (DHC 127) remained active until late 1952. She was acquired by Stan Reynolds of the Reynolds Pioneer Museum, Wetaskiwin, Alberta and stored until rebuilt to flying condition in 1987. Reynolds Pioneer Museum

Once the racing DH.60G Coupé Moth owned by Sir Nigel Norman at Heston, G-AAHI survived the war after storage at Broadway Garage in Bournemouth. Although some parts were used in the reconstruction of G-AAWO, G-AAHI was rebuilt by John and Nigel Reid at Pulborough between 1993 and 1996 when she was reflown at Lee-on-Solent, her current base. Phil Shaw

Classically painted American-built DH.60GMW, the Wright Gipsy engined G-AAMY, with historic wooden DH.60G Moth G-AAWO, soaking up the sunshine during the de Havilland Moth Club Rally at Woburn Abbey in 1991. Ian Oliver

First registered to Bentley Motors in 1930, DH.60G Moth G-ABAG was operated by a number of private owners before the war. The aeroplane was stored at Witney from 1940 until she was re-certificated in 1946. Owned by the Hull family from 1950 to 1955 and again from 1974, she was donated to the Shuttleworth Collection in 1977 but sold to Bentley dealers P & A Wood in 2001 and is currently airworthy at Audley End. Ian Oliver

The ex-Spanish wreck of EC-AAO was rebuilt in England to become G-AAOR (*AAO Rebuild*), registration letters issued at a time when the CAA had a more understanding attitude in the allocation to period aircraft of previously unused letters. Gordon Bain

DH.60GMW was built at Lowell in 1929 and registered NC237K to Curtiss-Wright Flying Services. She later became N298M and joined the Doyle Cotton Collection in 1978 until sold at auction in 1986. Acquired by Cliff Lovell, the aeroplane was shipped to England and allocated period letters G-AANF. Owned by Ralph Hubbard at Liphook, the Moth forced landed near Popham in 1989 and was badly damaged by fire when the hot exhaust came into contact with dry straw. The airframe was sold to Colin Smith in New Zealand and is under active restoration at Mandeville. Eric Darrah

Based on the remains of DH.60G Moths 1076 and 1293, both of Spanish ancestry, the aircraft was rebuilt by Cliff Lovell and fitted with a Gipsy II engine. Registered with the unallocated letters G-AAMZ, she was reflown in 1994 and in 1998 sold to David Watson, a Tiger Moth owner living in Acton, California. Re-registered N60MZ, the aircraft remains in her British scheme with the American details confined to a position under the tailplane. Cliff Lovell

A trio of DH.60G Moths and a DH.60M being judged for the premier award at the de Havilland Moth Club's Woburn Rally: The Flying Duchess Trophy. The appearance of the large diameter, spoked wheels of DH.60G G-AAMZ, nearest the camera, compared with the air-wheels of the three other aircraft, well illustrates a major advance in wheel and tyre technology. Richard Grundy

DH.60G G-ABDA was impressed into wartime service as an instructional airframe with an Air Training Corps Squadron in Worcestershire. Airframe remains were subsequently located by Ian Castle and by coincidence the original Gipsy II engine fitted to G-ABDA at Stag Lane in 1930 was discovered in store with the Shuttleworth Collection at Old Warden. The airframe was rebuilt by Aero Antiques at Durley and the engine overhauled by Rex Ford at Sywell, where, following completion, the aircraft first flew during the summer of 1998. The Moth was seen there during the visit of American-based Tiger Moth owner Dr John Burson whose offer to buy was accepted. Ian Castle

The aeroplane was packed into a container and shipped to Georgia in December 1999, where she was registered N60GD and based at Gum Creek Airfield, Roopville. During the summer of 2005, the aircraft was offered for sale and following a flying visit by Roy Palmer, returned to England in May. Via Dr John Burson

DH.60G No 13 was built by Morane Saulnier in Paris in 1930 and sold to Switzerland in 1932 where she remained airworthy until 1964 when she was withdrawn from use. Acquired by Ron Souch of Aero Antiques in 1983, restoration began at Old Sarum. Registered with period letters G-AANV, the sole surviving Morane Moth is owned by Richard Seeley and based at Durley.
Gordon Bain

DH60M VH-ULM was active with the Tasmanian Section of the Australian Aero Club from 1929 to 1941 and with the Royal Victorian Aero Club and many different private owners between 1944 and 1971. In 1977 the aircraft was acquired by Joe Drage and exhibited at the Wangaratta Airworld Museum until closure in 2002 when she was sold to Mrs Louise Redmond of Brisbane for restoration to airworthy condition. Darryl Cott

The sole survivor of the batch of 32 DH.60X Moths contracted for manufacture by the Larkin Aircraft Supply Co of Coode Island, Melbourne in 1929 is No 22, originally supplied to the RAAF as A7-44, issued free of charge to the Royal Queensland Aero Club in 1944 and registered VH-AFN. The aircraft was sold to the USA in 1968 and registered N168G, an identity retained following resale to the Early Birds Foundation at Lelystad in The Netherlands, where the aircraft is maintained in airworthy condition. Barry Dowsett

Currently fitted with a Cirrus Hermes II engine, this DH.60X was built in Finland's State Aircraft Factory as No 8 and delivered to the Finnish Air Force in 1929. Due largely to his Finnish ancestry, in 1975, the aeroplane was sold to Ken Orrman in Shepparton, Victoria, Australia, where she was registered VH-SSC and rebuilt to airworthy condition by May 1979.
Ken Orrman

G-ABDX, flying in company with DH.60G Moths G-AAHI and G-AAWO in humid summer conditions in England, watched as both other aircraft suffered engine semi-failure and forced landed in a field near Lasham. Idling overhead, G-ABDX experienced precisely the same symptoms, believed to have been the result of carburettor icing. Discretion being the greater part of valour, G-ABDX was folded up, placed on the back of a car transporter and safely returned to her base at Durley while her companions, after consultation, continued on their voyage. Michael Souch

Plymouth Airways of New Hampshire was the first owner of Moth Aircraft Corporation's DH.60GM No 125, manufactured in 1930. After an accident in 1932 the remains were stored until 1982 when they were acquired by Cliff Lovell in England. As a project registered G-AAMX, the parts were sold to John Parkhouse who undertook the complete rebuild at his home in Harpenden. G-AAMX flew from Hatfield in the hands of Desmond Penrose in August 1987. Following the death of John Parkhouse in 1994, the aircraft was donated to the RAF Museum and displayed at Cosford before moving to the 'Milestones of Flight' Hall at Hendon in 2003. Left photograph via author; Lower photograph Gordon Bain

Built in the USA in 1930, Moth Aircraft Corporation DH.60GM No 157 was active with two American owners from the Sixties until sold to Cliff Lovell in England in 1982. Registered G-AAVJ, the aircraft was rebuilt by Ron Souch for Robin Livett and was airworthy by February 1985. Sold at auction in 1993, the Moth was delivered to Mrs Rita Sholton in Fairbanks, Alaska where original registration N573N was restored in August 1994. Richard Riding

Hamish Moffatt's interest in Bugattis and other mechanical devices with a vintage flavour, led to his purchase of DH.60GM N939M from Bert Brooks of Falls Church, Virginia, USA, in 1985. The aircraft was overhauled by Cliff Lovell and period registration G-AADR allocated in June 1986. The aircraft is maintained in an airworthy condition on a private airstrip in Herefordshire. Peter Henley

Before everybody realised the speed potential of a DH.80A Puss Moth, de Havilland Chairman Alan Butler arranged for the design of a special Racing DH.60M Moth whose most obvious difference from a standard aircraft was the arrangement of the centre section. Registered G-AAXG in May 1930 the aircraft was sold to France, then returned to England in 1933 before shipment to New Zealand. Currently owned by Gerald Grocott, the original specification has been largely retained apart from operating in a two-seat configuration. Gordon Bain

DH.60G Moth G-ABJJ was delivered to a private owner at Castle Bromwich in 1931. She survived active war service and in 1946, with a new Certificate of Airworthiness, was offered for sale at £450. In 1956 she was acquired by aircraft dealers R K Dundas and in 1962 was sold to George Neal, Chief Test Pilot of the de Havilland Aircraft of Canada at Downsview, Toronto, to whom she was registered CF-AAA. The aircraft is currently owned by Watt Martin at Milton. Gordon Bain

The green and silver painted DH.60G G-ABEV was the ideal vehicle to portray Amy Johnson's Gipsy Moth *Jason*, G-AAAH, when the BBC shot a feature film, *Amy,* at Sywell in 1984. Filming coincided with several days of blustery wind conditions and for the comfort of the crew and safety of the aeroplane, Mr Radcliffe, 'Theatrical and Exhibition Transporter' came to the rescue, acting as a portable windbreak. Stuart McKay

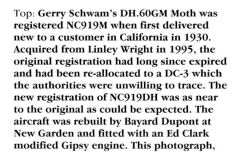

Top: **Gerry Schwam's DH.60GM Moth was registered NC919M when first delivered new to a customer in California in 1930. Acquired from Linley Wright in 1995, the original registration had long since expired and had been re-allocated to a DC-3 which the authorities were unwilling to trace. The new registration of NC919DH was as near to the original as could be expected. The aircraft was rebuilt by Bayard Dupont at New Garden and fitted with an Ed Clark modified Gipsy engine. This photograph,** taken soon after the Moth was airworthy, was used on posters to publicise the 2001 Air Show in support of the Colonial Flying Corps Museum. Via Gerry Schwam

Above left: **A glorious summer day in good company and with every reason to feel proud of the achievements of an age when slide rules and glue pots were of primary importance. A vision of the past and the present at the de Havilland Moth Club's Woburn Rally in 2004.** Mike Jerram

Above right: **De Havilland agent Sir Malcolm Campbell (London) 1927 Ltd sold DH.60G G-AALY to Edouard Bret in France in 1929 and in 1932 the aircraft was resold to make way for a DH.80A Puss Moth. As F-AJKM she was last heard of in Cannes in July 1939. A sufficiency of parts was recovered to Durley to permit Aero Antiques to restore G-AALY and her owner Kevin Fresson to take the Flying Duchess Trophy for Concours at Woburn in 2002.** Richard Riding

Delivered to Switzerland in 1933 as CH-353 and later HB-OBA, this DH.60G spent most of the next 27 years at Lausanne where she was photographed in 1960 in company with DH.85 Leopard Moth HB-OSE.
Erich Gandet

Edward Eves acquired HB-OBA and, as G-ATBL, flew her home to Sywell in April 1965. She was the first DH.60 restoration completed by Cliff Lovell and qualified for a Certificate of Airworthiness in 1971. When owned by Michael Vaisey in the early Eighties and based at RAF Henlow, the aircraft was marked G-AALG for use in a BBC documentary film to represent the DH.60M flown by Jean Batten in an attempt on the England-Australia record in 1933.

Painted green and silver and currently owned by Captain John Greenland, G-ATBL was delivered to him at Hatfield Aerodrome, where his father had been a de Havilland test pilot, early in 1993 and was flown home to his private airstrip in Wiltshire. The aircraft has been a regular visitor to the Woburn Rallies where she is seen touching down on the southerly runway heading in 2002. Barry Dowsett

Originally delivered to the Danish Army Air Corps in the last days of 1929, DH.60M No 1446 was sold into the civilian market in 1933 and in October 1942 was flown by Lieutenant Peer Perch during an escape from Jylland to England. Following wartime storage the aircraft was overhauled at Cambridge in 1946 and returned to Denmark. Following an accident in about 1956, major component parts were delivered to Southampton for reconstruction by Aero Antiques for new owner Derek Ellis. The aircraft was painted in the distinctive colours of National Flying Services (NFS) and registered G-AANL.

The DH.60GIII/Moth Major was an attempt to win back pilots of a sporting disposition in an age when club and private ownership was being directed towards cabin aircraft with modern conveniences. Powered by the Gipsy III and later the Gipsy Major engine (hence the model designation), it was rather too late to divert public opinion, although in a modified form the wooden fuselage allied with upgraded Tiger Moth wings became the successful Queen Bee target aircraft. G-ABZB had been sold to Sweden in 1939 and the crash-damaged remains were repatriated by Bob Ogden in 1980. Following some major restoration work the project was sold to Brian Morris and Richard Earl in 1997 and completed to prize-winning concours standard by The Newbury Aeroplane Company in 1998. Mike Jerram

Thought to be a possible competitor in the 1934 MacRobertson International Air Races, Moth Major G-ACNS was never formally entered and eventually was owned amongst others, by British Airways and the Hampshire Aeroplane Club. In 1940 the aircraft was sold to South Africa but in May 2000 was restored to Ron and Dianne Souch at Southampton. J D Gretton

Moth Major No 5078 was delivered to Basel, Switzerland, in 1934 as CH-348 and later HB-UPE, and in 1952 moved to Lausanne with the Aero Club de Suisse. Twenty years later she was acquired by the Lausanne based Groupe Avions Historique, under whose ownership the aeroplane paid a visit to the de Havilland Moth Club Rally at Woburn Abbey in 1999. David McIntosh

DH.60GM Moth G-AAMY is fitted with a RH rotation Wright-built Gipsy engine and fuel tank fabricated from flat panels, basic differences which expose her roots as American. In this setting one might suppose she was on location during her starring role in the film *Out of Africa*, but the photograph was taken in New Zealand in 2004 when G-AAMY was one of a number of British-based Moths shipped south for a major air rally. Via Henry Labouchere

1933 TO INFINITY

BY 1933, although much of the growth and development of the basic DH.60 had been wrung out of the design, there were still corners to explore. DH.60M K1864 (1604) was withdrawn from RAF Communications duties in September and sent to Martlesham Heath for tests with mass-balanced ailerons, an exercise which was to create much excitement when the bomb-equipped Tiger Moth was spun. Business confidence also returned and Stag Lane's workforce was increased to about 1,200, all of whom contributed towards the end of year's healthy gross profit of over £100,000.

In spite of attracting interest and attention from many parts of the world, sales of the DH.60GIII were very disappointing. The Gipsy Major was offered as an alternative engine from February 1933 and in this configuration the type was still referred to as the DH.60GIII but now carried a name: Moth Major. To enhance the sales potential the Company introduced what they termed the 'Tourist Model' in July. Apart from more comfortable seating based on adaptors for the parachute seat pan, Puss Moth cushions, back rests and cowling rolls, the doors of the first demonstrator, G-ACHH (5026), had been redesigned to incorporate higher and sculpted top edges in an attempt to reduce the inevitable draught which flowed into an open cockpit. This process was aided by a new style of windscreen frame, but the combination of doors and screen had an adverse effect as accessibility to the engine switches was hampered. The matter was not considered to be serious enough to warrant a mandatory change but de Havilland agreed to improve matters in respect of subsequent aircraft embodying similar modifications.

Maurice Wilson planned to fly his DH.60G G-ABJC to India, and then on to Mount Everest, crash-landing on the side of the mountain and completing the ascent to the summit alone and without oxygen. His training included walking circuits of Stag Lane Aerodrome. The plan was not approved but Wilson did fly to India where the Moth was sold. He subsequently disappeared during his single-handed climb, but a tent and diary discovered on the mountain proved he had made remarkable progress. A J Jackson Collection

In January, Lindsay Everard had a retractable 4in Harley landing-light installed in the front cockpit of his DH.60GIII G-ACBX (5020), positioned in the floor between the parallel arms of the rudder bar support box and operated by an arrangement of Bowden cables from the rear cockpit. In August 1933, DH.60GIII PH-AJI (5040) was supplied to a Dutch advertising agency, fitted with navigation lights, Holt flares, provision for lighting leads for illumination of adverts painted on the airframe and fuselage attachments for banner towing. ZS-ADF (5021), scheduled for the South African Company at Baragwanath in April, was fitted with an Eclipse self-starter, although it had to be wound up from outside the aircraft by hand.

The Gipsy III engine option was dropped altogether from September 1933, but sales did not improve in spite of enthusiastic reviews of the aircraft's lively performance on 130hp, and enthusiastic promotion from the late autumn of 'the 1934 Model' with a reduction in price to £695.

Flight Lieutenant David McIntyre flew the Marquess of Douglas & Clydesdale's DH.60GIII G-ABZK (5012) from Heston to India in February in support of the Houston-Mount Everest Expedition. The aircraft was badly damaged by gales in India in March but was repaired and flown back to England in May. Flying in the opposite direction, in DH.60G G-ABJC (1825), was Maurice Wilson, a member of the London Aeroplane Club, who had formulated a plan to crash land his Moth as near to the summit of Everest as he could manage and climb the rest of the way unaided. His applications to the various interested authorities seeking approval of the idea were all rejected, but Wilson flew to India anyway where he sold the aircraft, and disappeared during a solo assault on the summit, leaving just a diary in a small tent to mark his passing.

Alan Cobham, never far from the innovative face of aviation throughout his entire life, had established a company based at Ford in Sussex, which was experimenting with the prospects of refuelling aircraft in mid-air. The prize was a non-stop flight from England to Australia and, early in the spring of 1933, trials were flown over the south coast involving a DH.9 acting as mock-tanker aircraft and a DH.60G, chartered from the Rollason Aviation Company, as receiver. Flying the Moth behind and below the DH.9, alongside a suitably weighted trailing hose, the end of which would, in service, be fitted with a nozzle ready for capture by a crew member bravely positioned in the receiving aircraft, the aim was primarily to determine

Victor Dorée's DH.60M G-AALG was wrecked during a forced landing in India during Jean Batten's first record attempt to Australia. The aircraft was returned to England at a cost of £75 when the remains were sold to Brooklands Aviation for £25, repaired and re-sold to a private owner in Budapest. Victor Dorée

For a further attempt on the Australia record in 1934, Jean Batten acquired DH.60M G-AARB with the assistance of £400 donated by Lord Wakefield. Victor Dorée gifted all the long-range tanks salvaged from G-AALG, which were on board when this photograph was taken at Seletar in May 1934, outbound from Lympne to Darwin. Via Desmond Penrose

Thompson, a 22-year-old Australian, in DH.60GIII Moth Major G-ACUC (5084).

James Woods left Broome, Western Australia, on 7th July 1933 flying DH.60M VH-UPD (1558), in an attack on Jim Mollison's record to England. The aircraft was fitted with an auxiliary tank in the front cockpit and a canopy over the rear and arrived at Croydon six weeks later, on 17th August, having suffered from bad weather and technical delays, including an undercarriage collapse on take-off from Bandar Abbas. James Woods announced his intention of flying VH-UPD back to Australia in about eight days, aided by his wife acting as second pilot, but the aircraft was eventually shipped home and sold.

The 1933 King's Cup Air Race was run from Hatfield on the day after James Woods began his long journey. The course was three legs of about 200 miles each, starting and finishing at Hatfield, plus another of similar length for eight finalists. Only two DH.60s were entered, the GIII G-ABVW of Laurie Lipton and GIII Moth Major G-ACCW (5022) of his racing arch-rival, Richard Westenra. Amongst the other 33 entrants, seven were flying DH.80A Puss Moths and Hubert Broad was in a DH.84 Dragon. Geoffrey de Havilland was the winner in the new DH.85 Leopard Moth G-ACHD, his favourite amongst all the Moths.

Once Hatfield Aerodrome had been opened in 1930, there was little doubt that flying activities at Stag Lane would cease. Notice came just before the King's Cup that the greater part of the old Edgware aerodrome had been sold for £105,000 for house building, although the Works was to be retained indefinitely, principally as an engine factory. Other work in hand gradually would be transferred to the new facilities at Hatfield. All flying, other than for the benefit of the Company, ceased in September 1933 and the Air Ministry licence was withdrawn from 5th January 1934. The London Aeroplane Club was purchased by the Company as a business concern and all its assets transferred to Hertfordshire where

the length of hose needed for safe and practical deployment. The trials were successful and in the long run laid the foundation for a new strategy in military aviation.

Jean Batten learned to fly at Stag Lane in 1929 and on 9th April 1933 left Lympne for Australia. She was flying DH.60M G-AALG (1411), still painted in the Guards' colours carried when the aircraft was owned by The Prince of Wales, since bought and loaned to Jean Batten by her friend Victor Dorée. The flight ended near Karachi on 16th April as the result of engine failure and a crash landing which caused considerable damage.

With the assistance of Lord Wakefield, in 1934 Jean Batten acquired DH.60M G-AARB (1412), a veteran of flights to, around and home from Transjordan, and she took off from Lympne on 22nd April, again bound for Australia. Due to unexpectedly strong headwinds, G-AARB ran out of fuel in the

pitch dark and pouring rain over the centre of Rome. In the daylight it was seen that the forced landing had been made between a forest of wireless masts and cables. To ensure any chance of a record, Jean Batten flew G-AARB back to England to begin again. She arrived on 6th May and left Lympne two days later, arriving in Darwin after a flight of almost 15 days. She shipped the aircraft to her native New Zealand but in 1935 returned to Australia and flew back to Croydon, landing on 29th April, having endured poor weather and technical problems for most of the way. Jean Batten became the first woman to have achieved, amongst other records, an out-and-return solo journey and her 1935 flight is also credited as the last by a DH.60 Moth between the two countries. The last from England to Australia was flown in 44 days between September and November 1934 by Miss Freda

private owners and new members were encouraged to join its sociable surroundings, leaving the de Havilland School of Flying to concentrate on contract work for the RAF Reserve. The displaced Club membership found its own level, either moving to Hatfield or dividing itself between the rival attractions of Heston, Brooklands, Broxbourne, Hanworth or Woodley. From the beginning, it was clear that the new London Aeroplane Club was to be a showcase for the Company and when the Club's four DH.60G Moths arrived at Hatfield from Stag Lane, they were soon withdrawn from use and sold, immediately replaced by Tiger Moths, supplemented by a Puss Moth and other Moths as time went on.

Harold Evans flew DH.60GIII Moth Major G-ACII (5036), the sixth de Havilland aeroplane he had owned, from Heston to Karachi in September 1933, and declared that he was unlikely to make any further long-distance flights in connection with his business interests 'while the air traveller's life was made such a burden to him'. Evans was complaining about the rising level of bureaucracy which was now attaching itself to international air travel and the needless amount of paperwork littered with inappropriate questions. Similar frustration was experienced by de Havilland's Portuguese agent, Carlos Bleck, who, on 19th February 1934, left Lisbon in DH.60GIII Moth Major CS-AAI (5053), to fly to Goa, the Portuguese colony on the west coast of India. The aircraft had been prepared at Hatfield with long-range tanks and a Fairey Reed propeller and the leading edges of the lower wings were faced with ply. Bleck arrived in Goa on 5th March, having averaged 105mph over 62 hours' flight time. Like Harold Evans he was dismayed by the growing bureaucracy, and complained to the Portuguese Chargé d'Affaires in Alexandria that Customs were demanding that he pay 'import duties' before allowing him to transit Egypt.

There were no international complications for the 21-year-old Ted Harvie and Miss Trevor Hunter who, in a single day on

Friday 1st December, flew DH.60G ZK-ABP (1250) the 1,168 miles from North Cape to Bluff, the entire length of New Zealand, in a flying time of 16 hours 10 minutes. They started from Kaitaia at 2.00am and landed at Invercargill as the sun went down just before 8.00pm. Harvie had only qualified for his pilots' licence in June and within a fortnight, on 12th July, had set a New Zealand altitude record by climbing a Western Federated Flying Club Moth to 18,400ft in one hour and twenty minutes.

From March 1934, Dr Clyde Fenton was engaged as a self-piloting doctor for the Northern Territory Medical Service based at Katherine, servicing an area of half a million square miles of Australia. He borrowed £500 to purchase his first aeroplane, DH.60M VH-UNI (1431), having taught himself to fly and to be a proficient aircraft engineer during his previous post at Wyndham. During the next six years, until he joined the RAAF as a pilot in 1940, Dr Fenton became a leg-

end, flying and breaking and mending and flying again, mostly without any form of authority, a total of four DH.60 Moths, in addition to VH-UNI, DH.60G VH-UJN (987); DH.60M VH-UOI (1478) and DH.60M VH-UQV (783). The government paid him £100 per annum plus a shilling a mile flown to cover expenses, which was insufficient but welcome. He developed a natural instinct for flying at night, for landing in impossibly small paddocks, on roads and tracks, and for carrying seriously ill patients in the front cockpit over huge distances. One remarkable episode was related by Australian Moth historian Bruce Winley:

'In March 1936, Dr Fenton left Darwin in VH-UOI to fly to Swatow in China to visit his mother after receiving news of the death of his sister. With the aid of a local plumber he had installed an auxiliary tank taken from VH-UJN but the Department of Civil Aviation (DCA) suspended the C of A and refused permission for the flight because Dr

An arch-rival of Laurie Lipton on the racing circuit, due to their evenly matched aircraft, was Richard Westenra whose DH.60GIII G-ACCW, was an entrant in the King's Cup Air Race which started at Hatfield in July 1933. DH Moth Club Archive

Stag Lane Aerodrome, March 1933. Twenty-seven aircraft of many types can be seen on the site, which was closed to all club and private flying at the end of the year. The infill of housing between the airfield and the Edgware Road, running horizontally at the top of the picture, eventually encircled the site, stifling any thought of expansion and bringing a chorus of protests from new residents about noise and nuisance.
de Havilland

Fenton had not obtained permits to fly over foreign territory. Undeterred, he left Darwin and flew to Swatow, where he stayed for six weeks. On his return flight the aircraft was impounded at Hong Kong on the presumption of an inspection but Clyde Fenton was anxious to attend a study course on malaria in Singapore and escaped with the aircraft. While over the sea near Macao, the engine lost power and a forced landing was made on a beach. The tappet adjuster on one rocker had come undone releasing the push rod which fortunately was not lost and, after readjustment, the flight resumed. After spending six weeks in Singapore and three in Java, Dr Fenton returned to Australia where the

DCA again demanded an inspection of the aircraft, but he objected on the grounds that it was only six months since the last inspection, and in any case, it was too expensive!'

Although there was concern over some of Clyde Fenton's exploits, officialdom was reluctant to stop his operation, realising that he was providing a valuable and essential service to the people of the Northern Territory and many of the alleged breaches of the regulations could be accounted for by the extreme conditions prevailing at the time.

The Midland Aero Club which had proudly publicised its long and lasting relationship with its original DH.60 Cirrus Moth

G-EBLT (186), a fleet aeroplane since August 1925, bowed to the inevitable in April 1934 when the aircraft was traded-in with the Brian Lewis Company against three new DH.60GIII Moth Majors. G-ACOG, 'OH and 'OI (5070-5072) were handed over in a ceremony at Heston. These three were later joined by G-ACNR (5067) and G-ACTW (5091), also supplied through Brian Lewis, who resold G-EBLT to South Wales Airways. In 1936, whilst operating with the Witney and Oxford Aero Club, an arsonist set fire to her hangar and all the aircraft inside with her were lost.

On Friday 13th April, Frank Hearle called a meeting to discuss future Company plans. It was recognised that with so many types in production or nearly so, the Company was already dealing with a parts inventory of almost 18,000 different items, and an urgent review of the product range was advised. It was suggested, amongst much else, that the Fox Moth should be discontinued as soon as the current supply of components was used up; the Tiger Moth

The Midland Aero Club who had safely and successfully operated DH.60 G-EBLT since 1925, traded her in with the Brian Lewis Company at Heston and upgraded the entire fleet in April 1934, taking on a quartet of new DH.60GIII aircraft fitted with the Gipsy Major engine, and now known as the Moth Major. BAE Systems

Professor J C Cooke's DH.60G Seaplane, VR-SAQ, powered by a Cirrus III engine, was previously G-AADJ with the Singapore Flying Club, and in this shot is seen flying up the East coast of Malaya in 1938. The following year she was converted to a landplane. J C Cooke

should be replaced by a general purpose Advance Trainer and the Moth Major give way to the new DH.87 Hornet Moth, soon to fly from Stag Lane. It was after the good showing of that aeroplane in the 1934 King's Cup that Francis St Barbe admitted to his fellow Directors that the Moth Major was 'on its last legs' in spite of 43 sales having been achieved since Christmas. He was particularly concerned about the emergence of the new Miles Hawk, fitted with a Gipsy Major engine and selling at £750.

Jean Stampe bought a second hand DH.60GIII OO-GUT (5006) in the summer of 1934. Later, as the Company's Belgian agent, he and his colleague Maurice Vertongen visited the Hatfield factory and asked for permission to design their own light biplane which they assured de Havilland would be powered by a Gipsy Major engine. The result was the all-wood, highly aerobatic Stampe SV4.

Although there was some confusion in confirming the definition of particular Rules and Regulations for aircraft entered in the MacRobertson International Air Races from Mildenhall to Melbourne in October, applications were received for a great diversity of aircraft types including a number of different biplane Moths, none of which actually reached the starting line. DH.60GIII Moth Major G-ACNS (5068) was one example. She was flown in Great Britain during the summer of 1934 by an American, Hubert Julian,

At the Copenhagen Aero Show in August 1934, DH.60GIII OY-DAH was displayed under the collective banner of 'England' on a stand organised by the Society of British Aircraft Constructors. Mike Hooks

The Austrian Aero Club was a major customer for the DH.60GIII Moth Major, taking the last off the line. The Club was acting as a front for a Reconnaissance Squadron of the Austrian Air Force. Delivery flights from England had to be carefully routed and were flown by military pilots in civilian clothes who had been furnished with false documents. DH Moth Club Archive

A view of the de Havilland Canada workshops at Downsview in 1935, when the first DH.89 Dragon Rapide was being prepared for Canadian operation on floats. The Company was doing good business by refurbishing Moths, particularly for the RCAF, and substituting metal frames for old wooden fuselages. de Havilland Canada

who had announced his intention of taking part, but never did.

A second DH.60GIII Moth Major G-ACUR (5097) was specially prepared at Hatfield as a Race entry for owner Sydney Jackson. The aircraft was finished as a single seater with a fuel capacity of 58 gallons. She was painted bright red and silver and fitted with stub exhausts, luminous-faced instruments, navigation lights and faired wings that prevented them from being folded. In her completed state with a C of A, G-ACUR had cost £1,000 but was withdrawn from the Race and offered for sale against 'reasonable offers' through Brian Lewis.

Whilst at Lewis' aircraft store at Aldenham, G-ACUR was inspected by the Duchess of Bedford and following an agreement to purchase was flown to Hatfield by Philip

Gordon Marshall on 23rd June, where the de Havilland Service Department converted her to standard two-seat configuration and painted her dark green and silver. Brian Lewis took DH.60G G-ABXR (1905), in part exchange, and subsequently advertised her for sale 'with cockpit heating' at £435. G-ACUR was frequently flown solo by the Duchess from her private aerodrome at Woburn Abbey and by late March 1937 she was on the threshold of her 200th hour solo. To achieve the target she took off from Woburn during the afternoon of Monday 22nd March 1937 for an hour's triangular cross-country to Buntingford and Cambridge, but she never returned. Several days later, interplane struts identified as belonging to G-ACUR were washed up on the east coast.

While Jerry Shaw was in Australia, arranging fuel supplies for MacRobertson Race entrants during a Far East Tour in his capacity as Aviation Manager for Shell, he travelled with Qantas on their scheduled service between Daly Waters and Birdum. He was intrigued to discover that the 40 mile flight was conducted with DH.60G VH-UGW (834), which lived in a grass hangar at Daly Waters and carried her single passenger to connect with a one-coach train which took two days to travel 300 miles to Brisbane.

The Bombay Flying Club at Juhu took Moth Major VT-AFA (5054), in January 1934 and another, VT-AFW (5030), in December. The Club was already well known for its Moth formation tours around the sub-continent, and to Europe, and the Moth Major fleet was boosted in 1935 and 1937 when two more aircraft were added, VT-AGL (5142) and VT-AIO (5091) respectively. The Royal Indian Air Force took a single aircraft, K5055 (5116), for their Initial Training School at Lahore in February 1935.

St Barbe would have been delighted to accept the order from the Spanish Ministry of War for 12 DH.60GIII Moth Majors for use at their Fighter Combat School at Alcala de Henares, Madrid. The contract stipulated that the aircraft, 34-1 to 34-12 (5101-5112), were to be delivered by the end of December 1934. To achieve this, a winter ferry flight was essential and one of the School instructors, George Cox, recruited eleven other Hatfield pilots including Clem Pike, Eddie Fulford, 'Whizzy' King, J A Harris and Peter de Havilland, to leave Hatfield on Christmas Eve. They flew together via Tours and Perpignan before crossing the Pyrenees in marginal weather to land in Madrid on 30th December.

At the end of the year, DH.60X G-AAPH, an aircraft with a Cirrus III engine supplied to National Flying Services (NFS) at Hanworth in 1929, was sold to the locally-based General Aircraft Ltd and fitted with a new power unit developed by the company, the GAL V/4, an inverted Vee engine developing

Before the war, Royal Navy pilots were trained in the art of deck operations by flying Moths, first from marked runways ashore and later from Training Carriers. This picture shows DH.60M J9107, officially assigned to 769 Squadron, Donibristle, in May 1939, but here operating under RAF command from the flightdeck of HMS *Furious* in 1938. DH Moth Club Archive

Service Moths relegated to the status of ground instructional airframe, joined by impressed civil aircraft not considered worthwhile to maintain in airworthy condition, often survived intact to provide 'live' training for newly-recruited aircraft handlers, fitters and riggers. Practical demonstrations of engine starting and running could be provided at minimum cost. This Ground Instructional Airframe, 1593M, based at Cosford from July 1939, was once DH.60M K1901, delivered new to Kenley in 1931. Richard Riding

In semi-skeletal form, this anonymous Cirrus Moth, less the Cirrus engine, was donated to London University as early as November 1935, but origin and fate are unrecorded. Richard Riding

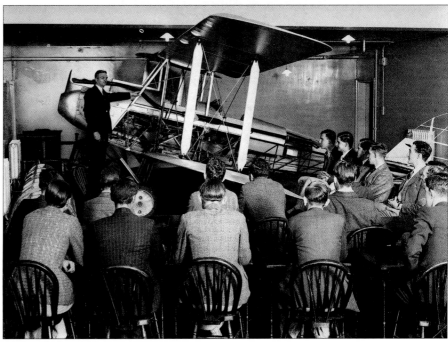

85hp. Flight trials were conducted during the late summer of 1935 but the engine was abandoned the following year. On 19th September, NFS had been involved in demonstrations at Hanworth of the Blanvac exhaust silencer system developed by C G Vokes Ltd. A series of vanes inside the exhaust pipe were arranged to damp out the pulsations of gas and convert them into a steady swirling stream. Static runs were conducted by a Cirrus III-powered DH.60M and flight demonstrations by a Puss Moth, but observers reported they could tell little difference between aircraft fitted with the system and those not.

As was customary, at an early stage in its life, performance figures were calculated for a DH.60GIII operating on a float chassis, but there were no customers until June 1935 when Moth Major No 5139 was due to be fitted with floats at Rochester. The aircraft left Hatfield as a landplane on 15th June for Madrid where she was registered EC-BBD, destined for use by an expedition setting off to study the Upper Amazon. Another coincident Spanish sale was No 5141, supplied to the Navy at Getafe without an engine.

That the Moth Major had survived for so long after Frank Hearle's rationalisation plans of April 1934 may be attributed to adoption of the basic fuselage, much modified, as the core of an Air Ministry requirement for a wireless-controlled target for anti-aircraft gunnery practice. Using a Tiger Moth centre section, wings and tail, and powered by a Gipsy Major engine, the aircraft became the DH.82 Queen Bee.

Four DH.60GIII Moth Majors had been supplied to the Austrian Aero Club in March 1935, OE-TAM and 'TEM (5125-5126) and OE-TIM and 'TOM (5129-5130). These were followed in June and July by six more, OE-TUM (5146), and the last off the line, OE-TAE, 'TEE, 'TIE, 'TOE and 'TUE (5148-5152), to complete a total of 131 production aircraft. At the same time, G-ADIO (2253), a DH.60GIII built by the students of the de Havilland Aeronautical Technical School,

was acquired for demonstration purposes by de Havilland's energetic Austrian agent, Niklaus von Eltz, and registered OE-DIO. In December two aircraft which had been built against an order that subsequently was cancelled, Nos 5144 and 5145, were also sold to Austria as OE-TAT and 'TET.

All the aircraft listed to the Austrian Aero Club were in fact destined for service with the Austrian Army and were flown to Vienna by military pilots furnished with false documents. The last two aircraft avoided heavy snow conditions in Switzerland by operating from Hatfield via Brussels, Frankfurt and Nurnberg to Aspern Aerodrome, Vienna, where they were accepted by No 2 Reconnaissance Squadron on 27th January 1936.

With the exception of a few special orders, the last DH.60M was built at Stag Lane in the spring of 1933 and the last wooden DH.60G in the late summer of the same year. The Aus-

trian order for the Moth Major ended DH.60 type production although the Queen Bee was built in parallel with the Tiger Moth at Hatfield until 1939.

Moths in military service continued in a wide variety of roles aided by the needs of the Expansion Programme. In September and October 1936 an RAF DH.60M based at Northolt was flown over Harrow in a co-operative exercise for anti-aircraft training purposes. News reached the BBC Television Service at Alexandra Palace and on 5th December, flown by Flight Lieutenant J W Donaldson, the Moth repeated its performance in conjunction with the Anti Aircraft and Searchlight Battalion of the Royal Engineers and in so doing, became the first aircraft in the world to feature in a public service television broadcast.

The question of Moth wing structural failures was again raised by the Air Ministry's

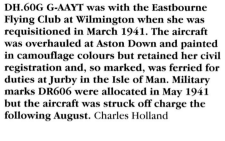

DH.60G G-AAYT was with the Eastbourne Flying Club at Wilmington when she was requisitioned in March 1941. The aircraft was overhauled at Aston Down and painted in camouflage colours but retained her civil registration and, so marked, was ferried for duties at Jurby in the Isle of Man. Military marks DR606 were allocated in May 1941 but the aircraft was struck off charge the following August. Charles Holland

Accident Investigation Branch in 1938 following the accidents to DH.60M K1893 (1643) during an aerobatic routine in Aden, a Tiger Moth in England and a Hornet Moth in New Zealand. They were aware that ten accidents had been reported in ten years and that the first four occurrences, in 1928 to 1932, had been referred to the Aeronautical Research Committee which had abandoned further investigation, having arrived at no firm conclusion. After careful consideration of all the available evidence the new report published in June 1938 could identify no single cause, except to suggest that the most likely explanation was failure as the result of damage caused by a blow, a bad landing or contact of the planes with the ground. In addition, splits had been discovered in spars at the bolt holes of the drag strut fittings. The Board's recommendation was that much greater care should be exercised in the inspection of spars during a C of A examination and particularly after an acci-dent that necessitated a repair of any kind to the wings.

The inevitability of a major war in Europe had caused hundreds of Tiger Moths to be ordered by the Air Ministry, many operating in the colours of Reserve flying training schools administered against military requirements by civilian contractors. The emergence of the Civil Air Guard ensured that the Clubs associated with the scheme were flooded with new recruits, most not eligible for military service, anxious to learn to fly at practically no cost to themselves, and largely in support of the prospective needs of the nation rather than as a social pastime. DH.60 Moths carried much of the burden, as they had done when subsidised flying was introduced in 1925, until September 1939 when, in Great Britain, all civil flying ceased and the aircraft were grounded pending a decision on their future disposition.

It was a slow and painful process. Of 1,740 aircraft on the British Civil Register at the outbreak of the Second World War, 956 were 'impressed' into the service of the Crown. The usual procedure was that following a survey of each individual aircraft, arranged on behalf of the Ministry of Aircraft Production (MAP) by officials from No 41 Group Headquarters at Andover, the owner was offered what was regarded as a fair price. The prospect of protracted squabbling was settled by the threat to requisition the aircraft against a lesser payment and to continue haggling on appeal after the shooting had stopped. Almost 150 civil-registered DH.60 Moths were allocated military markings in Great Britain, about 20 in India and the RAF took control of eight DH.60Ms formerly owned by the Iraqi Air Service. Aircraft not in first class condition were either scrapped or reduced to spare parts. Many were allocated to Technical Training Schools for dissection; others to units of the Air Training Corps as educational tools. RAF and Royal Navy Squadrons, Commands, miscellaneous units and stations inherited DH.60s to fly as hacks. Even before the war, during the summer of 1939, the Royal Navy was using DH.60Ms borrowed from the RAF, to acclimatise new pilots in the art of carrier deck landing, first on dry land and later on board the training carriers HMS *Argus* or HMS *Courageous* moored off the Scottish coast. Badly damaged aircraft mostly were reduced to components. With the factories engaged on more urgent tasks, apart from dwindling stocks of original spares, cannibalisation was the only other source.

As part of lavish deception plans, in 1940 decoy airfields were established, mostly in Eastern England, complete with 'lighted runways', buildings, facilities and small detachments of RAF personnel. They

During the Second World War, the British firm of W S Shackleton provided a number of civil aircraft to overseas customers, and in 1941 they shipped DH.60G G-AAKM from Hanworth to India, where she was registered VT-APU to the Madras Flying Club. The aircraft was impressed into the Indian Air Force as MA953 in September 1942 and, whilst her military serial was applied to the rudder, her civil identity remained on the fuselage. The photograph was taken at 322MU Cawnpore as late as 1946 when she was registered to the Government of India and probably painted yellow overall. Reg Webster

needed their own fleets of 'decoy' aircraft to add authenticity and many Moths were allocated to Shepperton Film Studios, operating under the name 'Sound City Films', where, in collaboration with the RAF Unit at nearby Chessington, Moths were either painted in camouflage colours to represent current trainers or physically modified to become, to the passing eye, Hurricane fighters. These inventive creations of the film industry were staked out in open fields, exposed to the British climate for over a year, after which they were good for nothing but the bonfire.

In Australia, New Zealand and throughout Africa, civil Moths also were requisitioned for military training purposes but with a higher chance of survival. Most DH.60 Moths in Canada and certainly in the USA, remained on the civil register throughout the war years, their numbers diminished only by attrition, lack of spares and their replacement by more modern equipment, often Tiger Moths, available as military surplus, released at the end of hostilities for little more than scrap value.

On a worldwide basis, an extraordinarily large number of Moths had been badly damaged or wrecked before the Second World War, not primarily as the result of design or mechanical failure, but due to acts of poor airmanship, bravado, inexperience, bad weather and lack of judgement on the part of their pilots. Before the days of intense regulation, anybody who could afford to was able to buy a light aeroplane and, with the minimum of tuition, step into what for many was unknown territory. The war created the definitive barrier beyond which, for many reasons, few Moths managed to survive.

In 1949 an aircraft built from spares by Veljekset Karhumaki in Finland was registered as a de Havilland 60G and allocated letters OH-VKM. The aircraft was powered by a Gipsy Major engine and featured a neat canopy, free of obstruction, faired into a high rear decking. OH-VKM was sold to Sweden in 1956 and rebuilt to standard open cockpit configuration for display in a museum. Karhumaki via Eino Ritaranta

DH.60X Seaplane G-CAPA was supplied to the Ontario Provincial Air Service in May 1928. In 1930 she was rebuilt with a metal fuselage, fitted with a Gipsy I in 1932 and a Gipsy II in 1934. In 1955 the aircraft was sold to Warner Bros for use as a camera ship in making the film *The Spirit of St Louis* **for which purpose she was registered N1510V. During filming, her wings caught fire when stored on a trailer and were destroyed, to be replaced by a set sourced in Canada which on delivery proved to be from a Tiger Moth. Harlan Gurney, Technical Director on the film, and a stand-in pilot for his friend Charles Lindbergh, adapted the wings to fit and installed an inverted Gipsy Major engine … and it all worked!** Via David Watson

In the 21st Century, it is the efforts of the enthusiasts who managed to salvage what they could, and to re-manufacture what they could not, that have preserved the flickering flame first kindled in 1924 by Geoffrey de Havilland and his friends and working colleagues. They genuinely fashioned a dream into what quickly became an icon, and from a muddy field in North London established their Enterprise, globally recognised and admired.

In October 1933, Francis Bradbrooke wrote about the DH.60 Moth in his regular column in *Flying* magazine. The words were appropriate then, at a time when hundreds of aeroplanes were still in full cry and were penned under the heading *The Universal Aeroplane*:

'The Gipsy Moth comes about as near to being the universal aeroplane for amateur pilots as any type in the world today. Its popularity is not even bounded by civilisation, and besides being the standard training machine in use by more flying clubs than any other type, it has also long distance and overseas flights to its credit far too many to mention here and a striking record in commercial service.

'The Gipsy Moth has now come upon the days of its obsolescence, the DH.60 design being nine years old, but although we expect better aeroplanes in the light of modern knowledge and increased facilities, we may be assured of getting many worse. Its years have added to it such well-tried dependability that modern rivals start with a big practical and psychological handicap.

'From the maintenance standpoint the Moth is hard to beat. Not only has it been designed and developed with that aspect in mind, but there is service for Moths almost everywhere in the world. In all its details it has been evolved by practical day-in and day-out pilots for others of like kidney, and the fact that the Man in the Street still regards every light aeroplane as something lepidopterous shows the immense effect that the Moth has had on aviation at large.'

DH.60 MOTH – THE SURVIVORS

BRITISH BUILT AIRCRAFT

188	DH.60	1925	G-EBLV	BAE Systems	Old Warden	Airworthy
192	DH.60	1925	VH-UAE	David & Carolyn Salter	Walcha, NSW	Airworthy
261	DH.60	1926	SE-ABS	Ugglarp Museum	Ugglarp	Rebuilding
340	DH.60M	1928	G-AACD	Unknown	Huntingdon	Stored
411	DH.60X	1927	VH-UGN	Nick Challinor	Murwillumbah, NSW	Rebuilding
447	DH.60X	1927	OH-ILA	Central Finland Avn Mus	Tikkakoski	Static
503	DH.60X	1928	G-CYYG	Reynolds Alberta Museum	Wetaskiwin, Alberta	Airworthy
506	DH.60X	1928	N1015V	David Watson	Santa Paula, CA	Rebuilding
552	DH.60X	1928	G-EBWD	Shuttleworth Collection	Old Warden	Airworthy
604	DH.60X	1928	VH-JGS	Mick Betts	Breakwater, Victoria	Rebuilding
608	DH.60X	1928	G-EBZN	Jane Hodgkinson	Kent	Rebuilding
613	DH.60X	1928	VH-UAO	David McCallum	Sydney, NSW	Airworthy
614	DH.60X	1928	VH-UAU	Power House Museum	Sydney, NSW	Static
627	DH.60X	1928	G-EBXU	Gilbert Pugh	Stapleford	Airworthy
630	DH.60X	1928	G-CAUA	Canada Aviation Museum	Rockliffe, Ottawa	Static
711	DH.60M	1929	VH-UKC	C Edmonds & D Clarke	Lilydale, Victoria	Rebuilding
757	DH.60M	1929	CF-AAJ	Watt Martin	Milton, Ontario	Airworthy
781	DH.60M	1929	CF-ADI	Western Dvpt Museum	Moose Jaw, Sask	Rebuilding
783	DH.60M	1929	VH-UQV	Ken Ruff	Mt Waverley, Victoria	Rebuilding
804	DH.60G	1928	G-AAAH	Science Museum	London	Static
859	DH.60G	1928	VP-TAA	Chaguaramas Museum	Port of Spain	Parts only
878	DH.60G	1928	VH-UFV	Jim Starr	Walbundrie, NSW	Rebuilding
898	DH.60G	1929	VH-ULC	Jim Starr	Walbundrie, NSW	Rebuilding
910	DH.60G	1928	CF-AQF	Watt Martin	Milton, Ontario	Parts only
940	DH.60G	1929	G35	National Aero Museum	Santiago, Chile	Static
1027	DH.60G	1929	G-AAEG	Ian Grace	Ada, MI	Rebuilding
1052	DH.60G	1929	G-AAGT	Malcolm Paul	Lee-on-Solent	Rebuilding
1060	DH.60G	1929	VH-ULT	Harold Thomas	Camden, NSW	Stored
1066	DH.60G	1929	VH-UKV	Moorabbin Air Museum	Moorabbin, Victoria	Static
1074	DH.60G	1929	VH-ULJ	Historical Aviation Mus	Salisbury, SA	Static
1075	DH.60G	1929	G-AAOR	Ben Cox & Nick Stagg	Bristol	Airworthy
1076	DH.60G	1929	N60MZ	David Watson	Santa Paula, CA	Airworthy
1082	DH.60G	1929	G-AAHI	Nigel & Louise Reid	Lee-on-Solent	Airworthy
1101	DH.60G	1929	ZK-ADT	Lee Middleton	Wellsford, NZ	Airworthy
1175	DH.60X	1929	G-AALY	Kevin Fresson	Pulborough	Rebuilding
1233	DH.60X	1930	G-AAYT	Paul Groves	Lee-on-Solent	Rebuilding
1235	DH.60G	1930	G-AAWO	Nigel & Louise Reid	Lee-on-Solent	Airworthy
1253	DH.60G	1930	G-AAZG	Cliff Lovell	Chilbolton	Rebuilding
1259	DH.60G	1930	G-ABAG	Paul & Andrew Wood	Audley End	Airworthy
1284	DH.60G	1930	G-ABDA	Roy Palmer	Durley	Airworthy
1294	DH.60G	1930	G-ABDX	Michael Souch	Durley	Airworthy
1316	DH.60M	1929	CF-ADW	Canadian Museum of Flight	Langley BC	Rebuilding
1322	DH.60M	1929	CF-APA	Canadian Museum of Flight	Langley BC	Rebuilding
1323	DH.60M	1929	CF-AGF	Canadian Museum of Flight	Langley BC	Fuselage
1325	DH.60M	1929	N443	Pacific Southwest	Los Alamitos, CA	Airworthy
1343	DH.60M	1929	CF-AGK	Ed 'Skeeter' Carlson	Spokane, WA	Stored
1362	DH.60M	1929	G-AAHY	David Elliott	Thruxton	Airworthy
1379	DH.60M	1929	VH-UMO	Donald & Robert Bunn	Bungowannah, NSW	Stored
1403	DH.60M	1929	VH-ULM	Louise Redmond	Brisbane, Queensland	Rebuilding
1405	DH.60M	1929	VH-ULO	SA Aviation Museum	Adelaide, SA	Stored
1406	DH.60M	1929	VH-ULP	Grant Cowlie	Campbell's Creek, Vic	Airworthy
1431	DH.60M	1929	VH-UNI	Royal Flying Doctor Mus	Katherine, NT	Static
1446	DH.60M	1929	G-AANL	Andrew Berry	Perth	Airworthy
1488	DH.60M	1930	ZK-ABS	Unknown	Unknown	Rebuilding
1542	DH.60M	1930	ZK-AEJ	Gerald Grocot	Napier, NZ	Airworthy
1561	DH.60M	1930	ZK-ACE	Colin Smith	Mandeville, NZ	Rebuilding
1563	DH.60M	1930	ZK-ACH	Keith Trillo	Auckland, NZ	Stored
1673	DH.60M	1930	LV-RZR	Unknown	Unknown	Stored
1685	DH.60M	1931	VH-UQH	Ed Field	Lilydale, Victoria	Rebuilding
1702	DH.60T	1931	SE-AZW	Flygvapenmuseum	Kajtumjaure	Parts only
1718	DH.60T	1931	SE-BFH	Flygvapenmuseum	Linkoping	Static
1720	DH.60T	1931	SE-BFI	Kjell Franzen	Gusum	Rebuilding
1823	DH.60G	1930	G-ABEV	Ron & Simon Darch	Yeovil	Airworthy
1840	DH.60G	1931	CF-AAA	Watt Martin	Milton, Ontario	Airworthy
1878	DH.60G	1931	HB-AFO	Christopher Tucker	Grenchen	Airworthy
1883	DH.60G	1931	G-ABSD	Michael Vaisey	Hemel Hempstead	Rebuilding
1906	DH.60G	1932	G-ABYA	Cobby Moore	Cranbrook	Airworthy
1917	DH.60G	1933	G-ATBL	John Greenland	Holt	Airworthy
5011	DH.60GIII	1932	G-ABZB	R Earl & B Morris	Wing	Airworthy
5030	DH.60GIII	1933	G-ACGZ	Nigel Lemon	Cookham	Rebuilding
5068	DH.60GIII	1934	G-ACNS	Ron Souch	Durley	Airworthy
5078	DH.60GIII	1934	HB-UPE	Groupe Avions Historique	Lausanne	Airworthy
5098	DH.60GIII	1934	G-ACXB	David Hodgkinson	Kent	Rebuilding
5105	DH.60GIII	1934	G-ADHD	Michael Vaisey	Hemel Hempstead	Rebuilding
5132	DH.60GIII	1935	SE-AGF	Luftmuseum	Nordkoping	Stored
-	DH.60G	-		Peter Winters	Antwerp	Project
-	DH.60GIII		EC-INK	Jose Villar	Gerona	Airworthy
-	DH.60GIII		G-BVNG	John Pothecary	Wiltshire	Rebuilding
-	DH.60GIII	-		Bruno Vonlanthen	Switzerland	Project
-	DH.60GIII	-		Michael Maniatis	New York	Project

AIRCRAFT BUILT OUTSIDE GREAT BRITAIN

Australia

1A	DH.60	1927	VH-UFV	Jim Starr	Walbundrie, NSW	Rebuilding
Larkin 22	DH.60G	1931	N168G	Early Birds Foundation	Lelystad	Airworthy

Canada

DHC111	DH.60M	1930	CF-CFU	Tom Coates	Saskatoon, Sask	Rebuilding
DHC127	DH.60M	1930	CF-AGX	Reynolds Alberta Museum	Wetaskiwin, Alberta	Airworthy

Finland

4	DH.60GIII	1949	OH-VKM	Technical Museum	Malmo	Static
8	DH.60X	1930	VH-SSC	Ken Orrman	Shepparton	Airworthy
10	DH.60X	1929	OH-EJA	Central Finland Avn Mus.	Tikkakoski	Static

France

13	DH.60G	1930	G-AANV	Richard Seeley	Durley	Airworthy

Sweden

-	DH.60G	1991	SE-BBT	Bjoern Blomstrand	Vastervik	Composite

United States of America

1-L	DH.60G	1929	N373H	Unknown	Unknown	Stored
1-R	DH.60G	1929	NC829H	Walt Wayda	Bethlehem, PA	Rebuilding
48	DH.60GM	1929	NC236K	Gary Sewal	Huntingdon Beach, CA	Airworthy
49	DH.60GM	1929	NC-AANF	Colin Smith	Mandeville, NZ	Rebuilding
65	DH.60GM	1929	NC965H	John Schildberg Collection	Greenfield, IA	Stored
86	DH.60GM	1929	G-AAMY	Totalsure	Seppe, Netherlands	Airworthy
117	DH.60GM	1930	NC916M	Gary Clark	La Cresenta, CA	Stored
118	DH.60GM	1930	NC917M	Yanks Air Museum	Chino, CA	Static
120	DH.60GM	1930	N919DH	Gerald F Schwam	New Garden, PA	Airworthy
125	DH.60GM	1930	G-AAMX	RAF Museum	Hendon	Static
138	DH.60GM	1930	G-AADR	Mrs E V Moffatt	Bosbury	Airworthy
157	DH.60GM	1930	N573N	Mrs Rita Sholton	Anchorage, AK	Airworthy
160	DH.60GM	1930	N1686	David Baumbach	California	Airworthy
165	DH.60GMW	1932	G-AANO	Tony Jenkins	Comberton	Rebuilding
179	DH.60GMW	1932	N617V	Melvin Lindgren	Helena, MT	Static
-	DH.60GMW	-		Unknown	Nevada	Stored

INDEX